MW01027722

Interpreting Solar Returns

Interpreting
Solar Returns

James A. Eshelman

Copyright © 1979, 1985
by James A. Eshelman

All rights reserved. No part of this book may
be reproduced or used in any form or by any
means — graphic, electronic or mechanical,
including photocopying, mimeographing,
recording, taping or information storage and
retrieval systems — without written permission
from the publisher. A reviewer may quote brief passages.

First Edition Published 1979
Astro-Analytics Publications

Library of Congress Catalog Card Number: 83-70661
International Standard Book Number 0-917086-40-6

Cover Design by Larry Ortiz
Author Portrait by Thea Day

Printed in the United States of America

Published by ACS Publications, Inc.
P.O. Box 16430
San Diego, CA 92116-0430

Dedicated

to
Anna-Kria

Also by ACS Publications, Inc.

All About Astrology Series
The American Atlas: US Latitudes and Longitudes, Time Changes
    and Time Zones (Shanks)
The American Book of Charts (Rodden)
The American Book of Nutrition & Medical Astrology (Nauman)
The American Book of Tables
The American Ephemeris Series 1901-2000
The American Ephemeris for the 20th Century [Midnight] 1900 to
    2000
The American Ephemeris for the 20th Century [Noon] 1900 to 2000
The American Ephemeris for the 21st Century 2001-2000
The American Heliocentric Ephemeris 1901-2000
The American Sidereal Ephemeris 1976-2000
The Asteroid Ephemeris: Dudu, Dembowska, Pittsburgh, & Frigga
    (Stark & Pottenger)
Astrological Insights into Personality (Lundsted)
Astrological Predictions: A Revolutionary New Technique (Whitney)
Astrology: Old Theme, New Thoughts (March & McEvers)
Basic Astrology: A Guide for Teachers & Students (Negus)
Basic Astrology: A Workbook for Students (Negus)
The Body Says Yes (Kapel)
The Cosmic Clocks (M. Gauquelin)
Cosmic Combinations: A Book of Astrological Exercises (Negus)
Expanding Astrology's Universe (Dobyns)
The Fortunes of Astrology: A New Complete Treatment of the
    Arabic Parts (Granite)
The Gauquelin Book of American Charts (F. and M. Gauquelin)
The Gold Mine in Your Files (King)
Healing with the Horoscope: A Guide to Counseling (Pottenger)
The Horary Reference Book (Ungar & Huber)
Horoscopes of the Western Hemisphere (Penfield)
Instant Astrology (Orser & Brighfields)
The International Atlas (Shanks)
Interpreting the Eclipses (Jansky)
The Koch Book of Tables
The Lively Circle (Koval)
The Mystery of Personal Identity (Mayer)
The Only Way to...Learn Astrology, Vol. I
    Basic Principles (March & McEvers)
The Only Way to...Learn Astrology, Vol. II
    Math & Interpretation Techniques (March & McEvers)
The Only Way to...Learn Astrology, Vol. III
    Horoscope Analysis (March & McEvers)
Planetary Planting (Riotte)
Planting by the Moon 1983/84 including Grower's Guide (Best &
    Kollerstrom)
The Psychic and the Detective (Druffel with Marcotte)
Psychology of the Planets (F. Gauquelin)
Secrets of the Palm (Hansen)
Small Ecstasies (Owens)
Stalking the Wild Orgasm (Kilham)
Tomorrow Knocks (Brunton)
12 Times 12 (McEvers)

Contents

Acknowledgments

First Edition

This book is an anniversary present to myself. It represents, in many ways, a culmination of my first decade of serious involvement with astrology. Even in that short time, a major shift has been perceptible in the consciousness of astrologers as a whole, and of other people with regard to astrology. In acknowledging those people who have contributed to this book you now hold in your hands, I want to place at the top of the list all who have contributed to this evolution. They have both shaped my thoughts and provided me with a receptive audience.

During that decade of immersion in the stars, one man had a more profound influence on my life and thoughts than any five other people. This man was **Donald A. Bradley,** who entered my life in 1970. Don was the nearest approximation to an astrology teacher I have had, poking little holes of understanding in the veil of murk, while delicately paring away at my irrationalities and lightly nudging me in more fruitful directions. Appropriately, Don authored, in 1948, the first book to describe the techniques developed in this present volume.

Anna-Kria King has had a considerably more current impact on my life through our ever-tightening personal and professional relationship in recent years. Those who have neither written a book nor lived with an author can probably not understand the extent of personal sacrifice required of an author's living-mate in adapting to that altered state of being called obsessive-compulsive, creative self-expression. Anna-Kria's support has been consistent beyond reasonable expectations of human endurance. I want to publicly express my appreciation for her constant input and love, and for her careful preparation of the

Precession Tables in Appendix B of the first edition.

Every now and then, but not often enough for my tastes, one encounters an individual whose interest in, devotion to, and competence with a subject so nearly matches one's own that equality is a fact of life and all interaction evokes stretching, pushing limits and growth. Spurred by a ferocious number of Mars interaspects, my relationship with **Matthew Quellas** has been of this type. Sometimes it is hard to tell where my ideas leave off and his begin, where I have given birth to thoughts and where I have borrowed his. Until I find a way to chain Matthew and his typewriter in one place with no chance of rescue, and compel him, at threat of burning all of his lion posters and statues, to write a book of his own, I want to acknowledge his unavoidable contributions to my opinions.

Had **Robert Jansky** not urged me two years ago to write this book, I would probably never have done it. I therefore wish to thank Bob, my publisher, for his encouragement and enthusiasm every step of the way.

Maritha Pottenger, Erin King and **Michael Douglas-Llyr** have, by force of proximity to me these last few months, displayed noble tolerance of the perverse idiosyncrasies I develop when pressured by a deadline. Along with the dozens of friends who were warned not to approach my home during writing season, and who usually complied, these three special people have earned my love and gratitude for the faith, endurance, kindness and other wonderful things each of them contributed.

No less appreciation goes to **Joanne Clancy,** editor of *American Astrology* magazine, for permission to reproduce two diagrams in Chapter 2 of this book, which originally appeared in the February and March 1957 issues of that periodical. Mrs. Clancy's publication has pioneered the research and development of techniques described in this book. Without her support, astrology overall would be far poorer today than it is.

JAMES A. ESHELMAN
October, 1978

Second Edition

Like the eternally winding spiral of the Earth in its path through space, life goes on. Old friends continue to contribute in new ways. Today, six years after the above acknowledgments went to press, **Maritha Pottenger**, sitting in a chair I warmed for two years, is the editor to whom I will hand this revised manuscript. **Matthew Quellas** has traded his typewriter for an Osborne 1 microcomputer and still has not committed his wisdom to paper. **Anna-Kria** and I approach our ninth anniversary together, closer than I could have dreamed six years ago.

And **Robert Jansky** has left Earth for the stars.

Only a month ago I stood on the beach of Miami overlooking the broad Atlantic, a continent from my home in Los Angeles. I had spent the day talking to new friends whose lives had been touched years ago by the man who tenderly brought forth this book from my potential. Across the vast seas, I pause to thank Bob again for all he contributed to me and to this field I so love.

Neil Michelsen played a major and valued role in my life for the two years of my residency at Astro Computing Services. To Neil, and the dear friends at ACS who have worked so hard on this book, I offer warm thanks.

Also deserving special mention are **Mark Pottenger**, who did more than any other to expand my computer skills and abilities; **Althea Day**, because she deserves acknowledgment; **Jan Kennedy**, because, when I'm with her, it's always harder to forget; and **Phyllis Seckler**, for continuing to lead me into the Light of the Sun.

October, 1984

CHAPTER ONE

INTRODUCTION

Each year the Earth on which we live makes a 584-million-mile circuit of the blazing, yellow Sun at the core of our planetary system. Astrologers on Earth designate by ecliptical (zodiacal) longitude the **direction** in space where the Sun is located — for instance, the direction in which one might point a telescope to observe the Sun. At any given moment, the Sun's longitude is identical to its longitude about 365 days and six hours earlier. This is the period of time required for the Earth to make one complete orbit about the Sun.

Once a year, close to our birthdays, each of us experiences the renewal of the Earth-Sun-space alignment that existed at the exact time we were born. Astrologically, we say that the Sun has returned to the precise apparent geocentric longitude it held at the moment we entered the world. An annual astrological map computed for this precise instant is called a **Solar Return**. Each Solar Return summarily describes one year of a person's life. It is one of the most valuable long-term diagnostic devices available to astrologers.

This book is designed to explain the **theory, calculation,** and **application** of Solar Returns. Most of the book is devoted to (a) interpretations of various components of a Solar Return, (b) tactics for integrating these into meaningful, informative, human descriptions, (c) numerous examples and (d) techniques for timing important specific periods during the year. It is not a beginning astrological textbook; rather, it is written for the professional astrologer and those students who already understand the basic structure of a horoscope.

It is not correct to say that the Sun (or Earth) returns to the same **place** from one year to the next. In twelve months the Sun has considerable motion of its own, traveling approximately 375 million miles through space with its cargo of planets and gravel in tow. This means that the Earth's orbit is neither a circle nor even an ellipse, but a **corkscrew**, spiraling outward through space toward a point in the vicinity of the constellation Hercules, a little north of the Milky Way. Nothing ever returns exactly to a previously held state, in either cosmology or human life. Only the relationship, the alignment, can be duplicated, and each time from a new perspective, a new location within the galaxy.

When we calculate a chart for the Sun's **apparent return** to its place at an individual's birth, we are in effect mapping this **reinstatement of that person's natal alignment with the totality of space.** This will be further explained and explored as we proceed. Right now, I just want to begin to direct your thinking toward matters cosmic rather than terrestrial, to a scale representative of the framework within which astrology truly exists.

The Problem of Precession

Down through the years, Solar Returns were mentioned from time to time in the writings of leading astrologers. Rarely, though, did they appear very convincing. It was only through the renascence in astrological thought of the last forty years that the correct ways of calculating and interpreting these charts have come to light, providing us with the most lucid and helpful tools ever to appear in an astrologer's repertoire.

Such brilliant astrologers in their times as Alan Leo, Elbert Benjamin and Charles Carter either dismissed Solar Returns entirely, or gave them only passing, superficial attention in the midst of other techniques. Dr. Zipporah Dobyns once told me that, after monitoring her own Solar Returns for a few years, she had been unable to credit them with any reliability. This is typical of the opinions of many objective, thinking astrologers who have examined these charts computed the commonly accepted way.

To paraphrase Shakespeare, the fault lies not in our stars but in our manner of measuring them. The secret of consulting Solar Returns lies first of all in a mathematical refinement which now has been applied for many years with sometimes astounding results. That refinement is based on the realization that **while the zodiac, as recognized by most astrologers, is a moving, precessing framework, the astrological universe as a whole is precession-free, or "fixed."**

The zodiac used by most astrologers in the West is based on twelve equal divisions of the Ecliptic (the mean orbital plane of the Earth about the Sun), measured from the vernal (spring) equinox, or vernal point (VP). The vernal point and the autumnal point (which exactly oppose each other) mark the intersections of the Ecliptic with the plane of the Earth's Equator. They are defined, respectively, as 0° Aries and 0° Libra of this measuring framework, which is called the **Tropical Zodiac**.

Due to a combination of factors, most of which involve the fluctuating effects of solar and lunar gravitational influences on the body of the Earth, these equinoctial points are unstable. The Earth's poles rotate through a small circle over a 25,000-year period, much like the slow spinning of the crown of a dying toy top or gyroscope. As the poles move, this automatically changes the location of the Equator, which is always 90° from both poles by definition. As the Equator moves, so do the places where it intersects the Ecliptic.

In short, this movement in the Earth's poles causes the equinoxes to regress along the Ecliptic at the (current) average rate of 50″.27 per year, or 1° in about 72 years. This movement is called **precession**. Because the starting point of the Tropical Zodiac is moving, it is also known as a **moving zodiac** — moving in reference to the remainder of space as we know it. It may also be called a **precessing zodiac**.

We can remove the effects of precession in two ways.

If an astrologer prefers to use this Tropical Zodiac, a regular correction must be applied to solar and other horoscopic placements to compensate for precession. How to apply this correction (of about 50″ per year) is explained in Appendix A, which shows how to calculate Solar Returns.

A second method of overcoming the effects of precession is to use **a precession-free reference system**, that is, a zodiac which by its very nature is unaffected by precession in the first place. Such an alternative framework exists. It is called the **Sidereal Zodiac**. Like the Tropical Zodiac, it is based on twelve equal divisions of the ecliptic circle. Unlike the Tropical Zodiac, it is not beholden to the equinoxes and is therefore totally undistorted by precession.

The issue here is not so much one of zodiacs, as of something far more fundamental to the essence of things astrological. Therefore, one can achieve the desired effects with Solar Returns by either (1) using the Tropical Zodiac and correcting for precession or (2) using the precession-free Sidereal Zodiac.

If neither of these methods is used, a Solar Return will be six hours in error by age 18, twelve hours in error by age 36, and an *entire day* off by the time a person attains the age of 72.

I personally choose to use the Sidereal Zodiac in my work. I switched to this zodiac initially because I felt it was more consistent with the **aprecessional** (precession-free) concept which was proving so essential in calculating transits and return charts. I continue to employ the Sidereal Zodiac because I find much greater clarity and accuracy in natal delineations through Sidereal sign placements than Tropical ones. However, I might add that Robert Hand, who also advocates a precession-free system, holds the precisely opposite view to mine with regard to choice of zodiac. He writes:

> I personally feel that the signs of the tropical zodiac give interpretive results that are more useful than those of the sidereal, but I recognize that it is possible to treat the tropical zodiac as if it were moving. In other words, one should treat the natal positions of the planets as if they were fixed stars. Since the vernal equinox moves backwards, the positions of the fixed stars move forward in the tropical zodiac. Opinion differs on this point, but many astrologers agree that at the very least, determining the positions of the natal chart corrected for precession helps significantly in timing events.[1]

Indeed, once a correction for precession was applied, astrologers of note, such as Hand, went on record with enthusiastic support of this new sort of Solar Return. Llewellyn George, Dean of American Astrologers in his day, financed the publication of Donald A. Bradley's *Solar and Lunar Returns*[2] with money from his personal funds, not those of his publishing company. In the Foreword to that book, George stated:

> Long ago I discontinued using the conventional 'standard' system of Solar and Lunar Returns because their indices were usually unsatisfactory. Nevertheless, a belief remained that 'there was gold in those fields' and this hope enhanced the urge to investigate. Sure enough, 'gold' was found in this modern revival of ancient practice which involves the sidereal zodiac of the Constellations.[3]

Yet, as Llewellyn George was surely aware, the issue was one of fixed versus moving reference systems, not one of zodiacs. Tropical and Sidereal astrologers alike have used the techniques described in this book to great advantage.

Chart diagrams in the following chapters have been drawn in both the Tropical and Sidereal Zodiacs to enable astrologers of either

---

1. Robert Hand, *Planets in Transit* (Gloucester, MA: Para Research, Inc., 1976), 20.
2. Donald A. Bradley, *Solar and Lunar Returns* (Los Angeles: Llewellyn Foundation for Astrological Research, 1948).
3. Ibid., 5.

conviction to feel comfortable in reading them. However, only rarely will we be discussing the sign placements of planets in this book, so I anticipate no difficulty on the part of either group of astrologers in following this material.

This is a book on **astrology,** plain and simple, not one "brand" or another.

Contrasting Period-Analysis Techniques

Astrologers have access to a variety of techniques designated as **forecasting** or **predictive tools.** I prefer to call these **period analysis techniques,** since they can be used to evaluate not only the future, but also the past and (especially) the present. Wherever we are looking along the client's private time-line, the intent is consistently to learn how human blends with moment, and what is being done (or can be done) with that coupling.

Period analysis techniques can be divided into (1) transits and (2) progressions/directions. Transits are planets in space at any given moment. Progressions and directions are more symbolic than literal, involved either with advancing all points in the horoscope by the same given increment (directions), or reapportioning time so that a lesser period of time is taken as representative of a greater period (progressions). An example of the latter is secondary progressions, where planet motions one day after an individual's birth are considered to represent a year of "real time," each planet moving at its own rate. A sample directional system is solar arc directions, which accelerate **every** chart component at the same rate as the secondary progressed Sun.

Progressions are more geared toward unleashing or developing traits inherent to the individual: situations generally arising from within, and basic maturations of the potentials stated in a birth chart. Transits, on the other hand, are more inclined to trigger situations arising from encounters with the environment, the world outside of us. This has been oversimplified in the past to where transits were often described as triggering overt events, while progressions were described as the agents of "psychological changes." However, any event is intimately bonded to a history of psychological factors. Internal states of being are capable of inciting external happenings. Transits definitely represent periods of psychological change, just as the inner shifts signaled by progressions often distill into concrete events. The distinction between transits and progressions is not one of "events" versus "psychological changes," but rather a distinction in **the perceived source of the motivation** for the life-shift, whether principally from within the individual, as a natural development of the natal condition, or principally from interaction with the environment.

Solar Returns are **transit-based** techniques. They arise from a precise aspect (conjunction) of the transiting Sun with the natal Sun. They consist of transiting planets at a given moment in time, near or on one's birthday, locked into collusion with natal planets for a year to follow.

It is necessary, therefore, to differentiate between Solar Returns and "just transits." To begin with, transits at the time of a Solar Return are imprinted for an entire year. They take on special significance because they map an individual's **new way of being** for twelve months. Secondly, transits in a prominent spot in the Solar Return (near the angles) can be strongly manifest even if relatively inexact.

This sheds some clarity on what is often a confusing question of transit orbs. As a rule, transit aspects to natal planets become noticeable when less than 1° from precise contact. These are times when feelings, attitudes and blatant events come to a head and demand attention. However, transits with wider orbs are surely operating below the surface of consciousness. A. G. Farnell, who for years wrote the "Astro-Dream Analysis" column for *American Astrology* , wrote me that he allows as much as a 10° orb (or more) for a transiting conjunction when studying dreams. These energies are making themselves known in the subconscious layers of mind well in advance of their cresting in consciousness. It is, therefore, no surprise that when a 5°-wide transit falls near the angles of a Solar or Lunar Return, its effects are most definitely felt. Issues connected with the transit do not culminate, at such a time, in the same way they crest at the exact transit phase. Instead, this angularity simply brings ongoing processes to the surface of awareness.

A Generation of Learning

Over thirty years ago, Bradley's *Solar and Lunar Returns* became the first book to publicize the astonishing potency of return charts calculated in an aprecessional reference system. His book continues to sell quite well today, and represents a landmark in astrological thinking and education.

However, in three decades we have learned many, many things about astrology in general and the application of Solar and Lunar Returns in particular. Along with the bounty of answers, those three decades have also raised questions that had not been (perhaps could not be) asked in 1948. Some of these new questions have been answered. Some have not.

This book came into being for one primary reason: specifically, that the most authoritative and widely consulted book existing on this subject was written a generation ago, with little published in the interim that has materially added to, or improved upon, Bradley's original work. *Interpreting Solar Returns* is the first of two planned books aimed at presenting the advances in technique, interpretation and application which have been gathered by students and serious practitioners working more than a score of years to polish and develop a remarkable set of tools.

Also, Solar Returns have never been adequately treated in their own right. Lunar Returns have dominated the literature since there are thirteen times as many of these monthly charts. Lunar Returns tune into a much finer period of time and therefore give more dramatic results. But Solar Returns are capable of very dramatic results as well. It is now time that these two types of charts were discussed separately, so that their specific differences in delineation can be better understood. These differences will be explored in greater detail in the second work covering Lunar Returns.

Certainly this present book will also reach new astrologers who will thereby be introduced to Solar Returns for the first time. This book has thus been organized with these new astrologers in mind, moving from basic precepts to interpretations of major astrological factors, then to discussions (with examples) of organizing the map into an understandable and complete delineation. Calculations are covered in Appendix A and can be learned whenever the student feels the need to do so. The new student will feel most comfortable by proceeding from the front to the back in orderly fashion, perhaps just skimming the interpretations in Chapters Three and Four at first, returning to them again later for more detailed study.

Try these methods on your own. They are easy in both calculation and interpretation. You will never learn to use Solar Returns just from reading this (or any other) book. Prepare yourself for a new adventure in astrology so literal you will be tempted to think that it has something to do with real life — because it does! Solar Returns are an important key to understanding the many lives you live and the identities you play in the process of becoming yourself as wholly as you possibly can.

CHAPTER TWO

SPEAKING THE SAME LANGUAGE

There is a fiction, in many quarters of the astrological world, which goes something like this: If a technique or variable or rule can be proven valuable and workable in one area of astrology, it must work in all of them; and, conversely, if a factor can be demonstrated by some means **not** to work in certain circumstances, it may therefore be labeled totally invalid and cast aside.

This is comparable to saying that if a thatched roof hut provides a superb home for a family on a South Pacific island, it would also be a most adequate substitution for an Eskimo's igloo near the North Pole.

My experience in astrology is that different areas of investigation have their own ground rules. We cannot assume that just because something works in one place, it will necessarily work in another place. As an example, consider aspects of planets with fixed stars. Most astrologers who have had considerable experience with fixed stars agree that the conjunction, and probably the opposition, are valid aspects to these points. Many would also add the square. Virtually no one would put much weight, if any, on trines or sextiles of natal planets with fixed stars, although trines and sextiles are generally acknowledged as being very significant in interpreting natal planet interaction. Here we have a good example of an astrological factor — trines or sextiles — being very important in one place but quite inconsequential in another.

In Chapters Five and Six of this book, I show how to read a Solar Return in two separate ways. First, it is read as the new birth chart which overlays the basic character indications of the true natal horoscope. Then it is examined a second time as a period analysis chart, in what might be called "return chart style." The Solar Return becomes a key to environmental circumstances the individual will encounter and the basic tone of life for the ensuing year. On the first reading, the Solar Return may be examined with exactly the same rules that have been found valid in delineating a natal chart. When we come to the second reading, the approach changes. In this chapter we are going to discuss some of the differences. In Chapter Six these differences will be developed further.

Waves versus Zones

Astrological factors may be conveniently divided into two broad groups. Some factors are rhythmic, wave-like and cyclic. These, which include aspects and angularity "power curves," have no sharp beginnings or endings. They gradually increase from nil to maximum intensity and fade out in a similar fashion.

Other astrological variables, such as signs and houses, represent discrete, separate categories boxcarred end to end with apparently sharp boundaries between them.

The dividing lines (cusps) between houses seem less sharp than those between signs. This could be attributed to several factors, including slightly inaccurate birthtimes in the horoscopes available for study and the persistent confusion over which house system is most viable. There is indecision about whether house positions should be measured ecliptically or *in mundo*. Another possibility, which I presently believe is a correct view, is that astrology's dividing lines are not based on space at all, but upon time. A planet, in its daily rotation, crosses a house cusp and moves 1° past it in about four minutes of time. It may require four to eight minutes of time for a planet to readjust or acclimate itself to a new house position; but during the same interval, the fastest astrological body, the Moon, only moves 2-3 ' along the Ecliptic, and no other planet moves even half a minute of arc. This may be the explanation for why sign boundaries seem more acute than house boundaries.

John Addey, one of England's most valiant astrological researchers, claimed that even signs and houses have no boundaries and that **all** astrological factors (except the planets themselves, which are the actual moving pieces in astrology's multidimensional chess game) are based upon wavelike action. His writings[1] are strongly recommended

1. Most important of these are: John M. Addey, *Harmonics in Astrology* and *Harmonic Anthology* (both Green Bay: Cambridge Circle, Ltd., 1976).

to all who wish to look deeply at astrology's foundations.

However, I do not agree with all of Addey's conclusions. I feel that his basic premise — that in astrology "the operative force is one which fluctuates gradually round the circle rather than one which has distinct boundaries or cusps"[2] — is very valid for aspects and for measuring the planets' relationships to the horoscopic angles (which is a type of aspect). Addey and his co-workers have done some impressive work with aspects in this fashion. Yet, when the same techniques are applied to planetary positions along the Ecliptic (the circle of signs), the evidence is not nearly so convincing or conclusive. Despite this, the harmonics theory provides a superb **modeling tool** for studying and seeking to conceptually understand the bases of astrology. Addey's insistence to the contrary, it is possible to model a "boxcar" type of zodiac, composed of discrete signs with precise boundaries, using a harmonics model. This is done by depicting the zodiac as what is called a "standing wave."

This subject is too involved to adequately cover here in a short space, and all findings are still tentative in this relatively new field of research. I refer the reader, therefore, to Addey's own publications for further background.

The major point I wish to make here is that **at least *some* astrological factors can best be described by the rising and falling action of waves, such as are found elsewhere in nature; and that those factors which have been most definitively proven to behave in wavelike fashion are the most significant individual factors in the astrologer's arsenal.**

Planets are the fundamental operating agents in astrology. They are conditioned in four separate ways: (1) by aspects, (2) by proximity to the horoscopic angles, (3) by sign placement and (4) by house placement. Angularity and house position are related but separate considerations.

In my experience, the order in which these four factors are here listed reflects their relative importance.

Different astrologers attach different significances to different astrological elements. Before plunging into an exposition of how Solar Returns are interpreted, I feel it is important to make sure you and I are speaking the same language — that is, that you, the reader, understand how I see the basic operating components of astrology. The remainder of this chapter covers each of these primary factors, one by one, with an emphasis on trying to understand the unique import of each.

---

2. Addey, *Harmonics in Astrology*, 34.

Angularity

One of the biggest controversies among contemporary astrologers centers on which house system, of the several available ones, is the right system. Inherent in this controversy is the belief that one house system embodies all of those individual elements which we think of when we hear the words, "house interpretation." Actually, astrologers traditionally delineate several different types of information from houses.

In my personal practice, and throughout this book, I use the Campanus system of domification. My major reason for this is that what few statistics we do have on house systems point to the superiority of Campanus in specific areas which are particularly important to the study of Solar Returns. Primary among these is the principle of **angularity**.

One of astrology's basic doctrines, handed down through the centuries, is that the angles of the horoscope — the horizon and meridian — represent the most powerful, active, dynamic areas of the map. A thesis became formalized in which the first, fourth, seventh and tenth houses were called **angular houses** and considered the most powerful; the second, fifth, eighth and eleventh houses were called **succedent houses** and considered less strong than the angular ones; and the third, sixth, ninth and twelfth were called **cadent houses** and said to be the weakest parts of the horoscope, wherein planets have little power to manifest their individual natures.[3]

Modern astrological research undertaken over the last thirty years has shown that this doctrine of angular, succedent, and cadent houses is only a useful, convenient simplification of a more fundamental

---

3. An important matter of language usage needs to be clarified before we go further. Throughout this book, unless we are speaking of specifically **astronomical** positioning, the word "planet" refers not to a distant ball of matter, but to an inner aspect of self.

Therefore, when we speak of "Mars" causing accidents, we mean that the cause lies with an individual's own impetuousness, hastiness and daring. "Saturn" only "causes" us to grow up because by the word "Saturn" we mean that inner tendency to maturation. The same applies to any of the planets, as used throughout this book.

The power of choice always originates within the individual being, as an unfolding of diverse needs, intentions and tendencies. The "predestination" of any event is nothing more than the certainty of that being's power to experience reality as it most deeply desires. Fate **is** free will, when that will is truly free — when the inner voice, the Truth-of-Self, is clearly heard and joyfully followed.

principle. In fact, two sets of principles appear to have become intermeshed because it has been convenient to do so. These are (1) the existence of houses and (2) the existence of a kind of **power curve** or **angularity curve**. Though these two things hang on the same frame, they are actually separate and distinct.

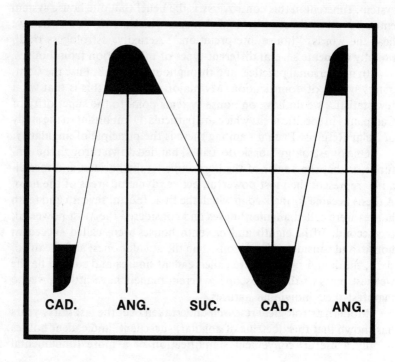

CAD.   ANG.   SUC.   CAD.   ANG.

Figure 2-1

Figure 2-1 shows a theoretical model, based on a combination of statistical research and personal experience. Although we may loosely speak of it as a "power curve," what it reveals is not the power of a planet *per se*, but the degree to which the planet's own nature may be easily expressed. It reflects how close to the surface of awareness are the needs, feelings and drives designated by that planet.

The highest point on the curve is exactly at the angular cusps. The lowest point is exactly at each of the cadent cusps. The succedent cusps show intermediate values.

Figure 2-2 is a statistically-derived angularity curve which resembles our theoretical model very closely. This diagram is reprinted from the March 1957 issue of *American Astrology* with the kind permission of

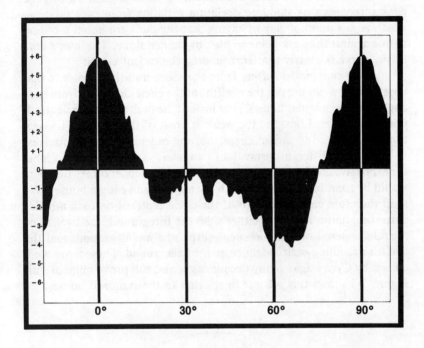

Figure 2-2
Suggested angularity curve, statistically derived from planetary
positions in Lunar Returns. (From Garth Allen, "Statistics to the
Rescue," *American Astrology*, March 1957. Courtesy of Clancy
Publications.)

the editor. In an article entitled "Statistics to the Rescue," Garth Allen
plotted planetary placements in relation to the angles of the Lunar
Returns preceding 75 childbirths, 120 weddings and 60 serious accidents.
He found much of what tradition would suggest. The Moon and traditional "benefic" planets preferred the angles in parturition returns,
while Mars and Neptune clustered around the cadent cusps. Jupiter also
dominated the angles in prewedding maps; but Jupiter and Venus avoid-
ed the angles of return charts covering periods of serious accidents,
their traditional protective natures being suspended, while Mars and
Saturn grouped around the angles and were only rarely posited near
the cadent cusps in these violent events.

By combining the graphed curves in each of these separate studies,
Allen arrived at the angularity index shown in Figure 2-2, upon which
I have based Figure 2-1. Unquestionably, the most positively significant

areas are shown to be those immediately around angular cusps. The peak surpasses a six standard deviation variation from expectancy — which is just another way of saying that the odds are about a billion to one against the peak being so high by chance alone. The lowest area of the curve is clearly that surrounding the cadent cusps.

Where this model differs from the more traditional view is that the strongest areas are not the twelfths of the circle clockwise from each angle (i.e., the angular houses), but instead the twelfths of a circle **straddling** the angles. Likewise, the weakest areas of the chart are the sections straddling the cadent cusps, not the cadent houses themselves.

We need different terms than "angular" and "cadent" to label the expressive and inexpressive portions of a horoscope; otherwise, there would be continual confusion with the angular and cadent houses. We shall therefore call the twelfth of the circle centered on each angular cusp (i.e., half a house on either side) the **foreground;** the twelfth of a circle centered on the succedent cusps, the **middleground;** and the twelfth straddling each cadent cusp, the **background.** These terms were coined by Cyril Fagan many decades ago, and still prove quite useful. Figure 2-3 shows this scheme in relation to the standard houses.

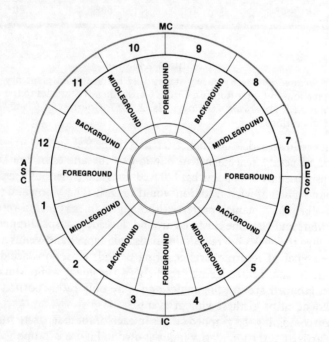

Figure 2-3

Planets in the **foreground** of a chart — whether a natal map, Solar Return, ingress or whatever — are the most prominent and important. **Background** planets acquire importance also because they are **least** able to manifest themselves and thus represent qualities which are held in abeyance. The **middleground** areas are neither particularly strong nor particularly weak, but reflect a measure of easy moderation.

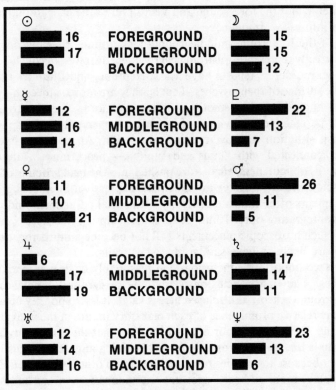

Figure 2-4

Frequency of individual planets in the three GROUNDS of 42 murderers' natal horoscopes. (From Garth Allen, MURDER WILL OUT!, *American Astrology*, February 1957. Courtesy of Clancy Publications.)

Supporting this basic tripartite division is another set of statistics that were published in the February 1957 issue of *American Astrology*. This data is summarized in Figure 2-4. Garth Allen tabulated the frequency of each planet's placement in each of the three "grounds" for timed birth charts of 42 murderers. It is immediately apparent that

Mars, Neptune, and Pluto prefer the foreground areas an outstanding number of times. Nearly as dramatic is their avoidance of the background. Though Saturn's positions are perfectly normal from a statistical point of view, it is noteworthy that they are **tiered** so that the foreground is slightly favored, the middleground is perfectly normal, and there is a slight avoidance of the background.

Now move your eyes to the other side of this graph. Notice how Jupiter avoids the foreground and Venus prefers the background, again with impressive frequency.

If the foreground-middleground-background scheme is accepted as correctly representing astrological realities, then we can conclude that known murderers tend to have Mars, Neptune, and Pluto traits close to the surface of their psyches. That is, they are more subject to overall stress and exaggerated emotional states, are more vulnerable to anxiety, hyperreactive to any type of pressure or coercion, and respond in a crisis situation with overt, aggressive action. At the same time, the traits connected with Venus and Jupiter — peacefulness, tolerance, warmth, obligingness, etc. — are pushed into the backgrounds of their consciousness where they are much less expressive. Such background placements often indicate difficulty with social adjustment and problems integrating oneself into peer relationships. Of course, everyone with such horoscopic placements will not become a murderer, though they **are** likely to have similar character traits.

Two important conclusions can reasonably be drawn from these figures. The first conclusion is that **the foreground-middleground-background scheme as displayed here is valid**. It is a major key in assessing the relative prominence of each planetary nature in the individual's psyche. The second important conclusion is that **the Campanus house system is the most appropriate for determining angularity.** This is apparent because the studies presented here, and others which could also be replayed, are all based upon the Campanus system and surpass in significance any other tested system when comparisons are made on this issue. This makes logical sense, too: Campanus is a **spatial** system, the only house system to accurately depict the appearance of the heavens in a spatial sense (with the possible exception of the ill-regarded Horizontal system), and therefore seems most suitable for measuring the closeness of a planet to the horizon or meridian.

Note, however, that the angular cusps themselves will be identical in the Placidus, Koch, Regiomontanus and similar house systems, only the intermediate cusps being different.

Figure 2-3, as a rigid scheme of twelve divisions, should not be taken literally. The angularity curve shown in Figures 2-1 and 2-2 is the truer representation of Nature's plan, revealing a graduated scale of increasing and decreasing values in a rhythmic cycle. The discrete foreground-middleground-background zones are a handy division that holds up in practice; but I urge you to be aware of the broader principles underlying this idea.

A few words also ought to be added regarding the research of Michel Gauquelin, whose well-known work[4] deals with the mundane (domal) placements of planets at the births of large groups of professionals, including athletes, scientists, artists, soldiers, writers, actors, politicians, business executives and medical doctors. Gauquelin discovered that there are certain dominant planets for each profession (each personality type), such as Jupiter for actors and politicians, and that these key planets prefer the areas **at or just past the angles** — that is, conjunct or just above the Ascendant, conjunct or just west of the Midheaven, and conjunct or just below the Descendant. The peaks near the Ascendant and Midheaven appear strongest, which agrees with astrological expectation; but the peaks were biased toward the cadent side of the angle, not the angular house side.

Two considerations are significant here. First, this angularity curve isolated by Gauquelin substantially resembles my recommended model. There is little difference between the two. Though the Gauquelin results are usually displayed in twelve sectors (approximating astrological houses), the high- and low-scoring areas are not bounded by house cusps. In most cases, the actual peaks fall on or near the angles themselves, and drop to their low somewhere in the middle of each quadrant.

However, all Gauquelin research has been performed using natal horoscopes; and there is no reason to presuppose that nativities and Solar Returns respond to the same angularity model. They may — but this has yet to be demonstrated. We began this chapter stating that a proven principle in one situation does not necessarily apply in another. To the slight extent that the Gauquelin results contradict research on angularity in return charts, we are nonetheless obligated to respect the latter in its own arena. It is the foreground-middleground-background scheme, and the potency curve shown in Figure 2-1, which will be the basis for all interpretations and delineations in this book.

---

4. The best summary to date is in: Michel Gauquelin, *Cosmic Influences on Human Behavior*, trans. Joyce E. Clemow (New York: Stein & Day, 1973).

Auxiliary Angles

There is one type of exception to the general angularity curve. Aside from the horizon and meridian, there are other sensitive points in an astrological map which can accentuate a planet posited there as though the planet were in the immediate foreground. Speaking very loosely, these are the points in square aspect to the Ascendant and Midheaven.

I say speaking loosely, because in reality these most important aspects to the chart angles are themselves other angles. For instance, the square to the Ascendant which falls above the horizon, often called the nonagesimal, is the true longitude of the **Zenith**. This is the highest degree of the zodiac (whereas the Midheaven is merely the most southern degree).[5] The square to the Ascendant which falls below the horizon is the true longitude of the **Nadir**, which is exactly opposite the Zenith. For instance, with an Ascendant of 9° Gemini, the Zenith is 9° Pisces and the Nadir is 9° Virgo. Both mark the longitudes of the meridian circle's intersections with the prime vertical.

Squares to the Midheaven are a little more complicated. Although ecliptical squares to the Midheaven within about 1° seem quite valid, evidence indicates that these aspects are more profitably measured along the Equator — that is, in right ascension. The points 90° from the meridian in right ascension are called the **East Point** and **West Point**. Extremely significant positions, they mark the intersections of three important great circles: the horizon, the celestial equator and the prime vertical. The **East Point** lies due east on the horizon, and the West Point lies due west.[6] To compute the degree of the Ecliptic on the East Point, add six hours to the sidereal time of the birth chart or return chart and extract the Midheaven from your table of houses for this new sidereal time. This is the East Point which is listed on the chart. The West Point is exactly opposite the East Point. Both points should approximately square the Midheaven in longitude.

Each of these four points acts like an angle, intensifying the significance of a planet conjoining the point. While the East Point and West Point behave much like squares to the meridian (which they are),

5. This is only consistently true north of the tropic of Cancer. If the Midheaven's declination is more northerly than the geocentric latitude of birthplace, it is the most **northern** degree of that horoscope.
6. Technically, this is not true of the **longitude** of the East Point and West Point, but of the points themselves. They are not ecliptical (zodiacal) points, but reside, instead, on the celestial equator. Their longitudes as placed in a horoscope are merely conveniences to enable us to more easily see when planets are nearby.

they have, respectively, a first house and seventh house quality. Similarly, the Zenith and Nadir are basically squares to the horizon, but have, respectively, a tenth house and fourth house coloration. I allow a 2-3° orb for these angles. The East Point and West Point are substantially more powerful than the Zenith and Nadir.

Though often of a much more subtle character, the **Vertex** is also important in assessing the focus of an astrological map. To find the Vertex in the birth chart: (1) subtract the birth latitude from 90°; (2) add twelve hours to the natal sidereal time; and (3) for this latitude and the new sidereal time, compute the Ascendant. This resulting longitude is that of the Vertex.

I do not consider the Vertex an angle so much as an important "sensitive point." Planets conjunct, opposite, or square the Vertex are highly accented, but any actual manifestations seem to be unconsciously motivated. For instance, Mars conjunct the Vertex in a return chart may indicate suddenly finding yourself in the middle of a fight that you did not expect, which you may swear you did nothing to initiate. However, an in-depth and honest examination of the situation and your own feelings is likely to reveal that you actually did much to prompt the argument, however unaware of this you were at the time. I believe it is this component of unconsciousness which gives the "fated" or "predestined" quality which other writers have associated with Vertex-sponsored occurrences.

The Vertex is always on the west side of the wheel and (except for certain instances in extremely neutral latitudes, near the Equator) in the opposite hemisphere, north or south, from the East Point. Opposite the Vertex is located the **Antivertex**. A seventh house quality colors the Vertex because other people are commonly involved in its workings; while the Antivertex has a first house cast. These two points are the most important in the Vertex system.

Also worth noting are the squares to the Vertex: the **South Point** of the horizon (SP), which has a tenth house coloration, and the horizon's **North Point** (NP), which is somewhat like the fourth house in nature.[7] The recommended orb here once again is 2-3° for the Vertex and Antivertex; perhaps less for the South Point and North Point.

Aspects

Aspects between planets are the keynotes in examining any type of astrological map. When two planets are separated by specific angular

---

7. Remember that for locations in northern climes, south is at the top of the wheel and north is at the bottom.

distances along the ecliptic, their natures are merged, indicating a dynamic link between the two principles they represent.

Each aspect used in astrology is formed by dividing the circle of 360° by some whole number. The most important aspects are those generated when the circle is divided by 1 (360°= 0° = conjunction), 2 (180° = opposition), and 3 (120° = trine), then successively halving these aspects to produce the square (180°/2 = 90°) and the sextile (120°/2 = 60°), which are divisions of the whole circle by 4 and 6, respectively. These five aspect configurations seem to be the most important in general astrological work.

In my personal work with natal charts, I use these five aspect-distances as well as the semisquare (45°) and the sesquisquare (135°). There are other aspects I also consider to be somewhat valid but do not regularly use, including the semisextile (30°) and quincunx (150°). The 22½° series (22°.5, 67°.5, 112°.5, 157°.5) seem quite valid in directions but are scarcely useful in natal work. Also, the quintile series, based on the division of the circle into fifths (72°, 144°) gives very reliable information natally, though these aspects are not readily discernible in a drawn horoscope.

Setting the quintile series aside for a moment, all other aspects mentioned above can be grouped into two categories: those based on successive halving of the opposition to produce the series 180°, 90°, 45°, 22°.5 and all their multiples, which are usually called **hard aspects**; and those based upon successive halving of the trine to produce the series 120°, 60°, 30°, and multiples of each, which are usually called **soft aspects**. The conjunction belongs to both groups since it is both 2 x 180° and 3 x 120°.

Rather than call these aspects "hard" and "soft," I prefer to use the terms **dynamic** and **static**.[8] The Opposition Series represents dynamic action, incentive and movement, whereas the Trine Series seems to signify placidity, quietness and stillness. John Nelson's work with predicting sunspots has clearly shown that the dynamic aspects are most important in triggering major solar flare-ups and activity. On the other hand, what I have termed the static aspects, especially the trine, will put a damper on the likelihood of solar activity, actually creating a situation where the release of solar energy is inhibited. The exception to this

---

8. In the first edition of this book, I suggested the terms **kinetic** and **static**. "Kinetic" was selected to imply not only energy but, especially, movement. In some ways, I still prefer it to "dynamic." However, **dynamic** is the precise antonym of "static," and indicates activity, force, energy, change, process (see Webster). Static means at rest, in equilibrium, quiescent. I agree with one author's criticism that this is a dynamic equilibrium; however, the net result is typically a lack of visible change.

is when the soft aspect connects directly to a hard aspect pattern, as when a planet trines one end of an opposition and sextiles the other. In that case, the soft aspect enhances and reinforces the energetic quality of the hard aspect.[9]

In natal astrology, these same principles hold true, with the soft aspect by itself representing a **status quo** in the personality where a person does not really care to change. A soft aspect connected to a hard aspect pattern, though, will reinforce and modify the latter configuration, augmenting whatever the basic hard aspect pattern represents.

Both dynamic and static aspects are important in natal astrology. However, my experience has convinced me that soft aspect transits are unreliable and only occasionally worth noting. Transits elicit a behavior change and provide an opportunity to take definite action, or grow. Because of their static quality, trines and sextiles bring no such likelihood.

Therefore, **in examining Solar Returns, our attention must be focused entirely on the dynamic aspects**. Remember, however, that we will be reading each Solar Return **twice**. When we read it as though it were a new birth chart, without recourse to the actual natal planets, we can use exactly the same rules which are valid in natal astrology. Even then, though, static aspects should take a back seat to dynamic aspects in any case of doubt. And, when Solar Return planets (which are actually transits) are compared to natal planets, only the dynamic aspects are important.

Parans

This brings us to another type of aspect with which many astrologers are not familiar: the **paran**. When present, this aspect often determines the central theme of a Solar or Lunar Return (or even a natal chart) quite succinctly. "Paran" is an affectionate shortening of the full Greek term, *paranatellon* (pl., *paranatellonta*).

Parans may sound very complicated, but in practice they are quite easy to apply and use. Simply stated, a paran exists when two planets simultaneously occupy a major angle (horizon or meridian) of whatever horoscopic wheel you happen to be studying.

This gives us three possible types of parans: (1) The planets may be conjunct each other and on the same angle. In this case we have

9. John H. Nelson, *Cosmic Patterns* (Washington, D.C.: American Federation of Astrologers, 1974), and Zipporah Pottenger Dobyns, *Finding the Person in the Horoscope* (Los Angeles: T.I.A. Publications, 1973), 36-39. (This latter summarizes Nelson's practical results in a way that is particularly meaningful for the astrologer.)

a **paran-conjunction**. Technically, this special case is known as a **synanatellon** — "synan" for short. (2) Our planets may also be in opposition to one another and simultaneously angular, such as one planet rising while the other sets. In this case we have what is technically termed a **paran-opposition**. (3) The third case occurs when two planets occupy **adjacent** angles, such as one planet rising while the other is on the Midheaven. This **paran-square** is too often overlooked because it does not always approximate an ecliptical square. However, it is an extremely powerful aspect.

Below are three examples of close paran-squares in the natal maps of famous people. The chart calculations for these examples are based upon birth certificate times.[10]

DAVID SCOTT, Astronaut

Midheaven	= 10° ♑ 59'	
Saturn	= 10° ♑ 33'	{−0°26'}
Ascendant	= 26° ♈ 09'	
Mars	= 24° ♈ 41'	{−1°28'}

LEE TREVINO, Golfer

Midheaven	= 15° ♑ 30'	
Moon	= 19° ♋ 41'	{+4°11'}
Ascendant	= 03° ♉ 28'	
Mercury	= 07° ♏ 32'	{+4°04'}

JOSEPH WAMBAUGH, Author

Midheaven	= 17° ♎ 36'	
Mars	= 14° ♎ 54'	{−2°42'}
Ascendant	= 23° ♐ 12'	
Mercury	= 22° ♐ 39'	{−0°33'}

Parans are not measured along the Ecliptic, but along another circle, called the **prime vertical,** which is oriented to the individual's own place on the Earth. For any given locality, the prime vertical rises due east, passes directly overhead, and sets due west. Along this great circle, the meridian and horizon are exactly 90° apart. Thus, the existence of a paran implies both that (1) two planets are simultaneously angular, thus at their greatest strength, and (2) they form either a conjunction, opposition or square to each other **as measured along the prime vertical.** In David Scott's nativity, Saturn is almost precisely on his Midheaven (actually, half a degree west in longitude). Mars is a degree and a half above the Ascendant. We can therefore estimate that a Mars-Saturn paran-square exists here with an orb of about 1°. (If Mars had

---

10. Katherine Clark, Allen Gilchrist, Janice Mackey and Charles Dorminy, *Contemporary Sidereal Horoscopes, Book I* (San Francisco: Sidereal Research Publications, 1976). All longitudes are sidereal.

been **below** the Ascendant, the orb would have been about 2°.) Lee Trevino has the Moon 4° west of the fourth-house cusp and Mercury 4° above the Descendant, so they are in virtually precise paran-square, according to their longitudes. Joseph Wambaugh's Mercury-Mars paran looks wider than the other two, for while his Mercury is only half an ecliptical degree above the Ascendant, his Mars is nearly 3° west of the upper meridian. The estimate paran orb is therefore a little over 2° in his case.

I speak of **estimated orbs** because parans, when correctly deter-mined, are not measured in longitude. Unless a planet is exactly on the Ecliptic (i.e., has no appreciable latitude, like the Sun), it will not rise, culminate, set or anticulminate with the degree of the zodiac it occupies. My own Moon, for instance, falls at 27≈24 in the Sidereal Zodiac (21)(31 Tropical), but is 4°45′ north of the Ecliptic. This causes it to cross the MC or IC when the longitude of either of those angles is 25≈22 (Sidereal). At the latitude of Los Angeles, where I live, the position the Moon held at my birth rises physically when the Ascendant is 20≈03, and sets when the Descendant is 28≈19. The procedures for making these exact measurements are easily managed if one is familiar with trigonometric functions,[11] and not much more problematic otherwise, provided one has tables such as are given in De Luce's *Complete Method of Prediction*.[12]

Nonetheless, in everyday practice the average astrologer usually will not take the time to do more than estimate parans from the longitudes of the planets. This is totally adequate in most (but not all) instances. Examples of active parans in Solar Returns will be given in the latter part of this book.

We may classify parans as being either **active** or **potential**. The three examples given above are all cases of active parans, where two planets actually occupy chart angles and actively form their paran-aspect. Using Scott's horoscope as an example, we can isolate the two requirements for an active paran: (a) the sidereal time at which his Saturn crosses the Midheaven is very close (nearly identical) to the sidereal time at which his Mars rises; (b) the sidereal time of his birth chart is very close to both of these sidereal times.

Let us suppose, though, that Scott had been born an hour or two earlier. Neither his Saturn nor his Mars would have moved very much, except for their house placement. If we were to compute the sidereal time, for this earlier birth, at which Saturn would occupy the Midheaven

---

11. Cyril Fagan and Brig. R. C. Firebrace, *Primer of Sidereal Astrology* (Isabella, Mo.: Littlejohn Publishing Company, 1971).
12. Robert De Luce, *Complete Method of Prediction* (New York: ASI Publishers, 1978).

and Mars the Ascendant, we would still find them virtually identical, fulfilling condition (a). However, the earlier birthtime would drop Mars far into the first house and Saturn well into the tenth, so condition (b) would not be fulfilled — that is, the planets would not actually be on the angles. The Mars-Saturn paran would only be **potential**.

One further example should further clarify this difference, and one from my own nativity is convenient. For the latitude of my present residence, three planets cross angles with the following sidereal times:

	Sidereal Time	Sidereal Longitude	Tropical Longitude
Uranus on Asc.	00:59:16	3°20′ Cancer	27°27′ Cancer
Jupiter on Asc.	01:01:22	3°36′ Cancer	27°42′ Cancer
Sun on IC	01:02:18	22°28′ Virgo	16°34′ Libra

These are spread over 3^m02^s of sidereal time, equal to 0°45′. The Sun-Jupiter paran-square is only $56^s(0°14′)$ wide. Because these three sidereal times are so close, they fulfill condition (a) above and thus form a **potential paran**. Every day that I live at my present geographical latitude (34N05), these planets will come to the actual angles once, as the local sidereal time rotates through the full 24-hour cycle. Thus, every day that I live here, I will, if only for a few minutes, feel as though I have the Sun in major dynamic aspect to my Jupiter-Uranus conjunction.

This **potential** paran becomes an **active** paran when a period-analysis chart, such as a Solar Return, has approximately the same sidereal time as the three tabulated above, fulfilling condition (b). So, when my 1977 Solar Return occurred at 12:41 AM PDT on October 10, with a sidereal time of 1:03:21, an **active paran** was formed for the duration of the Solar Return period. The sidereal angles of that chart were: MC = 22♓45, ASC = 3♋56. Note that this paran was visible merely from the longitudes of the planets, without need for elaborate math work.

Calculating all of the potential parans in a Solar Return often adds useful corroborative information. Still, they do not seem to be as important as the ecliptical aspects with which we are all familiar and, because this information is only corroborative, it may be overlooked without losing the vital themes symbolized in the return chart. In this book, our attention will be directed primarily to the active parans which are visible on the face of the Solar Return chart itself, formed by planets occupying the all-important angular cusps of the Solar Return.

Houses

Houses are used very little in the interpretation of Solar and Lunar Returns, but they do have a certain measure of importance.

Bradley's original work, *Solar and Lunar Returns*[13], put a far heavier emphasis on house placements than experience proves is warranted. At the other extreme, contemporary Siderealists have, as a rule, totally abandoned any use of houses[14] without an apparent sense of a middleground. I recommend **a moderate use of houses**, always keeping in mind that **angularity and aspects are the two prime delineative elements which must always be given top priority**.

Once more, it is necessary to recall that a Solar Return is routinely delineated **twice**. When the Solar Return is rendered into behavior terms as if it were a new nativity, its houses are as revealing as they would be in a birth chart. My own experience in astrology is that house dispositorships (in either zodiac) are irrelevant and misleading, but that a planet's position in a given house does reveal important information. Luminary house placements, or those of planetary clusterings (stellia) are the most important.

Angularity is the primary factor in the mundane (diurnal, domal) situation of a planet. Remember that a planet can be foreground and simultaneously in either an angular or cadent house; middleground and either angular or succedent; or background while either succedent or cadent (see Figure 2-3). Since planets in the foreground of a Solar Return have the greatest freedom of expression, the houses related to these areas are rightly subject to the most comprehensive delineations. Background bodies have only a small likelihood of manifesting their characteristic traits, except perhaps at deep levels outside the reach of normal conscious awareness. Accordingly, houses in background fields of the Solar Return need not be treated so extensively. Over a lifetime, an individual can develop, strengthen, elaborate and incorporate the most subtle implications of his or her natal horoscope; but in the year of a Solar Return's duration, only the most salient portents will generally materialize.

Solar Return houses and angles mean essentially the same thing that natal houses and angles mean, except that they apply specifically to unfolding patterns and events within a certain time frame. Meanings of Solar Return planets in Solar Return houses, therefore, resemble

13. Bradley, *Solar and Lunar Returns*.
14. Andrew B. Howard, "Angles vs. Houses: A Realignment of Priorities," *Astrology Now* (December 1975) I, no. 9, 7ff.

published delineations of planets transiting through natal houses. I have never found a whit of evidence that individual natal planets in Solar Return houses are significant.

However, natal planets on Solar Return angles do seem to manifest most often through the field of experience designated by the particular angle they contact. Due to the primacy of angular cusps, below are given specific characteristics of each major angle in the Solar Return. Sometimes the qualities of a foreground planet seem undifferentiated with regard to its particular angle-of-residence, its **emphasis** alone being the most important consideration. Most of the time, though, the following correlations will be useful in assessing details.

THE MERIDIAN (fourth/tenth-house cusp axis) pertains to very personal, individualizing factors within the person, probably deeply rooted in his or her sense of identity. **Identity**, in fact, is the fundamental key word of the meridian, in the sense of awareness of what constitutes ''I'' within each of us. There is also a relationship between the meridian and **authority**.

More specifically, *the Midheaven* is connected with **public authority**. This means either one's own authority exercised in a public sphere, outside of the home, i.e., one's **public identity**, or the authority one acknowledges in an outerworld ''superior'' (employer or ''the authorities,'' for instance; or, to a child, one of the parents). The Midheaven fundamentally signifies the unfolding of a personal sense of direction, the outcome of which is to be more truly and fully oneself, so in natal astrology it is most definitely the key to identity as measured by outerworld standards. In Solar Returns, it characteristically pinpoints circumstances affecting one's experience of ''highness'' (prestige, prominence, culmination). Reputation and status are often involved, because one's career is a frequent (though not exclusive) area of manifestation. For a public figure, it can reveal the overall tone of one's interaction with the public.

At the lower extreme of the Solar Return we find the *IC* (*Imum Coeli*), or *Lower Heaven*, the most personal, private focal point of awareness in a horoscope. **Privacy** is clearly the basic key word of this angle. Though, due to their angularity, planets on the fourth cusp are highly expressive keynotes of the year in question, the realm of manifestation is within emotional (if not physical) close quarters to home. The IC is usually considered the weakest, least important angle, but I think its effects are simply more private and therefore hidden from the casual observer. Domestic concerns, property, family and other resources may all be affected if we feel a need to look for specific outer manifestations. What seems more important to me, however, is the orientation to one's roots, the profound sense of inner self, and a reinvestment of energy into the psychic foundations of life. Sometimes the inward-turning brings about a re-evaluation of priorities; or ongoing decisions at a subconscious level can emerge into consciousness. As a result of either, an emphasized Lower Heaven may indicate a major cycle shift ("the beginning and end of the matter," as the old books called it), particularly if the Sun, Pluto or Uranus is placed there.

Relationships and interactions with the environment are fundamentally shown by *the horizon* of an astrological map. Personal relationships are composed of two parts: oneself and some "other," shown by the two ends of the horizon axis — respectively, the Ascendant and Descendant. Squares to the horizon aspect both the Ascendant and Descendant, thereby specifically describing the interaction of Self with Other, i.e., relationships *per se*.

THE ASCENDANT signifies one's experience of oneself in the process of interrelating with another. This projected self-image is how we extend ourselves to others. While the Ascendant is one of the two most important angles (the MC being the other), I believe it has been misunderstood by those astrologers who think of it as "self," existing in a vacuum, devoid of the balance of "other." Selfhood is a function of the entire horoscope, expressed primarily through the Sun and meridian, whereas the Ascendant implicitly signifies the existence of **relationship**.

Rather than the traditional "**I Am**" interpretation, the rising angle can perhaps best be rendered "**I Do**," especially in return charts. It indicates experiential participation. Though the Sun rising in a natal or return chart can be interpreted as self-interest, since the Sun always indicates primary focus of attention, the Ascendant by itself can be thought of more purely as meaning **self-involvement**.

Contrary to this, *the Descendant,* when involved in an angularity emphasis, signifies an **others-consciousness** — an increased focal awareness on other people — and the way we choose to experience other people. Bradley suggested **cooperation** and **competition** as polar keynotes designating the Descendant's attributes. I can think of no better summary. The fundamental principle of the retiring angle is **focus of attention away from self,** thus to others. This accounts very nicely with the traditional (and apparently valid) association of the Descendant with death, since death is the passing out of existence, or setting aside, of selfhood in the sense that it is represented by the horizon. The fundamental symbolism, however, is not explicitly that of death, but of any instance of stepping outside of the highly specialized and particularized selfhood which differentiates one incarnated individual from another.

Signs

Sign placements are among the least significant factors conditioning Solar Return planets. Certainly they have some importance, but it is extremely limited. If a planet has any close aspects at all, these seem to overwhelm the coloration of the sign. Subtleties can be perceived by the alert observer but, as has been stated before, we are not as interested in the subtleties as in the overall impression. Solar Returns are not given the opportunities for full development and expression which a natal chart receives as its birthright.

The primary exception to the relative unimportance of signs is that the sign tenanted by the Solar Return Moon seems to leave its impress on behavior for the year, augmented strongly, of course, by the lunar aspects. As the Moon is the most receptive, responsive, adaptive planet we have, representing, *inter alia*, easily shifting moods, it can be expected to reflect new traits more easily than any other planet.

Such is my personal experience. At the same time, the reader is strongly encouraged to make up his or her own mind on each issue discussed in these pages. What I am presenting is a compilation of my own working procedures, opinions and findings based on several years of using Solar and Lunar Returns, and several more in general astrology; but, fortunately, I do not at the present time have any delusions of infallibility. The most competent astrologers I have ever known have been those who have been willing to challenge any authority and test any rule for themselves. I hope my readers will do as much.

If you decide to examine the importance of Solar Return sign placements for yourself, a little common sense will keep you from getting lost in left field. The Sun's sign in a Solar Return is naturally identical to that of natal Sun. Mercury and Venus will also be in their natal signs often, though not always. Along with that of Mars, the signs of the latter two planets will be the only nonluminary positions worth consideration. Planets from Jupiter outward will be in the same sign in almost every Solar Return occurring anywhere in the world in a given year. Surely, this explains in part how outer planet sign transits have key effects on everyday life of individuals; but because of that, they belong in the sphere of mundane astrology, not genethliacal. Little **personalized** significance will be found in them.

Locality

Solar Returns consistently appear to score their best on accuracy tests when computed for the longitude and latitude that the individual occupies from minute to minute. If a man were born in New Orleans, permanently moved to Portland, Oregon, and was there for his birthday when the Solar Return set up, but fell deeply in love while in New York on vacation, it would be the Solar Return calculated for Manhattan which would sport a prominent Venus, rather than either of the other two locations.

The other two may show the event too; but experience proves that you cannot rely on this. In every case that I have seen, if an event was described by a return chart calculated for the coordinates of the birthplace, and the individual no longer lived there, the return for that person's current location would give a still clearer, more vivid picture of the situation. Something has always been missing in the birthplace return which the residence version supplies.

The nearest exceptions to this have been in connection with an event someplace other than where the Solar Return year actually began. Angles for the site where the Solar Return actually occurs (the place of residence on the birthday) seem to retain **some** of their significance as a basic "imprint" for that year, just as the angles of a natal chart never lose their significance no matter where on Earth a person chooses to relocate.

A recent Solar Return from my own life gives striking corroboration of this view, showing how significant even a small location shift can be in altering the portents of these charts. While living and working in San Diego, I experienced a Solar Return with natal Jupiter and Uranus 0°06′ and 0°11′ (respectively) from the Midheaven. Motivated by very strong commercial indicators, I conceived the idea of returning to Los Angeles and starting a new type of computer education business. We were at a peak in the "computer boom." Support for microcomputer owners could not begin to keep up with sales, and the trend was expected to continue in that direction. Already, while in San Diego, the number of calls in this new area were beginning to interfere with my regular employment, with much of the interest coming from the Los Angeles vicinity. It was time to move.

My Solar Return looked almost identical in Los Angeles and San Diego. The meridian and horizon shifted little more than a degree between the two cities. Yet, with my natal Jupiter-Uranus moved to just over a degree from the Midheaven for the City of the Angels, transiting

Saturn was now a mere 0°08′ from the Ascendant! Well-meaning friends suggested I might reconsider the move. Astrologer Ken Irving, tongue firmly planted in his cheek, said that under these charts I might return to L.A. and find that computers had already gone out of style.

Well, he wasn't **exactly** right.

However, the first year was one of the most trying and disappointing periods of my life, drawing on every bit of endurance and effort I could muster. For instance, the very **hour** I planted myself in Los Angeles, I learned that the previous tenant had not yet been vacated from my office space as promised and would not be gone for over a month. Difficult start-up years are not uncommon in new businesses, and we did manage a tiny profit. The remarkable thing, however, is that within two months of the subsequent Solar Return, the trend shifted again. The company began to bear its own weight. Our second year is assured of producing a substantial profit.

All for a degree and a half on the angular cusps!

Examining Solar and Lunar Returns for events far from an individual's birthplace stimulates thoughts on how our position in space, as well as time (a matter essentially under each person's individual control), strongly determines how we interact with and experience the world. A set of return charts comes to mind of a couple on the West Coast who had a most remarkable wedding, far removed from even some of the more liberal conventions by which our society regulates such affairs. Within their groups of friends, this affair was exciting, dramatic and quite enjoyable for all involved. Their return charts for the wedding site described this event extremely well.

However, both were originally from small towns in conservative areas of the Midwest. When their return charts were computed for their birthplaces, the wheels described restrictive conditions, anxiety, critical family pressures and overall discomfort. This is exactly what they would have experienced, in their opinions, if this same event had occurred in either of their hometowns, rather than in Southern California.

Vocabulary and Usage

Before closing this chapter on "Speaking the Same Language," there are a few word meanings I would like to clarify insofar as these words will be used in the next several chapters.

Whenever I use the term **Solar Return**, unless I state otherwise, you should understand that this refers to any Sun-based return discussed in this book, including Demi-Solars, Quarti-Solars and Enneads (discussed in Chapters 7 and 9).

Solar and Lunar Returns shall be referred to collectively as **Solunars** or **Solunar Returns,** terms originally coined by Cyril Fagan to simplify his own writings on this subject.

Whereas "foreground" and "background" mean roughly half a Campanian house on either side of the angular and cadent house cusps, respectively, we need other terms to indicate close conjunctions of the planets with the angles themselves. Planets within no more than, say, 5-7° from the horizon or meridian will be referred to as being located in **the immediate foreground.** Likewise, planets within close orb of conjunction with the cadent house cusps will be acknowledged as being located in **the immediate background.**

Just as planets in the natal chart are labeled "natal planets," "radical planets," etc., so shall I call planets in the Solar Return the **solar planets**. For instance, "solar Moon" means "transiting Moon at the time of the Solar Return."

CHAPTER THREE

INTERPRETING PLANETARY ANGULARITY

Seven million people have the same birthday you do (give or take a hundred thousand or so), though they were not all born in the same year. This is approximately the population of the greater Los Angeles area. Every one of those people will have fundamentally the same planetary longitudes in their Solar Returns for any given year, only the Moon's position being significantly different. Even here we find that half a million people will share the same identical Solar Return planet positions (including the Moon) for every birthday in the year.

Common sense suggests that these five hundred thousand people will not have identical, or even nearly identical, years. What makes the difference? What astrological factors, we must ask ourselves, discriminate between each of these many, many Solar Returns?

The answer, of course, is the mundane construction of the return chart, i.e., the relationship of each planet to the horoscopic angles with the subsidiary house divisions. Each planet's prominence by mundane placement reveals how great a part it plays in the unfolding drama of the new year of life. Basic themes are established which guide us in properly interpreting how the aspect dynamics are apt to manifest.

This "theme setting" function is of vital importance. Imagine a Solar Return with an extremely close Mercury-Pluto aspect, which usually coincides with a "demand for the answers" in some sense. In a basically Saturnian chart (Saturn closely conjunct an angle), this could suggest being backed up against the wall by an interrogator who does the demanding. An essentially Jupiterian return chart with this aspect, on the other hand, could suggest a philosophical period during which one is rewarded for one's probing search for answers. When one's freedom needs call the shots as signaled by Uranus' occupation of the immediate foreground, a close Mercury-Pluto aspect can signify an exciting discovery as the end product of investigation and asking questions. Should Venus set the theme, however, Mercury tightly configurated with Pluto may indicate that continual probing, introspection, question-asking and intellectual confrontation of an issue will center around romantic or social matters; for these are the concerns which will most likely dominate an individual's conscious and near-conscious awareness when transiting Venus holds the executive chair in a Solunar.

Don't take the foregoing delineative skits as "rules" for pairing a foreground Saturn, Jupiter, Uranus or Venus with a Mercury-Pluto aspect. They are only examples of **possible** outcomes which must make sense within the context of the remainder of the chart, given here as examples of a key principle. That principle is: **Foreground planets, both natal and solar, set the tone of the entire period covered by a Solunar return.** All planetary dynamics (shown by aspects) manifest within the context of these theme setters.

It is quite possible to read Solunars using only a list of foreground planets. At first introduction to the subject, this is a very good way to get clear, accurate, sometimes even vivid delineations which reinforce students' confidence in their own skills. Other details can be added later.

An important adjunctive consideration is noticing which planets are in the **background** of a return chart. Such planets require attention because they represent the least-manifest themes of a period. For instance, if one set aside a period of time during which to write a book, script, thesis or whatever, background Mercuries would be serious impediments to easy self-expression. In this chapter, brief interpretations are offered for Solar Return planets occupying the background, as well as foreground.

Setting the Psychological Tone

Astrological forecasting is based on two types of information.

First, we want to know which psychological factors within the individual are likely to have the freest, most active play. These may be needs, habits or other behavior motivations.

Also, it is important that we learn the nature of conditions **outside of the individual,** within the environment, which (s)he is likely to encounter.

Environmental factors and components within the self represent the total experiential reality of the individual. Nothing else has any personal significance. Gestalt psychologists sometimes refer to the sum of these two elements as the **life space** of the individual.

Through astrology, we can examine how a prescribed set of conditions **outside of oneself** interacts with, or is attracted by, certain conditions or factors **within oneself**. Often this enables us, through our working knowledge of human behavior, to predict events; but it is **only the psychological tone or conditioning** which can actually be shown astrologically.

In the interpretations of individual factors given in this book, primary emphasis is given to the psychological tone they imply. Any specific events suggested are mostly based on experience of how these factors will manifest, and partly based on logical extrapolation of the psychological principle. Remember that with astrology we can come uncannily close to describing how a person feels, almost from hour to hour. What we cannot do nearly so accurately is specify what events generate those feelings or what actions the person takes in response to the feelings.

Natal = "Inside" — Transits = "Outside"

Active elements in an individual's personal behavior are shown by planets in his or her natal horoscope. Similarly, the tone of the exterior circumstances which affect the individual can be deduced from studying the cosmic environment; that is, the transiting planets.

Transiting planets describe exterior input, usually (but not always) in terms of active participation with the environment. This is because transits (including transiting positions at the time of a Solar Return) are continually "new" factors, ever shifting, coming into awareness for a short time, but normally carrying a "foreign" feel to them. Transiting Mars, for instance, is an aggressive, energetic factor distinct from our own Mars. It is therefore harder for most people to recognize this transient aggressive quality as part of themselves.

If an individual does not identify with a need or quality (s)he is experiencing, that quality is **projected** onto a part of the environment; that is, the individual experiences it as a trait outside of himself or herself, "awarded" to someone else in the vicinity.

Because of this, transiting Mars' input is **interpreted** as aggression **aimed at the individual by someone or something in the environment**. Whereas natal Mars could indicate the individual's own aggression or energy, transiting Mars generally signifies others' aggression, energy from the outside or an otherwise Martian environment, in practical astrological interpretation.

Each of the planets can be similarly dichotomized as a general guideline. Discriminating between the natures of, say, natal Mars and transiting Mars, as above, is extremely important to correct interpretation. The two can mean, in some ways, completely opposite things.

At the same time, people more psychologically self-aware will be better equipped to accept the qualities of a transiting planet as their own, and not project these entirely onto the environment. Transiting Mars may signify "aggression directed at the native" in the form of an attack, but at least we can ask what we have done to bring such an attack on ourselves. If Mars transits natal Mercury, our ideas may be attacked; but if a writer or speaker is sufficiently critical of his own work in advance (accepting transiting Mars as part of himself), outside criticism is apt to be much less frequent or intense.

Transiting Planets in Solar Returns

Solar Return planets are, themselves, transits to the natal horoscope. Thus, they are generally interpreted as **outside influences operating centripetally,** i.e., inward upon the native.

Yet, when the Solar Return occurs, these transiting planets are **captured and frozen** into personal significance for the considerable period of one year. This makes them less "foreign" or "alien" than other transits. An individual will commonly regard solar Mars much as (s)he would natal Mars.

Solar planets are neither entirely "outside" like transits nor "inside" like natal planets. They lie somewhere between. They are like transiting planets which the individual does not entirely project. A convenient and useful approach, I have found, is to think of them as essentially transiting planets, but indicating **circumstances** described by the planet's nature. Thus, solar Mars symbolizes "competitive or angry circumstances" or some variation. This approach actively involves the individual in the planet's qualities, rather than making him or her completely separate from the Martian manifestation.

Solar Return Planets: Foreground and Background

TRANSITING SUN FOREGROUND OR BACKGROUND
Because a Solar Return is, by definition, a chart wherein transiting Sun precisely conjoins natal Sun, there is no way to differentiate between the positions of these two Suns. The Solar Return Sun, therefore,

has no real significance of its own. See the sections later in this chapter for **Natal Sun Foreground** and **Natal Sun Background**.

One place it is possible (although fairly rare) for transiting Sun to be foreground and natal Sun otherwise is in the Quarti-Solar Return. This is computed for transiting Sun's square to natal Sun (see Chapter 7). The Ennead (Chapter 9) also allows for one Sun to be foreground and the other background.

In these latter types of return charts only, a foreground transiting Sun will indicate special attention received during the period under consideration. Aspects made to the Sun by other transiting planets will indicate the type of attention, whether supportive or critical, and perhaps what part of the individual's life will be affected. Transiting Sun signifies "authorities" in the environment — those people to whom we somehow give away power, and whom we consider "higher" than ourselves (employers, legal authorities, clergy, parents, God, a revered friend, etc.).

Unless afflicted, a foreground transiting Sun brings with it recognition, honors, strokes for achievement and similar rewards. When subjected to stressful aspects, these same traits can become notoriety, condescension from others, criticism and other severe forms of attention.

TRANSITING MOON FOREGROUND

Emotional excitement surrounds the individual with this placement of the Solar Return Moon. Being strongly responsive to the emotional quality of the immediate environment, such a person is keenly attuned to the fluctuating, unstable circumstances of his or her world. Changing conditions require the native to adapt to new situations, so the year is apt to be one of acclimating oneself to an impermanent or uncertain life-style.

Not only are the appetites easily aroused, including the sexual ones, but these people display intensive desires and considerable emotional force in whatever activities they seriously undertake. Sensation and feeling are dominant keynotes for the period in question.

A foreground Moon is one of a few astrological factors which hypersensitize people to the astrological themes presently operating in their lives. Due to an acute awareness of the "feeling tone" of a place, anyone with this luminary active is apt to more fully experience whatever their Solunars, transits, etc., describe. Such people are quite vulnerable, susceptible, readily seduced. They react more spontaneously to impromptu situations, giving way to whims and impulses which spring from their sensitized desire natures.

At the root of any lunar manifestation are the nurturance needs nestled inside all of us. When the Solar Return Moon is foreground, we either respond to the nurturance needs of someone nearby, or stand to receive somebody's affection, support, care and general emotional sustenance. Either way, the need to belong or merge with another living being is accentuated. Emotional security is an alluring payoff, commonly rooted in the sensual tactile immediacy of a loved one's (or coveted one's) presence. Popular attention by friends, family or community is a variation of this same principle, publicity being a common outworking of a foreground transiting Moon.

TRANSITING MOON BACKGROUND
Unless Mercury, Uranus or Neptune occupies the Solar Return foreground, this will be a relatively calm, stable period. One's emotional antennae are retracted, so the feeling tone of the outside world does not intrude on everyday life. An individual's overall emotional involvement with people and circumstances in the environment is held to a minimum.

Barring contrary indications by foreground planets, a background Moon points to a relatively stable, solid, settled time in life. Little effort is wasted on distractions. Personal affairs can be given primary attention because the individual is not likely to be wrapped up in the frantic scatter of outerworld circumstances.

TRANSITING MERCURY FOREGROUND
Transiting Mercury signifies the curiosities, learning needs, and open eyes and ears of the people in one's environment. This is another way of saying that transiting Mercury, as it interacts with an individual's natal planets, represents that person's own need to communicate an idea, make an announcement, share a piece of informative data or otherwise personally express himself or herself to someone else. When transiting Mercury occupies the foreground of a Solar Return, these needs occupy the foreground of the native's consciousness.

Solar Mercury, prominent and unafflicted, indicates a year in which a person can be most effectively self-expressive. If it is well-aspected, say by a foreground Jupiter, the ideas are apt to be well received and bring considerable favorable attention. If traditionally "malefic" planets configure Mercury, however, the thoughts begging to be voiced are much more likely to incite adversely critical reactions. This does not alter their need for expression.

Mercury "rules" transportation. A prominent Mercury often points to travel. More generally, it sponsors busy, active circumstances with rapid movement, scurrying, liveliness and a constant give-and-take of information. Such quickness can be an asset if the individual does not get lost in wasted motion.

Not only busy-ness, but the world of business is in high focus with a foreground solar Mercury. For a year, at least, the individual is strongly oriented toward commercial production. (S)he displays a knack for organization and is highly resourceful. Mercury's aspects will usually have plenty to say about how successful any business venture will be and in what directions they are apt to be headed.

Finally, transiting Mercury in the immediate foreground of a Solar Return provides an opportunity to further develop one's intellectual and communicative faculties, whether through formal education or independent endeavors. The native will be very involved with the world on an intellectual level. Problems may arise, though, if a pronounced intellect supplants feelings. The individual is likely to identify with his or her ideas, possibly becoming wedded to them and perversely dogmatic.

TRANSITING MERCURY BACKGROUND
It seems, during these times, as though nobody is listening to you! With a background Mercury, self-expression seems blocked for lack of a ready ear to hear or eye to see what a person wants to communicate. Little overt activity marks the time (unless it is shown by other factors in the foreground).

Private thoughts characterize the time. Meditation may be well undertaken if other indications support the idea.

TRANSITING VENUS FOREGROUND
This is likely to be one of the most enjoyable years an individual experiences, provided Venus is not too harshly aspected. The fundamental meaning of a foreground transiting Venus is **affection received**, which can take a variety of forms. The common denominator in all such manifestations is that an individual experiences the affectionate, friendly, loving, caring emotions available in his or her environment, usually in a supportive, harmonious, pleasant sort of way.

This implies that the native is likable and able to attract the affection of others. People with foreground solar Venuses are characteristically charming, congenial and friendly. They make inviting companions. This placement typically implies a love of social life and a strong sense of comradeship.

Complex instances occur when, for instance, the foreground transiting Venus configures natal Saturn. An accentuated natal Saturn suggests that a person is holding his own feelings in check and being keenly conscious of his own inadequacies. This triggers survival behavior, such as aloofness or tenacious possessiveness (it can go either way). In such cases, the native's personality may not seem at all attractive. Almost despite this, friends and family are apt to act supportive and affectionate. Apparently, the individual, beneath a hard exterior, is still somehow making room for love in his or her life.

Basically, this person gravitates toward the beautiful, rather than the coarse. The environment is apt to be quite pleasant and harmonious. Softness characterizes the life. Trust grows, as the world is seen as an essentially safe place to be. Vulnerability can be risked without likelihood that the world will betray.

Typically Venusian circumstances prevail. The individual will be more popular and socially active. Others are available to care for him, or lovingly look after him if he's down in the dumps. Gifts may be received or exchanged, though these are only Venusian if they are tokens of affection. Venus' aspects will provide details on how these social contacts are experienced.

Others are very likely to express romantic or erotic interest in the individual. For the duration of this Solar Return, the native will feel most comfortable in close pair-bonds (with friends, romantically, etc.). Love unions are quite common, particularly with Venus in the rising or the setting foreground.

Biological matters are brought to the forefront of the individual's awareness. Children may suddenly be desired, for instance, by a person of the right age. Oriented to a life of the flesh, such people may find it all too easy to dally in sensual delights at the expense of life's more practical, workaday concerns.

TRANSITING VENUS BACKGROUND
Having fun and being entertained are probably not high priorities this year. Social involvement is held to a minimum. Any new romances cultivated are likely to remain rather casual, unless other Solar Return placements indicate heavy attachments. In times of stress, that "soothing something" does not seem to be on hand to wipe away the weariness.

TRANSITING MARS FOREGROUND
Involvement with Mars-related occurrences, situations, feelings and activities naturally dominates the year when transiting Mars holds a prominent spot in the Solar Return. The atmosphere will be tense, heated, aggravating, irritating, strenuous and confronting in a variety of ways. Most people, though, move right into such a period with little

forethought, adopting the martial life tone quite naturally. Suddenly, their personal worlds become very active and hectic.

Such a person does not usually realize that he has become more confrontive, candid and obstinate than normal. **Competition** becomes a theme word for this individual, who now rarely backs down from anything. At the roots of these reactions is a scarcely conscious belief that the world is an inherently threatening place, against which one must defend oneself.

Physical aggression is pronounced, whether in business drives, sexual desires or other personal passions. The individual is restless and edgy, feeling driven in his activities, and relating to the world in a forthright and direct style. Tempers may be easily lost (and not so willingly regained) as outside provocations play on the individual's vulnerable stores of anger.

The sex drive is apt to be intense, and jealousies dominant. In men, their malehood and virility become keenly important. Women with this placement incorporate into their personalities more of the traits socially attributed to men, including aggressiveness, assertiveness, ego-dominance and establishing themselves as strong, independent people. The most sexually active periods of one's life are those years when transiting Mars falls close to the angles of the Solar Return.

Overall discomfort, especially physical discomfort, is characteristic of the martial years. One is apt to push oneself hard, putting heavy strains upon the body, particularly the nervous system. Newfound courage in facing life can cause hastiness, impulsiveness and recklessness with one's own safety, so injury from accidents can occur with increased frequency. Excessive energy not burnt off in constructive ways will certainly find more destructive outlets.

Yet the high vitality and drive can be made constructive with so little effort, provided a person is willing to be creative and expressive. Mars is simply saying, "Come on, keep busy!" **How** to keep busy is up to each person. Unless Mars is problematically configured, significant advances can be made in one's ambitions. The drive for accomplishment of personal goals can find fulfillment. **Achievement** is a major key word of a positively operating Mars in an individual willing to accept life's challenges head-on.

TRANSITING MARS BACKGROUND
Overall, life's irritants seem to take a backseat this year. Circumstances do not feel very threatening. Although a foreground natal Mars can still stimulate aggressive competition, life is relaxed and pretty much at ease, with a basic trust in the safety of one's own world. In

this relatively passive, inactive period of life, an individual is generally inclined to be cooperative, willing to listen to other people's ideas, and happy to let them live their lives, without feeling threatened by their differences.

TRANSITING JUPITER FOREGROUND
Happy birthday, indeed! Jupiter transiting the foreground of a Solar Return points to a year when life seems to treat an individual quite well. Symbolizing **fortune coming from without**, transiting Jupiter **can** indicate a year when other people contribute money, time, gifts, support in the form of a stipend and other indications of favor. Their generosity can be incredible. Even when the rewards are not nearly so material, an unafflicted, prominent solar Jupiter promises tokens of esteem, congeniality, social recognition and respect.

People strongly attuned to Jupiter have a general dislike of problems. They focus their attention on pleasant things and are attracted to what is good and qualitative in life. When transiting Jupiter beckons, people gravitate to fortunate circumstances which make them happy, contented and secure. Almost always it marks a step upward on the self-improvement ladder (either socially, financially or morally), raising people a rung or two above their usual life station, whatever that may be. Creating, being, living and growing simply feel good at such times.

Jupiter signifies the superior and excellent. A list of characteristically Jupiterian manifestations includes luck, advantage, material gain, honors — all things which elevate and put at ease by generating a feeling of blessedness.

Unfortunately, this can turn into laziness. The most negligent years of my life have been those when transiting Jupiter was foreground, a pattern I have regularly seen in other people's return charts as well. This can undermine Jupiter's cornucopia of apparent luck. There is a strong belief in personal success, a feeling of being gifted, elaborate confidence and a refusal to seriously believe in failure. Mixed with an urge to climb socially, these positive, optimistic attitudes can generate fabulous opportunities; but if taken for granted, they can point to an ostentatious wastrel, overextending himself and alienating others with his arrogance and blind pretensions.

Sometimes, Jupiter can signify ill health, even death. Usually, it promises good health, a result of high spirits. Sickness, in a Jupiterian time, coincides with favorable attention from family and friends, gifts, sympathy and a genuine effort to help one feel well and good. A Jupiter-signaled death will typically be the end of a long period of pain and suffering, thus a relief. Also, the funeral (a religious ceremony, thus Jupiterian) will loudly proclaim the individual's virtues and otherwise bestow honors.

The same occurs in life, where Jupiter indicates elevation, recognition and the fulfillment of ambitions. Relative prosperity reigns, and the mind might be quite materialistic. Jupiter aspects will describe the specific attitudes toward, and feelings about, "the good things in life."

TRANSITING JUPITER BACKGROUND
Barring a prominent natal Jupiter, the silver spoon will slip from your lips at this time. Opportunities will seem scarce, particularly if transiting Saturn is foreground. The mind is less programmed for confident searching out of advantage, more sensitive to problems and roadblocks. While progress hopefully will not come to a halt, major gains will be made more through individual effort than luck.

TRANSITING SATURN FOREGROUND
Barring contrary indications, this will not be an easy year. It can certainly be a good one, though, in the sense of practical experience acquired.

Transiting Saturn, simply put, makes one sharply aware of the demands and expectations of people and institutions in the environment. This fundamental principle can, of course, manifest in many ways; but all have the same basic characteristics. Hard reality stands in the path of progress, emphasizing immediate survival before expansion. Limitations, delays, frustrations, obstacles, disappointments — in fact, any manifestation of Saturn's important **restriction** motif — characterize the basic flavor of large portions of this year. Financial hardship is not at all unlikely, this being the most common way in which people are brought to face the stern, practical verities of day-to-day existence.

Actually, most of these hindrances have been around before. Transiting Saturn in the foreground only times one's awareness of them. This is a vital point. Time after time, I have seen people enter Saturnian periods and suddenly find themselves weighted under by what appear to be monstrous burdens, responsibilities and demands. However, careful questioning regularly discloses that circumstances have not drastically changed, only the individual's attitudes and reactions to the circumstances.

Such people are very conscious of authority. Their sensitivity to expectations makes them more cautious. Personal resources have to be mobilized so that the person becomes more capable at manipulating his or her environment. Other people may be shut out emotionally because their motives are not entirely trusted, so the individual may not be in much of a mood to accept assistance. A self-fulfilling expectation can be actualized whereby other people really do abandon the individual because they feel excluded and alienated.

Others in the environment are apt to seem highly critical and severe. Perhaps the person with this placement will feel harshly disciplined, unpopular, unloved and unwanted, therefore retiring from the rest of the world for a while and forgetting about pleasurable social interaction. Separations (or any other type of loss) are typical Saturnian occurrences.

Strange to relate, many children respond to this influence better than most adults. Though some of the fun may be taken out of their lives, youngsters are called upon by transiting Saturn to grow up more quickly and typically take giant strides in becoming skilled, experienced, competent and able to exist realistically in their environment. Years with Saturn transiting the Solar Return foreground will be hardening, toughening and maturing.

TRANSITING SATURN BACKGROUND

Outerworld demands do not press heavily on an individual with this placement of solar Saturn. Though a simultaneously foreground **natal** Saturn may indicate a strong sense of responsibility and the push of **internal** demands, external expectations can be ignored rather easily. Without the feeling of being held back or restricted, a person can "get out from underneath" a pressing load more easily if responsibilities get heavy. The native can relax as the critical, punitive elements of his or her environment are held at bay.

TRANSITING URANUS FOREGROUND

If you like surprises, you will adore this year. Uranus heralds changes, new directions and probably a milestone and turning point in your life. Usually these events burst into our awareness suddenly, with little warning.

Uranian circumstances can be either thrilling or frightening, depending on how much a given individual enjoys change. Make no mistake, the presence of this planet in the Solar Return foreground can be totally uprooting, and in extreme cases separate an individual from every tie to the past that (s)he tenaciously clutches. But this is because Uranus, in its simplest and purest form, signifies **freedom**. It opens the individual to new areas of involvement and requires an honest, clear, objective viewing of feelings and experiences. Look to the specific angle or house Uranus occupies for clues to where in this person's life you can expect to find an adventure, an awakening and the need to adjust to altered conditions. Remember, though, that such adventures are probably things these people have wanted to do for a long time, consciously or otherwise. Uranus transiting the foreground sponsors new feelings of freedom which allow them now to risk or try something new.

Transiting Uranus is commonly interpreted as "changes sponsored by something in the environment." This means that the individual is attracted to the novel and is open to experiencing change. Each day is lived for its excitement. Uranian events can include a change of residence or vocation, travel or variation of scenery closer to home. They are characteristically surprising and electrical (which **can** mean shocking!).

The pervasive state of excitement and excitability may indicate considerable tension. In particular, this results when a person does not want change, preferring instead to maintain the *status quo*, not reevaluate his or her biases and continue with old, familiar patterns. In these instances, Uranus will be experienced as unsettling and upsetting. Tension is a sure sign that the individual is resisting openness or change in some important area of life.

Hopefully, a year with transiting Uranus in the Solar Return foreground will be enlightening and progressive. Some inhibitions will be cast aside most likely, but the freedom acquired may be the freedom to say "no" as well as "yes." Personal limits need to be redefined at this time. This period can be stimulating, colorful and future-oriented, opening original pathways to spontaneity and creativity. Above all, this is a year in which to move toward a clearer self-perspective founded in honest, objective self-evaluation.

TRANSITING URANUS BACKGROUND
Very little takes an individual by surprise when transiting Uranus lands in the background of his or her Solar Return. Life seems much more quiet; or, should a foreground Moon, Mercury, Mars or Neptune indicate instability, busy-ness, activity or hysteria, the Uranian qualities of novelty, excitement and discovery are still noticeably absent. Such a person is far more willing to routinely accept familiar patterns, attitudes and ways of doing things than when Uranus transits the foreground.

TRANSITING NEPTUNE FOREGROUND
Neptunian circumstances are marked by an exaggerated state of emotional excitement. This can be negative in the sense of hysteria,

fluster or worry, or it can manifest in much more enjoyable ways, like the excitement which clutches the bleacher crowd near the end of a major sporting event.

People with this placement thrive on the emotional vitality which surrounds them, getting caught up in the flurry and madness of the moment. Other factors in the Solar Return will show how each person experiences and reacts to such drama-filled occurrences (whether they feel elated, frightened, shaken, enchanted, trapped, etc.).

In transit, Neptune offers a temptation. It is the "Forbidden Fruit" from the Garden of Eden, alluring with its mystery and elusiveness. When Neptune occupies the solar foreground, an individual is therefore open to seduction of all types. Pleasure-seeking is pronounced.

An active imagination may play havoc with the practical reality to which most people relate. Much of what fills the individual's private daydreams may suddenly appear to be attainable, though such an image cannot necessarily be trusted. The person is apt to more frequently indulge sexually, sensually, in food, drink or drugs. Whether induced by chemicals or the simple insanities of daily existence, inebriation may seem a way of life.

These individuals are impressionable and easily influenced. Frequently, therefore, transiting Neptune symbolizes the threat of victimization brought on by one's own misled and misplaced vulnerabilities. When others are involved, the native can be sucked into something which looks promising, and then be disappointed, if not betrayed and exploited. People can victimize themselves, as well, especially through oversensitivity to physical and emotional impressions resulting in illness. While Uranus represents freedom, Neptune commonly indicates dependency and overinvolvement — either by being dependent on other people (as when recovering from sickness or injury) or by finding another person depending on them, vampirizing their resources.

At its worst, transiting Neptune manifests as confusion, anxiety, despair, hopelessness, defeat, lack of self-confidence, resignation, procrastination and a general lack of perseverance or sense of direction. The person dislikes change or surprise, and rarely risks when (s)he thinks something is really a gamble. Dealing with problems by avoidance is characteristic. In fact, an avoidance syndrome characterizes the Neptunian's behavior in many different ways.

On the other hand, Neptune can show captivation by drama, music, fantasy, mystery, mysticism and the psychic realms overall. Imagination can border on inspiration. Neptune's presence extends an illusion, a vagueness; but our reactions to the mystical and **mist**-ical promise has much to say about how happily we get through the year.

TRANSITING NEPTUNE BACKGROUND

Rationality prevails, as the individual with a background solar Neptune typically goes through life with a reasonable amount of assurance. Highly immune to being emotionally led, caught up, or seduced, such a person is not likely to form highly dependent relationships (unless other patterns specifically suggest the contrary). In fact, with natal Uranus prominent, this can be an exceptionally independent, self-sufficient period.

TRANSITING PLUTO FOREGROUND

Once Pluto conjoins an angle of a Solar Return, it tends to be foreground for several consecutive years. This is not a perfect rule, but holds true with a high degree of reliability, provided the individual does not relocate to a new city. During these several years, one's life stands an incredible chance of being entirely transformed. New phases begin while others are brought to a close. A persistent need for readjustment and reevaluation dominates the individual.

Pluto **transforms**. Rather than bringing simple hindrances or interruptions, Plutonian beginnings and endings feel absolute and final. When Plutonian circumstances are brought to a head, they seem climactic, breathtaking, intensive and sensational. Propelling the individual into a crisis situation (that is, a turning point with the promise of significant change and growth), such events are often described as unbelievable, having an "other worldly" quality about them.

By projecting the transforming power within themselves onto the outside world, individuals strongly influenced by Pluto find themselves confronting what appear to be forces descending upon them with mind-boggling might. This is the basis of transiting Pluto's nature. Yet, while it seems that a Deity-wielded blowtorch is redesigning, reshaping, remolding a person's very way of being, the power to transform is entirely within the individual at all times and completely under his or her control.

When people will not own up to their own magical capabilities, they may feel that awesome power trying to dominate them. Many try to break free or rebel. In these cases, where Pluto feels very much like a transiting Saturn, there can be a battle to regain control from the outer world. Transiting Pluto's nature is basically **separative**, whether from people, ideas, institutions, lifestyles or whatever. This can manifest in a great many ways, including (but not limited to) travel, saying farewell to friends and loved ones, changing jobs or, on occasion, someone's death.

Pluto **isolates**. An individual is apt to feel himself to be the exception to the rules, singled out from the herd whether alone as a hermit or elevated to a spot of singular personal significance. This can mean power and sudden promotion, or arrogance and overestimating oneself. Precedents are set. As a part of the "singling out" motif, Pluto also symbolizes the truly miraculous and awesome, those circumstances which break all odds, revolt against every established pattern and leave conformity in the dust. The normal rules and expectancies of the world "just do not work" anymore.

Over the course of a few years, as Pluto obstinately falls close to the Solar Return angles, precious inner changes can occur as well. Alterations of the physical environment are symptomatic of the internal metamorphosis taking place. The mystical experience, as William James described it, is Plutonian in every way. As one stands aware of powers greater than oneself, a deep potential for spiritual understanding emerges, often in dramatic soul-clutching instances of cosmic insight, which lay bare the source of Divine Consciousness within the individual's own soul.

TRANSITING PLUTO BACKGROUND
Except for those periods when transiting or natal Pluto is emphasized, most people are willing to take the world as it is offered to them. Or, if they seriously question their world, they only do so in the way that world taught them. The average person in the streets feels comfortable living the relatively naive existence of one absorbed in the patterns of our present civil-ization. Such a tendency is abetted by Pluto's absence from prominence in the annual picture.

Natal Planets Foreground

Like the slow-transiting planets, once a natal planet conjoins a Solar Return angle, it will tend to occupy the foreground of several consecutive Solar Returns. It may occasionally miss one and then return on the next, marking out a stage in life when the personality attributes associated with that natal planet have the fullest opportunity for development.

Natal planets signify the ingrained basic life pattern of an individual. As they come to the foreground in a Solar Return, these intrinsic factors are emphasized. Natal planets conjunct Solunar angles essentially show how an individual is reacting personally to the foreground transiting planets which dominate the Solunar.

Even more so than with prominent transiting bodies, it is very important to observe what aspects a foreground natal planet makes. These condition its operation. **Configurations with other natal planets** reveal any complex aspect system in the geniture — which is to say, any complex character structure in the individual's psyche — that is being focused through the angular planet. **Dynamic aspect transits it receives** will indicate the type of dynamic interaction with the environment which will bring the foreground natal planet into play.

NATAL SUN FOREGROUND

Astrologically, the Sun represents a quest for accomplishment as a natural development of an unfolding identity. The glyph that we use for the Sun (☉) can be looked at in many ways, but I like to think of it as a target or bull's-eye. Within a horoscope, the Sun also symbolizes a target, a sense of aim, direction and motivation.

When the natal Sun occupies the foreground of a current Solar Return, an individual is most conscious of this propelling drive toward an objective. The inner, blazing Truth-of-Self which we call the Sun is more of a catalytic spur to action than even Mars, but with one special difference: Sun-sponsored activity is guided and has a sense of purpose about it. At its best, it manifests an awakening of selfhood, the acquisition of a greater sense of meaning in life and creative individual expression.

Desire for recognition, if not some form of immortality, is a key motivator with natal Sun prominent. Typically, natal Sun indicates personal pride. This usually implies that the person is or does something (s)he can be proud of. Ideally, we find satisfaction in personal accomplishment. Unless inhibited by restrictive aspects, a prominent natal Sun designates organizational skills, willingness to make definitive decisions and other traits which come under the general heading of "leadership ability." Most people with this placement relate smoothly to power, theirs as well as others', and acquire a greater comfort with their own assertiveness and sense of command. If mishandled, this can lead to alienating arrogance and generally obnoxious behavior. Handled well, the same traits can have the exactly opposite effect, making the individual a magnetic, charismatic lure that others naturally respect and heed.

During this time, an individual is definitely putting his or her identity on the line. To the extent that such people are self-aware, their sense of identity is set out for all to observe. If this identity-concept is strong, it will endure and grow. If it is weak, there is also a good chance that the foreground Sun will signal the chance for the identity-concept to strengthen and develop. Still, a terribly insecure individual whose Solar Return sports a prominent Sun has the chance of seeing a weak self-concept crumble. The foreground Sun will, in this case as in others, show the need for self-expression, self-identification and self-assertion, but the weakness of personal will can make the task abominable against the heavy blockades such a person attracts and encounters.

Only a very few are apt to fail such a test. Those who do fail have entered the fray with a poor product and now have the opportunity to reconstruct a new identity-concept and find new goals under the impetus of the repetitively foreground Sun.

NATAL SUN BACKGROUND
Years when natal Sun is shy of the Solar Return, angles are more assimilative and preparatory than expressive. Individuals experiencing this may withdraw from much active participation in long-term objectives, being drawn hither and yon, instead, by more transient preoccupations. There is less propelling the individual toward any creative unfolding of his or her life-pattern, so the likelihood of special attention or recognition is greatly diminished. Vitality is typically lowered as well: a background Sun involved in health-depleting aspects is a characteristic indicator of sickness and waning strength, as a result of diminished spirits.

NATAL MOON FOREGROUND
Receptive, impressionable and vulnerable, the individual with natal Moon in the solar foreground responds to most things and most people in his or her environment with a keen, and sometimes pungent, sensitivity. This potentially indiscriminate reaction to whim and vagary leaves such a person shifting, changeable, perhaps moody and readily adaptive to circumstances.

Simply stated, these people are strongly affected by all that happens around them. Emotional "antennae" are extended to probe and explore the surroundings. The feeling nature is apt to be intense, so the individual will probably relate to life much more through the emotions than normally. Sentiments may dominate the decision-making processes. Any transiting planets aspecting a foreground natal Moon are likely to incite a strong emotional response to whatever circumstances the transiting planet signifies.

Notice which particular angle the Moon conjoins. This will reflect in what part of the individual's life the heightened responsiveness will be most apparent. A person will get drawn into, or wrapped up in, circumstances suggested by the particular angle. For instance, any foreground natal Moon implies a pronounced need to take part in nurturing experiences and share an emotional contact with another.

However, natal Moon in the setting foreground (conjunct the Descendant) further emphasizes the "merger" needs of a person, while making close, reciprocal, emotional interaction with someone else very attractive.

Other typical lunar manifestations can be expected. The individual will probably exhibit "nesting behavior" or increased domesticity. Sensuous desires will be strong as the individual seeks fulfillment of appetites on all levels. Active, carefree, at times juvenile, such people may dramatize everyday situations as a tactic for attracting attention to themselves. Emotional creativity can be based on strong powers of imagery.

NATAL MERCURY FOREGROUND
This is a time to learn. Natal Mercury symbolizes one's own curiosities and desires for information, as well as the anatomical sensory mechanisms which make data accessible. **Perception** keynotes a year under such a Solar Return. By studying, discussing, listening, exploring, a person broadens his or her intellectual picture of the world. No single astrological factor is better for learning than this one.

These people are primarily oriented to an **exchange of data** in a variety of forms. Their curiosities are heightened. They carefully assess information they obtain, typically subjecting it to their whetted critical and analytical abilities. Communication becomes very important, especially the acquisition of new knowledge.

Commerce is another familiar Mercurial expression. During this time, one is apt to focus on business matters, with plenty of opportunities for developing one's practical talents. In fact, since most types of learning are prone to go smoothly, this period is excellent for picking up new skills or honing old ones to a keener edge.

Mercurial years are notably laden with busy hours and abundant activity. Unlike lunar periods, when distractions seem indiscriminately to pull one in many directions at once, times when Mercury is strong will more often indicate constant preoccupation with one or more **projects** which keep an individual constantly on the go.

NATAL VENUS FOREGROUND
Venus relates to very deep feelings, in contrast to lunar feelings which tend to be less profound. Expect a clear, vital, emotional expression to emerge (or be heightened) when this planet is downstage in a current Solar Return. The individual has a full reservoir of love to tap and is inclined to share it generously. Compassion and sentimentality prevail. Highly affectionate, social and honestly caring, such a

person wants very much to be with others and share some genuine touching, whether of flesh or of souls.

There is a need to be part of a pair. Love unions are commonly formed and bonds of friendship tightened while natal Venus is emphasized. The individual extending himself or herself to a special other person is reminded in a moment of contact that life does not require us to proceed alone.

During such a Solar Return period, the individual wants life to be pleasant. Harmony and beauty are coveted luxuries. Congenial, friendly and compliant, these folks seek to establish easy living conditions for themselves and others, fulfilling a primary need to make life as nonthreatening, unharried and comfortable as they possibly can. Physical beauty has the power to raise their spirits. Their appreciation of the lovely and graceful is heightened. Other chart factors being in easy agreement, this can also coincide with a streak of exaggerated vanity, or at least close attention to one's own personal appearance.

NATAL MARS FOREGROUND
Natal Mars occupying the immediate foreground of a Solar Return marks an extremely competitive time in a person's life. Among the very young, sibling rivalry is intensified; among older (and hopefully wiser) people, other relationships may be exposed to the same kinds of stress and tension. Unless the individual involved is, by nature, very caring and egalitarian, odds are that (s)he will not share the spotlight with anyone if it can be helped.

This planet signifies one's own need to be aggressive, to approach life dynamically and to physically expend energy outward into the world. Willfulness is a companion of Mars. Mixed with the keynoted competitive streak, this can lead to argumentativeness, to obstinacy and, in peripheral cases, to violence. Such people are not inclined to back down from anything. Instead, they constantly seek to prove themselves in battle, whatever the front. If the war zone is one's domestic scene, for example (as when Mars sets or anticulminates), this can mean self-initiated disruption of one's personal life. One should be careful not to annoy or aggravate others during this year, since it seems most natural to tease and grate on anyone who happens to be in the vicinity.

A natural inclination to take charge makes this a prime time for promotion, particularly if Jupiter is strong. Ambition flares. Major accomplishments are possible. During the several years this planet may be foreground, an individual's accelerated need for unencumbered expression can push limits and barriers farther and farther away. Unfortunately, important people in one's life may also be pushed farther and farther away if restless self-involvement is not countered by reasonable consideration of others. Energy is abundantly available, but nearly always squandered. Beware of burn-out or overstrain!

With natal Mars highlighted, the competitive theme may indicate fierce sexual jealousies. Sexual desires are among the specific passions Mars ignites. The red planet enhances virility, i.e., the masterful, ardent, robust, potent component of maleness present in men and women alike. However, I have found **transiting** Mars foreground much more often than natal Mars for such occasions as one's first sexual experiences and the most sexually bountiful periods of life.

NATAL JUPITER FOREGROUND

Probably the most notable characteristic of a year such as this is that people feel well and good. Security in their competence breeds self-esteem, confidence and an overall impression that luck is on their side for a while. Of course, over-confidence can lead to serious problems; but the individual with Jupiter to the fore probably will not notice (let alone worry about) such things until the year is over. **Helpful hint:** If you are not covering your own blind spots, be sure that someone else is!

Jupiter signifies the need for advancement. Self-improvement is a major aim in this period of life. Astrological tradition avers Jupiter to be a planet of unbounded quantity; but this is Jupiter operating at a rather immature level. More rightly, Jupiter clamors for **quality**. Healthy Jupiterian growth takes the form of refinement and polish, not mindless accretion. When natal Jupiter occupies the Solar Return foreground, an individual moves unerringly into enhancing, expansive acts such as buying a new house, enlarging the scope of a business or taking steps which make some part of life run a little smoother. Irresponsible Jupiter manifestations lean toward compulsively "keeping up with the Joneses," pretentiousness and ostentation, heedlessness and negligence.

Equally characteristic of Jupiter periods is an insistent need to be liked, accepted and included. The Jupiterian soul needs to be important to someone else. (**One** of the pieces of astrological suicide patterns is a heavy involvement of Jupiter. Crisis counselors have long been aware that a suicide crisis involves two people: the suicidal individual and someone important in his or her life from whom the person feels isolated.) Amiable, tolerant and generous to the point of extravagance, these people respond to a social impulse that outdistances any Venus aspect and a drive for recognition more insistent than that of the Sun. Jupiter's call to the world is, "Please support me in completely believing I'm special and important."

Usually this call is answered before it becomes very loud. As a rule, little will interfere with the self-assurance, optimism and good humor of the individual who has natal Jupiter well-aspected in the foreground of a current Solar Return.

NATAL SATURN FOREGROUND
Just as transiting Saturn represents the demands and expectations an individual experiences coming from the outer world, natal Saturn personifies one's own demands and expectations.

Saturn, at root, is the tenacious, possessive, economical, serious facet of people which learns from experience and is vital to the perpetuation of existence. Saturn's prominence highlights basic self-preservation needs. An individual's focus on material security insists that essential food and shelter requirements be met first, and then, in our complex culture, turns to whatever other demands the individual associates with autonomous survival.

Put more simply, the selfish side of a person comes to the foreground alongside natal Saturn — and selfishness is **not** a bad characteristic, provided it is not carried to an extreme. A Saturn personality only runs into problems when the need for self-reliance and a basic distrust of others leads to emotional alienation from the herd. Skill at manipulating the physical environment is an asset in any growth process as long as it does not include enforcing control over others in a way that robs them of their own free will.

Probably the worst side of this ringed planet appears when unrealistic expectations are set for oneself. Self-driven by a compulsion to meet improbable standards, an individual nourishes not himself, but feelings of inadequacy instead. Insecurities and self-doubts can grow in such an environment, but not the individual who is fostering them. Faith in oneself gives way to exaggerated self-criticism if this process goes too far. A store of favorite bad feelings can rise to the surface.

A common defense reaction for these people is to stick only with factors they can "put their fingers on," and take few risks, thus gravitating to the stable, proven, sure and self-limiting. Many different specific manifestations are possible, including retreating from the world into personal isolation (thus feeling all the more alone against the world) and health problems (for a variety of reasons obvious to the psychologically aware). Encroachments on one's personal territory or available time can bring a hostile reaction. Caution and skepticism increase.

The above refers, as was stated, to a misdirected Saturn turned upon oneself rather than rightfully applied to the environment. But self-care is not only allowable, it is requisite to personal existence, despite the early training to the contrary most of us receive. By guiltlessly directing one's own Saturn toward this purpose, it can be a sustaining and strengthening force rather than demoralizing and melancholy.

NATAL URANUS FOREGROUND
Freedom is the Uranian's most valued treasure. When this natal planet lands in the Solar Return foreground, personal liberty is sought in increasingly diversified areas and ways.

What people normally experience, as their tolerance for limitation drops, is a stifled feeling, a sensation of living in a narrowing world with far too few options. In this sense, natal Uranus shares something with transiting Saturn. However, under Saturn's external pressures an individual may sit back and accept restraint. Not so when natal Uranus shines! Independence is claimed, roughly if necessary. Routine is set aside as these people rebel against what they now view as outmoded ways of being. Typically, one's outlook on the world is clarified and sharpened — though in an initial emancipatory thrust, such an individual can act in a very one-sided manner, carelessly disregarding others' rights or boundaries while delighting in his or her own new-found release.

Life can become quite exciting. Finding themselves on the brink of adventure, these people are inclined to abandon security chains and boldly hurl themselves into risk. Challenges to old beliefs are met head-on, come what may. Mentally stimulating subject matter fascinates the mind. Desire flares for a change of pace, novelty or discovery. Enthusiasm for the fresh and brisk carries this intellectual daredevil toward exhilarating insights and adventures which are quite unlikely to allow as prosaic a view of life afterwards as was present before.

NATAL NEPTUNE FOREGROUND
As with a foreground transiting Neptune, feeling reactions are exaggerated and sensory experiences intensified while natal Neptune predominates in a Solar Return. Sensitivity to physical and emotional impressions is magnified. Individuals may become immersed in drama or music, enraptured by mysticism or fantasy, or totally absorbed in some other interest that has the same type of personalized fascination for them.

Natal Neptune's essential nature seems centered around this need to be absorbed in or by something. Attention becomes focalized, but not in the Saturnian or Mercurial sense of meticulous concentration. Instead, the individual displays a very selective perception style, only paying attention to what is interesting and nonthreatening to his or her picture of the world. (Paranoia, to cite an extreme manifestation of Neptune, is characterized by remarkably acute perception, mobilized for the sole purpose of verifying one's preconceptions.) Susceptibility to deception comes from this same need to be absorbed into the whole, manifesting in the specific form of "being taken in."

The Neptunian is highly responsive to experiences — sometimes too much so for personal comfort — thus vulnerable to fierce embarrassment or anxiety. Disorientation and confusion result when the person is overloaded with input and cannot seem to coherently organize thoughts. Yet, imagination can be used creatively, not just for blowing situations out of proportion. Idealism running rampant is apt to end in frustration and futility but, matched by practical application, can make dreams very real.

The most serious problems faced by people currently experiencing a very active natal Neptune are their tendencies toward self-doubt and a liability to solve problems by avoidance or procrastination. Insecurity in their own competence makes them sensitive to rejection (if not betrayal), especially by those with whom they choose to pair. It is imperative that self-confidence be sustained and enhanced. If this is done, many gains can be made. Otherwise, the year is apt to be one in which a person does very little except fret about his or her "inability" to get anything done.

NATAL PLUTO FOREGROUND

People withdraw from the world when natal Pluto conjoins a Solar Return angle. This is not to say that they vanish altogether; only that they are typically in a stage of pulling back from others around them, or retreating from pressing circumstances, and finding (at least, seeking) a place where external demands are few.

Pluto is inherently **separative**. At root, the Pluto side of each of us knows we are distinct, different creatures with very personal identities and ways of being. Pluto within us refuses to conform to the expectations others have of how we should act, what we should like or dislike, where we should go with our lives, etc. In fact, the word "should" is antithetical to everything Pluto represents. Seeing no need to conform to life-styles not their own, Pluto people write their own behavior codes and want to be left alone to live their lives without interference.

All of these feelings are dominant when natal Pluto occupies the solar foreground. The individual with this placement is apt to appear aloof, unresponsive and antisocial, avoid human contact as much as possible, and essentially play a lone wolf's part. (S)he wants to pull away from control and expectations of others, and may even personally take the reins of power to accomplish this. Such people simply want to be left alone.

Depending on other chart factors, this is possibly a time of confrontational introspection, when meaning is sought through in-turned consideration of the "whys" of the cosmos. More generally, circumstances seem to require that critical decisions be made with little hesitation. A time of reevaluating many personal issues, this year is most likely to see the culmination and transformation of conditions which have been present or building for some time.

Planets on the Various Angles

Sometimes, foreground planets seem undifferentiated with respect to the particular angle they occupy, their **emphasis** alone being the chief consideration. Often, though, the specific angle will distinctly modify the way a foreground planet operates. This is especially so when a planet is within 5 to 7° of the angle; i.e., actually **conjunct the angle** rather than just broadly occupying the foreground region.

The capsule interpretations below are meant to be **supplemental** to the interpretations given previously, not to replace them. They were written to apply equally well to natal and solar planets.

SUN conjunct ASCENDANT or EAST POINT
Identity is under focus. Self-expression is easier, more vital. Seeking to draw attention to self. Conscious of goals or desires; motivated to take action and **do** something significant. Assertive, bold, leading, maybe overbearing.

SUN conjunct MIDHEAVEN or ZENITH
Receiving special attention, especially from people in authority. Ambitious: emphasis on career or life-goals as an expression of identity to the world at large. Self-aggrandizement. Probable advantage. Enthusiasm, clarity, drawing on barely suspected resources and abilities.

SUN conjunct DESCENDANT or WEST POINT
Emphasis on close relationships of all types (common placement for weddings). Sociable; oriented to **others** in cooperation or competition. Seeking attention and ratification of your importance from others. Watch the ego!

SUN conjunct LOWER HEAVEN or NADIR
Emphasis on personal, private, domestic matters. Things "close to home" (physically or psychologically) draw your attention. Strength from reflection, introspection, exploring one's inner roots. Closing some fundamental cycle or life-stage while beginning another.

MOON conjunct ASCENDANT or EAST POINT
Personality is under focus. Need for response, acceptance, feedback, recognition from others. Responsive, reactive, reflexive; receptive, sensitive, sensuous. Subject to whim and impulse; volition wavers in face of temptation or distraction. Emotions heightened, moods far-ranging.

MOON conjunct MIDHEAVEN or ZENITH
Receiving special attention (scrutiny), especially from people of higher rank or position. Visibility, publicity. Ambitious: emphasis on professional identity, development of public image; "on stage" to the world. Change and fluctuation in professional/occupational areas. Probable advantage. Possible parent issues.

MOON conjunct DESCENDANT or WEST POINT
Attracted to close, reciprocal, emotional interaction. Need for love, affection; to merge with another, take part in nurturing experiences and share emotional contact. Sociable, likely to receive attention or be in the spotlight. Heightened appetites, enhanced desire nature (few weddings with this placement, but many wild oats sown).

MOON conjunct LOWER HEAVEN or NADIR
Deep personal feelings are focus of awareness. Things "close to home" (physically or psychologically) draw your attention. It's important to trust and be conscious of your feelings, else unconscious patterns dictate reactive behavior. Domestic, nesting, emotional, affectionate, caretaking. Offering and requiring nurturing.

MERCURY conjunct ASCENDANT or EAST POINT
"Taking care of business." Communication, transportation, commerce, ideas. Curious, mentally quick, analytic, discriminating, practical. Flurry of communication and activity.

MERCURY conjunct MIDHEAVEN or ZENITH
Communication, ideas, transportation and business predominate. Business and busy-ness. Professional matters particularly benefit from lucid thought and careful communication. Publicity.

MERCURY conjunct DESCENDANT or WEST POINT
Communication and shared mental activity emphasized, either through cooperation or competition (dialogue, exchange of information, negotiation, consultation, debate). Mind clear, quick.

MERCURY conjunct LOWER HEAVEN or NADIR
Contemplative; magnifies any introspective streak in you. Personal matters require attention (domestic or family concerns; deep inner issues). Busy, practical, self-contained.

VENUS conjunct ASCENDANT or EAST POINT
Harmonious surroundings, pleasure, peace. Sharing love. Relationships draw your attention. Possible new romance or friendship. Beauty and harmony are important. Sensuous, comfy, perhaps ardent.

VENUS conjunct MIDHEAVEN or ZENITH
Feeling comfortable, happy, good about oneself. Enhanced self-image. Love and pleasure emphasized, affection received. Excellent for social events, public appearance, shared fun.

VENUS conjunct DESCENDANT or WEST POINT
Sharing affection and pleasure. Strong emphasis on relationships. Excellent for all one-on-one encounters. Cooperative, gentle, social, sensuous. Appreciative of beauty and comfort.

VENUS conjunct LOWER HEAVEN or NADIR
A wellspring of profound (probably positive) feelings opens around intimate, personal matters. Home and family give joy. New romance, sensuality, mutual pleasure. Deep sharing possible.

MARS conjunct ASCENDANT or EAST POINT
Assertive, competitive, physical, aggressive, irritating, willful, impatient, sexually demanding. Energetic time with possible angry conflict. Requires freedom of action. Capable of accomplishment and effective action.

MARS conjunct MIDHEAVEN or ZENITH
Aggressive individualism. Ego-energies intensified and applied to personal goals. Competitive, ambitious. Possible conflict from stressing one's own importance at cost of others' sensitivities.

MARS conjunct DESCENDANT or WEST POINT
Competitive. Possible conflict. **You** versus **another**, with each side going all out to win! Find cooperative uses for volatile energies. In intimate pairings, S.O.S. means "Sex or Strife."

MARS conjunct LOWER HEAVEN or NADIR
Ego-energies are roused. Competitive, stressing own needs over others'. Strife in personal life. Anger, moodiness or irritability tend to be reflexive, defensive, based on old, subconscious patterns.

JUPITER conjunct ASCENDANT or EAST POINT
Feeling especially good about yourself. Advantage from others' good will. Enhanced social image, self-esteem, opportunities. Self-improvement, refreshment. Interests in philosophical, religious, spiritual and/or professional and financial ideas. Beware of misplaced superiority and self-righteousness.

JUPITER conjunct MIDHEAVEN or ZENITH
A high point. Progress and advance come more readily, especially in profession. At its best: respect, recognition, gain, elevation, advantage, confidence. Feeling good about self and accomplishments (arrogance, inflated ego). Generally, the road looks pretty smooth, encouraging ambitions.

JUPITER conjunct DESCENDANT or WEST POINT
Increased respect. Gregarious, good-natured, sociable, inclined to cooperation. Sound relationships bring pleasure and comfort; while in strained relationships, a pause in the conflict is likely, providing space for tackling existing problems.

JUPITER conjunct LOWER HEAVEN or NADIR
Private life-elements become chief sources of pleasure and refreshment, especially home and those who share it. New value found in the traditions that underlie your mental, emotional and spiritual development. Improving the home, making promising investments, growth in family size, etc.

SATURN conjunct ASCENDANT or EAST POINT
Maturing self-sufficiency. Pressures build, demands increase. Work, discipline, aloof self-examination. You can take charge of life-areas where previously you have felt not in control. "Getting your act together." Loose ends seem naggingly obvious. Time to finish commitments and weed out the clutter in your life.

SATURN conjunct MIDHEAVEN or ZENITH
Identity and authority issues dominate. Learning much about who you are, what is important to you, how you handle power. Demands increase; basic needs are accented. You have only yourself to rely on! May signal professional maturity; or, if you have built poorly, a setback.

SATURN conjunct DESCENDANT or WEST POINT
Relationships require extra attention. Emphasizes incompatibility or unwillingness to cooperate. Accumulated grievances raise their heads. Be more willing to drop barriers between yourself and others. Solid relationships are not taxed as badly as shaky ones. Committed partnerships can be secured.

SATURN conjunct LOWER HEAVEN or NADIR
Get your feet squarely under you! Laying a foundation. Security and property issues become important. Family relationships possibly strained. Assuming greater self-reliance and encouraging it in your dependents.

URANUS conjunct ASCENDANT or EAST POINT
Awakening to truths about who you are; resetting your life course. Freedom needs increase. Relationships change. Desire for reform or revolution. Tension if you resist change; but excitement and renewal reward self-reliance and self-exploration. Progressive, stimulating.

URANUS conjunct MIDHEAVEN or ZENITH
Need for freedom. Individuality is emphasized. A basic Truth-of-Self emerges. Changes in career, status, life-goals. Maybe crisis involving authority. Needing to be more your own boss. Tension shows that you are resisting **appropriate** changes. Enthusiasm signals that you are probably on the right track.

URANUS conjunct DESCENDANT or WEST POINT
Changes in relationships, which now require more attention and energy. Exciting new relationships possible; while existing ones demand redesigning. Separations possible; but a strong pair-bond will be renewed if both are willing to rework it. Dependency and possessiveness do not work. **Self-reliance** is the keynote.

URANUS conjunct LOWER HEAVEN or NADIR
Inner restlessness prompts life-style shifts. Changes in home and domestic matters (maybe a move). Important shifts occur inside you.

Self-discovery. Possible disruption, separation. Need to refresh or renew close family relationships.

NEPTUNE conjunct ASCENDANT or EAST POINT
Shift in self-image and personality. Self-doubt while discovering a more sensitive self. Increased sensitivity requires refinement of habits. More responsive to emotional stimuli, prone to dramatize feelings.

NEPTUNE conjunct MIDHEAVEN or ZENITH
Identity and life direction confused, uncertain. Easier to dream than to transform dreams into reality. Applying imagination in successful, functional ways is the main need. Practical matters require focused, conscious attention.

NEPTUNE conjunct DESCENDANT or WEST POINT
Quest for something meaningful, probably involving close relationships. Either dissolving rigid views that separate you from others, thus new intimacy; or your prejudices are dramatized and trigger struggles and distress. Sensitive, vulnerable. Perhaps confused relationships, frustration, dependency, disillusionment in relationships, unrealistic views.

NEPTUNE conjunct LOWER HEAVEN or NADIR
Chance to explore your psychological and spiritual roots. Emotionally sensitive, vulnerable. Matters rise to consciousness involving early life. If not confronted: possible childish behavior, dependence, increased security needs, despair. Emotions may interfere with practical affairs.

PLUTO conjunct ASCENDANT or EAST POINT
Self-discovery. Liberation from inherited attitudes. Existential recognition of yourself as sole monarch of your inner universe. Rebellious, uncooperative; a need to be free of others' arbitrary values. Pivotal spiritual experiences possible.

PLUTO conjunct MIDHEAVEN or ZENITH
Transformation. Life-purpose gains new clarity. You assume more power over your life. May feel alienated from an irrational society. Reputation, rank, career and other outer tokens of identity change. Capable of unprecedented contribution.

PLUTO conjunct DESCENDANT or WEST POINT
Dramatic changes, particularly in close relationships. Turbulent self-examination through projection. Issues handled by direct confrontation.

Emphasis on competitive, separative aspects of relating; but a profound alliance is now possible.

PLUTO conjunct LOWER HEAVEN or NADIR
Changes in environment or family relationships. Substantial psychological changes. Private, reflective, more free of others' opinions. You stand close enough to touch the essence of yourself **if only you will**. Benefit from self-exploration techniques.

CHAPTER FOUR

INTERPRETING LUNAR ASPECTS

Once through the veil of the foreground planets, which focus our attention on the paramount themes of a Solar Return, our eyes should always turn next to the Solar Moon and its aspects.

In the previous chapter, we examined planetary angularity in great detail. Such an extensive treatment seems justified, since the primacy of foreground regions is the most important single key to clear, penetrating understanding of Solunar returns. But angles are not in themselves dynamic. The horizon and meridian (and their squares) lend potent expressiveness to planets which attend them and suggest the issues in a person's life with which the planetary motifs are apt to be associated; but they are themselves static constructs, like the setting of a stage before the actors arrive.

The verbal quality in astrology is represented only by the planets. And, of the ten moving bodies we normally place in an astrological map, two exceed the others in importance. These are, of course, the Sun and Moon, the director and stage manager of our stellar drama, known when paired as the **luminaries**. ALL of the planets are important, but these two hold a unique significance in the way they affect our lives.

Angles and luminaries comprise the **personal points**. The Midheaven, Ascendant, Sun and Moon provide emphasis, drawing attention to the most essential elements of a chart. When utilized to their fullest capacity, applying techniques native to Cosmobiology, they provide the "plumbing" of a horoscope, indicating which planetary pairings are most critical to the various areas of personality development, human interaction and individual creative expression. As we are employing them here, in a much more orthodox fashion, they retain their specialness, and are used in very direct, no-nonsense ways.

Uniquely, in the Solar Return there is not a **transiting** Sun distinct from the **natal** Sun. Solar and natal Sun are one and the same by definition. The active solar component becomes *dif*fused throughout the entire map, every angle and planet becoming *in*fused with a quality of the Sun's essence (thus a rationale for calling them "solar" planets). Therefore, the Sun's placement in a Solar Return is, ironically, far less important than in any other type of astrological chart.

This, then, isolates the Moon as the most crucial agent in a Solar Return, after the angles. Lunar aspects to natal and solar planets can never be treated lightly, even when rather wide in orb. So remarkable is this single factor that, if lunar aspects are nearly exact while the foreground planets are not exceptionally close to the angles, the solar Moon can be considered the primary theme-setter of the chart for the year ahead, bar none.

Meaning of the Solar Moon

Information on the basic nature of the Solar Return Moon can be distilled from the previous chapter where its foreground and background placements are delineated. However, the following summary may help to clarify some key points. By your understanding of fundamental principles, it becomes easier for you to assimilate the interpretations of lunar aspects later in this chapter.

The Solar Return Moon and its conditioning factors indicate:

1. Circumstances which evoke the most vivid feeling responses, described by the Moon's aspects to solar planets. (House and sign placements often give important added information; but we must let aspects have their say first.)
2. The type of feelings easily elicited from the native, indicated by the Moon's aspects to natal planets.
3. The emotional quality of the environment as the individual experiences it.
4. More specifically, the emotions, nurture-needs and other feelings of people in the environment; how the individual experiences (solar planets) and responds to (natal planets) other people's feelings.
5. By implication, those things which appear to happen to the individual, as differentiated from things (s)he purposefully seeks or initiates. (The quiescent reaction principle inherent in the Moon's symbolism typically shows the individual responding passively to circumstances promised by lunar aspects, rather than a willful and

conscious participation. An openness to a certain kind of experience attracts the individual to the event. The strong emotional response to that type of event singles it out as being especially significant for the individual.)

The Solar Moon and Health

One other area exists where we can supply important information by examining the solar Moon's placement and aspects: personal health. So potent are the medical implications and indications from this one factor that they deserve special mention and attention. In looking through dozens of Solar Returns with case histories, I was extremely impressed by how often years of important illnesses showed afflictions to the solar Moon, commonly in the appropriate constellation.

Usually these were foreground, but not always. The old rule was that background luminaries play havoc with health, while foreground luminaries indicate wellness. Though the Sun's angularity seems to be a major key to vitality, supporting the rule, a critical examination of the Moon's mundane placement in Solar Returns reveals a much more logical truth: that this luminary, which symbolizes feelings, softness, receptivity and vulnerability, is afflicted in a strong or medium-strong zone of the chart in most serious health problems.

All years will not bring extreme health problems, though. Those men and women fortunate enough to be having the Sun foreground in their current run of Solar Returns will have relatively few sicknesses, in fact. Nonetheless, the solar Moon will probably point to those bodily concerns which most attract attention during the year, though perhaps only through nagging aches. As "the Moon of the Sun," the solar Moon signifies **the responsiveness and vulnerability of the biological organism**. The feeling responses become oriented to a particular part of the body, frequently shown by the Sidereal constellation holding the Moon. This is one of the fascinating pieces of evidence which regularly reinforces my security with the zodiac I have chosen for my personal work.

This does **not** mean that an astrologer can or should use this finding to try to become a diagnostician without proper medical training. For one thing, the severity of the affliction cannot be determined by this rule. An afflicted, foreground Leo Moon might inspire an astrologer to predict heart problems; but if the prediction comes true it could very well be because the astrologer scared the client into a coronary arrest! This same lunar symbolism could just as easily indicate a backache.

Luminary Importance In Terms of Angularity

A tendency was noted above for the Moon's placement and aspects to have more severe indications for the health when in the foreground or middleground. Even though the Moon is the primary significator of reaction in the Solar Return, it is still subject to the angularity curve, which indicates how readily the lunar nature can manifest.

Cyril Fagan regularly suggested, in the sixteen years he wrote the column "Solunars" for *American Astrology*, that foreground planets are the most important in Solunar Returns. But, he would add, special attention should **always** be given to the Moon in a Solar Return. I have found both of these rules valuable and accurate for the most part, although they leave an ambiguity where the cadency of luminaries is concerned: We are told that luminaries are important, but are also told to disregard any planet in the background!

This is one of those questions for which only approximate rules can be given. So much depends on how well various elements of the return chart fit together and whether the luminary agrees or disagrees with the rest of the chart. The guidelines below are blatantly artificial and contrived, but do seem to be suitable and workable in practice.

SOLAR RETURN MOON
1. If **foreground** or **middleground** — give its aspects full priority.
2. If **background** — only consider its indices if the rest of the chart points in the same direction. (As we shall see later, all partile aspects — 1° orb or less — are worth noting, so they should be considered regardless of cadency.)

SOLAR RETURN SUN
1. Remember that this is identical to its natal namesake.
2. If **foreground** — give full priority to its aspects.
3. If **middleground** — only consider its indices if the rest of the chart concurs.
4. If **background** — forget it altogether. (Partile aspects, however, are an exception, and always potent.)

Reinforcement and Activation

Sometimes the Moon acts only to trigger or reinforce a planetary combination which it aspects. When this happens, the specific lunar nature, though probably still present, is harder to discern. It is as though the Moon's only function at such times is as an activator.

Primarily, this occurs when more than one other planet is involved, not with single planet aspects to the Moon. The combination is activated as a unit.

The November 1900 Solar Return of King Edward VII had a wide (6°) middleground square between Venus in the seventh house and Saturn in the eleventh house. Under normal conditions, it would have attracted very little attention from an experienced delineator of Solunar Returns. Seemingly of much greater importance was the transiting Jupiter-Uranus conjunction just west of the Midheaven, conjunct natal Jupiter and opposed by transiting Pluto. The latter configuration suggested a rather extraordinary year filled with outstanding promotion, marked increase of income or stature and in many ways a revolution in his life situation in the direction of improvement. Only the likelihood that the very basis of then Prince Edward's life was being overturned (Pluto conjunct the IC and opposed by Uranus) could possibly be considered stressful. In the context of this chart, even that type of Plutonian separation was apt to be to his greatest benefit.

However, the Moon (though weakly placed just below the sixth cusp) provided an important piece of "background information" (pun legitimately intended). By opposition to Saturn and square to Venus, it triggered the Venus-Saturn quadrature. With Pluto exactly on the IC, this highlighted square could very easily be read as the loss of a loved one, especially someone within Prince Edward's immediate family circle. Only 73 days after the Solar Return, Queen Victoria died, placing Prince Edward on the throne of England.

A similar incident occurred in my own life. My sixteenth Solar Return featured Venus at 29° Libra opposite Saturn at 27° Aries. This opposition was in the middleground, from the first to the seventh houses Jupiter was rising. From the fourth house, at 23° Capricorn, the Moon widely squared the Venus-Saturn opposition, activating an otherwise benign, neutralized aspect. Four months later, when solar Moon had progressed to 27° Capricorn in exact square to Saturn, my grandfather died. This was the first death of someone close to me. While England's throne was not my legacy, I did receive my grandfather's ring which I continue to wear to this day.

In both cases, we could isolate a feeling of **emotional loss** (Moon-Saturn) connected with an experience of **love feelings** (Moon-Venus). The aspects can be analyzed and dissected. More simply, though, we have an activation of a Venus-Saturn principle in a way which elicited an emotional response (solar Moon) from the persons involved.

Sun-Moon Aspects in the Solar Return

Of all of the forty-five possible planetary pairings, the aspectual blendings of the Sun with the Moon are the most archetypal. By this I mean that the mutual aspect cycle of the luminaries (from conjunction to conjunction) epitomizes the essence of the aspect cycle which all other planetary pairs also experience. The solilunar relationship is visible for all to see in the monthly phase cycle of the Moon, from New Moon (a Sun-Moon conjunction) to Full Moon (a Sun-Moon opposition) and back to New Moon again, with an infinite number of gradations in between.

The purity of a specific aspect's nature is most apparent when viewed as part of the Sun-Moon relationship. In fact, probably the best way to learn exactly what a given angular separation between planets means is to study many charts with the Sun and Moon in that aspect. The fundamental structure of an individual's personality will visibly carry the imprint of his or her Sun-Moon phase.

Dane Rudhyar discussed the significance of this relationship at great length.[1] His writings are worthy of study if you wish to acquire a more complete understanding of the meaning of the lunation cycle than it is possible to cover here.

In general, Sun-Moon aspects in a Solar Return represent **crisis**, i.e., significant turning points where the individual is most assuredly passing from one phase to another (just as the Moon is). Typically, there is a major involvement with other people. Significant pairings are established. The aspect may even indicate marriage, though in such a case a warning is in order: Because the life of the individual is coming to a transition point, it is important to examine relationship expectations and wants closely. A hasty pairing at such a time may meet with a premature end if the normal, healthy changes in one partner, accelerated by the Sun-Moon aspect, exceed the parameters of the original bonding.

Nonetheless, there is a natural inclination to get together with other people. Someone of singular importance may take a strong personal interest in an individual with this aspect in the current Solar Return. Self-assurance and pride are generally increased. Sun-Moon aspects are dynamic, so this will be an exceedingly active and busy period.

Others may find themselves expected to adapt to this individual's long-term goals. This is fine, when those others are willing to do so.

---

1. Dane Rudhyar, *The Lunation Cycle* (Berkeley, Calif.: Shambala, 1971).

In fact, this is why Sun-Moon co-aspects between two birth charts are so fortunate for partnerships of various kinds. On the other hand, enhanced self-assertion can stimulate emotional domination tactics. The rest of the chart should at least suggest which eventuality is most likely.

More specifically, **conjunctions** of the Sun and Moon represent the birthing of a new cycle or emerging phase, while an old phase eases away. Doors can be ripped open and slammed shut! There is a refocusing upon the direction in which that life is proceeding. The individual is apt to acquire a new basic orientation to life. This conjunction seems heavily infused with a solar quality, with assertiveness strong and with awareness of direction paramount for the life of the return chart.

In his book, *Interpreting the Eclipses*,[2] Robert Jansky explored this "crisis" characteristic of the Sun-Moon conjunction in great detail. A solar eclipse is, of course, a very special case of a Sun-Moon conjunction, which Jansky found affects people and nations, throws their lives into crisis and forces a reexamination of existing situations and the setting of new goals. Jansky also emphasized the primacy of the solar quality of this conjunction.

By contrast, the **opposition** (Full Moon) carries with it much more of a lunar quality. Change, responsiveness and adaptation are the requirements life places on the individual during this period. At opposition to the Sun, the Moon is at its fullest and most whole-appearing stage. This translates almost literally into life terms, for an astrological Full Moon signals some sort of culmination, and with it a stage of maximum extension in some area for the time being. Rudhyar comments, "In any case, some kind of concrete limits have been reached."[3] While determination and the full focus of one's talents could allow one to continue beyond the present state, a fitting climax is slated to occur **naturally** now. This, too, is an aspect that calls for a reorientation of some sort.

Squares between the luminaries sponsor the greatest amount of ego involvement. The impetus to **do something** is pressuring. Therefore, the individual is apt to feel his or her options unduly limited. In truth, they probably are not; however, the driving intensity of the quadrature seems to impart that there is little time to slow down and think. Of all the Sun-Moon aspects, these are least likely to produce successful relationships but are probably best suited for accomplishment. Major adjustments to the needs of others may be requisite to close, comfortable interaction in an otherwise competitive period.

2. Robert Jansky, *Interpreting the Eclipses* (San Diego: ACS Publications, Inc., 1980).
3. Rudhyar, *The Lunation Cycle*, 108.

Trines and **sextiles** of the Sun and Moon are characteristically different from conjunctions, oppositions and squares for two reasons. First, they are static aspects. Though all couplings of the lights are inherently robust, there is not the pressure to "do something" with trines and sextiles which is built into the dynamic aspects. Rather than primary phase changes, they are more likely to indicate personal reevaluation from an introspective point of view.

The second difference is that, while the previously interpreted aspects are actually solar Moon **transits** to natal Sun, soft aspect transits do not seem viable. Therefore, Sun-Moon trines and sextiles are more truly blendings of a transiting Moon with a **transiting**, rather than natal, Sun, personalized by their presence in the Solar Return. Two things result from this. First, there is a greater chance that the individual will receive special attention from some significant personage or authority in the outer world. Secondly, relationship opportunities seem to be more numerous, but far less climactic, than with dynamic aspect contacts.

Solar Moon Aspects with Solar Planets

The delineations that follow are capsulized, focusing on primary principles and some of the most important expected manifestations of the Moon's aspects to solar and natal planets. The words in parentheses represent variations, possible specific occurrences and some of the more negative outworkings which we sometimes see with these aspects. These parenthesized portions should not be expected to appear in every case; in fact, some are exceptions to the rules, rather than manifestations we would expect routinely to see. Tune into the basic principles given and extrapolate the most apt delineation in each case, based on the entire chart. Usually, the more important the principle, the earlier it appears in the delineative paragraph.

MOON-MERCURY
Life and personality overwhelmed by an intellectualism; prolific mental output and activity. Caught up in a Mercurial environment (academe, technology, commerce, "thinking people," etc.). Called upon to express oneself (desire to teach stronger than desire to learn); circumstances require one to "speak up," reveal information or commit oneself. Publicity. Easy exchange of information. Travel may be necessary.

MOON-VENUS
Vivid feeling responses, intense emotional life (moodiness). Temperamentally hungry for affection (affection received, being in love); need for gentleness, tenderness, caressing, touching, holding; responding with full sensual vigor to another's enamored advances. Responding to beauty (aesthetics, art-minded). Marked predominance of female component in behavior (any problems arise from inability to accept full scope of feminine side); desire for children. High frustration tolerance, usually happy state of mind (shared happiness).

MOON-MARS
Circumstances arouse a fierce emotional response in the native, inciting anger and inflaming passions. Strongly sexual. Extremely busy (drive, feeling of strength; highly competent, productive, hasty). Needs elbow room and freedom to act (will not be held back). Competitive (quarrelsome). Environment seems threatening, harsh, confrontive (native is attacked, prone to irritation, intolerant). Other people can be seen as very critical, toxic, not emotionally safe. Possible sickness, injury, accidents, physical discomfort (see rest of chart).

MOON-JUPITER
Circumstances give native reason to be joyful, enthusiastic, optimistic, happy, good-humored. Others are emotionally supportive, nurturing, encouraging. Receiving honors, gifts, opportunities, advantages, pleasantries (object of others' generosity; red carpet treatment). Feeling of personal specialness. Identification with the superior (desires only best in life; elitism may lead to snobbery; seeks qualitative life-style; spends time with others considered important or superior). Attunement to personal belief system (religious, mythological). Money matters go well, income and luck probably bountiful. (Perhaps ideal time for actualizing personal ambitions.)

MOON-SATURN
Emotional survival needs emphasized. Low frustration tolerance, increased security needs (wanting to "settle in" with someone or achieve domestic security). Others appear harsh, cold, nonsupportive, unsympathetic, unresponsive, placing severe emotional demands on the native. Pleasing others instead of oneself. Emotional loss (separation, estrangement). Cautious with emotions, private, distrustful, reserved. Lonely, pessimistic, anxious, little self-confidence, low spirits. Possible health problems. Hardworking, furious self-drive, insistent (advancement difficult; wounded pride; financial obligations).

MOON-URANUS

Emotional excitement (thrill, hectic circumstances, dullness is rare). Being taken by surprise; responds to variety. Time of change (new directions, turning point, renewal; may be introduced to new life-style). Emotional stress (body and mind kept in sustained tension; nervous strain; possible anxiety or paranoia; watch your blood pressure!). Captivated by new areas of exploration (inquisitive, investigative, interests vary). Freedom from stereotyped attitudes (adventure, travel). Creativity, originality (manifestation of genius).

MOON-NEPTUNE

Circumstances evoke an exaggerated (irrational) feeling response (not **necessarily** bad, but inclined to mood swings, emotional confusion, hyperbolic reactions or instability). Sensitivity (impressionable, vulnerable, easily wounded then withdraws; or attuned to others, empathic, psychic, sympathetic). Prone to psychic overload. Imagination active (painting, music, drama, fantasy). Idealism. Seduction, victimization, deception, exploitation. Sluggishness (slowed circulation?). Worry, fear of rejection, frustration, anxiety, feeling cornered (threatened).

MOON-PLUTO

Sharp, intensive alterations in life situation; dramatic transformations; revolt against format. Experiences elicit a profound, climactic emotional response (crisis, shock). Others seem aloof, distant, emotionally removed, implacable. Refusal to be categorized, but feels sharp impact of others' expectations. Independent, rebellious. Separations, emotional alienation, withdrawing from participation. Deep feeling levels tapped (nervousness, emotional stress, compulsive behavior). Encountering the unlikely, improbable, unbelievable. Intuitive insights into underlying causes of occurrences (touching something divine).

Solar Moon Aspects with Natal Planets

MOON-MOON

Strong emotional responsiveness toward (affinity with) the environment and its occupants. "Feelers" extended (strongly affected by what happens); feelings experienced more immediately, intensely (moodiness). Adaptation (change, vacillation, confusion). Nurtured by attention (center of attention, rapport with public or audience). Familiar surroundings augment security (domesticity, "nesting").

MOON-MERCURY
Curiosity, willingness to learn (learning, reading, speculation, conversing, travel). Data storage and retrieval (active mind, quick perception). Communication flows well (psychic; talkative, large phone bills). Apt to respond to emotional issues using objective (analytic, intellectual) criteria and tactics. Sensitized nervous system (high-strung; insomnia, proclivity to use stimulants and depressants).

MOON-VENUS
Loving, affectionate, caring feelings are easily aroused in the individual. Emotional component pronounced (much love to give, greater need for reciprocal involvement with others; moods dominate). Shared fun and happiness (enjoying life; pleasing behavior). Beauty and harmony are important. Others respond to native's amorous advances (desire to make emotional/sensual contact with another). Mutual desire to touch, caress, cuddle, hold, fondle (sensory enrichment, nourishing environment, love affair).

MOON-MARS
Emotionally aggressive, or aggressively emotional (heated emotions, strong passions, hot-tempered, quarrelsome, buried hostilities stir). Competitive feelings easily aroused in native. Trying to incite an emotional response in another (Be careful — you might get one!). Tendency to pick on others, seek out their vulnerabilities (then hurt them). Dynamic, physically expressive (strongly sexual). Impulsive, rash, hasty, excited.

MOON-JUPITER
Feeling superior (others regard native as an important person or exalted being). Much esteem, high prestige (desire to please, trying to win a popularity contest, entertaining others). Faith in life to treat him/her well (optimism, happy feelings; high expectations characterize the individual). In best form, outgoing, social, congenial, generally pleasant.

MOON-SATURN
Security needs emphasized (tenacious, possessive, needs roots; material ownership is basis for security; resists ending toxic relationships). Emotionally exhausting experiences (depression, sad feelings, frustration, resignation, psychosomatic illness). Being insensitive/unresponsive to others' feelings and needs (being uncommunicative, blocking others' free emotional expression). Space/time sensitive. Feeling inferior or inadequate (one's own shortcomings emphasized; anxiety, waning

confidence). Dutiful, thoughtful, conscientious, disciplined. Holding own feelings in check (need to "be strong" precludes active feeling involvement).

MOON-URANUS
Restlessness. Desires freedom, change of pace, thrill, novelty and discovery (dullness is rare). Native is rebellious, less inhibited than before, experimental, individualistic (greets life's changing emotional currents with excitement and curiosity). Intellectual aptitudes acute. Drawn to continually keep in touch with what is new, different and liberating (interest in metaphysics, unorthodox medicine, scientific innovations, human growth movements). Emotional tension (fluctuating moods; freedom demands can threaten close interpersonal involvements). Willful (obstinate).

MOON-NEPTUNE
Refined sensitivity (empathy or vulnerability; easily influenced, open to experiences, psychic). Intense emotional component (exaggerated reactions, taking things too personally). Imagination, idealism, inspiration, fertile power of visualization. Embarrassment, frustration, anxiety, hysteria, confusion, disorientation as a likely reaction to stress. Emotional security needs are emphasized (overdependence, exaggerated need to merge with another, clinging to a degenerate pair-bond). Retreat into one's own private world (distorted perceptions). Indulgence (thirst for sensation; tendency to excess). Be more aware of your subconscious motivations.

MOON-PLUTO
Refusal to comply with others' expectations or limitations; little regard for convention. Others perceive the native as "different" from the rest, alien, a curiosity (and are hypnotized, enthralled or awed). Remaining aloof and distant (marshaling one's most imposing personality traits; being inconsiderate of others' feelings). Deep feelings easily elicited from native (reactions to serious issues are profound, personally moving). Separation (isolation, escape from pressing conditions, another's death). Culmination (decisions may be forced by impulsive actions as festering emotions erupt).

CHAPTER FIVE

FIRST TIME THROUGH —
A NEW WAY TO BE

At this point in the history of the Earth, particularly in our Western civilization, one of the most powerful factors motivating human behavior is **the desire to have one's world be and stay exactly as one believes it to be.**

Constantly in tension with this primary desire is another force which sometimes gains the upper hand for a while. This is a **desire to change,** a **willingness to accept life in an open and experiencing fashion;** or, in summary, **a need for *growth, wholeness*, and *transcendence of the past*.** This is the dilemma we all live.

Change occurs whether or not an individual accepts or acknowledges it. I am today neither the person I was yesterday nor the person I shall be tomorrow. This is true for all people; the contrary is not within our power. Stagnation is the equivalent of death.

One of our options is to accept change as an ongoing process, making life an adventure of discovering oneself and one's world. On the other hand, those who choose to view change as something that only rarely occurs stand a greater chance of experiencing traumatic circumstances that seem to invade life when growth needs become too strong to be further repressed.

Crisis is an invitation to grow, but certainly not the only opportunity. There are more pleasant ways. Some are suggested in the Solar Return.

Resolutions for a New Year

As each January approaches, numerous people whom we all know are busily engaged in writing their resolutions of how they plan to act during the ensuing twelve-month period. Much of it is lighthearted, few vows are seriously kept; but still a sense prevails that this is a time for some kind of new beginning, a turning point if we so wish, at which we can start to become someone different than we are now, or have been previously.

Birthdays have this same feel. Often I hear statements like, "Twenty-three has been a strange year, but things should start to mellow out when I'm 24." More simple are comments along the lines of, "I'm having a birthday next month. I wonder what the new year will bring me."

There are moments which touch women and men closely, so that instant and human partake of each other's natures. As astrologers, we are aware of the birth moment's importance in shaping an individual's potential for life. A kind of sympathy can also exist between a person and some impactful experience, thereby shaping the life in profound ways for years after. Evidence strongly suggests that another of these pivotal moments is marked by the annual return of the Sun to the precise position it held at birth — the Solar Return. This represents a moment of identification with the surrounding presence of the universe similar to, but not quite the same as, the primal experience of this sort at the moment of birth.

The Solar Return acts in many ways as a new nativity for the duration of one year. It does not replace the original horoscope. It certainly does not negate or deny all of the preceding life experiences of the individual, which have been mirrored in the original horoscope. Yet it sets a new direction, provides a different sense of selfhood and acts as a superimposed mask or modification. The Solar Return provides a part-time alternative to the birth map. It offers us **another way to be**.

Priorities in Delineation

Different astrologers have different ways of delineating horoscopes. In fact, there are probably as many varied interpretive styles as there are astrologers to do the interpreting. While you are naturally welcome to use whatever strategy you choose to read a birth chart or Solar Return, I think it is important to have some sense of **priority** in relating an astrological figure to an individual. While many astrological techniques have been demonstrated to work, equally important is the need for a fair assessment of how obvious these "workings" become when placed in the context of a typical person's whole nativity along with dozens of other ingredients.

We should always look for **the unusual** in a chart. Typically, this means those most emphasized components, although extreme **under-emphasis** is equally significant, and too regularly overlooked.

The most important signs or houses are those holding the luminaries or a stellium. The most significant planets are those close to the angles, aspecting the luminaries or otherwise strongly configurated. Aspects with the smallest orbs will always be the most outstanding and, to my mind, are the best place to start an interpretation. Of these, the dynamic aspects should always be given priority over the static ones, all else being equal. One must also be conscious of multiplanet configurations (three, four or more planets mutually aspected), particularly when close midpoint contacts are involved. These can dominate a chart at times, even with somewhat wider orbs.

Planets are the active agents in astrology. All other considerations qualify their activity. Especially in Solar Returns, but also with natal horoscopes, aspects and angularity provide us with the most critical information. Signs and houses are valid, but to a lesser extent. For the most part, signs and houses detail how aspects are likely to manifest, or make us aware of an emphasis when several planets are lumped together into one-twelfth of the ecliptic or prime vertical.

A frequent question raised by students involves the interaction of angularity and closeness in orb of an aspect. For example, is a wide foreground conjunction more important than a very close background conjunction, all other things being equal?

Both angularity and partility are commonly described as being determinants of strength. Various theorists have even devised numerical grading systems for blending these two considerations in order to objectively evaluate an aspect's potency.[1] While such theories have been earnest, progressive attempts at quantification for certain kinds of research, they are also much like mixing orange juice and milk — and not much easier to swallow! Partility and angularity show **different** things. To my mind, the actual strength of an aspect is determined **solely** by the smallness of its orb (and possibly the type of aspect). Angularity, instead, indicates **ease of expression**, not the strength of a drive.

Therefore, a person with a close (1° or 2°) Venus-Jupiter

The Astrodyne method devised by the Church of Light, and the aspect and angularity potential scales provided by Garth Allen in the April 1974 *American Astrology*, are two such proposals.

conjunction at birth would have **an urgent need** for appreciation and social involvement, no matter where in the horoscope the conjunction fell. If it were background while Saturn conjoined an angle, this social impulse would have a hard time finding expression. The individual might seem more cautious, perhaps cutting himself (or herself) off from other people emotionally in an effort to maintain autonomy and resist entrapping involvements, despite feeling down deep (in the background) a need for that very involvement. This will be a far lonelier person than one who does not have the Venus-Jupiter conjunction.

Similarly, a partile Mars-Uranus aspect will indicate a fierce need for freedom and the chance to be aggressively independent. However, if these planets hover near cadent cusps (such as Mars square Uranus from the third cusp to the twelfth), these freedom needs will be actualized only with the greatest difficulty. The drive is still present; thus, we must consider the aspect to be operating very strongly due to its tiny orb. Cadency just inhibits the likelihood of manifestation.[2]

The remainder of this chapter is a study of heiress Patty Hearst's Solar Returns for 1973, 1974 and 1975, the years in which her kidnap by, and later apparent alliance with, the Symbionese Liberation Army (SLA) made her one of the hottest news items in the nation.

According to her birth certificate, Patty Hearst was born on February 20, 1954, at 18:01 PST, in San Francisco, California. The Solar Returns considered here have been used previously by other writers in a different way[3]. Here, we will consider them as alternative nativities for the years in question, to see what behavior could be expected as **natural** during each of the three years.

Patty Hearst: 1973 Solar Return

In these charts, four planets conjoin major angles (Figures 5-1, 5-2). Jupiter is just above the western horizon, while Pluto, the Moon

2. For the technically minded reader, I include here the theoretical model that I use to evaluate aspect strength. The following formulae give a score between 1.00 (maximum strength) and 0.00 (minimum operational strength), where **X** is the orb of the aspect, measured in degrees.

For a **conjunction** or **opposition**:   score = cos (9X)

For a **sextile, square** or **trine**:   score = cos (12X)

Other aspects, which I feel have much smaller allowable orbs, have different coefficients. For semisextiles, semisquares, sesquisquares and quincunxes, try **cos (45X)**. Play with the figures if you are inclined, and adjust the numbers to fit your own experience.

3. Bob Paige, "A Bonanza of Solar and Lunar Returns," *Astrology Now* (December 1975) I, no. 9, 3ff.

and Uranus cluster about the Lower Heaven (IC). This is a formidable quartet and deserves in-depth attention before approaching any other part of the figures.

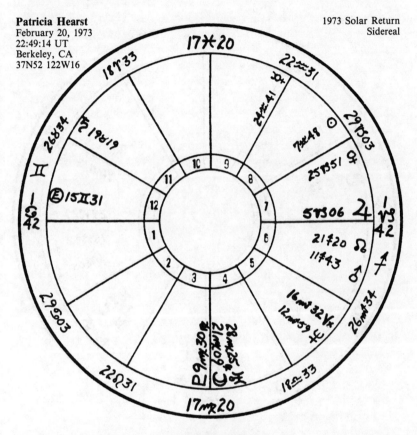

Patricia Hearst
February 20, 1973
22:49:14 UT
Berkeley, CA
37N52 122W16

1973 Solar Return
Sidereal

Figure 5-1

To achieve this, turn to Figure 5-3. This is the same Solar Return, but drawn in a different format called a **mundoscope**. It is actually a horoscope where planetary locations are given along the prime vertical, rather than the Ecliptic. Since the Campanus house system is based on equal divisions of the prime vertical, all houses in the mundoscope are precisely 30° in length. Therefore, Pluto 29° 24 ′ into the third house is actually only 0 °36 ′ from the IC (fourth-house cusp). Due to the extreme celestial latitude of Pluto during the 1970s, Pluto bodily crossed the MC, IC, EP and WP when it appeared about 7 ° away in longitude.

Adding 7° to Pluto's ecliptical longitude in Figure 5-1 (Sidereal) at 9°30′ Virgo gives 16°30′ Virgo, which is less than a degree from the 17° Virgo IC, verifying this calculation.

Patricia Hearst   1973 Solar Return
                                                           Tropical

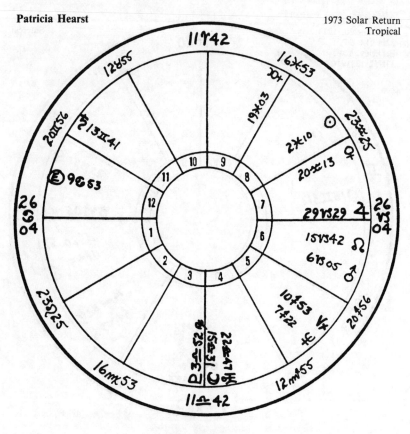

Figure 5-2

Parans are also readily seen in the mundoscope. In the ecliptical chart (Figures 5-1 and 5-2), the Moon and Jupiter are separated by 103° 57′, which is not even close to any aspect of note. But, in the mundoscope, we see Jupiter 3° 12′ above the Descendant and the Moon 1° 41′ west of the Lower Heaven, forming a 1° 31′ paran-square. Jupiter is also only 3° 48′ from an exact paran-square with Pluto, greatly reinforcing their ecliptical trine. The Moon and Pluto are in synan (paran-conjunction). Therefore, the Moon, Jupiter and Pluto form an extremely potent three-planet paran configuration.

If only the Moon and Jupiter were foreground, we would expect an individual with strong emotional ties to her family. These two angular planets co-indicate Patty's considerable need for appreciation, attention and recognition. Jupiter on the Descendant usually indicates a strong social orientation in practice, but at the root of this is something more pointed: a need for acceptance, esteem, respect and approval from other people.

Patricia Hearst

1973 Solar Return
(Mundoscope)

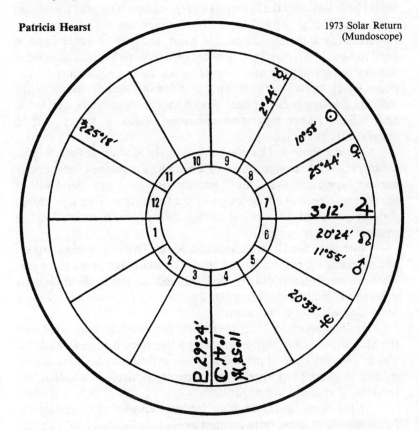

Figure 5-3

When the Moon squares Jupiter in a Solar Return, there is a need to identify with things thought superior. Patty Hearst was born into one of America's wealthiest, most prestigious families. She was accustomed to a Jupiterian life-style. She already had, so it would seem, many of the things her nineteenth Solar Return demanded for her in life.

But, there is more to this chart than security and society. There is also a reigning indication of disruptive separation.

Pluto is less than half a degree from the IC *in mundo*, and conjunct the Moon. Dominating the entire chart, Pluto signals a dramatic chapter in this young heiress's life when much that she had held onto in her past was to be interrupted and challenged.

Had I not known in advance how this Solar Return unfolded, I would have ventured the following interpretation: The primary tension motivating this individual is a stress between the need for security, respectability and tradition on one hand, and, on the other hand, a need to be her own person, follow her own rules rather than another's, and try to sort out her own way of being. Events seem scheduled to occur which violate the emotional and familial security bases of the individual as they presently exist. Major issues here are values, priorities and beliefs. Either reputation, financial status or career will be significantly challenged.

Consider **Pluto** and **Uranus** conjoining **the Moon** near Patty's Solar Return **IC**. All four ingredients which are here combined show one or another type of change. Transformation occurs at very deep levels of the psyche. She may not be aware of the festering need to have things different until, like Athena, it springs fully grown from her head, a matured product.

Pluto is squared by a background Mars. This is an outlaw aspect, adding much aggressive, willful energy to Plutonian needs to be free from arbitrary regulations. To state this another way, only through its square to Pluto, the sole foreground planet that Mars aspects, can this Mars find active manifestation.

To whatever extent Patty Hearst was or was not later involved with the SLA as an active participant, this Solar Return suggests that she was at a very deep level primed for their arrival into her life. She attracted to herself the type of experiences required to actualize the fermenting changes within her.

At the same time, transiting Jupiter indicated the considerable funds mobilized in her behalf within days of her February 1974 abduction. Transiting Venus had been retrograding back and forth over the solar Jupiter and Descendant when this occurred.

An eighth house Sun squared Neptune. The domal placement, aside from pointing to the involvement of money (dare we say that she was wasting her **inheritance**?), suggests more of what Moon-Pluto indicates: strong subconscious factors surging into consciousness which must be dealt with if the individual is not to be overwhelmed. Identity is diffused by this Sun-Neptune aspect, and power given over to others.

This entire Solar Return describes a time when unfamiliar forces seemed to descend upon Patty Hearst with awesome, engulfing presence, sponsoring more than a little apprehension. It coincided with an age (19) when most people are already facing freedom-dependency struggles, even without the reinforcing kick given by an annual chart such as this.

Patty Hearst: 1974 Solar Return

Patricia Hearst
February 21, 1974
5:04:33 UT
San Francisco, CA
37N47 122W25

1974 Solar Return
Sidereal

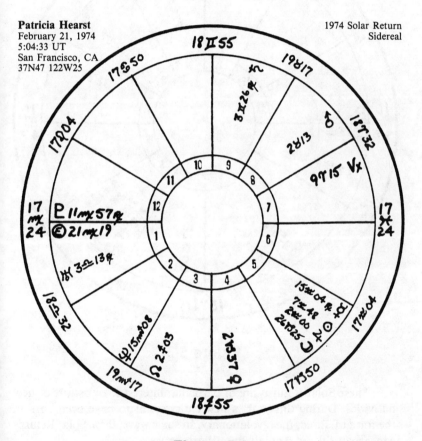

Figure 5-4

Almost immediately after her abduction by the SLA, Patty attained 20 years of age and entered a new Solar Return period. Figures 5-4 and 5-5 show her 1974 Solar Return charts. They are computed for San Francisco, although her location on her twentieth birthday is uncertain.

Much of the key activity of this year did, however, center about that general geographic area.

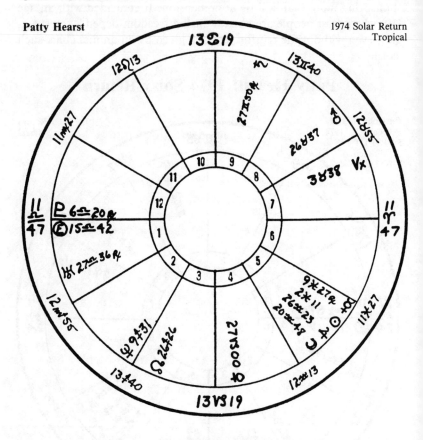

Patty Hearst   1974 Solar Return
                                                                    Tropical

Figure 5-5

These Solar Returns are of particular interest to our study of new nativities. During this year, a new entity seems to have been born in the form of Tania, the revolutionary. In some ways, these Solar Returns can be considered **Tania's natal horoscopes.**

Pluto conjoins the Ascendant and the East Point. (Its exact East Point contact is made when that angle is 19°20′ Virgo.) Along with Uranus in the rising foreground, this correlates nicely with Tania's "I am a revolutionary" pronouncement.

Let's examine the entire Solar Return in a systematic way to see what it might have told an astute astrologer in advance.

In an earlier book on natal delineation, I wrote the following about Pluto foreground:

> Pluto people are the loners of society, those unique individuals who refuse to melt into the mire of conformity and have their lives structured by precedent and custom. They are the exceptions to the rule, writing their own codes of behavior if necessary. In order to escape constant persecution for being 'different' from the masses, they draw within themselves and remain remote from the rest of the world. . . . [4]

This is the basic personality type the astrologer would have expected to see during 1974, especially since it reinforces the strong Pluto in Patty's natal chart. Pluto is further emphasized by a 0°32´ sesquisquare to the Moon, repeating all of the Moon-Pluto symbolism from the 1973 Solar Return.

A Venus-Uranus square is also foreground. This is a two-fold aspect. While it often signals emotional tensions that put the physical body under stress, it also basically means **social freedom**. The need for close, reciprocal relationships becomes inescapably connected to freedom needs. Usually, Venus-Uranus aspects mean a lot of fun! Relationships formed under this influence are not of the clinging variety but give all concerned plenty of opportunities to express their individual styles. Unless other factors interfere, **new romance** can flourish. With a fifth-house Aquarian stellium, this is precisely what we would have expected. In truth, it appears that Tania did develop an important love relationship which ended tragically in her beloved's death.

Notice the series of close 30°-multiple aspects involving Venus, Mars, Jupiter, Saturn and Uranus, which reflect different parts of these incidents.

In fact, this horoscope is rather unique in its number of extremely close contacts. Aside from the 36´ Venus-Uranus square, there are also Mercury square Neptune (4´), Mars square Jupiter (13´), Venus trine Mars (24´) and Saturn trine Uranus (13´). Saturn is also only 1°23´ from the south lunar node, wider than the others but still very close, and indicative of the end of an association. Let's take a look at the others, one at a time.

Mercury square Neptune: Perception and mentality are hypersensitized, leading perhaps to exaggerated responses to input. The mind is inclined to substitute fantasy for fact — the two do not integrate well — and, with everything so far considered, it is possible that the ability to deal with an objective, pragmatic world would be diminished.

---

4. James A. Eshelman and Tom Stanton, *The New Instant Astrologer* (Los Angeles: The Astro Press, 1976), 96.

Idealism flourishes. But anxiety may also be high, as this aspect points to a feeling of being hunted or hounded, sometimes only paranoid and sometimes justified. (This is a prime example of how significant partile aspects are, even when background. Usually, a Solar Return's key themes can be read from the very close aspects manifesting in the framework described by foreground planets.)

Mars square Jupiter: An aspect of extremism, this pairing is enthusiastic and exuberant. The individual puts considerable faith in personal resources and seems to seriously doubt her ability to lose. These resources are expended with abandon — money is rarely conserved, for instance — as confidence swells. Ideals get aggressively pursued. Beliefs are bantered about with something of a missionary, proselytizing zeal. It is also a lusty, sexual aspect (especially with Venus-Uranus and a fifth-house stellium present), just as it abets any other physical activities.

Venus trine Mars: Venus and Jupiter both aspecting Mars results in a well-aspected Mars. Strength, courage, fighting spirit, aggression, will, etc., are supported. Specifically, Venus-Mars aspects emphasize an intense passion pervading all activities (especially, but not exclusively, the sexual). Emotional strength is great.

Notice the subjective, feeling predominance of these aspects. Whatever she would actively do this year, Patty Hearst was scheduled to begin operating from her gut, perhaps more than in any previous period of her life.

Saturn trine Uranus: This is a very general aspect which is not exceptionally important here, but which is too nearly exact to be overlooked entirely. Saturn-Uranus is a tense aspect emphasizing needs for autonomy and independence. With Saturn background, survival needs can only be efficiently met through novel, creative, inventive (i.e., Uranian) tactics. As a first/ninth-house trine, it could be read as the need for autonomous self-expression of her ideals.

Consider all of this with the addition of a fifth-house stellium: an unbridled, ardent personality, somewhat unpredictable, uninhibitedly expressing herself and assuming her freedom, with no small amount of drama. Furthermore, solar Moon is applying to a conjunction with Jupiter. Along with a rising Pluto, this indicates a tendency to think of oneself as somehow special, perhaps superior to others.

I submit that this chart, interpreted systematically with as little bias as is possible when already knowing the outcome, does indicate the emergence of a new personality, tapping factors hitherto latent but always present in Patty Hearst. Rebellion, a love affair, dramatic self-assertion, a more visceral approach to life, and the possibility of identity confusion are the major themes present.

Patty Hearst: 1975 Solar Return

In Figures 5-6 and 5-7, we see the Solar Returns for Ms. Hearst's twenty-first birthday. From the beginning, they show marked departures from the previous year, even though some "old familiar faces" are still in sight.

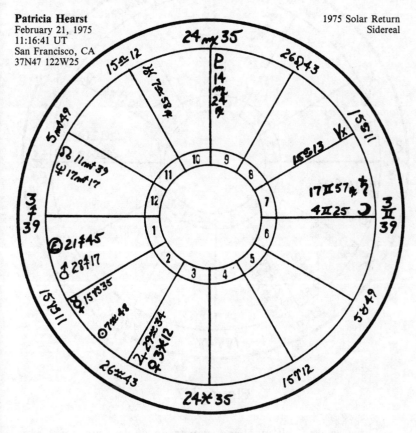

Patricia Hearst
February 21, 1975
11:16:41 UT
San Francisco, CA
37N47 122W25

1975 Solar Return
Sidereal

Figure 5-6

Among the familiar indications are: a foreground Pluto (culminating exactly with 21°49′ Virgo), a Moon-Pluto aspect (paran), and a Moon-Jupiter aspect (square). Uranus and Venus are again prominent, but in a different sense than before.

The departures are found in the totaled tone of the map. Despite the prominence of fluctuation planets (Moon, Mercury, Uranus, Pluto), this is much more stable and surefooted than either of the two preceding. Stresses are still abundant; but there are now new resources for handling stress.

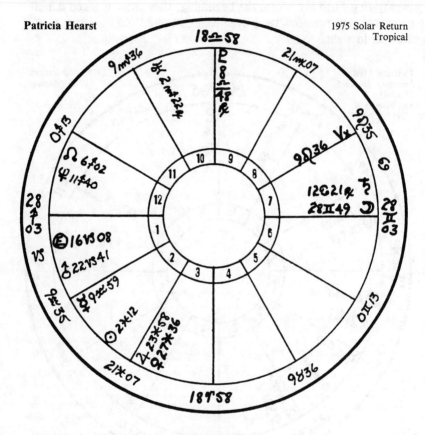

Patricia Hearst

1975 Solar Return
Tropical

Figure 5-7

Three aspects, all involving planets on angles, are novel and primary in this chart. They are Moon square Venus, Saturn square Pluto, and Mercury trine Pluto. Sun trine Uranus, only 10′ wide, claims a close fourth place.

Moon on the Descendant square an exalted Venus (Pisces, either zodiac) indicates strong feelings inclined toward the peaceful, and a marked desire for close emotional involvement with others, including close family members. There is desire for harmony, and a special receptivity to the loving feelings that are expressed by others. Frustration tolerance increases with this aspect, which is neither self-destructive nor others-destructive. Stresses can therefore be handled much better than before, even with the strong, high-strung Gemini Moon (either zodiac).

Saturn square Pluto is less congenial:

> Shouldering unwanted burdens, a person with this natal configuration often feels he is carrying the weight of the world on his shoulders ('Atlas syndrome'). He has a fear of being manipulated, hence he is not interested in confederations or alliances. This lone wolf tries desperately to dissociate himself from all labels and categorizations. The Saturn-Pluto aspect normally causes one to disregard any opinions or beliefs which do not immediately fall in line with his own established attitudes and ideas.[5]

In addition to the above, I read this as very sobering. There is an increased need for independent self-reliance, far greater than that shown before. There has been a maturing, even if a hardening as well. The calluses may be thick. In the Tropical Zodiac, this square reaches from Cancer to Libra and could be interpreted as affecting nurturance and pair-bonds. In Sidereal Gemini-Virgo, I prefer to interpret it as quite shrewd, drawing on our subject's best mental and strategic resources for survival.

At the same time, with Saturn near setting, this is bound to affect alliances adversely. That fact contradicts, at first look, what was said about Moon-Venus above. I would, therefore, clarify the latter as specifically suggesting a need for loving, caring relationships in a secure, supportive environment, perhaps in reaction to increasing doubts about the reliability of the people with whom she has been up until that time.

Mercury on the Antivertex is sensitized. One thing that this placement meant (with the setting Moon) was ongoing publicity. It also underscored activity and changing scenes, as well as the requirements placed on her mind. Solar Mercury on an angle means that other people want information from the native. Mercury-Pluto aspects (such as the trine in this chart) are "demand the answers" configurations which **can** sometimes go so far as to indicate being given the third degree. Neptune here sextiles both planets from their midpoint, stating the likelihood of much uneasiness, if not intense anxiety and apprehension, while the questions are being asked. Without stating it in so many specific words, this chart is starting to warn us of the possibilities of the arrest which occurred on September 18.

5. Ibid., 106.

Much of the revolutionary is still apparent in this chart. Pluto is in the upper foreground, with a prominent Uranus in nearly exact trine with the Sun and in wider (but not wide) trine with the Moon. Uranus is certainly highlighted! Freedom needs are still pronounced, with surprises appearing more than occasionally.

More important, to my thinking, is the tendency for Sun-Uranus aspects to indicate a clarified self-perspective (in contrast to the distorted, exaggerated self-image of Sun-Neptune during the previous two years). Several things in this chart suggest a "return to the real world," including this Sun-Uranus aspect, an angular Saturn, and a second-house Sun, with Neptune now pretty much out of the picture.

Year-to-Year Consistency

I am fascinated by the ongoing process, each step sequentially shown from year to year, from Solar Return to Solar Return. I have observed this many times before, and am no less impressed with how clearly it appears in Patricia Hearst's Solar Returns for 1973, 1974 and 1975. Astrology displays life in a way that makes sense, every stage being a kind of natural development from the one before it. The integrating factor is the person who is living the horoscope.

In closing, I want to point out the startling similarities between these three charts, showing as they do the full extent of this chapter in a young woman's life. In a generalized sense, every one indicates separation, alienation and revolt. More specifically, notice that all have:

Pluto foreground. Dramatic transformation, intensive alterations in life, travel, revolt against format, a need for readjustment.

Moon-Pluto aspects (two parans and a sesquisquare). Experiences elicit a profound, climactic emotional response (crisis, shock). Others seem aloof or implacable. Refusal to be categorized, while feeling the sharp impact of others' expectations. Rebellious. Separations, emotional alienation. Emotional stress, compulsive behavior.

Moon-Jupiter aspects (a paran, conjunction and square). Circumstances give the native reason to be enthusiastic and joyful. Others are emotionally supportive. A feeling of personal specialness. Identification with the superior. Attunement to a personal belief system. Money matters go well.

A grand trine involving Uranus and at least one luminary. This intrigues me, because grand trines are not infrequent for the maps of criminals. It gives a locked-in quality. We can also read this as a luminary-reinforced Uranus bounded by static aspects. Certainly it indicates a constant novelty in Ms. Hearst's situation, but beyond that I can only offer conjecture. Opinions from readers are welcome on this most interesting situation.

CHAPTER SIX

SECOND TIME THROUGH — WHEELS WITHIN WHEELS

It has taken us five "warm up" chapters to get here; but now we are set to get into the real "meat" of interpreting Solar Returns.

Solunar delineation is marked not only by big rewards in accuracy and clarity, but also by simple ways of achieving them. In this chapter, you will find an easy approach to getting important, key information from a Solar Return quickly and efficiently. You do not need to master the thousand and one complexities suggested by sponsors of many astrological methods. Nor do you need an abundance of either luck or psychic precognition. Though "rule" is generally considered an obscene, four-letter word in my classroom, it is in the analysis of Solunars that I am most inclined to recommend a strongly routinized, carefully regulated delineative approach.

This applies to the **second interpretation** of a Solar Return. Throughout this book, I am emphasizing the importance of reading an annual Solar Return **twice**, involving two very distinct examinations. With experience, these may begin to merge into one. Still, after years of using Solunars, I to this day first compute, draw and study a Solar Return without recourse to natal planets, much as with the Hearst charts in Chapter Five. This gives an important added perspective. Only then do I place the individual's natal planets on an inside ring and apply the tactics suggested in this chapter.

Once I have added that inner wheel — the wheel of natal planets an individual has carried through life — my entire approach changes. It becomes much more tightly focused, disciplined and acute. I know **precisely** where to look, and systematically look there. What is more, I find what I am seeking. The chart's contents are not always perfectly clear, but with some thought they become understandable. You do not need several years of experience to develop this acuity. All that the experience adds is increasing confidence that you are doing things the right way, plus the special personal understanding of nuance and subtlety which arises from any prolonged study of astrology.

You only have to try a few of these charts to get unmistakably accurate, vivid examples which prove how powerful and valuable these charts really are. Furthermore, Solunars never cease to be impressive and exciting as you examine chart after chart after chart.

The Rules Change

In Chapter Two, individual astrological factors were examined in depth, and some of the differences were noted between their applications in the first and second readings of a Solar Return. Those differences can now be summarized and specified. When studying a Solar Return as a period analysis chart, the following should be kept in mind.

1. **ANGULARITY and ASPECTS** are the factors to observe. Recall, if you will, that these are the ingredients of a horoscope which are wavelike in their operations. The categorical divisions of signs and houses can be set aside at this point. Experience indicates that they are more likely to confuse and clutter than clarify.
2. For the most part, **only foreground planets should be considered operative**, including in this planets which occupy minor angles. There are exceptions to this guideline, mentioned below; but it is essentially sound. Middleground bodies, while not of outstanding note, are worthy of attention when involved in close, important configurations. Background bodies are significant solely because of their general **lack of activity**.[1]
3. **Only hard (dynamic) aspects are to be considered**, primarily the conjunction, opposition and square (including parans). The exception I make to this is that trines and sextiles of solar luminaries,

---

1. For clarification, please note that the angles and other house cusps are those of the Solar Return itself. The Solar Return planets are placed in the outer circle and natal planets on the inner wheel. These placements are constant and intentional reminders of the "inside-outside" mode of transit interpretation.

particularly the Moon, to solar planets seem useful in rounding out the luminary pictures. This is especially so if within about 3° of exact aspect. I do not advise examining soft aspects between solar and natal planets.
4. The **inside/outside** principles of transit interpretation (see Chapter Three) are to be carefully applied.

These considerations are unique to this particular category of chart. I would feel lost applying them to a natal horoscope, although their importance for Solunars is certain. They lead very naturally to the following outline of exactly how to delineate a Solar Return.

Procedure for Solar Return Analysis

1. Note which planets are foreground, both natal and solar. Frame the core of your delineation around these factors alone, trying to come to some kind of integrated assessment of the map's general tone.
   A. If the same planet is foreground in both the natal (inner) and solar (outer) wheels, it takes on **special significance** as a theme planet.
   B. The planets closest to the angles have the most to say. While the entire map has to fit together synthetically, this guideline will often help prioritize and weight planetary involvement.
   C. Solar planets are interpreted as describing **circumstances the world brings to the individual**. Natal planets represent **the individual's reactions to these circumstances** or, sometimes, **the actions which invoke them**.
2. Note aspects between/among foreground planets.
   A. Aspects to foreground solar planets help refine judgment on what to expect from the outside world.
   B. Interpret foreground radical planets in terms of what they represent in the nativity (shown by their natal aspects and, to some extent, sign placements).
   C. Note foreground solar (transiting) planets aspecting foreground natal planets.
3. Interpret aspects of solar Moon to both solar and natal planets. See "Luminary Importance in Terms of Angularity" in Chapter Four. Stop at this point to make sure the delineation is consistent and makes sense.
4. Observe which solar planets are background and how they color the picture so far obtained.
5. Interpret aspects of the Sun to solar planets. See "Luminary

Importance in Terms of Angularity" in Chapter Four.
6. Consider any remaining aspects within about 1°. These represent supplementary, background considerations.

Aspect Orbs

We still have to consider the important question of aspect orbs. On this matter, so much disagreement exists from teacher to teacher that an inexperienced but well-read student is certain to be either confused or frustrated. As an astrological teacher and writer, I have sometimes been frustrated myself in trying to give clear, useful answers on this question.

You see, orbs don't really exist.

But we need to pretend that they do.

By this is meant that no magic line exists which, when crossed, banishes an aspect's influences to some netherworld of nonexistence. Aspect strength gradually fades away as the orb increases; but in a very technical sense it never drops to absolute zero.

My experience suggests that the rate of this fade-out approximates a sine curve; ergo, the potency formulae given in the last chapter. By this rate, a conjunction with an orb of 3°00′ is twice as strong as a conjunction of 7°03′. The latter is twice as potent as a conjunction with an 8°34′ orb, and so forth. The exact numbers are not important. What **is** important is that this drop-off is along a sloping curve, not a straight line, and that an aspect's power diminishes **progressively**, rather than just vanishing at some cosmic cutoff point.

One thing can be said with great certainty, which shines a beacon of clarity through the opinions and biases. This is: **closer aspects are stronger than wider aspects. The extent of partility (exactness) determines priority**. Therefore, if there are many close aspects, we have no need to use large ones. If close aspects are sparse, we are justified in taking the closest we can find, even if that means stretching our normal limits.

But where, it is fair to ask, does this potency drop below the limen of perceptibility? Where, in other words, does it become so weak that, for all reasonable purposes, it is nonexistent? Or, to frame this query a third way, what orbs are practical to assign to aspects from the standpoint of using them in everyday astro-work?

My formal orb recommendations are based on the aspect strength formulae in Chapter Five, which in turn were devised to match my experience. The following guidelines should be helpful.

1. In practice, the ultimate orb I accept is 10° for a conjunction or op-position, and 7° 30' for a square, trine or sextile. In this range the strength has dropped so low as to be imperceptible.[2] Only rarely are such aspects worth any notice.

2. Conjunctions and oppositions are at about 50% strength with an orb just under 7°; squares, trines and sextiles at 5°. Even in natal work, the drop-off beyond these points is steep. Such aspects, in natal astrology, only generate subtle influences. I would recommend these as **maximum orbs in Solar Returns**, since weaker factors have very little to say in the course of a year.

3. Another key point is the 80% mark on the aspect curve. For con-junctions and oppositions, this is a 4° orb; for squares, trines and sextiles, about 3°. Aspects within this range, especially transits (for the dynamic aspects), should be eagerly attended when in the Solunar foreground. We are now encountering very serious influences.

4. Partile aspects (1° orb or less) reign supreme. According to my pro-posed formulae, a conjunction or opposition with a 1° orb is at 99% of its maximum strength. Squares, trines and sextiles register 98% of their full clout. For almost any purpose, they can indeed be con-sidered "exact."

   Aspects at this high (partile) level of potency are apt to manifest no matter what. For anything less strong, angularity is required to lend easy expressiveness to whatever configurations are present. It is when angularity and aspect partility coincide that outstanding in-cidents are most likely to come about.

A Delineative Example

"Phil" was born August 2, 1944, 18:00 CWT, 88W46, 44N37 (Figure 6-1). Eight planets were contained at his birth between the Descendant and the ninth cusp — four each in the seventh and eighth houses. A heavy concentration of planets in this particular corner of the horoscope often indicates that much psychic energy is invested in other people, their needs and opinions.

While Saturn conjoins the Descendant, Neptune is **precisely** con-junct the Zenith. Furthermore, the Sun is in Cancer, conjoining Pluto. The Cancer Sun and angular Neptune indicate strong needs to be

---

2. I am aware that harmonics of 10°0' and 7°.5 have been found to be valid micro-aspects in their own right; but these are little blips with tiny orbs, rising from a low point in the main aspect curve for only an instant in the life of the cycle. The space leading immediately up to these "maximum limits" is dismally inactive.

wrapped up in other people in a tight sense of belonging, nourishing and merging. Saturn insists on separateness and personal autonomy. On the one hand, we encounter the need to be dependent, absorbed and returned to conditions reminiscent of the very matrix of life, the womb. On the other, there is a need to be discrete and individual, to firmly define oneself by one's own boundaries and solidarity. Through it all, the volitional Sun conjoins the outlaw Pluto to seemingly require this man to enter life only by his own rules, to disregard some of the most hallowed taboos if necessary in order to live in a way he can truly call his own.

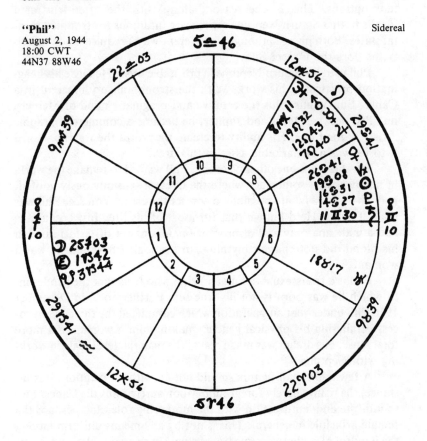

"Phil"
August 2, 1944
18:00 CWT
44N37 88W46

Sidereal

Figure 6-1

Saturn and Neptune do have some common ground between them. At their worst, for instance, they coincide with anxiety or sickness. In a more fundamental sense, however, they are world-defining. Neptune ultimately signifies the way we model our experience of the world: what we perceive, how we interpret it and what we choose to believe as the result. As none of us is physiologically or psychologically capable of perceiving everything in the objective universe, Neptune represents our capacity to shift and sort. Similarly, Saturn symbolizes objective structure, form and pattern. When combined, these planets symbolize the capacity to take a vision of the world and imbue it with material substance and believability. Saturn-Neptune people commonly have very unyielding models, which becomes a problem if they preclude important options. This is one reason, along with the often-frustrated idealism, that Saturn-Neptune aspects are infamous for troubled mental states. Both planets, though in different ways, require much security, as does the Cancer Sun.

Phil used his Saturn-Neptune in profitable ways. He made his imagination practical in his work. With the strong imagery inherent in a Cancer Sun-Venus, plus the creative and pragmatic mind of Mercury huddled between Mars and Jupiter, he became a commercial graphic artist. A good one. His ability to create the world the way he wished it to be was a remarkable asset in this area.

But there was one other place that Phil wanted to remake the world in his own way, someplace where the Creator had obviously goofed, and where it was quite possible to correct the error. You see, Phil was really Phyllis. He'd known that for most of his life. Just because he had a male anatomy and disproportionate amount of testosterone in his blood did not change anything. In his soul, Phil knew he was a woman.

Phil is a transsexual, a human being who feels that the gender into which he was born is not his true sex. Furthermore, in December 1976 Phil underwent an operation which completed the three-year process of altering his physical gender, making him a woman in a more total sense. His dream was made real at the material level, Saturn working with Neptune.

A few additional factors should not go without mention. For instance, the rising, barely foreground Moon surely joins the Cancer Sun to indicate an identification with the mothering role, and perhaps the female principle in general. This is not by any means uniform among the handful of male-to-female transsexual charts in my files, but is certainly appropriate for this situation.

Something which is uniform in those transsexual nativities I have seen is a difficulty with social adjustment. This is disturbing. I certainly do not want to generalize that all such men and women have these problems; yet, it has been consistent so far. Phyllis's setting Saturn, seventh house Pluto, Neptune-horizon square and Venus-Saturn semisquare have much to say about this. Relationships are shown as important to her, but as not particularly rewarding.

Finally, Mars squares Uranus from Leo to Taurus, a remarkably courageous configuration which features the lunar nodal axis at its midpoint: "the execution of extraordinary and unusual enterprise," according to Ebertin.[3]

Phil began psychotherapy in December 1973, a critical month for him astrologically even if only transits are considered. Neptune was making its second square to natal Mercury. Saturn retrograded across the natal Descendant, square natal Neptune. Anxiety was high. A lifetime of inner confusion and doubt was building in a world which seemed to take pride in its prohibitions. But Uranus was soon to turn stationary, sesquisquare its natal position, a signal of change; while Pluto was completing its first square to natal Saturn, urging old structures, limitations and patterns to be broken and rearranged.

Figure 6-3 is the Solar Return covering the last six months before Phil's surgical conversion to Phyllis, and her first months as an anatomical woman. According to convention, natal planets are on the inner ring, solar planets on the outer. Let's study this chart according to the specific rules given in this chapter. In fact, why don't you, the reader, go ahead and try your hand at delineation first. Just follow the guidelines carefully, consult the interpretations in Chapters Three and Four as needed, and turn to the next paragraph when you are through.

Now, here's my delineation, a little stilted perhaps, in an attempt to stick with the preplanned format for the sake of this demonstration.

1. **NOTE WHICH PLANETS ARE FOREGROUND.** Solar Neptune, Mercury and Venus conjoin major angles, with Jupiter on the Nadir and Mars on the Vertex. In fact, Neptune and Mercury are **exactly** on the meridian and horizon, respectively, with Neptune dominating from the Midheaven. Natal Venus, Jupiter, Mercury, Uranus and Mars are in the foreground, with Venus and Jupiter

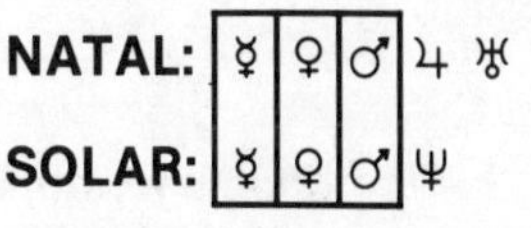

NATAL: ☿ ♀ ♂ ♃ ♅
SOLAR: ☿ ♀ ♂ ♆

FIGURE 6-2

3. Reinhold Ebertin, *The Combination of Stellar Influences*, trans. Dr. Alfred G. Roosedale and Linda Kratzch (Aalen, Germany: Ebertin-Verlag, 1972 edition).

straddling the Descendant while Uranus very closely conjoins the IC. Mercury is the most angular natal planet, however, being exactly on the West Point. We can list these for easy reference (Figure 6-2).

Both Mercuries, Venuses, Jupiters and Marses are foreground, though natal Mars is only weakly so. Certainly the Mars presences indicate the surgery itself.

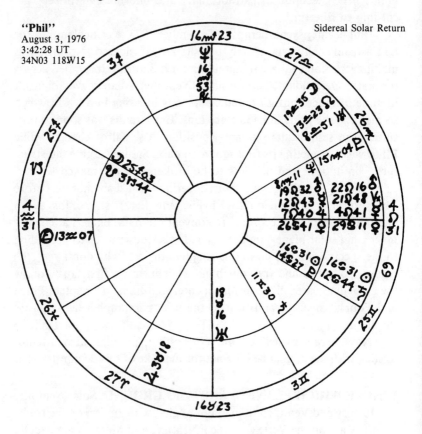

"Phil"
August 3, 1976
3:42:28 UT
34N03 118W15

Sidereal Solar Return

Figure 6-3

The Mercury emphasis indicates that this will be an exceedingly busy year, when the mind will be required to operate at high levels of performance. Much learning will be required (as indeed it was: these last months were lived in a female identity though still in a male body, learning everything necessary to function as a member of the opposite sex by doing it). According to this chart, a constant give-and-take of facts and dialogue will exist. With Venus conjuncting, and Jupiter squaring, solar Mercury, learning and communication will go smoothly. The native will feel that others are listening to him. There is also a strong possibility of travel.

A dual Venus emphasis promises an essentially pleasurable year when harmony and affection are leading themes. (Those few friends who knew what was happening became extremely supportive, helpful and caring, for instance.) On the Descendant, we could justifiably expect a significant romantic involvement. On the contrary, Phil lost the romantic relationship with his female roommate at this time due to the pending operation and, to my knowledge, no other developed.

Neptune and Mercury dominate the outer circle of the wheel, showing that this was a particularly anxious time, perhaps with a great deal of confusion and distortion. Under Mercury-Neptune aspects, an individual may feel pursued, or as though he is under close surveillance. Throughout this time of learning new behavior, Phil was regularly questioning how well his masquerade was working, wondering if people had "discovered the truth" and were whispering about him, and generally overreacting to other people in many kinds of interaction. Fortunately, solar Venus foreground indicated that the environment, overall, was not seen as intolerably threatening.

The wait seemed interminable. Then, as the date approached, came the worries and brief second thoughts. These passed, and the operation went well.

We can anticipate that the events of the year would draw a delighted response from the native. Natal Venus and Jupiter are setting, while the thrill planet, Uranus, anticulminates. Happiness is apparent, as is the personal need for change.

2. NOTE ASPECTS AMONG FOREGROUND PLANETS. Most important of these is Neptune's culminating opposition to natal Uranus. Transiting Neptune offers a vision or lure. When aspecting natal Uranus, a temptation or dream inspires the individual to boldly make changes in his or her life situation. Along the meridian, with Neptune also exactly trine the Sun, these changes were entirely volitional and involved the very identity of the person. Uranus on the IC suggests a personal escape from previous environmental conditions or elements from the past, with a possibility of breaking loose some deeply held, guarded feelings. External manifestations of this, such as a change of residence, can also be anticipated.

3. **INTERPRET LUNAR ASPECTS.** Solar Moon is just separating from a square to the Sun. Sun-Moon aspects always isolate years which are outstanding turning points in some way. Self-assurance and pride are reinforced, sometimes shining through the Neptunian tendency toward apprehension and worry.

4. **OBSERVE BACKGROUND PLANETS.** Natal Sun is in the background (minimizing the importance of solar aspects), along with solar Moon and Saturn. Solar Jupiter seems background at first glance, but is actually square the horizon and therefore considered angular.

The mutual aspect between the luminaries leaves them anything but weak. Nonetheless, a background Sun cycle is one of assimilation and preparation. This is not a period in the individual's life when creative unfolding is at a peak. That will come later. Instead, mental exploration and change are key themes (natal Mercury and Uranus repeatedly angular, from year to year). Personal affairs can be given primary attention, however (background Moon). Very little ultimately stands in the individual's way where major desires are considered (background solar Saturn).

5. **OBSERVE SOLAR ASPECTS.** Only the square to the Moon and partile trine to Neptune are important with this background Sun. These have been discussed.

6. **NOTE REMAINING PARTILE ASPECTS.** None exist.

I might add, in closing, that the surgery occurred at 104W59, 33N44, where the locality Solar Return Midheaven was 28♏41, and the Ascendant 24≈06, putting solar Mars within a degree of the Descendant where the knife was actually wielded.

CHAPTER SEVEN

TIMING

A Solar Return describes the life circumstances an individual experiences during the period of its effect. We have seen how it can be interpreted as an alternate birth chart for the course of the year. At the same time, the Solar Return is the basis of the most powerful forecasting system presently known to astrological technology.

So far, I have not emphasized the Solar Return's value in predicting events. I feel its greatest advantages lie in determining the path of evolving character. Nonetheless, when accompanied by certain accessory techniques, the Solar Return is capable of specifying events with great clarity and acuity.

However, it does not help much to predict specific events using a technique that can only pinpoint them to the nearest **year** of life. A Solar Return is operative 365¼ days. Whatever it describes will come to pass **sometime** during that period, but not less likely at the end of the year than the beginning. We require other, more finely tuned methods of designating times during the year when situations described by the Solar Return are most likely to appear.

This chapter presents those methods, under four headings: **Demi- and Quarti-Returns, Anlunar Returns,** two methods of **progressing the Solar Return** and **transits.**

Quarters of the Year

A **Demi-Solar Return (DSR)** is computed for the exact instant the transiting Sun **opposes** the natal solar longitude of an individual. This is a supplementary chart representing the last half of the Solar Return year.

A **Quarti-Solar Return (QSR)** is computed for the time when transiting Sun **squares** natal Sun. This accessory map has been found somewhat representative of the three months following its inception; i.e., until the next conjunction or opposition.

Demi-Solars and Quarti-Solars are most useful in timing the three-month period during which specific occurrences will manifest. The rules for this are simple, as well as reliable, to wit:

If a Quarti- or Demi-Return contains the same fundamental symbolism as the operative (conjunction) Solar Return, the major events or other manifestations of that symbolism will occur in the period specified by the quarterly chart. Otherwise, they will manifest in the first three months after the birthday.

By "same fundamental symbolism" I mean such blatant things as having the same planet(s) foreground or the same lunar aspects. For example, if the annual Solar Return set up with a conjunction of transiting Neptune and natal Venus in the immediate foreground, we would expect Neptune-to-Venus feelings, circumstances and events to dominate the year. One possible manifestation of this would be an idealized love affair. If the Demi-Solar had this same transit on an angle, then the affair would specifically occur in the last half of the year, probably in the three months immediately following the DSR. If one of the Quarti-Solars had this conjunction foreground instead, it would mark the three months subsequent to the QSR as the time for the affair. Should none of these accessory charts sport the same symbolism as the Solar Return, then the liaison will probably take off right after the birthday and either run its course or become far less idyllic by the time the first Quarti-Solar comes into power.

The Solar Return tells the year. The Demi-Solar or Solar isolates the six-month period. Within these boundaries, the Quarti-Solars may reveal the specific three months when Solar Return portents will be fulfilled. (See Figure 7-1.)

How valid, one might ask, are the Demi-Solars and Quarti-Solars by themselves?

Demi-Solars are potent charts. I regularly compute them for myself. If a client consults me near the middle of his or her birthday year, I am likely to compute the Demi-Solar. Sometimes I will do this in lieu of the regular Solar Return, sometimes in addition to it, depending on whether the consultation is to deal with immediate issues or those which have been ongoing for several months. The Demi-Solar

Return is a viable chart in its own right, though not so major as the conjunction return.

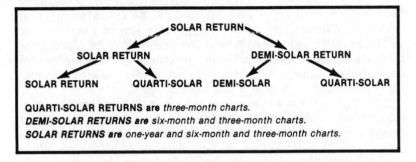

Figure 7-1

Unless I am specifically seeking to determine the quarter of a year in which an event will manifest, I almost never compute Quarti-Solars. By themselves, they are very minor charts. If they are in agreement with the Solar Return, they provide useful timing information. Otherwise, they have little to offer. Occasionally, when the Solar and Quarti-Solar are in major disagreement, it will feel as though someone is running interference across the path of your forward motion, though never to such an extent that the basic Solar Return's indications are offset.

Anlunar Returns

An- is a prefix originating with the same root as our word "annual," meaning "covering the period of a year." The Anlunar Return is based on the **annual Moon,** i.e, the Moon of the Solar Return. Every 27.3 days, transiting Moon returns to the same exact longitude it held at the time the Solar Return occurred. A chart drawn for this calculated moment is the Anlunar Return.

Lunar Return delineation will be detailed in a sequel and companion volume to this book, *Interpreting Lunar Returns*. For now, interpret Anlunars by the same rules given in Chapter Six for interpreting Solar Returns, but giving more attention to transiting Sun than it would receive in a Solar Return delineation.

Draw the Anlunar by placing current transiting planets in the outer ring and Solar Return planets on the inner ring of a two-ring chart blank. Natal planets can be ignored unless they are in partile dynamic aspect with a solar planet which is in the Anlunar foreground. (See Appendix A for calculation instructions.)

Anlunars have been used by several astrologers for as many as twenty years, and passed in and out of favor more than once during that time. Sometimes, they seem to be extremely valuable. Other times, they fizzle out with scarcely a spark to show. More confusing is that students of Solunars have reported Anlunars working very well one year and being totally worthless the next. While this observed fact may be somehow connected with the Moon's placement in the Solar Return, no clear patterns have emerged so far which allow us to say in advance when an Anlunar will or will not be effective

Therefore, when it is consulted as an independent chart, I cannot recommend the Anlunar as a reliable tool. Its greatest value — and here it works reliably — is in **pinpointing the month in a year when portents of the Solar Return are most likely to be actualized.** When used in conjunction with Quarti- and Demi-Solars, the Anlunar adds another layer to the stack of similar indications, summing influences of like kind, making the probability of overt events great by sheer weight of repeated symbolism.

If desired, Anlunar periods can also be broken into weekly time slots by Demi-Anlunars and Quarti-Anlunars. The latter are surely of little use for any purpose other than finely tuned timing.

An interesting fact I have never seen mentioned elsewhere is that, within a day, Anlunars occur on the same calendar dates for every year of a person's life. Count ahead 27, 55, 82, 109, 137, 164, 191, 219, 246, 273, 301, 328 and 355 days from your birthday and see if any of these are consistently red-letter dates in your life, or the beginnings of a month-long period during which the same type of events or feelings transpire. If so, it may correlate to an Anlunar regularly occurring then, accenting the Sun's exact transit to some planet in your natal chart.

Progressing the Solar Return

Because the Solar Return is a new inceptional figure, much like a birth chart, it can be progressed in the same ways a nativity can be progressed. Two methods have been proven especially valid and important: the **Solar Quotidian (SQ)** and the **Progressed Sidereal Solar Return (PSSR).**[1]

---

1. Tropical astrologers, it is hoped, will not panic over the label "sidereal" in the PSSR. These techniques were pioneered by Siderealists who gave them names that have (appropriately) stuck. Use of the system does not violate one's right to employ whatever zodiac one may wish. The "sidereal" naming of the system merely means that precession has not been allowed to interfere with the calculation of the chart. In other words, either the Sidereal Zodiac is used, or the Tropical Zodiac is used with accumulated precession removed.

"Quotidian" means "daily." Both the SQ and PSSR are daily charts in that their angles move approximately 1° per day.[2] Specifically, the SQ Midheaven advances about 1° per day, while the PSSR Midheaven is accelerated about 1¼°.

The Solar Quotidian is essentially the same as the standard Secondary (day-for-a-year) Progression, with an important refinement. Because in one day's time the Midheaven and other house cusps move through the entire zodiacal circle, a strict interpretation of the day-for-a-year equation requires that progressed angles also move through the entire zodiac in one year: 360° in 365 days.

Except for the Moon, progressed solar planets scarcely move in one year. Still, what progressed aspects they do form are important near the exact time of maturation. Progressed orbs seem to be based on elapsed time, not zodiacal arc. In a recent year, my Solar Return occurred the exact day of a Neptune-Pluto sextile. Although the orb of this aspect was less than 1' all year, the manifestation was unquestionably focused in the weeks when the progressed aspect was precise, as timed by the aspectarian of a reliable ephemeris.

Most important, though, with both the SQ and PSSR, are progressed lunar aspects and progressed angles.

The PSSR was discovered by Cyril Fagan in the fall of 1956. Seeds had been planted years earlier by another author, Sidney K. Bennett, known in astrological circles as "Wynn," who had the clear sight to recognize the inadequacy of period analysis techniques used in his day. In the 1930s, Wynn invented what he called the "Key Cycle,"[3] a way of progressing the Tropical Solar Return.

Simply put, Wynn's theory was this: the average difference in sidereal time between two consecutive Tropical Solar Returns is 5:48:46.0, never varying far from this. If this is spread evenly over the elapsed time between these two return charts (an average of 365.2422 days), we get a daily advance of 57 seconds of sidereal time, or about 0°14' on the Midheaven. A Key Cycle is, simply, a progression of a Tropical Solar Return by this rate.

Many astrologers find Key Cycles useful. I am not one of these. Instructions for using Key Cycles are provided for the curious and investigative in Appendix A in order to be fair to all concerned and to provide readers with an opportunity to compare systems. Although I respect Wynn's overall talents and sensibilities on other matters, I am not in any way endorsing his technique.

---

2. The method for calculating these charts is displayed in Appendix A. In this current chapter, some of their major characteristics will be discussed.

3. Wynn, *The Key Cycle* (Tempe, Ariz.: American Federation of Astrologers, Inc., 1970).

On the other hand, Fagan's PSSR, originally adapted from Wynn's innovative approach, succeeds admirably.

Each orbit of the Earth about the Sun takes 365 days plus about another six hours. In the precession-accelerated framework Wynn used, the average excess is 5:48:46.0 of clock time. In the precession-free system recommended by this book and mounds of research, the period is 365 days plus 6:09:09.5.

Wynn theorized that we should account for this six-hour discrepancy by progressing the Solar Return's sidereal time six hours a year. However, sidereal time is a measurement of the Earth's rotation. Look at the sidereal time column in any ephemeris and you will see each day's tabulated value is about 3^m57^s greater than that of the preceding day. This is because sidereal time increases 24:03:57 for every twenty-four hours of clock time. **In the period between two consecutive Solar Returns, the Earth rotates 366¼ times. The excess is *not six hours*, but rather *one day plus six hours:*** an average of 30:09:12.8 which, stretched over a year, amounts to about five minutes (1¼ °) per day.

This is the rate of the PSSR. Its calculation is a little cumbersome at first but well worth the effort (see Appendix A). Along with the Solar Quotidian, it provides a set of **daily angles.** When planets come within 1 ° (on rare occasions, up to 2°) of the PSSR or SQ angles, they dominate the day. These can be natal, solar, progressed solar or transiting planets.

The Moon's average daily motion is 13°11 ', which is also the average annual motion of the SQ Moon. This reduces to just over a degree per month (1°06 '). The PSSR Moon averages 16°33 ' a year, or about 1°23 ' a month. These figures will be useful in approximating when Solar Return progressions will mature.

Transits to the Solar Return

Solar Return planets and angles are at least as sensitive to transiting aspects as are the natal ones — perhaps more so. They are definitely more receptive to transits than are secondary progressed planets.

Essentially, transits to solar planets mean the same things as transits to natal planets. There are small differences, though, which the alert student can teach herself or himself by keeping personal records of what happens when these transits are present. The principle distinction is this: solar planets are basically transiting planets themselves, though highly personalized. Therefore, your solar Venus, for instance, actually has more to do with other people's love offered to you than your love offered to them. This can be stated in a very stilted way as, **the affection and pleasantries coming to you from the outer world which you carry around with you for a year.** When one's solar Venus is transited, the effects seem to be single-mindedly aimed at affecting relationships, particularly how one is treated by others. For instance transiting Mars conjunct **natal** Venus may signal an excellent time to pursue a sexual encounter; but transiting Mars conjunct **solar** Venus is apt to mean "stress in a relationship."

Solar Mars is "the aggression aimed at you by the outer world which you carry around with you for a year." It seems to keynote your confrontations for twelve months. Similarly, solar Jupiter might be considered your personal access to reward and opportunity, solar Mercury your "dialogue" planet, etc.

The concept is more important than the specifics. Examine actual examples. Keep notes of personal experiences and the transits to solar planets which accompany them. Before long, you will have registered the distinction at a body/feeling level and will begin responding to these astrological patterns from the gut.

In the past, published rules have stated that only transits to solar Sun, Moon, Mercury, Venus, Mars and angles were to be considered of importance, particularly when these planets are in the solar foreground. The reason for this is that Solar Return positions of the slow planets, especially Uranus, Neptune and Pluto, are shared within a very few degrees by billions of people around the world. How, other writers have asked, can a transit to solar Pluto possibly represent anything unique for a given individual?

I consider that a very fair question. I also agree with the implied answer, that such transits cannot possibly be intensely personal unless something isolates them as significant for a person (such as the intervention of a faster planet or angle). However, I do not think astrology exists only to anticipate those experiences a person has which are different from everybody else's experiences. When Mars squares Pluto in the sky, astrologers consider that the whole world will be feeling a little more Mars-Pluto-like than usual. Within only a few days of this aspect, Mars will also square the Pluto position in the Solar Returns of every person on Earth. Can anyone deny that **in a collective sense** we all will respond to this aspect? I contend that its effect on the individual is no less potent just because everyone else is going through the same thing. In fact, **because** everyone else is experiencing the same influence, and **because** there is also a Mars-Pluto square in space at the same time, this transit to solar Pluto is greatly reinforced and strengthened.

Transits to solar Neptune have produced Neptunian responses as strong as those to natal Neptune, and far more intense than those to progressed Neptune when the latter has gained any distance on its radical place. The same can be said for all solar planets. Transits to them deserve full attention.

One special situation exists involving transits to outer solar planets. Due to retrogradation, transiting Saturn, Uranus, Neptune and Pluto nearly always conjoin their solar placements sometime during the year. The effect of this is to expose the individual to what may be the purest essence of that planet one can experience. For instance, transiting Pluto precisely conjunct solar Pluto will mark the most intensely Plutonian week of a year. It is as though a personal window has been opened, giving the individual direct access to that planet's untainted central nature.

Example A

Two examples of these timing methods are given here to provide a sense of what is required to trigger an event and of how an astrologer might use these techniques in a rapid, efficient manner. The first is a private case involving a 19-year-old man and the date of his wedding.

In examining his Solar Return, one might not have isolated marriage as a definite possibility, although adequate appropriate symbolism was present in very simple ways. Also, the importance of surrounding issues, such as sex and finance, was clearly shown. Solar Jupiter was on the West Point (which acts much like the Descendant, as in marriage). Venus was 5 ° from Neptune (being "love drunk") in the fourth house (personal matters), closely sextile Jupiter (idyllic happiness through love). As with all nineteenth Solar Returns, solar Moon conjoined natal Moon.

Solar Moon was also about 7½ ° (applying) from the exact trine to solar Venus. By the SQ rate, this timed the progressed Moon-Venus trine as occurring about seven and a half months after his birthday; by the PSSR rate, a little less than six months. March and late May were isolated as the times when the Moon-Venus symbolism would manifest.

Scanning an ephemeris, it was quickly noticed that sometime in March, transiting Jupiter would square solar Venus. This is an important transit, showing a very fortunate, happy outcome of the Moon-Venus progression. Jupiter transits to solar Venus (and Venus transits to solar Jupiter) are quite common for weddings. Since there were no comparable transits in May, March seemed the most likely month for the event.

Jupiter's square to solar Venus was exact on March 13. Careful calculation showed that PSSR Moon trined solar Venus on March 14, within one day! Using this as a starting point, it was found that on March 16, close to the maturation dates of the major transit and progression, transiting Venus squared the solar Midheaven.

Without being aware of these factors, the man and his fiancée selected March 16 as their wedding date and consulted me to pick the time. This was done. However, last-minute delays postponed the wedding's start, throwing off the predetermined timing. When my client and his bride were pronounced husband and wife, the unscheduled local Midheaven had moved to precise opposition to solar Venus, triggering the pending astrological pattern and spontaneously timing the event to the minute!

Example B

In *The Sidereal Handbook*[4] I presented a series of charts for the suicidal plunge of former government official James Forrestal from the sixteenth story of Bethesda Naval Hospital. Forrestal was born on February 15, 1892, 14:30 EST, 73W58, 41N30. His death was at 1:45 EST, May 22, 1949, 77W06, 38N59.

Forrestal's Solar Return from the previous February featured a very exact, though middleground, opposition of Mars and Saturn. Solar Moon was applying to an eighth house conjunction with solar Neptune. Transiting Mars-Saturn aspects are potentially the most lethal of configurations. For an already unstable mind, these two aspects showed a strong tendency to overreact and dwell on the morbid, possibly leading to acute paranoia. A generally worrisome, anxious individual toward the end, Forrestal felt threatening outside demands and pressures invading his life, backing him into a corner. His fight-or-flight mechanism apparently drove him over the edge of sanity and out a sixteenth-floor window.

With Neptune at 20♍52 in the Solar Return progressions, PSSR Moon had reached 20♍44, four days short of precise contact.

Forrestal's Quarti-Solar occurred on May 18, 1949, at 17:41 UT, only four days before his leap. It duplicated the Moon-Neptune symbolism of the Solar Return and its progressions, while reinforcing certain other stress factors. The reader may wish to compute this chart for its general interest and bountiful educational value.

---

4. James A. Eshelman, *The Sidereal Handbook* (Anaheim, Calif.: Stymie Publications, 1975).

The Solar Return's most deadly combination was activated by the monthly and daily charts in clockwork-smooth fashion:

Solar Mars	=	9°≈40'	SQ ASC	=	6°♉18'
Solar Saturn	=	9°♌11'	Transiting Saturn	=	5°♌40'
Anlunar ASC	=	8°♌56'			
PSSR MC	=	7°≈59'			

Had we not examined the Quarti-Solar, we would still have had the lunar progressions to tell us the season and the Anlunar to reveal this particular month as one when the solar Mars-Saturn configuration was fully operative. This is a good example of aspects with small orbs landing excruciatingly close to return chart angles to produce extreme results. Finally, both sets of daily angles, the PSSR and SQ, activated the lethal pattern. Notice that the SQ horizon was just **separating** from transiting Saturn, while the PSSR meridian **approached** the Mars-Saturn opposition. This put the timing of the event close to the centerpoint of these concurrent contacts.

End-of-Year Mop-Up

Whatever is shown by the Solar Return will come to pass before the year is finished. This fact is axiomatic to the definition of what a Solar Return is and does. Particular events are not absolutely predetermined by this ruling, however; the same symbolism which seems to describe an event, in the common sense of the word, may work itself out in psychological ways. Yet, this symbolism must **somehow** be actualized in the twelve-month life span of the Solar Return, as our adopted way of being for the year greedily demands its right to life.

If, toward the end of the birthday year, important parts of the Solar Return have gone unexpressed, there arises within the individual a pressing urgency to see that this is done. This period has been labeled by Matthew Quellas and myself the Solar Return **mop-up period**. Its beginning point is well defined.

Recall, if you will, that the PSSR angles annually revolve through a full circle of the zodiac, plus an additional 92°. At some point, approximately 290 days after the birthday, PSSR angles will be **identical** to the Solar Return angles. Apparently, someone thought we needed an eleventh-hour reminder! From this point on, things move quickly.

Using the tables in Appendix C, finding the start of your own annual mop-up is easy. As explained in Appendix A, Appendix C provides tables for the easy calculation of the PSSR. These tables provide a value called the ASSI (Annual Solar Sidereal Increment) which increases annually from a value of 0:00:00 each March to a maximum value of 30:09:13. For the present purpose, you may use the table for any year, although when calculating the PSSR you should use the table for the year in question.

To find the date that your mop-up period begins, calculate the date on which the ASSI has advanced 24:00:00 since the birthday. If some-one were born on March 21 (any year) when the value of the ASSI is approximately 0:00, their mop-up period would begin every year on approximately January 6, when the ASSI reached 24:00:00.

Phyllis, in Chapter Six, was born on August 2. From the 1976 table (for example), we can extract the value of 11:04:43 for this date. Adding 24:00:00 gives a value of 35:04:43. Since this is greater than the maximum ASSI value of 30:09:13, we must subtract 30:09:13, leaving a remainder of 4:55:30. The ASSI next reached this value on May 18, 1977. Therefore, Phyllis's mop-up period begins each year on approximately May 18.

During these last ten or eleven weeks before a birthday, we are also in a preparation stage for the incoming Solar Return. Especially during the last month or so, be very aware of new people you meet and new situations you encounter. If you have birth data for these people, see how their planets aspect the angles and Moon of your approaching Solar Return. Many will have close, major contacts. These are people who will probably be important to you in the year to come, in ways described by their horoscopes' connections to your new Solar Return. By letting them into your life in advance, as well as (unconsciously) making a few other select moves at this time, you are setting yourself up so that when your birthday arrives you will be outfitted to begin immediately the activities and processes which will highlight the year before you.

Variations from Year to Year

Life is continuous. As shown by previous examples, the Solar Return reflects this continuity. There are a few important astronomical facts which predetermine some of this regularity, and which deserve mention.

Each Solar Return has a sidereal time approximately six hours nine minutes (92° of right ascension) greater than that of the preceding year's Solar (provided one does not change the longitude of residence). The actual value can vary as much as ten minutes, greater or less. So, if you add 2° to this year's East Point, you will be pretty close to next year's Midheaven. The Midheaven/East Point/Antimeridian/West Point cross will rotate about a quarter turn from Solar Return to Solar Return. Thus, natal and slow-transiting planets that occupy these angles will continue to do so for several years. (Note that the Ascendant changes at its own, much less regular, rate.)

At age 39, if you are still living at your birthplace, the Solar Return angles will exactly match those of your natal chart. The same occurs at age 78.

Solar Return Moon positions increase an average of 133° from one year to the next. This average, though, is not very useful in checking the accuracy of your calculations, since the true difference can vary from about 100° to 145°.

One regular feature of the Moon's positions is their house placements. While given to periodic exceptions, the Moon generally advances one house from year to year, sometimes skipping a house, sometimes staying in one house for a couple of years. (The Moon gains about 40° a year on the Midheaven, on the average, so it takes about nine years for the complete round of houses.) For instance, the house placements of the Moon for the first dozen years of my life, the only life for which I have computed every Solar Return, are: 6, 8, 9, 10, 12, 2, 2, 4, 5, 7, 7 and 9.

CHAPTER EIGHT

EXAMPLES

Only by examining chart after chart can any astrological principle be truly understood. This chapter contains a series of case studies which provide further examples of Solar Returns in action. Most of the examples were selected at random, some even before I had actually computed the charts. In this sense, they represent as homogeneous and unbiased a collection as I could gather.

To me, every horoscope is a new adventure. Rare is the chart that does not provide a new, exciting twist. I have sought, in these case histories, to place on paper my own thought processes, hoping thereby to share some of the excitement I personally find in first encountering a Solar Return "face-to-face."

Richard Nixon's Telltale Chart

Certainly the most dramatic chapter in modern American politics was the Watergate scandal and resulting resignation of President Richard M. Nixon, the only chief executive to abdicate his post in the two-century life span of the United States. The entire Watergate episode is a gold mine for astrological investigators, since accurate birth data are available for most key figures.

I am presenting here a lengthy discussion of the Solar Return and pertinent timing charts leading to Mr. Nixon's relinquishment of the presidency. This case is an important example because, based only on Nixon's Solar Return, I predicted his resignation in writing, to within a month, over a year in advance.

Let me make myself perfectly clear. I did not, in my written prediction, specifically state that Richard Nixon would resign from office in August 1974. Presidents had not been known to resign up until that time. Even as the momentum of Watergate accelerated, many questioned if such a thing were even allowed by the Constitution. What little innate caution I then had kept me from making so reckless a forecast.

However, I did explicitly state that during 1974 Richard Nixon's power and prestige would be greatly diminished; that his position as President would come under siege; and that these events would crest in some sort of political crisis in the summer, specifically in late July or early August of 1974.

These remarks were included in an article on world trends for 1974, written in the spring of 1973 and submitted to a major astrological magazine. The editor, whose innate caution was much greater than mine, rejected the article. It was never published. However, another article **was** published, likewise originally written in the spring of 1973, which came nearly as close to stating what actually happened. Appearing in the March 1974 issue of *American Astrology* were these words:

> What this spells is continued separation between the White House and Capitol Hill, at least during the remainder of a Republican administration. There is little chance for reconciliation between two groups so sharply divided. What may indeed happen is that in its effort to re-establish the system of checks and balances, and return much lost power to Congress, the minority lawmakers may unite with their erstwhile opponents in a front against executive authority. Thus, whether Democrat or Republican is elected in 1976 to the Presidency, we could expect little chance of conciliatory actions.[1]

It would be possible for me to select any number of examples to "prove" my theorem, that Solar Returns are magnificent predictive tools. However, this present example is particularly valuable because the forecast was made and put on record many months in advance of the event. I contend that this is far better than the *ex post facto* justifications which compose most astrological case studies.

Examine Figure 8-1, the telltale chart. This is Richard Nixon's Solar Return for January 10, 1974, representing the entire year to follow.

Most outstanding is the dual prominence of Saturn. Natal Saturn is within a degree of the Antivertex. Transiting Saturn and the south node are conjoined in the rising foreground, with the Grim Reaper only 15 ' from natal Pluto. Nixon's radix is dominated by Pluto's

---

1. James A. Eshelman, "Upheavals in World Structures," *American Astrology* (March 1974), 8.

opposition to Mars, Mercury and Jupiter; and this entire axis was under siege in the annual chart.

Richard Nixon
January 10, 1974
21:37:18 UT
Washington, D.C.
38N54 77W02

Solar Return

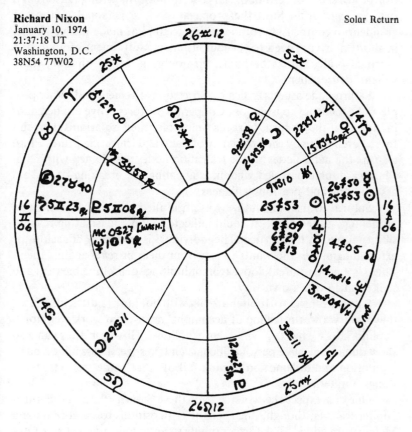

Figure 8-1

Taken by itself, transiting Saturn in the foreground signifies a burdensome year when an individual is extremely conscious of external demands and expectations. Financial obligations may loom. Without alleviating factors, it can be a frustrating, restrictive time when responsibilities and criticism seem too plentiful.

Natal Neptune rises, barely foreground but further emphasized by its opposition to the Sun, an opposition which also falls on the natal Midheaven relocated to Washington. The President, therefore, could be expected to respond to these problems in a Neptunian way, through avoidance, while feeling mounting pressures and anxiety. This did not promise to be an easy year for him. Perceptions were apt to be distorted. An accentuated Sun-Neptune aspect such as this further signifies an overblown sense of selfhood: self-assertion for the wrong reasons and (with a Sagittarian Sun) the propagation of a personal mythos of grandeur to compensate for increasing feelings of inadequacy. This is, in short, a driving need for accomplishment, fulfillment of goals and personal pride, with a hesitant, self-doubting, procrastinating trend which diffuses them.

Saturn-node aspects indicate restricted involvement with other people and a tendency to isolation. Cooperative efforts prove too demanding for what they return. Nixon's well-established isolationism is reinforced even more by the angularity of natal and transiting Pluto. Pluto transits the natal nodes, while transiting nodes are aligned with natal Pluto: a double-barreled whammy signaling the breaking off of old associations and previous alliances.

Saturn's transit to Pluto, by itself, is alienating, burdensome and hardening. Taken alone, it could indicate simply the isolating responsibility found in high office. The individual is extremely conscious of external demands and wants to run from them or rebel against them. There is a need to break loose from inhibiting, delimiting barriers and strike out in one's own way.

Saturn transits to Jupiter are likewise not **always** difficult. Often they signify a warm feeling of accomplishment from work well done. Jupiter-Saturn aspects are inherently political. However, they can also show diminishment of personal income and prestige, an assault on one's reputation and a demotion in rank (all of these being restrictions on things Jupiterian).

One can expect the worst side of these Saturn-Pluto and Saturn-Jupiter transits, though, once Saturn's oppositions to natal Mars and Mercury are added. The former points to antagonism, a feeling of impotence and the tendency to struggle fiercely against an unsympathetic world. The latter transit corresponds with a frustrating mental state and with times when it seems that nobody is listening to or valuing what one has to say.

Finally, we note solar Moon opposite natal Moon. Security needs are stressed. In the context of Saturn and Neptune, this transit points to moodiness, acute vulnerability, hyperreactiveness and perhaps a more subjective style of dealing with the world.

This was the Solar Return I first saw in April 1973 from which the earlier predictions were made. My timing device was Saturn's transit across the solar Ascendant in mid-July 1974. While this did represent the culmination of many month's pressure, and critical health problems for Mr. Nixon, the exact transit did not time his resignation. The remainder of this case study will be a rigorous appraisal of the timing factor based on the full application of techniques described in the preceding chapter.. I am not saying we should always use the full range of these techniques, nor that such is even practical. I am only providing one thorough example of what happens when the system is employed by the exacting rules given earlier. Knowing that an approach exists whereby events can be precisely timed is reassuring to me, even if I choose to apply it only rarely.

TIMING THE QUARTER
President Nixon's first Quarti-Solar Return in 1974 occurred April 10, 12:35 UT; his Demi-Solar, July 13, 0:45 UT; and his closing Quarti-Solar, October 14, 0:06 UT. All charts should be computed for Washington, D.C.

The first Quarti-Solar shows accumulating strain, but appeased by a soothing calm in the immediate environment. Transiting Jupiter and both natal and transiting Venuses square transiting Moon on the Descendant. Stressful placements exist, such as natal Saturn rising and natal Uranus at the Midheaven; but these are offset by this heartily benefic configuration.

Such good fortune is not sustained through the months colored by the Demi-Solar Return (Figure 8-2). Here, the natal Sun-Neptune opposition is once more across the horizon, duplicating the Solar Return symbolism. Transiting Mars exactly opposes natal Moon, indicating an aggressive attack on Mr. Nixon by others which ferrets out his weak spots and draws from him a wounded, emotional response. While natal Neptune is foreground, suggesting an uncomfortable emotional state, natal Uranus rising points to a need for change and freedom from repressive circumstances. Most significant, though, is the Demi-Solar Moon's opposition to Uranus and square to the Sun and Neptune. This isolates a major turning point in which the individual is feeling pressured to make changes in his life situation. Freedom needs are further underscored. A sustained emotional tension keeps the body under severe stress. Paranoia is a distinct possibility. Embarrassment, frustration, anxiety and disorientation accompany the individual's displacement in his private world of imagined insulation until Uranian revelation shatters the security of his fantasy prophylactic. Clearly, this is a painful, if not demoralizing, chart.

Nixon's final Quarti-Solar of that year was also rough. Transiting Neptune set, with natal Saturn rising and natal Uranus exactly culminating. A background but exact Sun-Mars conjunction squared

Saturn, the mark of impotence feelings, a seeming inability to accomplish anything and a paucity of pride.

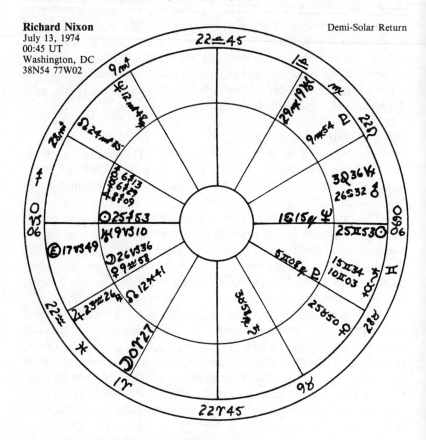

Figure 8-2

However, the Quarti-Solar Moon squared Nixon's Mercury-Mars-Jupiter-Pluto. While Moon-Pluto aspects can be separative and critical, they also grant an individual the ability to inspire awe in a way that leaves him appearing nearly invulnerable. Moon-Jupiter aspects show reason for gladness. Bad as it is, this Quarti-Solar is not as treacherous as the DSR. Furthermore, Saturn's transit across the solar Ascendant was scheduled for the summer months.

All things considered, the thirteen weeks following the Demi-Solar (July 13-October 13) seemed to isolate the time when Nixon's office was most threatened.

TIMING THE MONTH
Four Anlunars covered this period. They occurred:

1. June 23, 21:37 UT
2. July 21, 6:55 UT

3. August 17, 17:35 UT
4. September 14, 3:56 UT

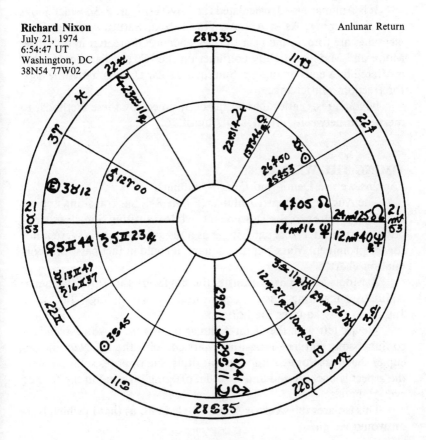

Figure 8-3

Anlunars Nos. 1 and 3 are not particularly difficult charts. Anlunar No. 1 has both natal and transiting Venuses closely hugging the angles, supported by Jupiter; while Anlunar No. 3 has a Sun-Moon-Mercury conjunction on the Zenith. Both charts have other, stressful elements (and, indeed, this entire period was surely stressful for Mr. Nixon);

but neither executed the Solar Return's original mandate in any visible way.

Anlunar No. 4 does have solar Saturn rising, squared by transiting Mars. However, a Venus-Jupiter opposition transits the meridian. Only Jupiter is inherently protective where titles and rank are concerned since Venus can indicate a need for peace arising from stressful circumstances; yet both, together, evoke a formidable Guardian Angel.

It is Anlunar No. 2, calculated for July 21 (Figure 8-3), which looks most threatening. As in Anlunar No. 4, solar Saturn is rising. Both Neptunes are foreground near the Descendant. Of greatest importance, Moon and Mars are tightly conjunct on the IC. No significant relief is offered by Venus or Jupiter. Sun square solar Uranus shows the need for freedom and change.

Nixon's resignation has so far been timed, by these methods, to the period between July 21 and August 16.

TIMING THE WEEK

For this we use Demi- and Quarti-Anlunars.

The August 11 Quarti-Anlunar (Figure 8-4) has transiting Jupiter in the very degree of the Descendant, while transiting Sun closely opposes solar Jupiter, disqualifying it as a resignation map. (Were it not for the prominent Mars-Neptune square, it could in fact pass for a coronation chart!)

A Moon-Mars paran transits the angles of the July 27 Quarti-Anlunar, suggesting less-than-comfortable surroundings; but solar Jupiter exactly squares the horizon.

We are left with the Demi-Anlunar of August 4, with Ascendant conjunct solar Saturn. Transiting Mars conjoins the IC. Neptune occupies the West Point. Although transiting Sun opposes solar Jupiter, the aspect is background and 5° wide, offering little aid in the face of everything else.

This isolates the week of August 4-11, 1974, as that in which Nixon would resign.

TIMING THE DAY

We can calculate PSSR and SQ angles for August 4 and 11 to estimate what planets they will conjoin during this critical week. Combined with transits to natal and solar planets, these would be expected to isolate the correct day of the event.

Below are the SQ and PSSR angular crossings by transiting, solar and radical planets for this week:

8/3   PSSR ASC ☌ r. ☽   8/5   PSSR MC   ☍ s. ♆
                                    PSSR DESC ☍ s. ☽
8/4   PSSR MC ☍ t. ♆   PSSR WP   ☍ t. ♀
      SQ   EP ☍ t. ♄
                              8/11 PSSR ASC ☍ r. ♂
                                    SQ   ASC ☍ s. ♄

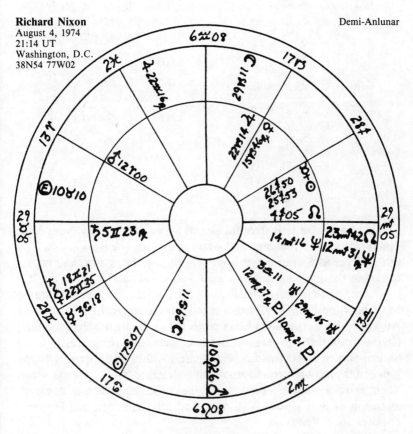

Richard Nixon   Demi-Anlunar
August 4, 1974
21:14 UT
Washington, D.C.
38N54 77W02

Figure 8-4

Two days are portrayed as emotionally severe. On August 4, transiting Neptune and transiting Saturn are simultaneously angular. The
following day, solar Neptune and Moon form an exact paran in the
PSSR, as transiting Mars perfects its contact with the PSSR West Point.

Beyond this are no further quotidian contacts until the "sweet and sour" couplet of Venus and Saturn on August 11.

Transits provide further information. During this entire time, transiting Neptune was semisquare solar Mercury (confusion, despair, disorientation, embarassment, anxiety), and transiting Uranus semisquare solar Neptune (truth penetrating the "fog," shifting emotional states, disrupted security). On a daily basis we observe:

8/4	t.	♂	⊒	r.	☉		8/9	t.	**♄**	**∠**	**r.**	**♄**

8/4   t. ♂ ⊒ r. ☉
      t. ☿ □ s. ♅

8/5   t. ♂ ⊒ s. ☿
      t. ♀ ⊒ r. ♀

8/6   t. ♀ ☍ r. ☉

8/7   t. ♀ ☍ s. ☿
      t. ☉ ∠ s. ♄
      t. ☉ ∠ r. ♇

8/8   t. ☿ □ s. ♂
      t. ☉ ⊒ r. ♂
      t. ☉ ⊒ r. ☿

8/9   **t. ♄ ∠ r. ♄**
      t. ♂ □ s. ♆
      t. ♀ ⊒ s. ♆

8/10 t. ☿ ☍ s. ♀
      t. ☉ ☍ s. ♃
      t. ☉ ⊒ r. ♃

8/11 t. ♀ ☌ r. ♆

Several particularly stressful aspects appear, including various combinations of Sun, Mercury and Mars, between August 4 and 8. The 6th emerges as a brief peace following the agonizing 5th, and is succeeded by the Sun's contact with solar Saturn and natal Pluto on the 7th.

Chief of all of these transits, however, is Saturn's slow semisquare to its natal position — a transit precise in the sidereal framework on August 9, just as transiting Mars perfected its square to solar Neptune. (In the tropical framework, without compensation for precession, the Saturn-Saturn aspect was 52 ' wide, barely within orb!) Mars-Neptune is one of the most severe and emotionally draining transits to experience. Then, as quickly as the following day, the crisis is past, the aspects eased, as transiting Sun aspects both natal and solar Jupiters, and Mercury opposes solar Venus.

August 9 brought unquestionably the most climactic and humiliating transits of the period. On that day, Richard Nixon flew from Washington in disgrace, the only U.S. President ever to resign his office.

Ascending the Throne

Examine Figures 8-5 and 8-6. Study them any way you wish. Then honestly ask yourself which is the horoscope of a monarch.

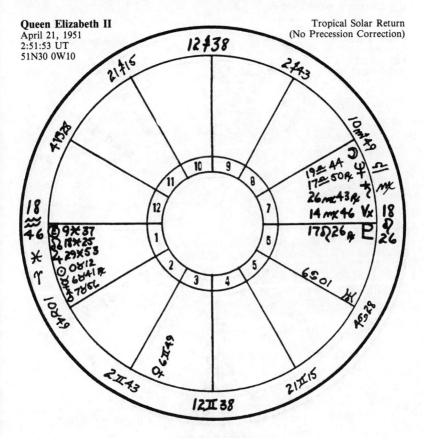

Queen Elizabeth II
April 21, 1951
2:51:53 UT
51N30 0W10

Tropical Solar Return
(No Precession Correction)

Figure 8-5

Nine and a half months after her twenty-fifth birthday, a traveling princess returned to England, at news of her father's death, to become Queen Elizabeth II. Figure 8-6, her Sidereal Solar Return, shows a rising Pluto complementing the culminating Sun, Mercury and Mars, clear signs of the assumption of power. Pluto's angularity also indicates dramatic, separative, life-altering circumstances, more often than not. Because the horizon is reversed between these two Solar Returns,

Pluto is angular in both. However, the first version does not have the mark of radiant pride, authority and grandeur shown in Figure 8-6. Either version contains Pluto's transits to natal Moon, Mars, Jupiter and Neptune, transits known for emotional separation, assumption to power, inheritance or other gain through separation, and a remodeling of one's world view.

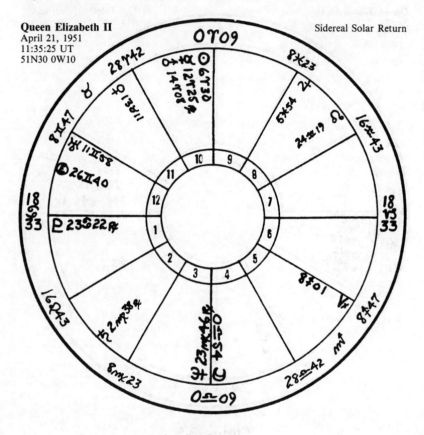

Figure 8-6

Angles and lunar aspects are the most important features within Solar Returns. Furthermore, they are the only features which clearly differentiate between two Solar Returns occurring on the same day. In both of these returns for Her Majesty, the Moon conjoins Neptune, suggesting strong, exaggerated emotional reactions to life, some emotional confusion, and great sensitivity. It can breed the self-doubts which certainly accompany the assumption of a throne. In Figure 8-5 the conjunction is much closer; but in Figure 8-6 it is angular — specifically on the fourth cusp, suggesting emotionalism related to her most private, familial areas of life leading to a powerful new beginning.

To my mind, the first house/seventh-house emphasis of Figure 8-5, including the setting of Pluto and the seventh-house Moon-Neptune conjunction, would be more indicative of a divorce than of what actually happened. Figure 8-6, on the other hand, has clear messages of a personal gain in authority, while suggesting that the most emotionally wounding issues would involve fourth-house life areas (parents!). Natal and solar Moons are both **precisely** angular, underscoring the presence of much emotion, as well as publicity; while the forming Sun-Moon opposition suggests a turning point, or "phase change," in life.

Without the precession deletion suggested throughout this book, I would have severely misjudged the tone of the year. Having removed the hampering, distorting precession by making the correction, we see the real results vividly displayed in Figure 8-6.

Monarch of an Era — Elvis Presley

Considerable controversy has existed regarding Elvis Presley's true hour of birth. Although sources have agreed on the date and place, nearly half a dozen birth**times** have been published. Most, reportedly, were from ostensibly reliable sources.

Thanks to the efforts of Clark, Gilchrist, Mackey and Dorminy,[2] we now know that Presley's birth certificate reads "4:35 AM (CST)." See Figure 8-7. I do not hold birth certificate data as sacrosanct by any means; however, when an officially recorded time accurately signals life events, I see absolutely no reason not to accept it as it stands.

For any birthtime, Elvis had reached the year of his secondary progressed Sun-Saturn conjunction in 1977. For the official birthtime, progressed Mars applied by a scant 2′ to a square with progressed Pluto in September 1977 when he died from a reported heart attack. These progressions suggest a severe overstrain on a weakening physical constitution. Transiting Neptune at the hour of his death was at 18♏58 (Sidereal), a mere 25′past the Ascendant which matches the recorded minute of birth. On this basis, I have accepted the recorded time.

Figure 8-8, Elvis's last Solar Return, is dominated by an incredible restatement of the Mars-Pluto symbolism which was apparent in his natal progressions. Not only does solar Pluto conjoin natal Mars

---

2. Clark et al., *Contemporary Sidereal Horoscopes* (see Chap. 2, n. 6).

within a degree, but it is joined in the immediate foreground by solar Mars. Progressions cannot be expected to match the Solar Return so exactly in most instances; but when they do agree, it must be interpreted as a potent reinforcement, each of the other.

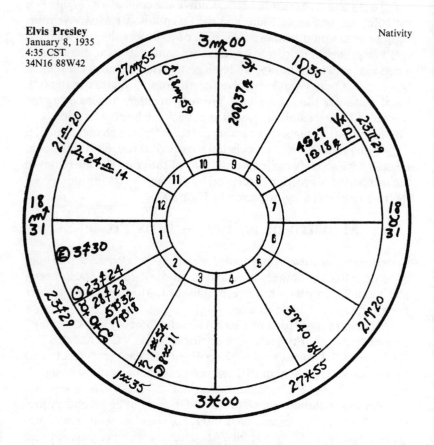

Figure 8-7

We again find the (to me) curious phenomenon of a strong Moon-Jupiter aspect in a fatal Solar Return. Solar Moon squares both natal and solar Jupiters. Dennis Elwell, whom I regard as one of astrology's greatest living thinkers, finds Jupiter a regular ingredient in death patterns. He writes, "At death Jupiter must bring the same feeling of extension, and perhaps overextension [as it does in life]. The evidence of psychical research is that after death consciousness, far from remaining the same or diminishing, undergoes an astonishing expansion."[3] I present this to the reader as a controversial astrological issue with important philosophical implications.

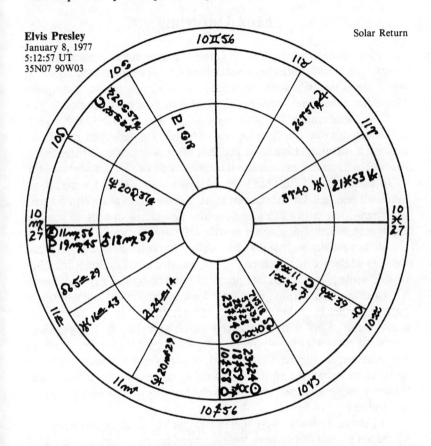

Figure 8-8

Solar Moon also conjoins Saturn, traditionally more appropriate for death since it commonly means poor health and depleted spirits. More important, though, are the solar Moon's progressions. At Elvis's death, it had reached 4♌09 by the SQ rate. This exactly semisquares 19♍09, triggering within minutes the Pluto-to-Mars transit which symbolizes the most emphatic strains on his physical system.

3. Dennis Elwell, "An Astrologer's Viewpoint on Death," *American Astrology Digest* (1978), 22.

Readers are advised to examine this Solar Return more carefully for other significant transits which add subtle details to the image presented.

Eros Unfurling

Pluto conjoined the East Point at the moment and place that Jo entered the world, initiating a years-long feeling of alienation from the world about her. With Saturn exactly on the Antivertex while conjunct Mars, her emotional withdrawal from full, free participation in her world was exacerbated by subtle assumptions that that world is inherently threatening; that emotions cannot be honestly experienced and openly expressed without a high cost; and that being alone or only superficially touching another person is a natural way to be. I know only a little of Jo's early family life; but what I know suggests that, for her, these inhuman realities may have been at least somewhat valid. When a person spends her entire life guarding and defending, it tells us she has encountered something really worth defending against.

Jo is a pessimistic idealist. My earliest impressions of her were that she viewed the world as a menace, but was driven by an inner idealism which, while it might insulate her with fantasy, would never abandon her to total desperation. Her closest aspect is Venus' opposition to Jupiter, Aries to Libra in either zodiac, falling in the immediate background of her nativity, where it suffered difficulty in expression. Her need for social involvement with other people, for appreciation and acceptance and companionship, was at cross-purposes with her needs to be immune and disclose nothing of herself. Even her more-than-noticeable tendency to be overweight was further insulation against her feelings.

In contemporary language, we might say that emotionally she would never really let anyone "get inside of her" or "touch some deep part of her." Jo's mind took these words all too literally, as minds are wont to do. The result was a paralyzed sexual development which further alienated her from meaningful contact with others.

She was referred to me at age 31, having had only a handful of sexual encounters, all within the preceding three to four years. None were satisfactory to Jo. She reported pain every time she attempted intercourse, which she thought was not unusual. Education about her sexuality was my first priority. I worked with her for several months, cooperating in a triadic therapeutic relationship with a sex surrogate, a highly trained, sensitive professional who served as her partner and teacher in exploring her sexuality. I role-modeled constructive interactive behavior, explored her relationship wants and styles, developed communication skills, encouraged reasonable vulnerability and self-disclosure, while exposing her to safe sensual and sexual experiences through her work with the surrogate. After a few months, she felt confident reentering a dating pattern, but from a different perspective. Through this, she established her first satisfying sexual relationship.

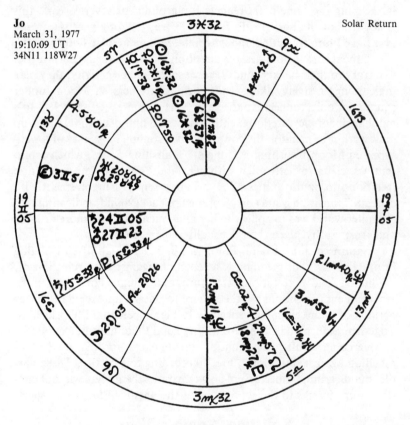

Jo
March 31, 1977
19:10:09 UT
34N11 118W27

Solar Return

Figure 8-9

Working with socially and sexually dysfunctional men and women is my trained specialty. Astrologers who are uneducated and inexperienced in this area will want to refer to competent outside professional help. Still, as agents of growth and change, astrologers need to know what astrological signals mark the times when major changes are most possible.

Checking an ephemeris, we see Pluto opposite Jo's natal Sun, on and off, from 1975 to 1978. Transit theory suggests an ongoing reevaluation of self during this entire period. Why, though, did she choose to take positive action shortly after her thirty-first birthday?

Figure 8-9 is her thirty-first Solar Return and gives the astrological portion of the answer. Pluto's opposition to natal Sun closely squared the horizon. Although the meridian advances about 92° a year, uniformly, keeping the same natal planets foreground for several years, this is not true of the horizon. In fact, **1977 was the *only* year she would *ever* have Pluto transiting opposite natal Sun on a Solar Return angle**.

Other chart factors deserve attention. Natal Mars and Saturn rise. Contrary to their background Vertex aspects in her nativity, they here indicate aggressively taking what is rightfully hers. A Moon-Jupiter square not only connects to the solar Vertex, but exactly touches Jo's natal horizon: increased joy, enthusiasm and optimism in relationship matters (not to mention the confident, blossoming sensuality of a well-aspected Moon transiting her angle). Transiting nodes, which represent associates, exactly align with her natal Venus-Jupiter opposition (relationship opportunities allow a happy sense of involvement with others). Transiting Mars and Neptune are background, indicating that the outer world was to appear to her as a much safer, far more rational and trustworthy place than it usually seemed to be.

Saturn conjoined natal Pluto within 5'. Though often isolating in practice, its root meaning is a rebellion against, and rejection of, the limits, rigid expectations, structures and demands of others in the environment. A Uranus partile square to natal Pluto regularly times periods of many changes, especially in highly personal life priorities. Together, Saturn and Uranus transiting natal Pluto indicate "the desire to overcome a difficult situation through extraordinary effort — rebellion against one's lot in life," according to Ebertin[4]. These partile, middleground aspects were able to express themselves without contradiction, thanks to the supremacy of the angular Pluto-Sun aspect.

Splitting Adam's Year

Adam is a regular client who called me last week. "I've decided it's time to come in for a 'checkup,' " he opened. I talked with this extremely successful businessman for a few minutes to try to establish why he chose this particular time to call.

"I've been very disturbed at the way I've been feeling the last two

---

4. Ebertin, *The Combination of Stellar Influences.*

or three months," Adam admitted. "I can't put my finger on precisely what's wrong."

"You sound as though things are generally vague and unfocused for you right now," I responded.

"Exactly. I guess that's the whole problem right there." We talked awhile longer, then set an appointment for a few days thence. Curiously, the appointment was for the eve of his mop-up period, I later learned. Concerns relating to his Solar Return were coming to a head, providing the opening basis of our session.

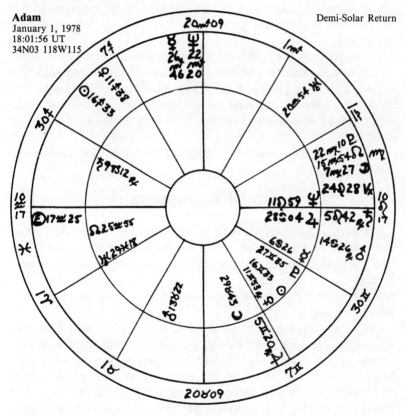

Adam
January 1, 1978
18:01:56 UT
34N03 118W115

Demi-Solar Return

Figure 8-10

However, it is not Adam's Solar Return which I have shown in Figure 8-10, but rather his Demi-Solar. Knowing his Sun sign to be Gemini, and that transiting Sun was currently in Pisces, it was quickly apparent that his "vague and unfocused" period of general uneasiness had begun with his Demi-Solar. After computing the chart, I could not help chuckling! It told me absolutely nothing I did not know already but was virtually a verbatim script of our phone conversation, written in astrological code.

Transiting Neptune crests the return chart in paran-square to natal Neptune and transiting Saturn on the Descendant. That tells the tale of the phone call in a nutshell. Natal Mars and Jupiter are on the outskirts of the foreground fields, emphasizing Adam's personal desire to expand his business and energetically accomplish something. Coming up against the lethargy of Saturn and the two Neptunes, all he felt he was doing was pouring money into something that was not returning a profit.

We explored the reality of his life situation. Demi-Solar Moon closely squared Jupiter, and the new business, I learned from him, was actually progressing at a promising rate. The twin Neptunes were urging him to ease back and relax for a while. Adam was deciding it was time to play but was feeling the heavy external demands of transiting Saturn.

The Demi-Solar proved to be an important tool for guiding our session.

Brutal Entrapment

Figure 8-11 is the Solar Return of Christine, a 19-year-old woman in the midst of a brutal, physically abusive relationship which lasted two years. This woman, now a powerful, maturing artist, has transformed some of the pain and anger of her battered years into gut-grabbing artistic statements — small compensation for the twenty-one months of hell at the "breaking out" stage of her life.

I include this example to make a special point. I worked for over a year with rape and violence victims and their families in a clinical setting. This included contact with battered women. Women under both headings suffer an after-the-fact social abuse and blame which sometimes rival in viciousness the original physical brutality. The humanistic astrological counselor, examining the charts of such women, will invariably find explanations of "attack-eliciting behavior"; yet the sensitive human being encountering these women cannot conceive of their being in any way to blame for the atrocities they have suffered. "Blame" and "responsibility" must be understood as different things: the former, a useless attending to the past; the latter, a constructive potency for dealing with the future. Without sacrificing one spot of sympathy and compassion for the victim, or shared anger at her assailant, we can counsel alternatives in behavior and character which free the individual from potentially destructive horoscopic patterns.

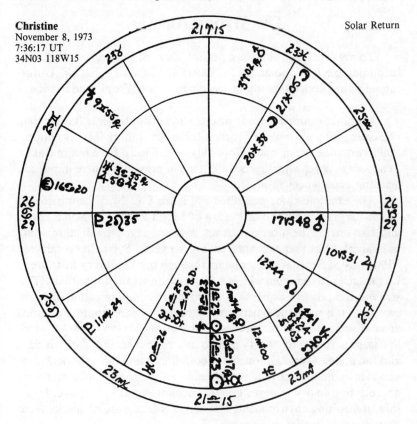

Christine
November 8, 1973
7:36:17 UT
34N03 118W15

Solar Return

Figure 8-11

Christine natally has a Sun-Saturn conjunction which squares Mars. This trio was occupying her Solar Return angles, along with a rising natal Pluto. Her inborn tendency to battle against the world, fighting limits on all fronts, crested in this instance in physical, abusive power struggles. Solar Moon, though background, exactly conjoined natal Moon, a mark of strong emotional responses and an unfortunate tendency to stick with a situation that is familiar and thereby secure, rather than bolting to safety.

This sort of emotional entrapment can be a sturdier prison than bars. The psychology is common in brutal relationships. Christine poignantly dramatized her attitude of the time in a series of bronze images of her face, each mask more broken and disfigured than the previous. Her title? "But I Love Him and Maybe He'll Change."

The Wrong Answer

To my mind, astrology is a perfect, flawless science, complete and incomparable in its potential for describing human behavior. Unfortunately, my understanding of astrology is not! From time to time, I goof.

My final example here is of one such misjudgment. Rather than presenting only examples of correct forecasts, I think it is also important to examine wrong ones. Hopefully we can learn from our mistakes. I encourage other astrologers to join me in presenting these important learning experiences in print.

The example chart presented in Figure 8-12 (with permission of the owner) is a recent Solar Return of Sylvia Kars — personal friend and also one of the most nurturing, encouraging, growth-stimulating individuals I have yet encountered. For six years, Sylvia has conducted "Pathway to Sensuality" seminars through her Discovery Institute in Los Angeles. Sylvia remarks in her promotional literature that "This seminar is a positive expression of growth in communication and sensuality...It is a unique experience." I could not agree more. Patterned around sensate-focus techniques pioneered by Masters and Johnson, Sylvia puts twelve to twenty people in a room together for two days and facilitates a magical touching, both literal and metaphorical, that generates communication, reevaluation of personal limits and self-appreciation in a way never exactly encountered anyplace else. It is a safe, nourishing environment. Her secret is a mixture of special techniques and a special personality.

Near her birthday in 1976, Sylvia called to say that she wanted to talk about her new Solar Return. At Sylvia's birth, the sky featured a close Sun-Jupiter conjunction in the eighth house, a partial indicator of her growth orientation and focus on expanding and improving other people's resources. When I calculated her new Solar Return, I found this pair of planets at the very top of her chart, qualified by the separating conjunction of transiting Pluto. A Moon-Neptune conjunction was rising, putting a wide Sun-Moon paran on the angles.

In recent years, Sylvia had been gaining considerable prestige in various quarters, including interviews internationally (she has appeared twice in *Der Spiegel*) and received invitations to speak before eminent groups in the therapeutic community. She was also trying to finish an important book at the time of our talk. Viewing her Solar Return, I thought it obvious that this year would be outstanding for her career, propel her to further heights and bring her even more public attention. Mercury was on the fringe of her upper foreground, a promising sign for her publishing hopes. Very likely the Neptune would indicate imagination and creativity needed in her writing, I thought. Looking further, I found that her Los Angeles natal Midheaven was 11♎10, with solar Uranus 11♎07 conjunct Venus, a sure indication of pleasant changes in her career. Reinforcement came from left and right to validate my original impression: that more than ever before, this year would put Sylvia Kars "on the map."

Sylvia Kars
September 28, 1976
19:39:46 UT
34N03 118W27

Solar Return

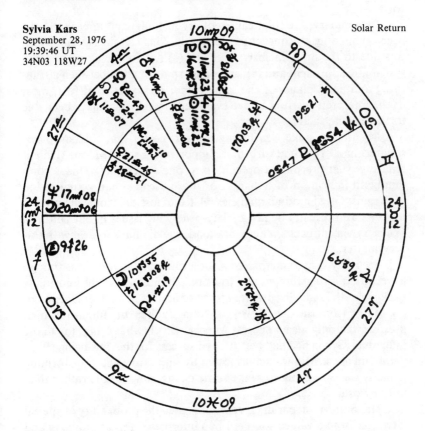

Figure 8-12

I was later to realize that this was a very sloppy delineation. It hooked into Sylvia's newly Neptunian hopes, and served her beneficially only by giving her faith and reinforcement to continue putting energy where she wanted until the time came for her to change her energy focus entirely.

What really happened? After several years of climbing to a peak in her career, Sylvia jettisoned half of her work, put the book in storage, took up tennis again and began a romantic live-in involvement with a man whose values and life-style were far removed from her own. It was the vehicle with which she could perform a mammoth overhaul on her life. The outcome? Sylvia had decided to stop and smell the roses, set aside her workaholic self-driver and be indulgently good to Sylvia for a while.

In summary, the chief causes of my misjudgment appear to have been (1) blinding preconception; (2) overlooking certain aspects, which was due to the more inclusive error of (3) not following an orderly, systematic approach; and (4) lack of sharp distinction between a transiting and natal planet of the same name. As a matter of fact, most of the interpretive errors I have ever made in astrology have been due to these same factors.

My first mistake was failing even to notice that solar Neptune squared natal Neptune (orb 6'), supported by solar Moon. (Isn't it amazing what preconception can do to one's eyesight?) This is commonly an indication of lethargy, of more dreams than actualization of dreams. Often it brings anxieties related to loss of income or employment (since those are highly anxiety-producing issues in our culture). When Sylvia cut back on her work load, she did have to deal with this very matter.

Secondly, I had interpreted a foreground natal Jupiter as though it were a transiting Jupiter; and transiting Jupiter was in the immediate background! Transiting Jupiter indicates honors and advantages coming to one from the outside world. Natal Jupiter often indicates high prestige, but only means success when success is what brings joy to the individual. Sylvia had had her share of success for the time being. With natal Sun at the Midheaven, aspected by supportive and transforming planets, she was going to make some changes in herself, rather than in the world.

Her Sun-Moon paran, at root, indicated the probability of special attention from a valued source. I had interpreted this as publicity and acclaim; but it is no less appropriate for a new romance. In fact, the solar Venus-Uranus-node conjunction on her locality natal Midheaven and solar South Point, and square natal Moon, was a stark statement of new romantic possibilities arising from the very alteration of professional matters I had rightfully — and wrongly — anticipated.

CHAPTER NINE

ENNEADS

Reinstating the use of Solar and Lunar Returns, computed and interpreted as suggested in this book and its sequel, has opened one of the most exciting chapters in the modern history of astrology. Some astrologers had previously suspected that our astrological universe was aprecessional (that is, based on a cosmic framework which is not beholden to precessing equinoxes). Studies both large and small have now shown that it is **only** in such a cosmos that Solar and Lunar Returns are viable. Once precession is expelled from our calculation processes, Solunars begin to speak in a language that is clear, lucid and expressive, delivering a message which is accurate, if not prophetic.

All of this has happened since 1944 when the American Federation of Astrologers published "Incidents and Accidents in Astrology," an article series by Cyril Fagan which introduced precession-free Solunars. Through the editorial courage of Ernest Grant, Llewellyn George, Joanne Clancy and Brigadier R. C. Firebrace, Solar and Lunar Returns began reappearing in major astrological publications with a force and reliability they had never before displayed in modern times. Most of the early researchers were proponents of the budding sidereal system of astrology; but, when all was told, Tropical and Sidereal astrologers alike were learning to respect and love these simple charts which only asked that their encumbering precessional loads be removed before they would sing their sweet songs of oracular poetry.

We astrologers tend to be idealists and dreamers. Even the most realistic and Uranian of us usually have our share of Neptune as well. Perhaps because of this, when we are given a new technique or approach which works magnificently, we begin wondering how it can be embellished, adapted or expanded, what adjuncts we can attach to it, and how we can further inflate the system, often to no end other than complications and confusion.

Innovativeness is admirable. Indeed, only through such diffuse trial-and-error applications can any field of knowledge grow. However, it is equally important that we be able to recenter ourselves, objectively survey the terrain after the intellectual orgy and seek a reasonable summation of what our explorations have uncovered that can be considered a real, valuable advance.

This mathematical revelry soundly struck the youthful system of Solunar Returns beginning in the 1950s, generating a monstrous proliferation of new return charts, mostly of questionable significance. In *The Sidereal Handbook*[1], I presented calculation techniques for fourteen similar predictive methods, trying to sort out their relative importance even while making the excess of charting theories available for those who wish to investigate them.

I do not use nearly that many techniques in my work as an astrologer, even on my own overly progressed horoscope. A few extremely reliable methods, used well, can normally provide all the information any astrologer will want.

Still, into the 1970s, a gnawing, nagging thought persisted that there was something missing. Our idealism sought just a little more than we had, while some inner prod pushed us toward finding a major misplaced piece of the predictive puzzle.

That major piece was a charting method called the **Ennead** (pronounced like "any-add," and meaning any group of nine things). It was discovered by Garth Allen shortly before his death and seems to be what the rest of us were seeking while wading through all those other near-hits.

Discovering the Ennead

Part of the flood of new cycle charts in the last decade was "the Duodenary System." Central to this lengthy thesis was something misnamed the Solar Monthly Return (SMR), computed for every thirty days or so when transiting Sun made any precise 30°aspect to natal Sun.

Garth Allen, ever the alert pragmatist, subjected the SMR to lengthy testing using charts of similar types of events (primarily deaths and accidents, which have an obstinate tendency to leave sharper

---

1. Eshelman, *The Sidereal Handbook*.

indications than other types of occurrences in most event-oriented systems). He found that some of the Solar Monthlies described the events admirably. Others, however, did quite poorly.

In trying to isolate why some charts scored well and others did not, Allen realized that the trine charts — transiting Sun 120° and 240° past natal Sun — rated better than any save the regular (conjunction) Solar Returns. Even the Quarti-Solars were poor by comparison.

"This circumstance was a bit disconcerting at first," he wrote in the September 1973 *American Astrology*,[2] "but it was quickly realized that the mystery was no mystery at all — and that what the figures were telling us was, simply, that the originally Egyptian, currently standard Hindu, system of 'novienic' or 'navamsa' divisions of the ecliptic also held true as viable returns. That is, there are nine basic 'solar returns' during each year, ticked off every 40°00′00″ from the position of the natal Sun."

The Navamsa is identical to what John Addey has called the "ninth harmonic chart." It is a mathematical way of representing the fact that the zodiac seems to be symbolically represented nine times in the standard zodiac we are familiar with. In other words, the entire zodiac from 0° Aries to 30° Pisces is symbolically duplicated in the one-ninth (40°) of the ecliptic from the "standard" 0° Aries to 10° Taurus; again from 10° Taurus to 20° Gemini; a third time from 20°Gemini to 0° Leo, etc. Other harmonic charts are possible; but Hindu astrologers and Garth Allen's statistics attribute a special importance to the ninth.

This means that, by considering the Navamsa framework, every degree of the zodiac is seen to be in pseudoconjunction with the points 40°, 80°, 120° and 160° from it in both directions around the ecliptic. Trines and conjunctions are the only 30° aspects which are also multiples of 40°, which is why the trine SMRs scored so well.

Allen named his discovery the **Ennead**. It forms a ruling triumvirate, along with the ordinary Solar Return and Lunar Return: three charts which, together, form the backbone and flesh of effective astrological forecasting.

Computing the Ennead

Beginning with your precise natal solar longitude, repeatedly add increments of 40°. This provides nine longitudes, corresponding to nine Ennead Suns. Think of 40° as 10° plus one sign.

2. Garth Allen, "Perspectives," *American Astrology* (September 1973), 34.

For instance, John F. Kennedy's Sidereal natal Sun was 14°♉15′07″. Therefore, the nine Ennead Suns were:

$$14° \ 15' \ 07'' \quad ♉ \quad ♍ \quad ♑$$
$$24° \ 15' \ 07'' \quad ♊ \quad ♎ \quad ♒$$
$$4° \ 15' \ 07'' \quad ♌ \quad ♐ \quad ♈$$

Notice that only three values actually need to be calculated, since we are dealing with three perfect grand trines with 40° between them.

Kennedy's Tropical Sun can provide a convenient second example. It was 7°♊50′36″, suggesting these nine longitudes:

$$7° \ 50' \ 36'' \quad ♊ \quad ♎ \quad ♒$$
$$17° \ 50' \ 36'' \quad ♋ \quad ♏ \quad ♓$$
$$27° \ 50' \ 36'' \quad ♌ \quad ♐ \quad ♈$$

A Tropical astrologer would use these longitudes, after first correcting them for precession as described in Appendix A. For instance, the Tropical longitude of the Sun at Kennedy's death (November 22, 1963) was 29° Scorpio. The Ennead immediately preceding this was timed with the Sun's passage across 18°Scorpio, about November 11. Precession from President Kennedy's birthday (May 29, 1917) until this Ennead date was 0°38′21″. Adding this correction to the uncorrected Ennead Sun longitude (17°50′36″ Scorpio) gives 18°28′57″ Scorpio, the exact longitude for which the return should be calculated.[3] Use the same approach as for calculating a Solar Return.

Subdividing the Ennead Period

Just as 40° of solar motion is taken as equivalent to a full 360° cycle with the Enneads, each additional 10° is equivalent to a square. Therefore, the forty days of the Ennead period can be subdivided into four periods of ten days each. Charts computed for these ten-day intervals are called **decilia** (singular, **decilium**).

For example, John Kennedy's final Ennead occurred with the Sun at 24♎15. During the subsequent forty days he was scheduled to have three decilia charts phase in — when the Sun reached 4°15′, 14°15′ and 24°15′ of Scorpio. At 4♐15, another Ennead would occur.

The second decilium (14♏15 in this instance) is equivalent to a Demi-Return and has been affectionately labeled the "Demi-Enny." I suppose the other two could be called "Quarti-Enneads," indicating

---

3. Siderealists need not make this correction.

their similarity to Quarti-Solar Returns; but "decilium" has done fine so far.

Interpreting the Enncad

Enneads are examined by the same rules as Solar Returns, with only a few modifications.

First of all, Enneads need to be interpreted only once, using the "second reading" approach offered in Chapter Six. These charts last just forty days and forty nights, to coin a phrase. Rather than signify a revamping of essential identity, they are much more event-oriented. However, keep in mind that this includes altered mental and emotional states, which are probably the underlying causes of more material events anyway.

There is a transiting Sun distinct from a natal Sun. An interpretation of "Transiting Sun Foreground" is given in Chapter Three for this specific reason.

Figure 9-1 is the final Ennead for President John F. Kennedy. Turning our eyes to the foreground, a major configuration leaps to our immediate attention: Venus and Mars straddling the Ascendant, square a Uranus-Pluto conjunction just west of the Midheaven (near the Zenith). Along with this, both natal and transiting Moons conjoin the Dallas Midheaven (their midpoint being 28 ♌ 19, within a degree of the angle), a major indication of publicity, popular attention, emotion-filled circumstances and a general openness and willingness to respond to whatever comes along. Furthermore, transiting Moon is in close paran with the rising Mars, the configuration which most dominates this Ennead, indicates an emotional and violent time when an individual is quite prone to physical discomfort, if not serious injury; and threatening surroundings in which the native is subject to attacks.

Of the first-mentioned quartet, the Mars-Pluto square is the closest individual aspect. Simply put, transiting Mars signifies aggression aimed at the individual from the outer environment, whereas transiting Pluto sponsors dramatic landmark incidents that force change in life, usually through separation or painful confrontation. Together, they can be incredibly violent.

Both natal and transiting Venuses are foreground. On the one hand, we can see in this the monumental love a nation displayed for its handsome, fallen leader. On the other hand, two Venuses, two Moons, a Mars and a close Sun-Neptune conjunction indicate strong emotions of many kinds engulfing the event.

Incidentally, Venus-Mars aspects are the most common configurations in murderers' nativities. All that could have been easily read from this chart in advance was that John Kennedy would be subjected to inflamed passions (Venus-Mars) in circumstances which would drastically alter, if not totally overthrow, his then-current life situation (Uranus-Pluto), particularly in terms of his profession and general public position (Midheaven/Zenith); however, a retrospective examination of the chart, showing the **specifically** homicidal tendency of the aspects, should not be discounted as an opportunity to learn something.

John F. Kennedy
November 11, 1963
14:43:07 UT
Dallas, TX
32N47 96W47

Ennead

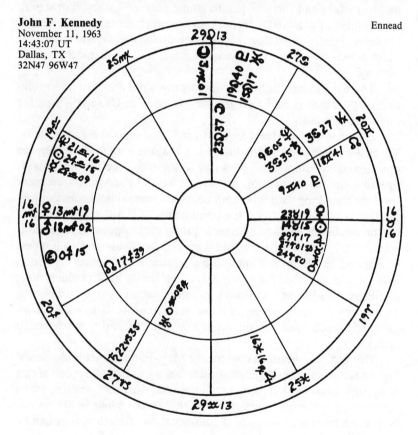

Figure 9-1

Most importantly: these four planets aspected President Kennedy's setting natal Sun! Attacked that day were his place of command, his power, his role as a leader, his very identity, which was also the surrogate ego of the United States — in short, his role as President. No other natal planet could be more appropriate for this. It also shows that he was to be attacked **personally** and probably **physically.**

That November, Saturn squared Neptune in space. Transiting Sun joined in this configuration the day of Kennedy's Ennead, further aspecting his own Mercury and Mars (and, to some extent, Jupiter). This is a classic pattern for the nefarious termination of a governmental leader's position, if not his life. Natal Saturn was exactly on the Ennead Vertex, sesquisquared within 33 ′ by the rising Mars. A seemingly fated (Vertex) fight (Mars) for survival (Saturn) was clearly signaled in advance.

Interpreting the Kennedy Ennead has proceeded in A-B-C fashion, with poignant and accurate results. No hedging or stretching of points was required. Such examples are typical, in my experience.

Students often ask if Enneads might be better "triggers" of events foreshadowed in the Solar Return than are Anlunars. I find that, in general, Enneads are far more potent individual charts than Anlunars, but that they do not specifically fulfill this "reinforce and trigger" function. An Ennead is not beholden to the Solar Return in any way, except that the latter is a powerful descriptor of the individual who is experiencing the Ennead.

As an example of this, the second chart offered here (Figure 9-2) is James Forrestal's final Ennead. Recall that the Anlunar and Solar Return progressions activated a particularly critical aspect in the Solar Return: Mars opposite Saturn at about 9° Leo-Aquarius. This is what I look for when I want a triggering mechanism.

This "fatal" degree (for Forrestal), so precisely isolated elsewhere, is not dominant in the Ennead. No triggering device is activated here. However, taken by itself, the Ennead does accurately describe the situation. Transiting Neptune is **exactly** conjunct the West Point, semisquared by Saturn: exaggerated negative emotional excitement, paranoia, etc. A rising Mars is in partile opposition to natal Uranus: threatening circumstances elicit a desire for change and freedom; also, commonly a transit for accidents and physical injury.

This opposition is reinforced by a semisquare/sesquisquare from the Ennead Moon, which also opposes natal Jupiter: normally, a feeling of superiority and faith that life will be kind. I shall not try to explain this seeming "miss" except to mention that Jupiter frequently appears prominently in death charts when the individual seems to be gaining release from miserable conditions.

Pluto squares the Sun, indicating a dramatic life-altering event, revolt against present circumstances and, specifically in this case, death.

Just to show that Enneads can anticipate happy events as well as hurtful ones, I am including a third example. As I sit here writing this final chapter of a book which has required (and gotten) the majority of my time and emotional/mental energy for several months, I have

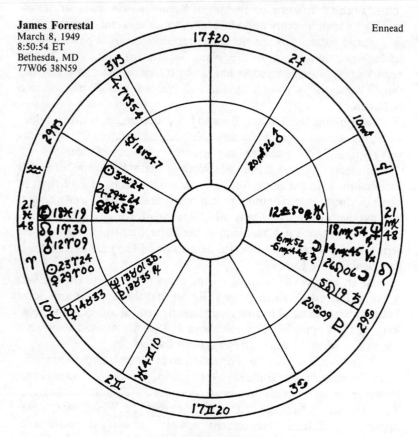

Figure 9-2

just received an invitation from out-of-state friends to visit them on a much-needed vacation in a few weeks. My new Ennead has just occurred. It is a classically auspicious map. Transiting Venus and Mercury are conjoined at the Midheaven in close square to a rising Moon. Jupiter is only 14′ from precise square to the (ninth house) Ennead Sun. This square is less than 2° from my natal horizon and meridian (Sun on natal Descendant for the social element) and almost precisely aspecting natal Mercury. My natal Jupiter-Uranus conjunction is on the Ascendant. Not only does this portray the celebration I feel at completing this book, but the promise of a pleasant, relaxing, fun time (after many months of work), involving travel, the chance to explore a new geographic area I have never before visited, and an opportunity to spend time with distant friends is all shown. (The trip is scheduled to occur at the tail end of this 40-day period.)[3]

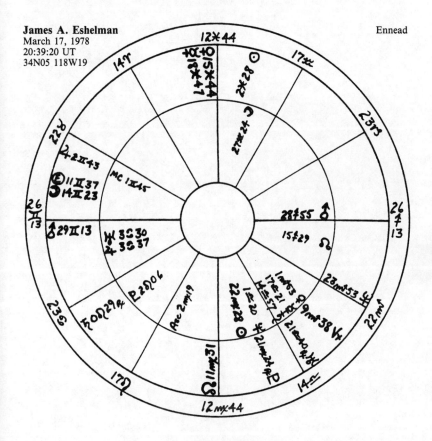

Figure 9-3

However, Mars is rising and transiting Saturn closely squares my locality natal Midheaven. There is still much work to do, turning the last piece of this manuscript over to the publisher. Duty calls, so let's finish this chapter quickly. Then I can start my vacation.

3. We had a marvelous time! J.A.E., 1984

Appendix A: Calculation

Preparation

It is essential that the natal Sun be accurately computed to the **nearest second of arc.** Traveling at its average speed, the Sun requires more than 24 minutes of time to travel 0°01′. By calculating to the nearest arc-second, our average maximum error is reduced to **plus or minus 24 seconds of time.**

Throughout the instructions which follow, three common calculation aids are explained: **diurnal logarithms, tables of diurnal planetary motion** ("DPM tables"), and **direct calculation,** as with an electronic calculator or slide rule. If you prefer to use logarithms, it will be necessary to have tables that provide logs to seconds, such as those in *Easy Tables.*[1] Of several sets of DPM tables available, by far the best are those published by Neil F. Michelsen,[2] which provide tables for every two seconds of the Sun's daily motion from 57′12″ to 61′10″.

Our sample chart for these examples will be that of President Ronald W. Reagan who was in Tampico, Illinois (41N38, 89W47), on February 6, 1911. His natal chart is displayed in Figures A-1 and A-2 in both Sidereal and Tropical forms for a birthtime of 1:20 AM CST.

Although any birth hour would serve the purpose of this Appendix (the demonstration of calculation techniques), a few words seem on order on why I prefer this time for Mr. Reagan. Several different birthtimes are available for him over the course of an hour. Most of these times seem to have originated from someone close to the President. Following his election in 1980, I retroactively studied the various

---

1. J. Allen Jones, Jr., *Easy Tables* (Hollywood, Calif.: Golden Seal Research Headquarters, 1973).
2. Neil F. Michelsen, *The American Book of Tables* (San Diego, Calif.: ACS Publications, 1976), which is contained in its entirety in *The American Ephemeris 1931 to 1980 & Book of Tables,* also by ACS Publications.

predictive charts to see what birthtime best depicted the election, focusing on techniques such as secondary progressions and solar arc directions of the natal angles which are highly sensitive to a precise birthtime. **Only** the 1:20 AM time accurately depicted the event, bringing his natal Jupiter (part of a Jupiter-Sun-Moon configuration) exactly to the Midheaven for the event. This time then proved extremely accurate in describing the subsequent events of his term of office.

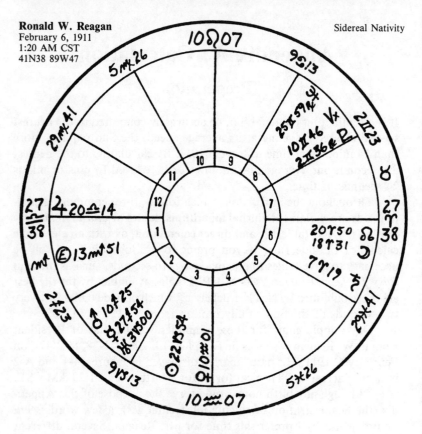

Ronald W. Reagan
February 6, 1911
1:20 AM CST
41N38 89W47

Sidereal Nativity

Figure A-1

Compensating for Precession

As explained in Chapter One, there are two ways to escape the distorting effects of precession. One is to perform all calculations using the

Sidereal Zodiac. Another is to use the Tropical Zodiac, but first to remove the precession accumulated since birth.

Should we wish to use the first method, we would note that Mr. Reagan's natal Sidereal Sun is at 22°54′17″ Capricorn. We would then open a Sidereal ephemeris to February 1985 to compute his seventy-fourth Solar Return.

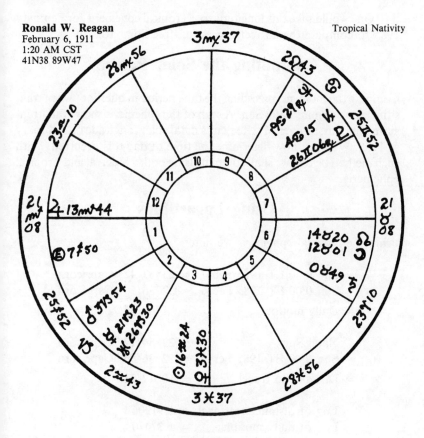

Ronald W. Reagan
February 6, 1911
1:20 AM CST
41N38 89W47

Tropical Nativity

Figure A-2

If we choose to employ the Tropical Zodiac, we can correct for precession using the Vernal Point Ephemeris in Appendix B. These tables give the moving position of the precessing equinox against a fixed, precession-free backdrop. Simply subtract the value given on the date of the Solar Return from the value given on the birth date, and **add** this to the Tropical longitude of the natal Sun.

VP 1911 Feb 6 (birth)	=	6°30'15"	
− VP 1985 Feb 6 (Solar Return)	−	5°28'16"	
= Precession Correction	=	1°01'59"	
+ Tropical Natal Sun	+	16°24'02"	Aquarius
= Corrected Natal Tropical Sun	=	17°26'01"	Aquarius

One would take this longitude to a Tropical ephemeris for February 1985 to compute the correct precession-free Solar Return.

Computing the Solar Return

Compute the moment, preceding the time period in question, when transiting Sun conjoins natal Sun. A scan of the ephemeris shows that transiting Sun passed over Mr. Reagan's natal solar longitude on February 6, 1985. We must now determine the time of day this occurred. With each method below, we shall compute using both a Sidereal and Tropical ephemeris.[3]

Using Logarithms

From the Sidereal ephemeris we note:

Sun 0:00 ET 1985 Feb 7	=	23°37'42"	Capricorn
− Sun 0:00 ET 1985 Feb 6	=	22°36'56"	Capricorn
= Daily motion	=	1°00'46"	

Natal Sun	=	22°54'17"	Capricorn
− Sun 0:00 ET 1985 Feb 6	=	22°36'56"	Capricorn
= Distance to travel	=	0°17'21"	

Log of distance to travel	=	1.91906
− Log of daily motion	=	1.37470
= Log 6:51:09	=	0.54436

The Solar Return is found to have occurred on February 6, 1985, 6:51:09 ET (= 6:50:15 UT = 1:50:15 EST).

---

3. Neil F. Michelsen, *The American Sidereal Ephemeris 1976-2000* (San Diego, Calif.: Astro Computing Services, 1981). Neil F. Michelsen, *The American Ephemeris 1981 to 1990* (San Diego, Calif.: ACS Publications, 1977).

From the Tropical ephemeris we note:

Sun 0:00 ET 1985 Feb 7	=	18°09′26″ Aquarius
− Sun 0:00 ET 1985 Feb 6	=	17°08′40″ Aquarius
= Daily motion	=	1°00′46″
Natal Sun (corrected)	=	17°26′01″ Aquarius
− Sun 0:00 1985 Feb 6	=	17°08′40″ Aquarius
= Distance to travel	=	0°17′21″
Log of distance to travel	=	1.91906
− Log of daily motion	=	1.37470
= Log 6:51:09	=	0.54436

These two approaches, as can be seen, give the same answer. It is possible that they could give slightly different results due to rounding errors of various kinds. A discrepancy of approximately half a minute of time is common.

Using DPM Tables

Using Neil Michelsen's DPM tables for the Sun,[4] we find a column for the Sun's daily motion of 60′46″.

Referring to the daily motion and distance-to-travel figures calculated above:

Distance to travel	=	17′21″
− Motion in 6 hours	=	15′12″
= Motion in 51 minutes	=	2′09″

The calculated time is then 6:51 ET, agreeing exactly (to the nearest minute) with the answer obtained by logarithms.

When using motion tables, one can only trust the answer to the nearest minute of time. These tables are less **precise** than either of the other methods, although sufficiently accurate and easy to use.

Using a Calculator

Referring to the daily motion and distance-to-travel figures calculated above:

$$\text{Distance to travel} = 17′21″ = 1041″$$
$$\text{Daily motion} = 60′46″ = 3646″$$

4. Michelsen, *The American Book of Tables,* Table V.

These minute-and-second values have been converted to seconds by multiplying the number of minutes by 60, then adding the seconds; for instance, 17 × 60 = 1020, to which we add 21 to get 1041.

Divide the distance-to-travel by the daily motion (1041/3646) to get the portion of the day elapsed (0.2855183763). Multiply this by 24 to get 6.852441031 hours. Subtract the 6, and multiply by 60 to get 51.14646188 minutes. Subtract the 51 and multiply by 60 to get 9 seconds.

The correct time of the Solar Return is therefore 6:51:09 ET. (If your calculator has a decimal-to-sexagesimal conversion, just multiply 0.2855183763 by 24, then use the conversion key to get the same answer.)

This method gives, in this instance, exactly the same answer as logarithms. Such meticulous agreement will not always occur.

Direct calculation with an electronic calculator is the fastest, most efficient and most accurate of these three methods. Only direct computation by a high-precision computer program is faster and more exacting. In this instance, one such computer program gave a time of 6:51:24 ET. The choice of technique is left to each individual astrologer.

Figures A-3 and A-4 are this Solar Return computed for Washington, D.C., in both the Sidereal and Tropical zodiacs. Notice that, while sign placements differ, everything else is exactly the same, including such things as house positions and aspects.

In contrast, Figure A-5 is Mr. Reagan's Solar Return computed from his Tropical Sun **without the precession correction.** At his advanced age, the difference is considerable when compared to Figure A-4. Although the house positions look approximately the same, this is not due to a small difference in the times of the returns because they occur **one entire day apart.** The Tropical Return is for February 5 — one day earlier — at 6:23 UT. The Moon's placement has shifted considerably. Without the precession correction, his year (1985) is described by natal Jupiter rising, natal Venus at the IC and the solar Moon opposing the Sun. When the precession correction is applied, the chart is dominated by Saturn rising exactly square solar Moon. These are substantially different maps! Both **cannot** be right at the same time! Readers are left to draw their own conclusions by comparing Solar Returns of both types, although this writer has little question in his mind of what your conclusion will be if you approach the question with open eyes and mind.

Anlunars are calculated using the same principles described for calculating a Solar Return, with minor changes. An Anlunar is computed for the moment when transiting Moon conjoins the Solar Return Moon. No precession correction is needed since an Anlunar always occurs within a year of the Solar Return on which it is based. Detailed instructions for computing extremely accurate Lunar Returns will be given in the forthcoming companion volume *Interpreting Lunar Returns*.[5]

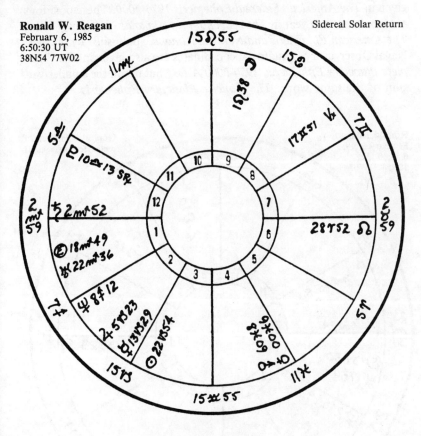

Ronald W. Reagan
February 6, 1985
6:50:30 UT
38N54 77W02

Sidereal Solar Return

Figure A-3

Solar Right Ascension

Before moving on to describe how the SQ and PSSR maps are calculated, it is necessary to show the method of determining the Sun's

---

5. Owners of Michelsen's *The American Sidereal Ephemeris 1976-2000* will find careful instructions in the Introduction for calculating Solar, Lunar and Planetary Returns, the SQ and PSSR. As some of these methods are dependent on special features included in that particular, extraordinary ephemeris, I am not reproducing them here.

right ascension. Right ascension (RA) is a positional measurement along the celestial equator, just as longitude is a positional measurement along the ecliptic. The right ascension of all planets was given daily in the *Omega Sidereal Ephemeris* for the years 1970 through 1975, and is also given in *The American Sidereal Ephemeris 1976-2000*. These positions are tabulated each year in *The Astronomical Almanac* (previously called *The American Ephemeris and Nautical Almanac*) published by the U.S. Naval Observatory. Equatorial coordinates are also given in *The Complete Planetary Ephemeris, 1950-2000 A.D.*,[6] but not in the smaller version of the same work, *The Concise Planetary Ephemeris*.

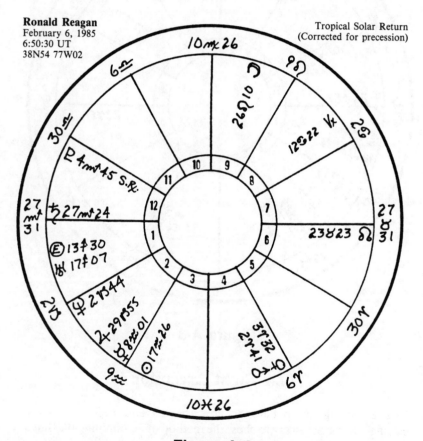

Ronald Reagan
February 6, 1985
6:50:30 UT
38N54 77W02

Tropical Solar Return
(Corrected for precession)

Figure A-4

6. *The Complete Planetary Ephemeris, 1950-2000 A.D.* (Medford, Mass.: Hieratic Publishing Co., 1975).

Even when these ephemerides are not available, the RA of the Sun is easy to compute once you realize that it equals **the sidereal time (ST) at which the Sun occupies the Midheaven.** For instance, at ST 12:44:00, the Tropical longitude of the Midheaven is 11≏58. Therefore, if the Sun were to be found at Tropical 11≏58, we could easily determine that RA Sun = 12:44:00. In performing this operation, it is important that the Sun's longitude and the table of houses be either both Tropical or both Sidereal.

Ronald W. Reagan
February 5, 1985
6:22:32 UT
38N54 77W02

Tropical Solar Return
(No correction for precession)

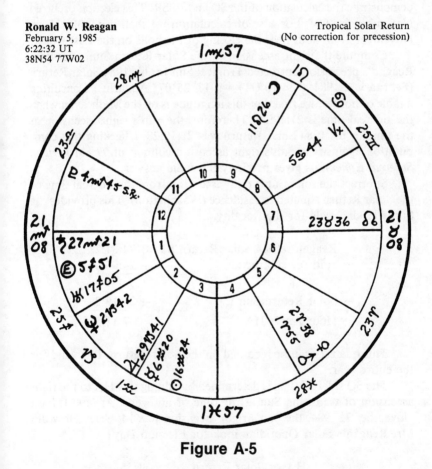

Figure A-5

Computing the Solar Quotidian (SQ)

The Solar Quotidian progresses the Solar Return at the rate of one rotation of the Earth on its axis (about 23:56 of clock time) for the one year duration of the Solar Return. It moves not at a linear rate, but at the same rate as the transiting Sun's right ascension. Its daily sidereal time can be computed with ease.

An **Hour Angle (HA)** is the distance of a planet from the Midheaven, measured in right ascension. The SQ is designed such that the Hour Angle of transiting Sun in the SQ will always equal the Hour Angle of the Solar Return Sun in the Solar Return.

President Reagan's re-election provides a suitable event to demonstrate the calculation of the SQ and PSSR. This election occurred November 6, 1984. For ease of calculation we shall use 0:00 UT on November 7, an hour near the closing of the polls on the East Coast.

Compute the right ascension of the Solar Return Sun. President Reagan's precession-corrected Tropical Sun for his 1984 Solar Return (February 7, 1984, 0:34:10 UT) was 17°25'07" Aquarius. Consulting a table of houses, we find that this longitude is on the Midheaven when the sidereal time is 21:19:28. Therefore, the Sun's right ascension at the time of his 1984 Solar Return was 21:19:28. Checking this computation against the Sun's right ascension column in *The American Sidereal Ephemeris* gives precisely the same answer.

Subtract the solar Sun's right ascension from the sidereal time of the Solar Return equated to residence (Washington). This provides the Sun's Hour Angle for that locality.

Reagan's 1984 Solar Return ST			4:31:23
+ Add for subtraction		+	24:00:00
			28:31:23
− Solar Return Sun RA		−	21:19:28
= Hour Angle HA		=	7:11:55

This quantity can be recorded on the Solar Return. It is valid for the entire year.

The SQ sidereal time is determined by adding this HA to the right ascension of transiting Sun at the time of an event. At 0:00 UT on November 7, 1984, the Sun's right ascension was 14:49:11. How did Mr. Reagan's Solar Quotidian look for Election Day?

HA of Solar Return		7:11:55
+ Transiting Sun's RA	+	14:49:11
= SQ sidereal time	=	22:01:06

Extract from a table of houses the angles for this sidereal time at the latitude of Washington, D.C. (38N54):

> Midheaven   3≈35
> Ascendant   26♉44   t. Venus 27♏02
> East Point   7♉50

Compare these angles to the natal, solar and transiting planets. In this instance, transiting Venus was found to be angular, indicating a happy, pleasurable day suitable for celebration.

Notice that this answer may be obtained in another way, using the same factors. The answer is exactly equal to the one obtained by subtracting the solar Sun's RA from that of transiting Sun, and adding the difference to the solar ST.

> | | Transiting Sun's RA | 14:49:11 |
> |---|---|---|
> | + | Add for subraction | + 24:00:00 |
> | | | 38:49:11 |
> | − | Solar Sun's RA | − 21:19:28 |
> | = | "Alpha-age" | = 17:29:43 |
> | + | Solar Return ST | + 4:31:23 |
> | = | SQ sidereal time | = 22:01:06 |

"Alpha-age" is simply the "age" of the Solar Return as measured by the Sun's right ascension. The Greek letter alpha is used by astronomers to designate right ascension.

These two methods give identical results. Only the order of the steps is different. The first method is quicker once the Sun's Hour Angle is computed and recorded. However, the second method has an advantage for the astrologer who is also computing the PSSR for the same date, in that the Alpha-age is necessary in the most accurate method of computing the PSSR.

Computing the Progressed Sidereal Solar Return (PSSR)

Another way of rotating the Solar Return angles is the PSSR. This method takes the difference between two consecutive Solar Returns (which averages 30:09:13) and distributes it over the year. See Chapter Seven for further explanation.

First, compute both the current Solar Return and the one which will follow it. Determine the sidereal time difference between them,

making sure that both are calculated for the same geographic longitude. We previously calculated President Reagan's 1984 Solar Return for February 7 at 0:34:10 UT and his 1985 Solar Return for February 6 at 6:50:30 UT. At Washington, the sidereal times of these two Solar Returns were, respectively, 4:31:23 and 10:47:47.

	ST 1985 Solar Return		10:47:47
−	ST 1984 Solar Return	−	4:31:23
		=	6:16:24
+	Add one day	+	24:00:00
=	"Solar Return Year" (SRY)	=	30:16:24

Two methods are presented here for using this information. One uses direct calculation, as with a hand calculator; the other uses special tables in Appendix C.

Direct Calculation

Reduce the SRY to a decimal of days. This is done by converting it to 30 hours and a decimal, then dividing by 24 hours. The answer will always be close to 1.26.

Divide the number of seconds by 60; add the number of minutes and divide again by 60; add the number of hours and divide by 24. (To be perfectly correct, one should divide by 24:00:03, which is 24.00083333 hours, since three seconds of precession accumulate between birthdays. We shall ignore this subtlety here for the sake of simplicity.)

$$30:16:24$$
$$= 30:16.4$$
$$= 30.273333 \text{ hours}$$
$$= 1.2613889 \text{ days}$$

I call this the **annual constant** or annual decimal.

For any given date and time, compute the Alpha-age as shown under "Computing the Solar Quotidian." The Alpha-age is the transiting Sun's right ascension minus the solar Sun's right ascension. Convert this to hours and a decimal. Multiply the Alpha-age by the annual constant to find the amount of sidereal time which the Solar Return has advanced by the PSSR rate. This is added to the Solar Return ST to get the PSSR ST.

Previously we found that Mr. Reagan's Alpha-age for Election Day 1984 was 17:29:43 (17.4952778 hours). Multiplying this by the annual constant (1.2613889) gives 22.068349 hours, or 22:04:06.

	Solar Return ST		4:31:23
+	PSSR Increment	+	22:04:06
		=	26:35:29
−	Subtract if necessary	−	24:00:00
=	PSSR ST	=	2:35:29

Once more, we turn to a table of houses and extract the angles which correspond with this sidereal time at latitude 38N54:

Midheaven 16 ♈ 47
Ascendant   24 ♋ 31
East Point   11 ♋ 58

There were no natal, transiting or solar planets conjoining PSSR angles. Approximately one and a half days earlier, however, Mr. Reagan's natal Sun had crossed the PSSR Descendant, no doubt adding to the President an aura of leadership and stability for the day or so before the election. Furthermore, the PSSR Sun, calculated as shown below ("Timing the Solar Return Progressions"), was 23 ♑ 50, within a degree of the Descendant throughout Election Day itself.

It should be noted that the SQ and PSSR generally work independent of each other so that, even if contradictory, neither cancels the other's indications.

Using the Tables

In Appendix C are "Annual Sidereal Solar Increment" (ASSI) tables useful in calculating the PSSR. These tables provide the ASSI on a daily basis.

The ASSI takes into consideration the changing rate of the Sun's RA throughout the year, and shows how much the PSSR advances from day to day. By necessity, these tables are based on the **average** SRY, 30:09:13. Used without correction, they can allow as much as a 2°.5 error in the PSSR angles by the end of the birthday year. However, it is possible to apply a simple correction which makes them accurate.

Calculation of the PSSR using these tables follows six steps:

STEP ONE: Find the current SRY, as shown above.

STEP TWO: Subtract 30:09:13 from the SRY. Call your answer "D." Be sure to note whether D is a positive or negative number.

STEP THREE: Calculate the ASSI of the Solar Return from the tables in Appendix C, interpolating the ASSI as though it were a planet. Being constant for the entire Solar Return year, this value is called the Annual Sidereal Solar Increment Constant (ASSIC).

STEP FOUR: Calculate the ASSI for the date and time for which you wish to calculate the PSSR. Subtract the ASSIC from the transiting ASSI. (If the transiting ASSI is smaller than the ASSIC, add 30:09:13 first, **not** 24:00:00.)

STEP FIVE: Add the Solar Return's sidereal time for the longitude of residence. If the sum is greater than 24:00:00, subtract 24:00:00. The answer is the **mean** sidereal time of the PSSR.

STEP SIX: To correct this mean value, determine the number of days elapsed from the Solar Return date to the PSSR (event) date. Multiply this number by D, and divide by 365.25, being careful to observe whether D is positive or negative. Add this to the mean PSSR ST calculated in Step Five.

Notice, incidentally, that D will readily tell you how much error is possible for the PSSR if not corrected this way. If the SRY is 30:05:53, D will be 30:05:53 − 30:09:13 = −0:03:20. Since four minutes of time averages 1° on the angles, 3m20s corresponds to a maximum error of 0°50′, a little less than 1°. This maximum error will only occur at the end of the Solar Return year. Half way through the year, it will be half of this, etc. This factor allows the user to determine easily whether (s)he wishes to bother with this correction.

President Reagan's PSSR for Election Day 1984 would be calculated as follows:

STEP ONE. The SRY was previously calculated to be 30:16:24.

STEP TWO. Subtract 30:09:13 from the SRY to get the value D:

$$
\begin{array}{r}
30:16:24 \\
-\ 30:09:13 \\
\hline
=\ \ \ 0:07:11 \\
=\quad 431 \text{ seconds}
\end{array}
$$

STEP THREE. The 1984 Solar Return occurred at 0:34:10 UT on February 7. From the 1984 table in Appendix C, we learn that the ASSI at 0^h February 7 was 26:47:20, and the ASSI at 0^h February 8, 26:52:22. Interpolating for 0:34:10 UT, we get an ASSIC of 26:47:27.

Notice that the three steps so far completed need only be done once for each Solar Return. The values of the SRY, D and the ASSIC are then constant for the duration of the Solar Return period.

STEPS FOUR AND FIVE. The ASSI for 0^h UT November 7, 1984 (also extracted from Appendix C), was 18:37:07. We subtract as follows:

	Transiting ASSI	18:37:07
+	Add for subtracting	+ 30:09:13
		= 48:46:20
−	ASSIC	− 26:47:27
=	Mean PSSR Increment	= 21:58:53
+	1984 Solar Return ST	− 4:31:23
		= 26:30:16
−	Subtract if necessary	− 24:00:00
=	Mean PSSR ST	= 2:30:16

STEP SIX. From February 7 (the Solar Return date) until November 7 (the PSSR date) is 274 days. D has been calculated as 431 seconds. We calculate the correction as follows:

$$
\begin{array}{r}
431\,'' \\
\times\quad 274 \text{ days} \\
\hline
=\ 118094\,'' \\
\div\ 365.25 \text{ days} \\
\hline
=\quad 323\,'' \\
=\quad 5'23\,''
\end{array}
$$

Since D is a positive number, this correction is **added** to the mean PSSR ST.

Mean PSSR ST	2:30:16
+ Correction	+ 0:05:23
= PSSR ST	= 2:35:39

This agrees within ten seconds with the sidereal time previously determined by the calculator method.

Timing Aspects in the Solar Return Progressions

Sidereal time moves 9.8565 seconds per hour faster than clock time. This totals to 3 minutes 57 seconds per day. Our methods of computing the SQ and PSSR tell us how much they advance in sidereal time, but not in clock time. To find the latter, we need to reduce the advance in sidereal time by 9.83 seconds per hour (note that this is different from the previous value), or about ten seconds per hour if one prefers to work with rounded numbers. Alternately, given an increase in clock time, we must accelerate this by 9.8565 seconds per hour to get the ST equivalent.

My own 1976 Solar Return occurred the exact day of a Neptune-Pluto sextile. According to *The American Ephemeris 1931 to 1980 & Book of Tables,* the sextile occurred at 9:46 ET on October 10 of that year. My Solar Return occurred at 1:37 ET of the same day. The question is, when **in my "real-time" life** was this progression exact?

First, subtract the Solar Return's time from the time of the exact aspect. This gives the clock-time advance. Accelerating this by ten seconds per hour provides the sidereal time advance.

Exact aspect	=	9:46 ET
− Solar Return occurrence	−	1:37 ET
= Difference	=	8:09
Acceleration	=	0:01:20
= Sidereal time advance	=	8:10

By the Solar Quotidian rate, this is equal to the Alpha-age. Simply add this advance to the solar Sun's right ascension to get the right ascension of the Sun on the day the progression is exact.

```
        Solar Sun RA              =  13:02
      + Advance                   +   8:10
      = Sun's RA on maturation date = 21:12
```

This is the right ascension of the Sun at Tropical 16° Aquarius (Sidereal 21° Capricorn), equating to February 4, 1977.

By the PSSR rate, the easiest approach is to add the sidereal time advance to the ASSI value for the birthday (Appendix C), then look for the date, later in the same table, corresponding to the sum. If the sum exceeds 30:09:13, this amount should be subtracted before consulting the tables.

```
        ASSI 1976 Oct 10  =  16:22
      + Advance           +   8:10
      = ASSI of event day =  24:32
```

The value of 24:32 equates to about January 11, 1977. Therefore, by the PSSR rate, the Neptune-Pluto progressed aspect was exact on that date. I experienced the effects most strongly throughout January and the first half of February.

For another example, we can calculate Mr. Reagan's SQ and PSSR planets for Election Day. Usually, only the progressed Solar Moon moves sufficiently to deserve notice. However, occasionally the other planets will complete an aspect or move sufficiently to otherwise have a distinct influence. One example of this is Mr. Reagan's PSSR Sun which had advanced sufficiently to conjoin the PSSR Horizon on Election Day, even though the PSSR angle had clearly passed the natal Sun.

To find the time for which to calculate the SQ and PSSR planets, follow these steps:

STEP ONE. Determine how much the SQ or PSSR sidereal time has increased since the Solar Return. For the SQ, this will be the Alpha-age. For the PSSR, this will be the PSSR Increment calculated by any of the above methods. (It is also, of course, PSSR ST minus Solar Return ST.)

STEP TWO. Subtract 10 seconds per hour (more precisely, 9.83 seconds). This gives the amount of clock time by which the Solar Return has progressed.

STEP THREE. Add this increase in clock time to the UT of the Solar Return to get the UT of the PSSR or SQ.

Beginning with the SQ, recall that Mr. Reagan's Alpha-age was previously found to be 17:29:43. As this is 17.5 hours, a correction of 10 seconds per hour would give 175 seconds, or 0:02:55. A more precise calculation shows the requisite decrement to be 0:02:52 (17.5 × 9.83 = 172).

Alpha-age	= 17:29:43	
− 9.83 seconds/hour	− 0:02:52	
= SQ Civil Time Increment	= 17:26:51	
+ UT of 1984 Solar Return	+ 0:34:10	2/7/84
= UT of SQ	= 18:01:01	2/7/84

The planets, especially the Moon, would be calculated for this time. It should be noted that SQ Moon had reached 26♓22, closely square natal Neptune (25♊59).

A similar process is applied to the PSSR. The PSSR Increment was calculated previously as 22:04:06. Because this is approximately 22.1 hours, the 10 seconds/hour correction would be estimated as 221 seconds, or 0:03:41. A more precise calculation gives 0:03:37.

PSSR Increment	= 22:04:06	
− 9.83 seconds/hour	− 0:03:37	
= PSSR Civil Time Increment	= 22:00:29	
+ UT of 1984 Solar Return	+ 0:34:10	2/7/84
= UT of PSSR	= 22:34:39	2/7/84

It is for this calculated time and date that the PSSR planets are calculated. PSSR Sun had therefore advanced to 23♑50, within half a degree of the PSSR Descendant of 24♑31. Furthermore, PSSR Moon had reached 28♓40, square natal Mercury at 27♐54.

Computing the Key Cycle

Wynn's Key Cycle is no more difficult to calculate than the PSSR. In fact, these two techniques are based on sibling concepts. One major difference between them is that the Key Cycle spins off the standard Tropical Solar Return; that is, a Solar Return calculated in the Tropical Zodiac without the precession correction found essential throughout this book. The second "key" difference is that, whereas the annual PSSR rate increase averages 30:09:13, Wynn's theory is based on a 5:48:46 increase throughout the year, on the average. Rather than accelerating the Midheaven about 1°.25 per day (the PSSR rate), Key Cycles only move the Midheaven about 1° in four days.

Because Key Cycles are rooted in a type of Solar Return that has never performed well in practice, the whole theory is questionable from the start. Yet, it was this very inadequacy of "standard" Solar Returns which inspired Wynn to investigate the Key Cycle in the first place. As he wrote:

> ...the [standard] solar return yielded only partially satisfactory results. It did not show conditions in my affairs or those of my friends except for a short time around the birthday. I tried using the transits over the chart for the solar return; fairly good for a short time after the birthday and mostly to slow movers, Neptune, Uranus, and Saturn. No good in the middle of the birthday year and thereafter.[7]

Wynn's solution was to progress the return chart by the method here described. However, after applying his approach to the dozen biggest events in my own life, to another dozen "pet" events by which I test any new system that comes along, and to a collection of accident charts, I can credit it with no consistent significance whatsoever.

I am taking space to describe how Key Cycles are calculated for one reason only: Many astrologers are captivated by them and would like to experiment. Any experimentation is laudable, when the results are evaluated with an objective, responsible mind. And no solid conclusions can ever be reached, verified and re-verified unless the investigators are calculating their charts accurately. Thus, the need for clear-cut directions.

Below are instructions for calculating the Key Cycle using an electronic calculator. As an example we shall use President Richard Nixon's resignation. Mr. Nixon's Tropical Sun is 19♑24'08". His Tropical Solar Return (TSR) preceding the resignation (computed without precession correction) occurred January 10, 1974, at 1:02:05 ET, when the sidereal time in Washington, D.C., was 3:10:45. The subsequent Tropical Solar Return occurred January 10, 1975, at 6:57:05 ET when the Washington ST was 9:04:59. His resignation speech began at 20:00 EDT on August 8, 1974 (= August 9, 0:00 UT).

Direct Calculation Method

(1) Determine the ST difference between two consecutive returns. This should be close to 5:49.

---

7. Wynn, *The Key Cycle.*

Washington ST (1975 TSR)	9:04:59
− Washington ST (1974 TSR) −	3:10:45
= Difference =	5:54:14

(2) Since the cuspal framework of the Key Cycle moves so slowly, we can for virtually any practical purpose assume that the elapsed **clock time** between these two Tropical Solar Returns is exactly 365.25 days. For maximum precision, we can subtract to find the true value in each case, though this should never be necessary.

1975 TSR	1975 Jan 10, 6:57:05	ET
− 1974 TSR −	1974 Jan 10, 1:02:45	ET
= 365 days =	5:54:20	
= =	365.246	days

(3) Next, find **how many days after the preceding Tropical Solar Return** the event occurred. In non-leap years like 1974, August 9 is the 221st day and January 10 is, naturally, the 10th day of the year:

$$221 - 10 = 211 \text{ days elapsed}$$

(4) Convert the answer found in (1) to hours and a decimal, rather than hours, minutes and seconds.

$$5:54:20 = 5.9039 \text{ hours}$$

This is a constant for the year. Multiply this by the number of days elapsed (211), and divide by 365.25.

$$\frac{5.9039 \times 211}{365.25} = 3.4106 = 3:24:38$$

(5) Add the value found in (4) to the sidereal time of the Solar Return calculated for residence (Washington, D.C.):

1974 TSR ST (Washington)	3:10:45
+ Increment +	3:24:23
= ST of Key Cycle chart =	6:35:08

This is the ST of the Key Cycle chart. Calculate the angles for the latitude of residence (38N54) and see if any natal, Tropical Solar Return or transiting planets contact them. Mr. Nixon's Key Cycle for his resignation had the following angles (Tropical longitudes):

Midheaven =   8♋08
Ascendant =   7♎08 − s. Pluto 6♎50
East Point =   9♎38
Vertex   = 20♈25 − r. Sun 19♑24
                                s. Mercury 19♑50

In this particular instance, we find remarkably appropriate planets contacting angles for the event. This single case is the most outstanding example of the Key Cycle I have ever seen; and while it is virtually the **only** example I have ever seen where the Key Cycle actually worked, it may serve as a basis for anyone else's research by demonstrating the kind of symbolic aptness any working system should be able to produce time after time after time.

Appendix B — Synetic Vernal Point

	COMMON YEARS				LEAP YEAR		COMMON YEARS				LEAP YEAR
DATE	1900	1901	1902	DATE	1903	DATE	1904	1905	1906	DATE	1907
	6°	6°	6°		6°		6°	6°	6°		6°
JAN 1	39 4.3	38 16.2	37 29.5	JAN 1	36 44.2	JAN 1	36 0.0	35 15.5	34 30.3	JAN 1	33 44.1
11	39 2.7	38 14.3	37 27.7	11	36 42.8	11	35 58.3	35 13.7	34 28.6	11	33 42.6
21	39 0.9	38 12.5	37 26.3	21	36 41.2	21	35 56.6	35 12.1	34 27.3	21	33 40.9
31	38 59.2	38 11.2	37 24.9	31	36 39.6	31	35 55.2	35 10.8	34 25.8	31	33 39.2
FEB 10	38 57.9	38 10.1	37 23.5	FEB 10	36 38.3	FEB 10	35 54.1	35 9.7	34 24.3	FEB 10	33 38.0
20	38 57.0	38 8.7	37 22.2	20	36 37.4	20	35 53.1	35 8.4	34 23.2	20	33 37.0
MAR 2	38 55.7	38 7.5	37 21.6	MAR 1	36 36.6	MAR 2	35 51.8	35 7.4	34 22.6	MAR 1	33 35.9
12	38 54.6	38 7.0	37 20.7	11	36 35.5	12	35 51.0	35 6.9	34 21.6	11	33 34.8
22	38 54.1	38 6.1	37 19.6	21	36 34.9	22	35 50.6	35 6.0	34 20.5	21	33 34.3
APR 1	38 53.1	38 5.0	37 18.9	31	36 34.3	APR 1	35 49.6	35 4.9	34 20.0	31	33 33.5
11	38 51.9	38 4.2	37 18.3	APR 10	36 33.2	11	35 48.6	35 4.4	34 19.2	APR 10	33 32.2
21	38 50.9	38 3.3	37 17.2	20	36 32.2	21	35 47.8	35 3.5	34 18.0	20	33 31.3
MAY 1	38 49.9	38 2.2	37 16.0	30	36 31.4	MAY 1	35 46.9	35 2.2	34 16.8	30	33 30.5
11	38 48.6	38 0.7	37 14.8	MAY 10	36 30.2	11	35 45.6	35 1.0	34 15.7	MAY 10	33 29.0
21	38 46.9	37 59.3	37 13.6	20	36 28.7	21	35 44.1	34 59.7	34 14.4	20	33 27.4
31	38 45.3	37 58.1	37 12.0	30	36 27.2	31	35 42.7	34 58.4	34 12.7	30	33 26.0
JUN 10	38 44.0	37 56.3	37 10.2	JUN 9	36 25.9	JUN 10	35 41.4	34 56.6	34 11.0	JUN 9	33 24.5
20	38 42.1	37 54.4	37 8.9	19	36 24.3	20	35 39.5	34 54.8	34 9.7	19	33 22.7
30	38 40.1	37 53.1	37 7.4	29	36 22.4	30	35 37.8	34 53.6	34 8.0	29	33 20.7
JUL 10	38 38.8	37 51.5	37 5.4	JUL 9	36 21.0	JUL 10	35 36.6	34 51.9	34 6.0	JUL 9	33 19.3
20	38 37.2	37 49.7	37 4.0	19	36 19.7	20	35 35.0	34 50.1	34 4.7	19	33 17.9
30	38 35.5	37 48.3	37 2.8	29	36 18.1	30	35 33.4	34 48.9	34 3.5	29	33 16.1
AUG 9	38 34.1	37 47.1	37 1.4	AUG 8	36 16.7	AUG 9	35 32.3	34 47.8	34 1.9	AUG 8	33 14.7
19	38 33.0	37 46.0	37 0.1	18	36 15.8	19	35 31.2	34 46.5	34 0.6	18	33 13.8
29	38 32.1	37 44.7	36 59.1	28	36 14.8	29	35 30.2	34 45.4	33 59.7	28	33 12.6
SEP 8	38 30.8	37 43.7	36 58.4	SEP 7	36 13.7	SEP 8	35 29.2	34 44.5	33 58.9	SEP 7	33 11.4
18	38 29.8	37 43.2	36 57.5	17	36 12.8	18	35 28.4	34 43.9	33 57.9	17	33 10.5
28	38 29.4	37 42.3	36 56.5	27	36 12.2	28	35 27.9	34 42.9	33 56.9	27	33 9.8
OCT 8	38 28.3	37 41.1	36 55.9	OCT 7	36 11.5	OCT 8	35 26.9	34 41.9	33 56.3	OCT 7	33 8.8
18	38 27.1	37 40.5	36 55.2	17	36 10.4	18	35 25.9	34 41.4	33 55.5	17	33 7.6
28	38 26.3	37 39.6	36 53.9	27	36 9.5	28	35 25.2	34 40.4	33 54.1	27	33 6.7
NOV 7	38 25.2	37 38.2	36 52.8	NOV 6	36 8.7	NOV 7	35 24.1	34 38.9	33 53.0	NOV 6	33 5.7
17	38 23.6	37 36.8	36 51.7	16	36 7.3	17	35 22.5	34 37.7	33 51.9	16	33 4.0
27	38 22.0	37 35.4	36 50.2	26	36 5.7	27	35 21.1	34 36.4	33 50.2	26	33 2.4
DEC 7	38 20.4	37 33.9	36 48.5	DEC 6	36 4.3	DEC 7	35 19.7	34 34.7	33 48.4	DEC 6	33 1.0
17	38 18.8	37 32.0	36 46.7	16	36 2.7	17	35 18.0	34 32.8	33 46.7	16	32 59.2
27	38 16.8	37 30.1	36 45.2	26	36 1.2	27	35 16.1	34 31.1	33 45.2	26	32 57.2
JAN 6	38 14.9	37 28.8	36 43.6	JAN 5	35 59.0	JAN 6	35 14.4	34 29.7	33 43.3	JAN 5	32 55.3

	COMMON YEARS				LEAP YEAR		COMMON YEARS				LEAP YEAR
DATE	1908	1909	1910	DATE	1911	DATE	1912	1913	1914	DATE	1915
	6°	6°	6°		6°		6°	6°	6°		6°
JAN 1	32 56.5	32 6.3	31 14.2	JAN 1	30 20.8	JAN 1	29 26.4	28 30.4	27 34.2	JAN 1	26 38.9
11	32 54.5	32 4.2	31 12.5	11	30 19.2	11	29 24.1	28 28.1	27 32.5	11	26 37.2
21	32 52.6	32 2.6	31 10.9	21	30 17.2	21	29 22.1	28 26.5	27 30.8	21	26 35.1
31	32 51.3	32 1.2	31 9.2	31	30 15.3	31	29 20.7	28 24.9	27 28.9	31	26 33.3
FEB 10	32 50.0	31 59.8	31 7.5	FEB 10	30 14.0	FEB 10	29 19.2	28 23.3	27 27.2	FEB 10	26 31.9
20	32 48.7	31 58.2	31 6.3	20	30 12.8	20	29 17.7	28 21.6	27 25.9	20	26 30.8
MAR 2	32 47.3	31 57.2	31 5.4	MAR 1	30 11.4	MAR 2	29 16.0	28 20.5	27 25.0	MAR 1	26 29.3
12	32 46.5	31 56.6	31 4.1	11	30 10.2	12	29 15.1	28 19.7	27 23.5	11	26 28.1
22	32 45.9	31 55.3	31 2.8	21	30 9.5	22	29 14.4	28 18.3	27 22.2	21	26 27.4
APR 1	32 44.7	31 54.1	31 2.3	31	30 8.5	APR 1	29 12.9	28 17.0	27 21.6	31	26 26.3
11	32 43.5	31 53.5	31 1.2	APR 10	30 6.9	11	29 11.7	28 16.3	27 20.4	APR 10	26 24.7
21	32 42.8	31 52.3	30 59.7	20	30 6.0	21	29 10.8	28 15.0	27 18.8	20	26 23.9
MAY 1	32 41.6	31 50.8	30 58.5	30	30 4.9	MAY 1	29 9.4	28 13.3	27 17.6	30	26 22.8
11	32 40.0	31 49.4	30 57.2	MAY 10	30 3.2	11	29 7.6	28 11.8	27 16.2	MAY 10	26 21.0
21	32 38.4	31 48.0	30 55.6	20	30 1.4	21	29 5.9	28 10.4	27 14.6	20	26 19.3
31	32 37.1	31 46.4	30 53.6	30	29 59.8	31	29 4.4	28 8.6	27 12.5	30	26 17.7
JUN 10	32 35.5	31 44.4	30 51.8	JUN 9	29 58.2	JUN 10	29 2.6	28 6.4	27 10.7	JUN 9	26 16.0
20	32 33.3	31 42.6	30 50.3	19	29 56.1	20	29 0.3	28 4.6	27 9.2	19	26 13.9
30	32 31.6	31 41.2	30 48.3	29	29 54.0	30	28 58.5	28 3.1	27 7.1	29	26 11.8
JUL 10	32 30.3	31 39.2	30 46.2	JUL 9	29 52.5	JUL 10	28 57.1	28 0.9	27 4.9	JUL 9	26 10.4
20	32 28.5	31 37.2	30 44.8	19	29 50.8	20	28 54.9	27 58.9	27 3.5	19	26 8.7
30	32 26.7	31 36.0	30 43.3	29	29 48.7	30	28 53.0	27 57.6	27 1.9	29	26 6.6
AUG 9	32 25.6	31 34.6	30 41.5	AUG 8	29 47.2	AUG 9	28 51.8	27 56.0	27 0.0	AUG 8	26 5.2
19	32 24.3	31 33.1	30 40.1	18	29 46.2	19	28 50.4	27 54.3	26 58.6	18	26 4.1
29	32 23.1	31 31.8	30 39.0	28	29 44.7	29	28 48.9	27 53.0	26 57.4	28	26 2.6
SEP 8	32 21.9	31 30.8	30 38.0	SEP 7	29 43.3	SEP 8	28 47.6	27 51.9	26 56.4	SEP 7	26 1.2
18	32 21.0	31 30.0	30 36.6	17	29 42.3	18	28 46.7	27 51.0	26 54.9	17	26 0.2
28	32 20.3	31 28.7	30 35.4	27	29 41.4	28	28 45.8	27 49.5	26 53.7	27	25 59.4
OCT 8	32 19.0	31 27.5	30 34.8	OCT 7	29 40.2	OCT 8	28 44.3	27 48.3	26 53.1	OCT 7	25 58.1
18	32 17.9	31 26.9	30 33.6	17	29 38.7	18	28 43.1	27 47.6	26 51.8	17	25 56.7
28	32 17.2	31 25.6	30 32.0	27	29 37.8	28	28 42.2	27 46.2	26 50.2	27	25 55.9
NOV 7	32 15.8	31 23.9	30 30.9	NOV 6	29 36.6	NOV 7	28 40.6	27 44.4	26 49.1	NOV 6	25 54.7
17	32 14.0	31 22.6	30 29.5	16	29 34.7	17	28 38.7	27 43.1	26 47.7	16	25 53.2
27	32 12.5	31 21.1	30 27.6	26	29 32.9	27	28 37.1	27 41.5	26 45.6	26	25 51.1
DEC 7	32 10.9	31 19.1	30 25.6	DEC 6	29 31.4	DEC 7	28 35.4	27 39.4	26 43.7	DEC 6	25 49.6
17	32 9.0	31 17.1	30 23.8	16	29 29.4	17	28 33.3	27 37.2	26 41.9	16	25 47.5
27	32 6.9	31 15.3	30 22.0	26	29 27.1	27	28 31.0	27 35.4	26 40.1	26	25 45.3
JAN 6	32 5.2	31 13.6	30 19.9	JAN 5	29 25.1	JAN 6	28 29.2	27 33.7	26 37.8	JAN 5	25 43.4

	COMMON YEARS			LEAP YEAR			COMMON YEARS			LEAP YEAR	
DATE	1916	1917	1918	DATE	1919	DATE	1920	1921	1922	DATE	1923
	6°	6°	6°		6°		6°	6°	6°		6°
JAN 1	25 44.6	24 51.0	23 59.3	JAN 1	23 10.1	JAN 1	22 22.7	21 36.3	20 51.3	JAN 1	20 7.3
11	25 42.4	24 48.9	23 57.8	11	23 8.5	11	22 20.7	21 34.5	20 50.0	11	20 5.7
21	25 40.4	24 47.4	23 56.2	21	23 6.6	21	22 19.0	21 33.2	20 48.4	21	20 3.9
31	25 39.0	24 45.9	23 54.5	31	23 5.0	31	22 17.9	21 31.8	20 40.9	31	20 2.6
FEB 10	25 37.6	24 44.3	23 52.9	FEB 10	23 3.8	FEB 10	22 16.5	21 30.4	20 45.6	FEB 10	20 1.5
20	25 36.1	24 42.8	23 51.8	20	23 2.8	20	22 15.2	21 29.2	20 44.7	20	20 0.4
MAR 2	25 34.5	24 41.8	23 50.9	MAR 1	23 1.5	MAR 2	22 13.9	21 28.4	20 43.8	MAR 1	19 59.4
12	25 33.7	24 41.1	23 49.6	11	23 0.5	12	22 13.3	21 27.7	20 42.7	11	19 58.6
22	25 32.9	24 39.7	23 48.5	21	23 0.0	22	22 12.6	21 26.6	20 41.9	21	19 58.1
APR 1	25 31.5	24 38.6	23 48.1	31	22 59.0	APR 1	22 11.5	21 25.8	20 41.5	31	19 57.1
11	25 30.4	24 38.0	23 47.0	APR 10	22 57.8	11	22 10.6	21 25.3	20 40.5	APR 10	19 56.1
21	25 29.5	24 36.8	23 45.6	20	22 57.1	21	22 9.9	21 24.2	20 39.4	20	19 55.5
MAY 1	25 28.2	24 35.2	23 44.6	30	22 56.1	MAY 1	22 8.7	21 22.9	20 38.6	30	19 54.5
11	25 26.5	24 33.9	23 43.4	MAY 10	22 54.5	11	22 7.2	21 21.9	20 37.4	MAY 10	19 53.0
21	25 24.8	24 32.6	23 41.8	20	22 53.1	21	22 5.9	21 20.6	20 35.9	20	19 51.8
31	25 23.4	24 30.9	23 40.0	30	22 51.7	31	22 4.6	21 19.1	20 34.4	30	19 50.5
JUN 10	25 21.6	24 28.8	23 38.4	JUN 9	22 50.1	JUN 10	22 2.9	21 17.3	20 33.0	JUN 9	19 48.9
20	25 19.4	24 27.2	23 36.9	19	22 48.2	20	22 1.0	21 15.8	20 31.5	19	19 47.1
30	25 17.7	24 25.7	23 34.9	29	22 46.4	30	21 59.6	21 14.4	20 29.6	29	19 45.5
JUL 10	25 16.3	24 23.6	23 33.0	JUL 9	22 45.1	JUL 10	21 58.2	21 12.5	20 28.0	JUL 9	19 44.2
20	25 14.2	24 21.8	23 31.8	19	22 43.5	20	21 56.3	21 11.0	20 26.9	19	19 42.5
30	25 12.4	24 20.6	23 30.3	29	22 41.6	30	21 54.8	21 9.9	20 25.4	29	19 40.9
AUG 9	25 11.3	24 19.1	23 28.6	AUG 8	22 40.5	AUG 9	21 53.8	21 8.5	20 23.9	AUG 8	19 39.9
19	25 9.9	24 17.6	23 27.4	18	22 39.5	19	21 52.6	21 7.2	20 23.0	18	19 38.8
29	25 8.5	24 16.4	23 26.4	28	22 38.2	29	21 51.4	21 6.3	20 22.0	28	19 37.6
SEP 8	25 7.3	24 15.4	23 25.4	SEP 7	22 37.1	SEP 8	21 50.5	21 5.5	20 21.1	SEP 7	19 36.7
18	25 6.5	24 14.6	23 24.2	17	22 36.3	18	21 49.8	21 4.7	20 20.1	17	19 36.0
28	25 5.6	24 13.3	23 23.3	27	22 35.6	28	21 49.0	21 3.7	20 19.4	27	19 35.3
OCT 8	25 4.2	24 12.3	23 22.7	OCT 7	22 34.6	OCT 8	21 47.9	21 3.0	20 18.9	OCT 7	19 34.3
18	25 3.1	24 11.7	23 21.6	17	22 33.4	18	21 47.2	21 2.4	20 17.8	17	19 33.3
28	25 2.3	24 10.3	23 20.2	27	22 32.8	28	21 46.4	21 1.2	20 16.6	27	19 32.7
NOV 7	25 0.7	24 8.7	23 19.3	NOV 6	22 31.6	NOV 7	21 45.0	20 59.9	20 15.9	NOV 6	19 31.5
17	24 59.0	24 7.6	23 18.0	16	22 29.9	17	21 43.6	20 58.9	20 14.6	16	19 29.9
27	24 57.5	24 6.1	23 16.1	26	22 28.6	27	21 42.3	20 57.4	20 12.9	26	19 28.7
DEC 7	24 55.8	24 4.1	23 14.4	DEC 6	22 27.2	DEC 7	21 40.7	20 55.7	20 11.4	DEC 6	19 27.3
17	24 53.8	24 2.1	23 12.8	16	22 25.3	17	21 38.9	20 54.0	20 9.9	16	19 25.4
27	24 51.6	24 0.5	23 11.1	26	22 23.4	27	21 37.0	20 52.4	20 8.1	26	19 23.6
JAN 6	24 50.0	23 58.8	23 9.0	JAN 5	22 21.7	JAN 6	21 35.5	20 50.8	20 6.2	JAN 5	19 22.1

	COMMON YEARS			LEAP YEAR			COMMON YEARS			LEAP YEAR	
DATE	1924	1925	1926	DATE	1927	DATE	1928	1929	1930	DATE	1931
	6°	6°	6°		6°		6°	6°	6°		6°
JAN 1	19 22.9	18 37.0	17 50.1	JAN 1	17 1.8	JAN 1	16 11.1	15 18.1	14 24.1	JAN 1	13 29.3
11	19 20.9	18 35.3	17 48.8	11	16 59.9	11	16 8.9	15 16.3	14 22.6	11	13 27.2
21	19 19.4	18 34.0	17 47.0	21	16 57.9	21	16 7.4	15 14.9	14 20.5	21	13 25.0
31	19 18.2	18 32.5	17 45.3	31	16 56.6	31	16 6.0	15 13.1	14 18.6	31	13 23.6
FEB 10	19 16.9	18 31.0	17 44.1	FEB 10	16 55.3	FEB 10	16 4.4	15 11.4	14 17.3	FEB 10	13 22.2
20	19 15.6	18 29.9	17 43.0	20	16 54.0	20	16 2.9	15 10.1	14 16.1	20	13 20.6
MAR 2	19 14.5	18 29.2	17 42.0	MAR 1	16 52.9	MAR 2	16 1.7	15 9.2	14 14.8	MAR 1	13 19.4
12	19 14.0	18 28.2	17 40.8	11	16 52.0	12	16 1.0	15 8.0	14 13.4	11	13 18.4
22	19 13.1	18 27.1	17 40.0	21	16 51.2	22	15 59.8	15 6.6	14 12.5	21	13 17.4
APR 1	19 12.0	18 26.5	17 39.4	31	16 50.0	APR 1	15 58.5	15 5.9	14 11.7	31	13 16.0
11	19 11.4	18 25.8	17 38.2	APR 10	16 48.9	11	15 57.9	15 5.0	14 10.2	APR 10	13 14.8
21	19 10.6	18 24.6	17 37.0	20	16 48.3	21	15 56.8	15 3.4	14 8.9	20	13 14.0
MAY 1	19 9.3	18 23.3	17 36.2	30	16 46.9	MAY 1	15 55.2	15 2.1	14 8.0	30	13 12.5
11	19 8.0	18 22.3	17 34.9	MAY 10	16 45.3	11	15 53.8	15 0.9	14 6.4	MAY 10	13 10.6
21	19 6.7	18 20.9	17 33.2	20	16 44.0	21	15 52.4	14 59.3	14 4.5	20	13 9.4
31	19 5.4	18 19.2	17 31.6	30	16 42.6	31	15 50.7	14 57.3	14 2.7	30	13 7.7
JUN 10	19 3.6	18 17.5	17 30.1	JUN 9	16 40.7	JUN 10	15 48.7	14 55.4	14 1.1	JUN 9	13 5.6
20	19 1.8	18 16.1	17 28.4	19	16 38.7	20	15 46.8	14 53.9	13 59.2	19	13 3.6
30	19 0.5	18 14.5	17 26.4	29	16 37.1	30	15 45.4	14 52.0	13 56.9	29	13 1.9
JUL 10	18 58.9	18 12.4	17 24.8	JUL 9	16 35.6	JUL 10	15 43.5	14 49.8	13 55.3	JUL 9	13 0.2
20	18 57.1	18 11.0	17 23.6	19	16 33.6	20	15 41.4	14 48.3	13 53.9	19	12 58.0
30	18 55.8	18 9.9	17 21.8	29	16 31.9	30	15 40.1	14 47.0	13 51.8	29	12 56.2
AUG 9	18 54.8	18 8.3	17 20.2	AUG 8	16 30.9	AUG 9	15 38.9	14 45.1	13 50.1	AUG 8	12 55.1
19	18 53.4	18 7.0	17 19.3	18	16 29.5	19	15 37.3	14 43.6	13 49.1	18	12 53.5
29	18 52.3	18 6.2	17 18.2	28	16 28.0	29	15 35.9	14 42.6	13 47.7	28	12 51.8
SEP 8	18 51.5	18 5.3	17 17.0	SEP 7	16 27.1	SEP 8	15 35.0	14 41.5	13 46.3	SEP 7	12 50.9
18	18 50.8	18 4.2	17 16.0	17	16 26.2	18	15 34.1	14 40.2	13 45.2	17	12 49.9
28	18 49.9	18 3.2	17 15.2	27	16 25.2	28	15 32.8	14 39.0	13 44.3	27	12 48.7
OCT 8	18 48.8	18 2.5	17 14.4	OCT 7	16 24.0	OCT 8	15 31.6	14 38.2	13 43.3	OCT 7	12 47.3
18	18 48.2	18 1.7	17 13.1	17	16 23.0	18	15 30.9	14 37.2	13 41.7	17	12 46.2
28	18 47.3	18 0.3	17 11.9	27	16 22.2	28	15 29.7	14 35.3	13 40.5	27	12 45.3
NOV 7	18 45.8	17 59.1	17 11.1	NOV 6	16 20.7	NOV 7	15 27.9	14 34.2	13 39.5	NOV 6	12 43.6
17	18 44.5	17 58.1	17 9.9	16	16 18.9	17	15 26.6	14 33.0	13 37.7	16	12 41.7
27	18 43.2	17 56.4	17 7.6	26	16 17.7	27	15 25.2	14 31.0	13 35.6	26	12 40.5
DEC 7	18 41.5	17 54.5	17 6.2	DEC 6	16 16.0	DEC 7	15 23.1	14 29.0	13 34.1	DEC 6	12 38.6
17	18 39.6	17 52.9	17 4.5	16	16 13.8	17	15 21.0	14 27.2	13 32.2	16	12 36.3
27	18 37.9	17 51.3	17 2.5	26	16 12.0	27	15 19.2	14 25.4	13 30.0	26	12 34.4
JAN 6	18 36.4	17 49.4	17 0.5	JAN 5	16 10.3	JAN 6	15 17.5	14 23.3	13 27.8	JAN 5	12 32.6

	COMMON YEARS			LEAP YEAR	
DATE	1932	1933	1934	DATE	1935
	6°	6°	6°		6°
JAN 1	12 33.3	11 37.0	10 41.9	JAN 1	9 48.3
11	12 31.0	11 35.2	10 40.4	11	9 46.1
21	12 29.5	11 33.7	10 38.3	21	9 44.1
31	12 27.9	11 31.8	10 36.4	31	9 42.8
FEB 10	12 26.2	11 30.1	10 35.2	FEB 10	9 41.3
20	12 24.6	11 28.8	10 33.9	20	9 39.8
MAR 2	12 23.3	11 27.9	10 32.5	MAR 1	9 38.7
12	12 22.5	11 26.5	10 31.2	11	9 37.7
22	12 21.2	11 25.1	10 30.4	21	9 36.8
APR 1	12 19.7	11 24.4	10 29.6	31	9 35.4
11	12 19.1	11 23.4	10 28.0	APR 10	9 34.4
21	12 17.9	11 21.8	10 26.8	20	9 33.7
MAY 1	12 16.1	11 20.5	10 25.9	30	9 32.2
11	12 14.7	11 19.2	10 24.3	MAY 10	9 30.5
21	12 13.2	11 17.5	10 22.4	20	9 29.3
31	12 11.4	11 15.5	10 20.8	30	9 27.7
JUN 10	12 9.3	11 13.6	10 19.2	JUN 9	9 25.7
20	12 7.3	11 12.1	10 17.2	19	9 23.8
30	12 5.8	11 10.1	10 15.0	29	9 22.1
JUL 10	12 3.8	11 7.8	10 13.4	JUL 9	9 20.5
20	12 1.6	11 6.4	10 12.0	19	9 18.4
30	12 0.3	11 5.0	10 9.9	29	9 16.7
AUG 9	11 58.9	11 3.0	10 8.3	AUG 8	9 15.7
19	11 57.2	11 1.5	10 7.4	18	9 14.2
29	11 55.8	11 0.6	10 6.0	28	9 12.6
SEP 8	11 54.8	10 59.4	10 4.6	SEP 7	9 11.8
18	11 53.8	10 58.0	10 3.6	17	9 10.8
28	11 52.4	10 56.9	10 2.7	27	9 9.7
OCT 8	11 51.1	10 56.1	10 1.7	OCT 7	9 8.5
18	11 50.4	10 55.0	10 0.2	17	9 7.5
28	11 49.1	10 53.3	9 59.1	27	9 6.7
NOV 7	11 47.2	10 52.1	9 58.1	NOV 6	9 5.0
17	11 45.9	10 50.8	9 56.3	16	9 3.4
27	11 44.4	10 48.8	9 54.4	26	9 2.2
DEC 7	11 42.2	10 46.8	9 52.9	DEC 6	9 0.4
17	11 40.1	10 45.1	9 51.0	16	8 58.2
27	11 38.2	10 43.2	9 48.8	26	8 56.5
JAN 6	11 36.4	10 41.0	9 46.8	JAN 5	8 54.8

	COMMON YEARS			LEAP YEAR	
DATE	1936	1937	1938	DATE	1939
	6°	6°	6°		6°
JAN 1	8 55.4	8 4.3	7 15.8	JAN 1	6 29.1
11	8 53.3	8 2.7	7 14.3	11	6 27.2
21	8 51.9	8 1.3	7 12.4	21	6 25.5
31	8 50.4	7 59.5	7 10.8	31	6 24.3
FEB 10	8 48.7	7 58.0	7 9.7	FEB 10	6 23.0
20	8 47.4	7 56.9	7 8.6	20	6 21.7
MAR 2	8 46.2	7 56.1	7 7.4	MAR 1	6 20.9
12	8 45.5	7 54.9	7 6.4	11	6 20.1
22	8 44.2	7 53.8	7 5.8	21	6 19.2
APR 1	8 43.0	7 53.2	7 5.0	31	6 18.2
11	8 42.5	7 52.3	7 3.7	APR 10	6 17.4
21	8 41.3	7 50.9	7 2.8	20	6 16.8
MAY 1	8 39.7	7 49.8	7 2.0	30	6 15.4
11	8 38.5	7 48.7	7 0.5	MAY 10	6 14.1
21	8 37.1	7 47.1	6 58.9	20	6 13.1
31	8 35.4	7 45.4	6 57.5	30	6 11.6
JUN 10	8 33.5	7 43.7	6 56.1	JUN 9	6 9.8
20	8 31.7	7 42.3	6 54.3	19	6 8.1
30	8 30.3	7 40.4	6 52.3	29	6 6.7
JUL 10	8 28.4	7 38.4	6 50.9	JUL 9	6 5.1
20	8 26.4	7 37.1	6 49.6	19	6 3.2
30	8 25.2	7 35.8	6 47.8	29	6 1.9
AUG 9	8 23.9	7 34.1	6 46.4	AUG 8	6 0.9
19	8 22.3	7 32.8	6 45.6	18	5 59.5
29	8 21.2	7 32.0	6 44.4	28	5 58.3
SEP 8	8 20.3	7 31.0	6 43.2	SEP 7	5 57.7
18	8 19.4	7 29.8	6 42.5	17	5 56.9
28	8 18.2	7 28.9	6 41.8	27	5 55.9
OCT 8	8 17.1	7 28.3	6 40.9	OCT 7	5 55.0
18	8 16.5	7 27.3	6 39.7	17	5 54.3
28	8 15.3	7 25.8	6 38.8	27	5 53.4
NOV 7	8 13.6	7 24.9	6 37.9	NOV 6	5 52.0
17	8 12.5	7 23.7	6 36.3	16	5 50.7
27	8 11.1	7 21.9	6 34.7	26	5 49.6
DEC 7	8 9.1	7 20.1	6 33.4	DEC 6	5 47.9
17	8 7.1	7 18.6	6 31.6	16	5 46.0
27	8 5.5	7 16.8	6 29.7	26	5 44.5
JAN 6	8 3.8	7 14.9	6 27.9	JAN 5	5 42.9

	COMMON YEARS			LEAP YEAR	
DATE	1940	1941	1942	DATE	1943
	6°	6°	6°		6°
JAN 1	5 43.4	4 58.5	4 14.5	JAN 1	3 29.8
11	5 41.6	4 57.2	4 13.0	11	3 27.8
21	5 40.4	4 55.7	4 11.1	21	3 26.3
31	5 38.9	4 54.1	4 9.8	31	3 25.2
FEB 10	5 37.5	4 52.9	4 8.8	FEB 10	3 23.8
20	5 36.4	4 52.0	4 7.6	20	3 22.5
MAR 2	5 35.4	4 51.1	4 6.5	MAR 1	3 21.9
12	5 34.8	4 50.1	4 5.7	11	3 21.0
22	5 33.7	4 49.2	4 5.2	21	3 20.0
APR 1	5 32.8	4 48.8	4 4.3	31	3 19.1
11	5 32.4	4 47.9	4 3.2	APR 10	3 18.5
21	5 31.3	4 46.6	4 2.5	20	3 17.6
MAY 1	5 30.0	4 45.8	4 1.6	30	3 16.2
11	5 29.0	4 44.8	4 0.1	MAY 10	3 15.0
21	5 27.7	4 43.2	3 58.7	20	3 14.0
31	5 26.1	4 41.7	3 57.4	30	3 12.3
JUN 10	5 24.4	4 40.2	3 55.9	JUN 9	3 10.6
20	5 22.9	4 38.7	3 54.1	19	3 9.1
30	5 21.5	4 36.9	3 52.4	29	3 7.5
JUL 10	5 19.7	4 35.2	3 51.0	JUL 9	3 5.8
20	5 18.1	4 34.1	3 49.6	19	3 4.0
30	5 17.0	4 32.7	3 47.8	29	3 2.8
AUG 9	5 15.7	4 31.1	3 46.7	AUG 8	3 1.7
19	5 14.4	4 30.2	3 45.9	18	3 0.2
29	5 13.5	4 29.4	3 44.6	28	2 59.1
SEP 8	5 12.7	4 28.4	3 43.6	SEP 7	2 58.5
18	5 11.9	4 27.4	3 43.0	17	2 57.6
28	5 11.0	4 26.7	3 42.3	27	2 56.5
OCT 8	5 10.1	4 26.1	3 41.3	OCT 7	2 55.8
18	5 9.6	4 25.1	3 40.2	17	2 55.0
28	5 8.4	4 23.3	3 39.5	27	2 53.9
NOV 7	5 7.1	4 23.1	3 38.5	NOV 6	2 52.5
17	5 6.1	4 21.9	3 36.8	16	2 51.3
27	5 4.7	4 20.1	3 35.4	26	2 50.1
DEC 7	5 2.8	4 18.6	3 34.1	DEC 6	2 48.2
17	5 1.2	4 17.1	3 32.2	16	2 46.4
27	4 59.7	4 15.3	3 30.4	26	2 44.9
JAN 6	4 58.0	4 13.5	3 28.8	JAN 5	2 43.1

	COMMON YEARS			LEAP YEAR	
DATE	1944	1945	1946	DATE	1947
	6°	6°	6°		6°
JAN 1	2 43.6	1 55.8	1 6.7	JAN 1	0 15.4
11	2 41.9	1 54.5	1 4.9	11	0 13.1
21	2 40.7	1 52.8	1 2.9	21	0 11.5
31	2 39.0	1 51.0	1 1.5	31	0 10.3
FEB 10	2 37.5	1 49.8	1 0.3	FEB 10	0 8.6
20	2 36.6	1 48.7	0 58.9	20	0 7.1
MAR 2	2 35.5	1 47.7	0 57.7	MAR 1	0 6.4
12	2 34.6	1 46.5	0 56.7	11	0 5.3
22	2 33.5	1 45.6	0 56.0	21	0 4.0
APR 1	2 32.7	1 45.0	0 54.9	31	0 3.0
11	2 32.1	1 43.8	0 53.6	APR 10	0 2.2
21	2 30.9	1 42.5	0 52.9	20	0 1.0
MAY 1	2 29.5	1 41.7	0 51.7	30	59 59.4
11	2 28.5	1 40.4	0 49.9	MAY 10	59 58.1
21	2 27.2	1 38.6	0 48.5	20	59 56.9
31	2 25.4	1 37.1	0 47.1	30	59 54.9
JUN 10	2 23.7	1 35.6	0 45.2	JUN 9	59 53.0
20	2 22.2	1 33.8	0 43.2	19	59 51.4
30	2 20.6	1 31.8	0 41.4	29	59 49.6
JUL 10	2 18.6	1 30.1	0 40.0	JUL 9	59 47.6
20	2 17.0	1 28.9	0 38.2	19	59 45.7
30	2 16.0	1 27.2	0 36.3	29	59 44.3
AUG 9	2 14.4	1 25.5	0 35.1	AUG 8	59 43.0
19	2 13.0	1 24.6	0 34.0	18	59 41.2
29	2 12.2	1 23.5	0 32.5	28	59 40.0
SEP 8	2 11.3	1 22.3	0 31.4	SEP 7	59 39.3
18	2 10.2	1 21.3	0 30.6	17	59 38.0
28	2 9.3	1 20.4	0 29.7	27	59 36.7
OCT 8	2 8.4	1 19.7	0 28.4	OCT 7	59 35.8
18	2 7.7	1 18.4	0 27.2	17	59 34.9
28	2 6.3	1 17.0	0 26.4	27	59 33.5
NOV 7	2 4.9	1 16.2	0 25.0	NOV 6	59 31.9
17	2 3.9	1 14.7	0 23.1	16	59 30.6
27	2 2.3	1 12.7	0 21.7	26	59 29.2
DEC 7	2 0.3	1 11.2	0 20.2	DEC 6	59 27.0
17	1 58.7	1 9.6	0 18.0	16	59 25.0
27	1 57.1	1 7.5	0 16.0	26	59 23.5
JAN 6	1 55.2	1 5.5	0 14.3	JAN 5	59 21.4

	COMMON YEARS			LEAP YEAR			COMMON YEARS			LEAP YEAR	
DATE	1948	1949	1950	DATE	1951	DATE	1952	1953	1954	DATE	1955
	5°	5°	5°		5°		5°	5°	5°		5°
JAN 1	59 21.8	58 27.1	57 32.0	JAN 1	56 36.1	JAN 1	55 40.0	54 45.1	53 51.9	JAN 1	52 60.0
11	59 20.1	58 25.7	57 30.0	11	56 33.7	11	55 38.3	54 43.7	53 49.9	11	52 57.8
21	59 18.7	58 23.7	57 27.8	21	56 32.1	21	55 36.9	54 41.6	53 47.8	21	52 56.4
31	60 16.7	68 21.7	67 26.4	01	00 00.7	01	55 34.0	54 39.7	53 46.6	31	52 55.0
FEB 10	59 15.0	58 20.4	57 25.0	FEB 10	56 28.9	FEB 10	55 33.1	54 38.5	53 45.2	FEB 10	52 53.3
20	59 14.0	58 19.2	57 23.4	20	56 27.3	20	55 32.1	54 37.2	53 43.7	20	52 52.0
MAR 2	59 12.7	58 17.8	57 22.0	MAR 1	56 26.6	MAR 2	55 30.7	54 35.9	53 42.4	MAR 1	52 51.3
12	59 11.5	58 16.5	57 20.9	11	56 25.4	12	55 29.5	54 34.6	53 41.5	11	52 50.2
22	59 10.2	58 15.4	57 20.1	21	56 24.0	22	55 28.1	54 33.7	53 40.7	21	52 49.0
APR 1	59 9.3	58 14.7	57 18.8	31	56 22.8	APR 1	55 27.3	54 32.9	53 39.4	31	52 48.0
11	59 8.5	58 13.3	57 17.3	APR 10	56 22.1	11	55 26.4	54 31.5	53 38.2	APR 10	52 47.4
21	59 6.9	58 11.8	57 16.6	20	56 20.8	21	55 24.8	54 30.1	53 37.5	20	52 46.2
MAY 1	59 5.4	58 10.9	57 15.2	30	56 19.0	MAY 1	55 23.4	54 29.3	53 36.2	30	52 44.6
11	59 4.4	58 9.4	57 13.3	MAY 10	56 17.8	11	55 22.3	54 27.7	53 34.4	MAY 10	52 43.6
21	59 2.7	58 7.4	57 11.8	20	56 16.5	21	55 20.5	54 25.8	53 33.0	20	52 42.4
31	59 0.7	58 5.7	57 10.3	30	56 14.3	31	55 18.5	54 24.2	53 31.6	30	52 40.4
JUN 10	58 58.8	58 4.1	57 8.3	JUN 9	56 12.4	JUN 10	55 16.7	54 22.6	53 29.7	JUN 9	52 38.7
20	58 57.2	58 2.1	57 6.1	19	56 10.7	20	55 15.0	54 20.7	53 27.7	19	52 37.2
30	58 55.4	57 59.9	57 4.2	29	56 8.9	30	55 13.2	54 18.6	53 25.9	29	52 35.4
JUL 10	58 53.1	57 58.1	57 2.7	JUL 9	56 6.8	JUL 10	55 10.9	54 16.8	53 24.4	JUL 9	52 33.4
20	58 51.5	57 56.7	57 0.7	19	56 4.8	20	55 9.3	54 15.5	53 22.5	19	52 31.7
30	58 50.3	57 54.8	56 58.7	29	56 3.4	30	55 8.1	54 13.5	53 20.7	29	52 30.5
AUG 9	58 48.4	57 52.9	56 57.5	AUG 8	56 1.9	AUG 9	55 6.2	54 11.8	53 19.6	AUG 8	52 29.0
19	58 46.8	57 52.0	56 56.2	18	56 0.1	19	55 4.6	54 10.9	53 18.4	18	52 27.4
29	58 45.9	57 50.7	56 54.5	28	55 58.9	29	55 3.7	54 9.6	53 16.8	28	52 26.4
SEP 8	58 44.7	57 49.2	56 53.4	SEP 7	55 58.1	SEP 8	55 2.5	54 8.2	53 15.9	SEP 7	52 25.7
18	58 43.4	57 48.1	56 52.5	17	55 56.7	18	55 1.2	54 7.2	53 15.0	17	52 24.5
28	58 42.3	57 47.1	56 51.4	27	55 55.4	28	55 0.1	54 6.3	53 14.0	27	52 23.4
OCT 8	58 41.3	57 46.2	56 50.0	OCT 7	55 54.5	OCT 8	54 59.2	54 5.4	53 12.8	OCT 7	52 22.6
18	58 40.4	57 44.7	56 48.7	17	55 53.5	18	54 58.1	54 3.9	53 11.7	17	52 21.8
28	58 38.7	57 43.2	56 47.8	27	55 52.0	28	54 56.5	54 2.7	53 10.9	27	52 20.5
NOV 7	58 37.2	57 42.3	56 46.3	NOV 6	55 50.3	NOV 7	54 55.1	54 1.7	53 9.4	NOV 6	52 19.0
17	58 36.1	57 40.5	56 44.3	16	55 49.1	17	54 54.0	54 0.0	53 7.6	16	52 18.0
27	58 34.2	57 38.4	56 42.8	26	55 47.6	27	54 52.0	53 58.0	53 6.3	26	52 16.5
DEC 7	58 32.0	57 36.8	56 41.2	DEC 6	55 45.3	DEC 7	54 49.9	53 56.6	53 4.8	DEC 6	52 14.4
17	58 30.3	57 35.1	56 38.9	16	55 43.3	17	54 48.3	53 54.8	53 2.6	16	52 12.8
27	58 28.5	57 32.8	56 36.8	26	55 41.8	27	54 46.4	53 52.6	53 0.7	26	52 11.3
JAN 6	58 26.3	57 30.7	56 35.1	JAN 5	55 39.6	JAN 6	54 44.3	53 50.6	52 59.1	JAN 5	52 9.3

	COMMON YEARS			LEAP YEAR			COMMON YEARS			LEAP YEAR	
DATE	1956	1957	1958	DATE	1959	DATE	1960	1961	1962	DATE	1963
	5°	5°	5°		5°		5°	5°	5°		5°
JAN 1	52 9.7	51 21.6	50 35.7	JAN 1	49 50.4	JAN 1	49 5.8	48 21.5	47 36.5	JAN 1	46 49.7
11	52 8.1	51 20.3	50 33.8	11	49 48.6	11	49 4.5	48 20.1	47 34.5	11	46 47.9
21	52 6.8	51 18.4	50 32.0	21	49 47.4	21	49 3.1	48 18.2	47 32.9	21	46 46.7
31	52 4.9	51 16.8	50 30.9	31	49 46.0	31	49 1.4	48 16.8	47 31.9	31	46 45.1
FEB 10	52 3.5	51 15.8	50 29.7	FEB 10	49 44.5	FEB 10	49 0.2	48 15.9	47 30.5	FEB 10	46 43.5
20	52 2.6	51 14.7	50 28.4	20	49 43.5	20	48 59.4	48 14.7	47 29.2	20	46 42.6
MAR 2	52 1.4	51 13.5	50 27.4	MAR 1	49 42.9	MAR 2	48 58.3	48 13.6	47 28.4	MAR 1	46 41.8
12	52 0.3	51 12.5	50 26.6	11	49 41.9	12	48 57.3	48 12.8	47 27.5	11	46 40.7
22	51 59.2	51 11.8	50 26.0	21	49 41.0	22	48 56.5	48 12.1	47 26.7	21	46 39.8
APR 1	51 58.6	51 11.1	50 24.9	31	49 40.2	APR 1	48 55.9	48 11.3	47 25.6	31	46 39.0
11	51 57.8	51 9.9	50 24.0	APR 10	49 39.6	11	48 55.1	48 10.2	47 24.8	APR 10	46 38.2
21	51 56.4	51 8.9	50 23.4	20	49 38.5	21	48 53.8	48 9.4	47 24.1	20	46 36.9
MAY 1	51 55.2	51 8.2	50 22.2	30	49 37.3	MAY 1	48 52.9	48 8.6	47 22.8	30	46 35.6
11	51 54.3	51 6.8	50 20.7	MAY 10	49 36.4	11	48 52.0	48 7.1	47 21.3	MAY 10	46 34.8
21	51 52.7	51 5.1	50 19.6	20	49 35.2	21	48 50.4	48 5.6	47 20.3	20	46 33.3
31	51 50.9	51 3.8	50 18.2	30	49 33.4	31	48 48.8	48 4.4	47 18.8	30	46 31.4
JUN 10	51 49.3	51 2.3	50 16.5	JUN 9	49 31.9	JUN 10	48 47.4	48 2.8	47 16.9	JUN 9	46 30.0
20	51 47.8	51 0.5	50 14.7	19	49 30.6	20	48 45.9	48 1.0	47 15.3	19	46 28.5
30	51 46.0	50 58.7	50 13.2	29	49 28.8	30	48 44.1	47 59.3	47 13.8	29	46 26.5
JUL 10	51 44.0	50 57.2	50 11.8	JUL 9	49 27.1	JUL 10	48 42.4	47 57.9	47 12.2	JUL 9	46 24.7
20	51 42.7	50 55.9	50 10.0	19	49 25.6	20	48 41.1	47 56.5	47 10.3	19	46 23.2
30	51 41.5	50 54.1	50 8.5	29	49 24.4	30	48 39.9	47 54.8	47 8.9	29	46 21.9
AUG 9	51 39.8	50 52.7	50 7.6	AUG 8	49 23.0	AUG 9	48 38.3	47 53.5	47 8.0	AUG 8	46 20.3
19	51 38.5	50 52.0	50 6.4	18	49 21.7	19	48 37.3	47 52.8	47 6.6	18	46 18.9
29	51 37.8	50 50.8	50 5.2	28	49 20.9	29	48 36.6	47 51.5	47 5.3	28	46 18.2
SEP 8	51 36.7	50 49.7	50 4.5	SEP 7	49 20.2	SEP 8	48 35.5	47 50.5	47 4.7	SEP 7	46 17.2
18	51 35.6	50 49.0	50 3.7	17	49 19.1	18	48 34.6	47 49.9	47 3.9	17	46 15.9
28	51 34.8	50 48.2	50 2.9	27	49 18.4	28	48 33.9	47 49.1	47 2.8	27	46 15.2
OCT 8	51 34.1	50 47.4	50 1.9	OCT 7	49 17.7	OCT 8	48 33.2	47 48.1	47 1.9	OCT 7	46 14.4
18	51 33.1	50 46.2	50 1.0	17	49 16.9	18	48 32.2	47 47.1	47 1.1	17	46 13.3
28	51 31.7	50 45.2	50 0.3	27	49 15.7	28	48 31.0	47 46.2	47 0.1	27	46 12.1
NOV 7	51 30.6	50 44.4	49 59.0	NOV 6	49 14.5	NOV 7	48 30.1	47 45.2	46 58.7	NOV 6	46 10.8
17	51 29.6	50 42.8	49 57.5	16	49 13.6	17	48 29.0	47 43.6	46 57.2	16	46 9.7
27	51 27.8	50 41.2	49 56.4	26	49 12.1	27	48 27.2	47 42.1	46 56.1	26	46 8.0
DEC 7	51 26.0	50 39.9	49 54.8	DEC 6	49 10.2	DEC 7	48 25.6	47 40.8	46 54.3	DEC 6	46 6.0
17	51 24.5	50 38.2	49 52.9	16	49 8.8	17	48 24.2	47 39.0	46 52.3	16	46 4.6
27	51 22.8	50 36.2	49 51.2	26	49 7.3	27	48 22.4	47 37.0	46 50.8	26	46 2.9
JAN 6	51 20.8	50 34.5	49 49.7	JAN 5	49 5.4	JAN 6	48 20.5	47 35.5	46 49.1	JAN 5	46 0.7

| | COMMON YEARS | | | LEAP YEAR | | COMMON YEARS | | | LEAP YEAR | |
DATE	1964	1965	1966	DATE	1967	DATE	1968	1969	1970	DATE	1971
	5°	5°	5°		5°		5°	5°	5°		5°
JAN 1	46 1.4	45 11.3	44 19.3	JAN 1	43 25.2	JAN 1	42 30.2	41 34.6	40 38.8	JAN 1	39 43.0
11	45 60.0	45 9.6	44 17.0	11	43 23.3	11	42 28.6	41 32.7	40 36.4	11	39 41.1
21	45 58.3	45 7.5	44 15.3	21	43 21.9	21	42 26.7	41 30.4	40 34.7	21	39 39.8
31	45 56.4	45 6.0	44 14.2	31	43 20.1	31	42 24.6	41 28.9	40 33.5	31	39 37.8
FEB 10	45 55.2	45 5.0	44 12.5	FEB 10	43 18.2	FEB 10	42 23.4	41 27.7	40 31.6	FEB 10	39 36.0
20	45 54.3	45 3.5	44 10.9	20	43 17.3	20	42 22.2	41 26.1	40 30.0	20	39 35.1
MAR 2	45 52.9	45 2.2	44 10.0	MAR 1	43 16.2	MAR 2	42 20.7	41 24.6	40 29.1	MAR 1	39 34.0
12	45 51.8	45 1.3	44 9.0	11	43 14.8	12	42 19.3	41 23.7	40 28.0	11	39 32.5
22	45 50.9	45 0.5	44 7.8	21	43 13.8	22	42 18.3	41 22.8	40 26.7	21	39 31.6
APR 1	45 50.2	44 59.4	44 6.6	31	43 12.8	APR 1	42 17.5	41 21.5	40 25.5	31	39 30.6
11	45 49.1	44 58.0	44 5.6	APR 10	43 11.8	11	42 16.1	41 20.0	40 24.5	APR 10	39 29.5
21	45 47.7	44 57.2	44 4.7	20	43 10.3	21	42 14.6	41 19.1	40 23.5	20	39 28.0
MAY 1	45 46.8	44 56.1	44 3.1	30	43 8.9	MAY 1	42 13.6	41 17.9	40 21.7	30	39 26.7
11	45 45.6	44 54.3	44 1.5	MAY 10	43 7.9	11	42 12.2	41 16.0	40 20.2	MAY 10	39 25.7
21	45 43.7	44 52.7	44 0.4	20	43 6.1	21	42 10.1	41 14.4	40 19.0	20	39 23.8
31	45 42.1	44 51.4	43 58.5	30	43 4.0	31	42 8.5	41 13.0	40 17.1	30	39 21.8
JUN 10	45 40.6	44 49.6	43 56.4	JUN 9	43 2.5	JUN 10	42 6.9	41 10.9	40 14.9	JUN 9	39 20.4
20	45 38.9	44 47.5	43 54.7	19	43 0.8	20	42 4.9	41 8.8	40 13.2	19	39 18.6
30	45 36.9	44 45.7	43 53.0	29	42 58.6	30	42 2.7	41 6.9	40 11.4	29	39 16.4
JUL 10	45 35.1	44 44.2	43 51.1	JUL 9	42 56.6	JUL 10	42 0.8	41 5.3	40 9.5	JUL 9	39 14.5
20	45 33.7	44 42.5	43 49.1	19	42 55.0	20	41 59.4	41 3.4	40 7.4	19	39 12.9
30	45 32.2	44 40.5	43 47.6	29	42 53.5	30	41 57.6	41 1.3	40 5.9	29	39 11.4
AUG 9	45 30.4	44 39.2	43 46.5	AUG 8	42 51.6	AUG 9	41 55.6	41 0.0	40 4.7	AUG 8	39 9.5
19	45 29.4	44 38.3	43 44.7	18	42 50.1	19	41 54.6	40 58.9	40 2.9	18	39 8.0
29	45 28.5	44 36.7	43 43.3	28	42 49.3	29	41 53.5	40 57.2	40 1.4	28	39 7.2
SEP 8	45 27.2	44 35.5	43 42.6	SEP 7	42 48.0	SEP 8	41 51.9	40 55.9	40 0.8	SEP 7	39 5.9
18	45 26.1	44 34.8	43 41.5	17	42 46.5	18	41 50.8	40 55.2	39 59.5	17	39 4.5
28	45 25.3	44 33.8	43 40.1	27	42 45.7	28	41 49.9	40 54.1	39 58.1	27	39 3.8
OCT 8	45 24.5	44 32.5	43 39.1	OCT 7	42 44.7	OCT 8	41 48.9	40 52.7	39 57.2	OCT 7	39 2.8
18	45 23.2	44 31.4	43 38.1	17	42 43.4	18	41 47.4	40 51.4	39 56.1	17	39 1.4
28	45 21.8	44 30.4	43 36.9	27	42 42.0	28	41 45.9	40 50.4	39 54.8	27	39 0.1
NOV 7	45 20.9	44 29.1	43 35.2	NOV 6	42 40.6	NOV 7	41 44.9	40 49.0	39 53.1	NOV 6	38 58.8
17	45 19.5	44 27.2	43 33.6	16	42 39.3	17	41 43.3	40 47.0	39 51.6	16	38 57.5
27	45 17.4	44 25.6	43 32.4	26	42 37.3	27	41 41.1	40 45.4	39 50.3	26	38 55.5
DEC 7	45 15.8	44 24.2	43 30.3	DEC 6	42 35.2	DEC 7	41 39.4	40 43.9	39 48.1	DEC 6	38 53.5
17	45 14.3	44 22.0	43 28.1	16	42 33.7	17	41 37.8	40 41.6	39 45.9	16	38 52.1
27	45 12.1	44 19.9	43 26.5	26	42 31.8	27	41 35.4	40 39.4	39 44.3	26	38 50.1
JAN 6	45 10.1	44 18.3	43 24.6	JAN 5	42 29.4	JAN 6	41 33.3	40 37.8	39 42.4	JAN 5	38 47.8

| | COMMON YEARS | | | LEAP YEAR | | COMMON YEARS | | | LEAP YEAR | |
DATE	1972	1973	1974	DATE	1975	DATE	1976	1977	1978	DATE	1979
	5°	5°	5°		5°		5°	5°	5°		5°
JAN 1	38 48.6	37 55.8	37 4.7	JAN 1	36 15.2	JAN 1	35 28.0	34 42.3	33 57.5	JAN 1	33 13.0
11	38 47.1	37 54.0	37 2.5	11	36 13.5	11	35 26.6	34 40.5	33 55.6	11	33 11.5
21	38 45.1	37 51.8	37 1.0	21	36 12.3	21	35 24.7	34 38.7	33 54.3	21	33 10.2
31	38 43.2	37 50.5	36 59.8	31	36 10.5	31	35 23.1	34 37.6	33 53.1	31	33 8.5
FEB 10	38 42.1	37 49.3	36 58.1	FEB 10	36 9.0	FEB 10	35 22.2	34 36.5	33 51.6	FEB 10	33 7.2
20	38 40.9	37 47.8	36 56.7	20	36 8.2	20	35 21.1	34 35.2	33 50.5	20	33 6.5
MAR 2	38 39.4	37 46.5	36 56.0	MAR 1	36 7.2	MAR 2	35 19.8	34 34.2	33 49.9	MAR 1	33 5.5
12	38 38.1	37 45.7	36 55.0	11	36 6.0	12	35 18.9	34 33.5	33 49.0	11	33 4.5
22	38 37.1	37 44.8	36 53.9	21	36 5.3	22	35 18.1	34 32.8	33 48.0	21	33 3.9
APR 1	38 36.4	37 43.6	36 52.8	31	36 4.5	APR 1	35 17.5	34 31.8	33 47.2	31	33 3.2
11	38 35.1	37 42.4	36 52.1	APR 10	36 3.5	11	35 16.3	34 30.8	33 46.6	APR 10	33 2.2
21	38 33.6	37 41.6	36 51.1	20	36 2.3	21	35 15.2	34 30.2	33 45.6	20	33 1.2
MAY 1	38 32.8	37 40.4	36 49.6	30	36 1.2	MAY 1	35 14.5	34 29.1	33 44.3	30	33 0.3
11	38 31.4	37 38.6	36 48.3	MAY 10	36 0.2	11	35 13.2	34 27.6	33 43.3	MAY 10	32 59.2
21	38 29.4	37 37.2	36 47.2	20	35 58.6	21	35 11.5	34 26.4	33 42.2	20	32 57.6
31	38 27.8	37 35.9	36 45.4	30	35 56.9	31	35 10.2	34 25.1	33 40.4	30	32 56.1
JUN 10	38 26.3	37 34.0	36 43.5	JUN 9	35 55.6	JUN 10	35 8.7	34 23.3	33 38.8	JUN 9	32 54.9
20	38 24.3	37 32.0	36 41.9	19	35 53.9	20	35 6.9	34 21.6	33 37.4	19	32 53.2
30	38 22.2	37 30.3	36 40.3	29	35 52.0	30	35 5.1	34 20.2	33 35.8	29	32 51.3
JUL 10	38 20.5	37 28.7	36 38.5	JUL 9	35 50.3	JUL 10	35 3.6	34 18.7	33 34.1	JUL 9	32 49.9
20	38 19.1	37 26.9	36 36.6	19	35 48.9	20	35 2.3	34 17.0	33 32.5	19	32 48.5
30	38 17.3	37 25.1	36 35.3	29	35 47.5	30	35 0.7	34 15.5	33 31.3	29	32 47.0
AUG 9	38 15.5	37 23.9	36 34.2	AUG 8	35 45.8	AUG 9	34 59.2	34 14.5	33 30.1	AUG 8	32 45.5
19	38 14.5	37 22.9	36 32.5	18	35 44.7	19	34 58.4	34 13.4	33 28.7	18	32 44.5
29	38 13.5	37 21.3	36 31.4	28	35 44.0	29	34 57.4	34 12.1	33 27.8	28	32 43.8
SEP 8	38 12.0	37 20.2	36 30.8	SEP 7	35 42.8	SEP 8	34 56.3	34 11.4	33 27.3	SEP 7	32 42.6
18	38 11.0	37 19.6	36 29.7	17	35 41.7	18	34 55.5	34 10.8	33 26.2	17	32 41.7
28	38 10.2	37 18.6	36 28.6	27	35 41.2	28	34 54.9	34 9.9	33 25.3	27	32 41.3
OCT 8	38 9.2	37 17.3	36 27.8	OCT 7	35 40.3	OCT 8	34 54.0	34 8.9	33 24.7	OCT 7	32 40.4
18	38 7.8	37 16.3	36 26.9	17	35 39.2	18	34 52.9	34 8.1	33 23.9	17	32 39.2
28	38 6.5	37 15.4	36 25.8	27	35 38.1	28	34 51.9	34 7.3	33 22.8	27	32 38.4
NOV 7	38 5.6	37 14.1	36 24.3	NOV 6	35 37.0	NOV 7	34 51.0	34 6.0	33 21.5	NOV 6	32 37.4
17	38 4.0	37 12.2	36 23.0	16	35 35.8	17	34 49.5	34 4.5	33 20.4	16	32 36.0
27	38 1.9	37 10.9	36 21.8	26	35 34.1	27	34 47.8	34 3.3	33 19.1	26	32 34.4
DEC 7	38 0.4	37 9.4	36 19.8	DEC 6	35 32.4	DEC 7	34 46.5	34 1.9	33 17.2	DEC 6	32 32.9
17	37 58.8	37 7.3	36 17.9	16	35 31.1	17	34 44.9	33 59.9	33 15.6	16	32 31.5
27	37 56.6	37 5.3	36 16.4	26	35 29.2	27	34 42.9	33 58.2	33 14.2	26	32 29.5
JAN 6	37 54.6	37 3.8	36 14.6	JAN 5	35 27.2	JAN 6	34 41.2	33 56.8	33 12.4	JAN 5	32 27.7

Table 1 (1980–1987)

	COMMON YEARS				LEAP YEAR		COMMON YEARS				LEAP YEAR
DATE	1980	1981	1982	DATE	1983	DATE	1984	1985	1986	DATE	1987
	5°	5°	5°		5°		5°	5°	5°		5°
JAN 1	32 28.5	31 42.9	30 55.5	JAN 1	30 6.4	JAN 1	29 15.7	28 22.9	27 28.3	JAN 1	26 32.8
11	32 27.0	31 41.0	30 53.6	11	30 4.9	11	29 14.0	28 20.7	27 26.2	11	26 31.2
21	32 25.2	31 39.3	30 52.3	21	30 3.3	21	29 11.9	28 18.8	27 24.8	21	26 29.4
31	32 23.8	31 38.2	30 50.9	31	30 1.4	31	29 10.0	28 17.7	27 20.1	01	26 27.3
FEB 10	32 22.9	31 36.9	30 49.2	FEB 10	30 0.1	FEB 10	29 9.3	28 16.0	27 21.2	FEB 10	26 26.0
20	32 21.6	31 35.5	30 48.2	20	29 59.3	20	29 7.8	28 14.4	27 20.1	20	26 25.0
MAR 2	32 20.4	31 34.7	30 47.4	MAR 1	29 57.9	MAR 2	29 6.3	28 13.5	27 19.2	MAR 1	26 23.4
12	32 19.7	31 33.9	30 46.3	11	29 56.8	12	29 5.5	28 12.5	27 17.8	11	26 22.2
22	32 18.9	31 33.0	30 45.3	21	29 56.2	22	29 4.6	28 11.3	27 16.6	21	26 21.5
APR 1	32 18.2	31 32.0	30 44.5	31	29 55.2	APR 1	29 3.5	28 10.1	27 15.6	31	26 20.3
11	32 17.1	31 31.1	30 43.7	APR 10	29 54.0	11	29 2.2	28 9.0	27 14.7	APR 10	26 18.9
21	32 16.1	31 30.4	30 42.5	20	29 52.9	21	29 1.1	28 8.1	27 13.2	20	26 17.6
MAY 1	32 15.3	31 29.0	30 41.0	30	29 51.9	MAY 1	29 0.2	28 6.5	27 11.5	30	26 16.6
11	32 13.9	31 27.5	30 40.0	MAY 10	29 50.5	11	28 58.4	28 4.8	27 10.5	MAY 10	26 15.0
21	32 12.3	31 26.4	30 38.7	20	29 48.7	21	28 56.6	28 3.7	27 8.9	20	26 13.0
31	32 11.1	31 25.0	30 36.7	30	29 47.2	31	28 55.4	28 1.9	27 6.7	30	26 11.5
JUN 10	32 9.6	31 23.0	30 35.1	JUN 9	29 45.8	JUN 10	28 53.6	27 59.7	27 5.0	JUN 9	26 10.0
20	32 7.7	31 21.4	30 33.7	19	29 43.8	20	28 51.4	27 58.0	27 3.5	19	26 7.7
30	32 6.0	31 19.9	30 31.8	29	29 41.8	30	28 49.7	27 56.3	27 1.3	29	26 5.6
JUL 10	32 4.6	31 18.2	30 29.9	JUL 9	29 40.3	JUL 10	28 48.1	27 54.4	26 59.3	JUL 9	26 4.1
20	32 3.1	31 16.5	30 28.4	19	29 38.7	20	28 46.4	27 52.4	26 57.6	19	26 2.3
30	32 1.5	31 15.0	30 27.1	29	29 36.9	30	28 44.4	27 50.8	26 56.1	29	26 0.3
AUG 9	32 0.1	31 14.0	30 25.6	AUG 8	29 35.3	AUG 9	28 43.0	27 49.6	26 54.4	AUG 8	25 58.6
19	31 59.4	31 12.7	30 24.1	18	29 34.2	19	28 42.1	27 48.0	26 52.7	18	25 57.4
29	31 58.2	31 11.3	30 23.2	28	29 33.2	29	28 40.6	27 46.5	26 51.8	28	25 56.2
SEP 8	31 57.1	31 10.7	30 22.4	SEP 7	29 31.8	SEP 8	28 39.2	27 45.7	26 50.8	SEP 7	25 54.6
18	31 56.5	31 9.9	30 21.2	17	29 30.8	18	28 38.6	27 44.7	26 49.3	17	25 53.6
28	31 55.7	31 8.8	30 20.2	27	29 30.2	28	28 37.6	27 43.3	26 48.2	27	25 52.9
OCT 8	31 54.7	31 7.9	30 19.5	OCT 7	29 29.0	OCT 8	28 36.3	27 42.3	26 47.4	OCT 7	25 51.5
18	31 53.7	31 7.0	30 18.5	17	29 27.7	18	28 35.2	27 41.3	26 46.1	17	25 50.1
28	31 52.7	31 6.1	30 17.1	27	29 26.8	28	28 34.0	27 40.1	26 44.6	27	25 49.1
NOV 7	31 51.7	31 4.6	30 15.8	NOV 6	29 25.6	NOV 7	28 32.8	27 38.4	26 43.1	NOV 6	25 47.8
17	31 50.1	31 3.0	30 14.6	16	29 23.9	17	28 30.9	27 36.7	26 41.8	16	25 46.0
27	31 48.5	31 1.9	30 13.0	26	29 22.1	27	28 29.1	27 35.4	26 40.0	26	25 44.0
DEC 7	31 47.2	31 0.2	30 10.9	DEC 6	29 20.5	DEC 7	28 27.8	27 33.4	26 37.7	DEC 6	25 42.4
17	31 45.5	30 58.0	30 9.3	16	29 18.9	17	28 25.7	27 31.0	26 36.0	16	25 40.7
27	31 43.4	30 56.5	30 7.8	26	29 16.7	27	28 23.4	27 29.4	26 34.4	26	25 38.2
JAN 6	31 41.9	30 55.0	30 5.7	JAN 5	29 14.7	JAN 6	28 21.8	27 27.7	26 32.0	JAN 5	25 36.2

Table 2 (1988–1995)

	COMMON YEARS				LEAP YEAR		COMMON YEARS				LEAP YEAR
DATE	1988	1989	1990	DATE	1991	DATE	1992	1993	1994	DATE	1995
	5°	5°	5°		5°		5°	5°	5°		5°
JAN 1	25 37.3	24 41.4	23 46.0	JAN 1	22 52.1	JAN 1	22 0.1	21 9.6	20 20.9	JAN 1	19 34.3
11	25 35.4	24 39.1	23 44.0	11	22 50.5	11	21 58.3	21 7.5	20 19.2	11	19 32.8
21	25 33.1	24 37.3	23 42.7	21	22 48.7	21	21 56.2	21 5.9	20 17.9	21	19 31.1
31	25 31.6	24 36.1	23 40.9	31	22 46.7	31	21 54.8	21 4.8	20 16.2	31	19 29.5
FEB 10	25 30.5	24 34.4	23 39.0	FEB 10	22 45.5	FEB 10	21 53.7	21 3.2	20 14.7	FEB 10	19 28.5
20	25 28.7	24 32.7	23 38.0	20	22 44.5	20	21 52.1	21 1.7	20 13.9	20	19 27.5
MAR 2	25 27.2	24 31.8	23 37.0	MAR 1	22 43.0	MAR 2	21 50.8	21 1.0	20 12.9	MAR 1	19 26.3
12	25 26.3	24 30.7	23 35.6	11	22 42.0	12	21 50.1	21 0.1	20 11.8	11	19 25.5
22	25 25.3	24 29.5	23 34.5	21	22 41.3	22	21 49.1	20 59.0	20 10.9	21	19 24.9
APR 1	25 24.1	24 28.2	23 33.5	31	22 40.2	APR 1	21 48.0	20 58.0	20 10.2	31	19 24.0
11	25 22.7	24 27.2	23 32.6	APR 10	22 38.9	11	21 46.8	20 57.1	20 9.3	APR 10	19 23.0
21	25 21.6	24 26.2	23 31.1	20	22 37.7	21	21 45.9	20 56.2	20 8.1	20	19 22.1
MAY 1	25 20.5	24 24.5	23 29.6	30	22 36.8	MAY 1	21 44.9	20 54.8	20 6.9	30	19 21.2
11	25 18.6	24 22.8	23 28.6	MAY 10	22 35.3	11	21 43.1	20 53.3	20 6.0	MAY 10	19 19.8
21	25 16.8	24 21.7	23 27.0	20	22 33.3	21	21 41.6	20 52.3	20 4.5	20	19 18.2
31	25 15.5	24 19.9	23 24.8	30	22 32.0	31	21 40.4	20 50.6	20 2.6	30	19 17.1
JUN 10	25 13.5	24 17.6	23 23.2	JUN 9	22 30.5	JUN 10	21 38.5	20 48.7	20 1.3	JUN 9	19 15.6
20	25 11.3	24 15.9	23 21.6	19	22 28.3	20	21 36.5	20 47.2	19 59.8	19	19 13.7
30	25 9.5	24 14.3	23 19.5	29	22 26.4	30	21 34.8	20 45.6	19 57.9	29	19 12.1
JUL 10	25 7.8	24 12.3	23 17.5	JUL 9	22 25.0	JUL 10	21 33.2	20 43.8	19 56.1	JUL 9	19 10.7
20	25 6.0	24 10.2	23 15.9	19	22 23.2	20	21 31.5	20 42.0	19 54.7	19	19 9.1
30	25 4.0	24 8.7	23 14.5	29	22 21.3	30	21 29.7	20 40.6	19 53.4	29	19 7.5
AUG 9	25 2.5	24 7.5	23 12.8	AUG 8	22 19.8	AUG 9	21 28.4	20 39.5	19 51.9	AUG 9	19 6.2
19	25 1.5	24 5.8	23 11.1	18	22 18.7	19	21 27.5	20 38.0	19 50.6	18	19 5.3
29	24 59.9	24 4.2	23 10.3	28	22 17.5	29	21 26.0	20 36.8	19 49.9	28	19 4.2
SEP 8	24 58.5	24 3.6	23 9.3	SEP 7	22 16.1	SEP 8	21 24.8	20 36.2	19 49.0	SEP 7	19 3.0
18	24 57.9	24 2.5	23 7.8	17	22 15.2	18	21 24.3	20 35.2	19 47.8	17	19 2.4
28	24 56.7	24 1.2	23 6.9	27	22 14.6	28	21 23.3	20 34.1	19 47.1	27	19 1.8
OCT 8	24 55.3	24 0.1	23 6.1	OCT 7	22 13.3	OCT 8	21 22.1	20 33.3	19 46.4	OCT 7	19 0.7
18	24 54.2	23 59.0	23 4.8	17	22 12.0	18	21 21.1	20 32.5	19 45.4	17	18 59.8
28	24 53.0	23 57.8	23 3.4	27	22 11.1	28	21 20.1	20 31.3	19 44.2	27	18 59.0
NOV 7	24 51.6	23 56.1	23 2.0	NOV 6	22 9.9	NOV 7	21 18.9	20 29.9	19 43.0	NOV 6	18 57.9
17	24 49.7	23 54.4	23 0.8	16	22 8.2	17	21 17.1	20 28.5	19 41.9	16	18 56.4
27	24 47.9	23 53.1	22 59.0	26	22 6.4	27	21 15.6	20 27.3	19 40.3	26	18 54.9
DEC 7	24 46.5	23 51.1	22 56.8	DEC 6	22 4.9	DEC 7	21 14.3	20 25.4	19 38.4	DEC 6	18 53.6
17	24 44.3	23 48.8	22 55.2	16	22 3.2	17	21 12.2	20 23.4	19 37.0	16	18 51.9
27	24 42.0	23 47.2	22 53.5	26	22 0.9	27	21 10.1	20 22.0	19 35.4	26	18 49.9
JAN 6	24 40.4	23 45.4	22 51.2	JAN 5	21 59.1	JAN 6	21 8.7	20 20.3	19 33.4	JAN 5	18 48.4

Appendix C — Universal PSSR Increment

1947 SSRY = 30:20:48

	January	February	March	April	May	June	July	August	September	October	November	December
1	0: 0: 0	2:48: 8	5: 5: 3	7:31: 7	9:51:30	12:26: 5	15: 3: 5	17:41:30	20: 8:51	22:25:26	24:51:32	27:26:53
2	0: 5:36	2:53:18	5:11:18	7:35:43	9:56:19	12:31:15	15: 8:19	17:46:25	20:13:26	22:30: 0	24:56:28	27:32:19
3	0:11:11	2:58:28	5:16:33	7:40:20	10: 1: 8	12:36:24	15:13:33	17:51:20	20:18: 2	22:34:35	25: 1:24	27:37:46
4	0:16:45	3: 3:37	5:22:17	7:44:20	10: 5:58	12:41:35	15:18:46	17:56:14	20:22:37	22:39:49	25: 6:20	27:43:14
5	0:22:20	3: 8:45	5:28: 7	7:49:32	10:10:49	12:46:45	15:23:58	18: 6: 8	20:27: 7	22:43:20	25:16:20	27:54:12
6	0:27:55	3:13:53	5:33:36	7:54: 8	10:15:40	12:51:58	15:29:11	18: 6: 0	20:31:45	22:43:45	25:21:20	27:59:42
7	0:33:27	3:18:57	5:38:17	7:58:46	10:20:32	12:57:10	15:34:25	18: 8: 0	20:36:10	22:52:56	25:26:25	28: 5:13
8	0:38:59	3:24: 1	5:42:56	8: 3:23	10:25:25	13: 2:22	15:39:37	18:15:43	20:40:53	22:57:33	25:31:25	28:10:44
9	0:44:31	3:29: 0	5:47:28	8: 8: 0	10:30:18	13: 7:35	15:44:48	18:20:34	20:45:27	23: 2:10	25:36:29	28:16:16
10	0:50: 3	3:34: 4	5:49:28	8:12:38	10:35:12	13:12:48	15:49:59	18:25:24	20:50: 0	23: 6:48	25:41:26	28:21:46
11	0:55:34	3:39: 4	5:56: 2	8:17:16	10:40: 7	13:18: 2	15:55:11	18:30:13	20:54:33	23:11:26	25:46:40	28:27:23
12	1: 1: 3	3:44: 9	6: 3:27	8:21:54	10:45: 3	13:23:16	16: 0:20	18:35: 1	20:59: 9	23:16:22	25:51:47	28:32:57
13	1: 6:33	3:49: 6	6: 6:33	8:26:33	10:49:59	13:28:30	16: 5:30	18:39:48	21: 3:39	23:20:44	25:56:55	28:38:31
14	1:12: 2	3:54: 2	6:12:44	8:31:12	10:54:56	13:33:44	16:10:39	18:44:35	21: 8:11	23:30: 6	26: 2:15	28:49:47
15	1:17:30	3:59: 6	6:17:22	8:35:51	10:59:54	13:39: 0	16:15:48	18:49:22	21:12:44	23:30:46	26: 7:15	29: 0:23
16	1:22:57	4: 4: 0	6:22:57	8:40:31	11: 4:52	13:44:15	16:20:46	18:54:52	21:17:16	23:34:46	26:12: 7	29: 0:53
17	1:28:24	4: 8:57	6:26:38	8:45: 2	11: 9:52	13:49:30	16:26:48	18:58:52	21:21:48	23:44:11	26:17:39	29: 6:29
18	1:33:50	4:13:53	6:31:15	8:49:52	11:14:52	13:55:2	16:31:10	19: 3:36	21:26:21	23:44:11	26:22:53	29:12: 2
19	1:39:14	4:18:47	6:35:52	8:54:33	11:19:54	14: 0:15	16:36:16	19: 8:20	21:30:53	23:53:38	26:28: 7	29:17:42
20	1:44:37	4:23:41	6:40:29	8:59:15	11:24:57	14: 5:16	16:41:21	19:13: 3	21:35:25	23:58:23	26:33:23	29:23:20
21	1:50: 0	4:28:33	6:45:42	9: 3:57	11:30: 1	14:10:32	16:46:25	19:17:45	21:39:58	23:59:19	26:38:40	29:28:56
22	1:55:22	4:33:24	6:49:42	9: 8:30	11:35: 6	14:15:48	16:51:29	19:22:26	21:44:30	24: 7:55	26:43:57	29:34:33
23	2: 0:43	4:38:15	6:54:18	9:13:20	11:40:12	14:21:4	16:56:33	19:27: 7	21:49: 2	24:12:42	26:49:16	29:40: 8
24	2: 6: 2	4:43: 5	6:58:55	9:18: 7	11:45:15	14:26: 19	17: 1:46	19:31:48	21:53:35	24:17:31	26:54:35	29:45:46
25	2:11:21	4:47:54	7: 1:31	9:22:37	11:50:19	14:31:36	17: 6:38	19:36:27	21:58: 7	24:22:19	26:59:56	29:51:23
26	2:16:41	4:52:42	7: 8: 7	9:27:37	11:55:19	14:36:50	17:11:39	19:41:45	22: 7:10	24:27: 0	27: 5:17	29:57: 2
27	2:21:58	4:57:30	7:13:43	9:32:22	12: 0:25	14:42:4	17:16:39	19:45:45	22: 7:13	24:32: 9	27:10:40	30: 2:36
28	2:27:18	5: 2:17	7:18:43	9:37: 8	12: 5:34	14:47:26	17:21:43	19:50:23	22:16:19	24:37: 9	27:16: 3	30: 8:13
29	2:32:29		7:21:55	9:41:55	12:10:43	14:52:26	17:26:39	19:55:1	22:16:10	24:41:44	27:21:28	30:13:49
30	2:37:43		7:21:55	9:46:42	12:15:47	14:52:41	17:31:36	19:59:38	22:20:52	24:41:44		30:13:49
31	2:42:56		7:26:31		12:20:56		17:36:33	20: 1:14		24:46:38		30:13:49

1948 SSRY = 30: 9:43

	January	February	March	April	May	June	July	August	September	October	November	December
1	0: 0: 0	2:47:13	5:10: 7	7:33:12	9:52:54	12:26:47	15: 2:53	17:40: 7	20: 6:19	22:22: 4	24:47:33	27:22:21
2	0: 5:34	2:52:22	5:14:50	7:37:47	9:57:41	12:31:51	15: 8: 5	17:45: 0	20:10:53	22:22: 4	24:52:28	27:27:46
3	0:11: 7	2:57:30	5:19:33	7:42:22	10: 2:29	12:37: 4	15:13:17	17:49:53	20:15:27	22:35:44	24:57:24	27:33:11
4	0:16:40	3: 2:37	5:24:16	7:46:56	10: 7:18	12:42:13	15:18:28	17:54:45	20:20: 0	22:35:44	25: 2:20	27:38:38
5	0:22:12	3: 2:37	5:28:59	7:51:31	10:12: 7	12:47:22	15:23:40	17:59:36	20:24:33	22:40:27	25: 7:18	27:44:35
6	0:27:42	3: 7:43	5:33:36	7:56: 6	10:16:57	12:52:33	15:28:51	18: 4:27	20:33:38	22:44:27	25:12:18	27:44:33
7	0:33:15	3:12:49	5:38:17	8: 0:42	10:21:48	12:57:44	15:34: 1	18: 9:17	20:38:10	22:49:27	25:17:16	27:55: 2
8	0:38:46	3:17:53	5:42:56	8: 5:18	10:26:40	13: 3: 8	15:39:11	18:14: 8	20:42:42	22:54: 2	25:22:17	28: 6: 0
9	0:44:17	3:22:58	5:47:35	8: 9:54	10:36:26	13: 8: 6	15:44:21	18:18:54	20:47:13	22:58:38	25:27:19	28: 6: 2
10	0:49:47	3:27:59	5:52:14	8:14:30	10:36:26	13:13:18	15:49:30	18:23:41	20:51:44	23: 3:15	25:32:22	28:11:32
11	0:55:16	3:32:59	5:56:52	8:19: 8	10:41:15	13:18:30	15:54:38	18:28:28	20:56:14	23: 7:59	25:37:26	28:17: 3
12	1: 0:44	3:37:57	6: 1:30	8:23:44	10:46: 4	13:23:44	15:59:46	18:33:24	21: 0:44	23:12: 7	25:42:35	28:22:35
13	1: 6:12	3:42:57	6: 6: 7	8:28:21	10:51: 9	13:28:55	16: 4:54	18:37:59	21: 5:20	23:17:27	25:47:36	28:28: 7
14	1:11:39	3:47:57	6:10:44	8:32:59	10:56: 6	13:34: 8	16:10: 7	18:42:44	21: 9:48	23:26:25	25:52:43	28:33:40
15	1:17: 6	3:52:55	6:15:21	8:37:37	11: 1: 2	13:39:21	16:15: 7	18:47:28	21:14:18	23:30:25	26: 3:11	28:39:13
16	1:22:31	3:57:50	6:19:33	8:42:15	11: 5:59	13:44:34	16:20:12	18:52:11	21:18:48	23:30:25	26: 3:11	28:44:46
17	1:27:58	4: 2:40	6:24:33	8:46:55	11:10:57	13:44:48	16:25:18	18:57: 3	21:23:19	23:35:27	26: 8:21	28:50:25
18	1:33:20	4: 7:40	6:29:33	8:51:34	11:15:56	13:55: 1	16:30:21	19: 1:35	21:27:49	23:40:27	26:13:22	28:55:53
19	1:38:42	4:12:33	6:33:44	8:56:14	11:20:55	14: 0:15	16:35:25	19: 6:16	21:32:20	23:49:52	26:18:34	29: 1:28
20	1:44: 4	4:17:26	6:38:20	9: 0:54	11:25:55	14: 5:28	16:40:28	19:10:57	21:36:50	23:54:36	26:23:47	29: 2:37
21	1:49:26	4:22:17	6:42:55	9: 5:35	11:30:56	14:10:42	16:45:30	19:15:36	21:41:21	24: 4:53	26:29: 2	29:12:37
22	1:54:46	4:27: 8	6:47:30	9:10:15	11:35:58	14:15:55	16:50:31	19:20:36	21:45:53	24:18:28	26:34:46	29:18:11
23	2: 0: 5	4:31:57	6:52: 4	9:14:58	11:41: 0	14:21: 8	16:55:31	19:25:36	21:50:22	24:18:28	26:39:59	29:23:46
24	2: 5:23	4:36:45	6:56:38	9:19:40	11:46: 2	14:26:22	17: 0:30	19:30:36	21:54:53	24:18:26	26:44:51	29:29:21
25	2:10:40	4:41:35	7: 1:13	9:24:23	11:51: 6	14:31:36	17: 5:30	19:34:10	21:59:24	24:23:15	26:50:10	29:34:56
26	2:15:56	4:46:22	7: 5:47	9:29: 7	11:56:10	14:36:50	17:10:30	19:38:47	22: 3:56	24:28:15	26:55:29	29:40:31
27	2:21:12	4:51: 9	7:10:20	9:33:51	12: 1:15	14:42: 5	17:15:28	19:43:23	22: 8:56	24:28:15	27: 0:50	29:46: 6
28	2:26:29	4:55:54	7:15:29	9:38:51	12: 6:19	14:47:22	17:20:28	19:48: 1	22:13:26	24:33:15	27: 6:14	29:51:44
29	2:31:33	5: 0:24	7:19:29	9:43:25	12:11:26	14:52:28	17:25:22	19:52:35	22:17:32	24:38:15	27:11:33	29:57:15
30	2:36:51		7:24: 4	9:48: 7	12:16:32	14:57:41	17:30:17	19:57:10	22:17:32	24:37:47	27:16:56	30: 2:49
31	2:42: 3		7:28:38		12:21:39		17:35:12	20: 1:45		24:42:40		30: 8:23

1949 SSRY = 30:18: 9

Day	January	February	March	April	May	June	July	August	September	October	November	December
1	0: 0: 0	2:47:41	5: 6:11	7:29:58	9:50:15	12:24:46	15: 1:35	17:39:37	20: 6:36	22:22:58	24:49: 3	27:24:25
2	0: 5:35	2:52:51	5:10:56	7:34:34	9:55: 5	12:29:56	15: 6:49	17:44:32	20:11:11	22:27:32	24:53:58	27:29:51
3	0:11:10	2:58: 0	5:15:40	7:39:10	9:59:53	12:35: 6	15:12: 2	17:49:27	20:15:46	22:32:41	25: 8:52	27:35:18
4	0:16:44	3: 3:10	5:20:23	7:43:46	10: 4:41	12:40:16	15:17:15	17:54:20	20:20:22	22:41:16	25: 8:51	27:40:44
5	0:22:19	3: 8:18	5:25:48	7:48:39	10: 9:34	12:45:28	15:22:28	17:59:13	20:24:54	22:45:52	25:13:51	27:46:14
6	0:27:51	3:13:21	5:29:48	7:52:59	10:14:25	12:50:39	15:27:40	18: 4: 5	20:29:28	22:50:28	25:18:51	27:51:44
7	0:33:23	3:18:25	5:34:24	7:57:35	10:19:17	12:55:51	15:32:52	18: 8:56	20:34: 1	22:55:41	25:23:53	27:57:13
8	0:38:55	3:23:28	5:39:10	8: 2:12	10:24:10	13: 1: 3	15:38: 3	18:13:46	20:38:34	22:59:41	25:28:56	28: 2:44
9	0:44:27	3:28:32	5:43:51	8: 6:49	10:29: 3	13: 6:16	15:43:14	18:18:36	20:43:40	23: 4:18	25:34: 0	28: 8:15
10	0:49:58	3:33:33	5:48:51	8:11:27	10:33:56	13:11:28	15:48:25	18:23:26	20:47:40	23: 8:56	25:39: 5	28:13:47
11	0:55:29	3:38:34	5:53:10	8:16:10	10:38:52	13:16:42	15:53:34	18:28:17	20:52:12	23:13:35	25:44:18	28:19:20
12	1: 0:57	3:43:34	5:57:49	8:20:43	10:43:47	13:21:59	15:58:44	18:33: 7	20:56:45	23:18:14	25:49:18	28:24:53
13	1: 6:25	3:48:32	6: 7: 6	8:25:27	10:48:41	13:27: 5	16: 3:54	18:37:46	21: 1:17	23:22:53	25:54:36	28:30:26
14	1:11:53	3:53:30	6:11:41	8:30: 0	10:53:48	13:32:23	16: 9: 3	18:42:32	21: 5:49	23:27:34	25:49:18	28:36: 0
15	1:17:20	3:58:27	6:15:?	8:34:39	10:58:38	13:37:33	16:14:18	18:47:17	21:10:28	23:32:15	26: 4:46	28:47:10
16	1:22:46	4: 3:23	6:20:58	8:39:58	11: 3:36	13:42:42	16:19:24	18:52:?	21:14:53	23:36:57	26: 9:57	28:52:45
17	1:28:12	4: 8:17	6:25:35	8:43:58	11: 8:36	13:48:51	16:24:28	18:56:46	21:19:24	23:41:39	26:15:10	28:58:21
18	1:33:36	4:13:11	6:30:12	8:48:39	11:13:36	13:53:22	16:29:28	19: 1:30	21:23:56	23:46:23	26:20:23	29: 3:56
19	1:39: 0	4:18: 4	6:34:48	8:53:19	11:18:36	13:58:37	16:34:33	19: 6:12	21:28:28	23:51: 7	26:25:38	29: 9:33
20	1:44:23	4:22:56	6:39:25	8:58: 1	11:23:33	14: 3:52	16:39:36	19:10:54	21:33: 2	23:55:52	26:30:44	29:15:10
21	1:49:44	4:27:48	6:44: 1	9: 2:41	11:28:40	14: 9: 7	16:44:44	19:15:35	21:37:37	24: 0:38	26:35:58	29:20:45
22	1:55: 5	4:32:40	6:48:37	9: 7:12	11:33:40	14:14:22	16:49:52	19:20:16	21:42:34	24: 5:24	26:41:28	29:26:22
23	2: 0:25	4:37:28	6:53:12	9:12: 8	11:38:40	14:19:37	16:54:57	19:24:57	21:46:36	24:10:12	26:46:47	29:31:58
24	2: 5:44	4:42:17	6:57:48	9:16:52	11:43:50	14:24:52	16:59:49	19:29:37	21:51: 8	24:15: 0	26:52: 2	29:37:35
25	2:11: 2	4:47: 5	7: 2:24	9:21:36	11:48:50	14:30: 8	17: 4:50	19:34:16	21:55:30	24:19:59	26:57:28	29:43:48
26	2:16:20	4:51:53	6:57:48	9:26:21	11:54: 0	14:35:23	17: 9:51	19:38:55	22: 0:15	24:24:50	27: 2:50	29:54:24
27	2:21:36	4:56:40	7: 2:24	9:31: 5	11:58: 2	14:40:37	17:14:49	19:43:33	22: 4:39	24:29:30	27: 8:12	30: 0: 0
28	2:26:52	5: 1:26	7:11:35	9:35:53	12: 4:13	14:45:52	17:19:49	19:48:10	22: 9:18	24:34:24	27:13:36	30: 5:36
29	2:32: 5		7:16:11	9:40:39	12: 9:21	14:51: 7	17:24:47	19:52:47	22:13:51	24:39:14	27:19: 0	30:11:12
30	2:37:18		7:20:46	9:45:27	12:14:29	14:56:21	17:29:45	19:57:24	22:18:25	24:44: 8		
31	2:42:30		7:25:22		12:19:37		17:34:41	20: 2: 0				

1950 SSRY = 30:21:17

Day	January	February	March	April	May	June	July	August	September	October	November	December
1	0: 0: 0	2:48: 4	5: 6:55	7:31: 0	9:51:29	12:26:12	15: 3:16	17:41:39	20: 8:57	22:25:34	24:51:48	27:27:18
2	0: 5:35	2:53:15	5:11:40	7:35:36	9:56:18	12:31:22	15: 8:30	17:46:35	20:13:33	22:30: 8	24:56:43	27:32:44
3	0:11:11	2:58:24	5:16:25	7:40:12	10: 1: 7	12:36:32	15:13:44	17:51:29	20:18:43	22:34:43	25: 1:39	27:38:10
4	0:16:45	3: 3:33	5:21: 9	7:44:49	10: 5:48	12:41:43	15:18:58	17:56:23	20:23:18	22:39:18	25: 6:38	27:43:37
5	0:22:19	3: 8:41	5:25:52	7:49:25	10:10:48	12:46:54	15:24: 9	18: 1:17	20:27:18	22:43:53	25: 6:39	27:49: 9
6	0:27:53	3:13:47	5:30:34	7:54: 4	10:15:40	12:52: 6	15:29:24	18: 6: 9	20:31:48	22:48:29	25:11:37	27:54:38
7	0:33:26	3:18:49	5:35:16	7:58:39	10:20:32	12:57:19	15:34:38	18:11: 1	20:36:26	22:53: 6	25:16:37	23: 0: 9
8	0:38:59	3:23:56	5:39:56	8: 3:18	10:25:25	13: 2:31	15:39:48	18:15:52	20:41: 0	22:57:42	25:21:38	23: 5:40
9	0:44:31	3:29: 0	5:44:39	8: 8:17	10:30:19	13: 7:44	15:45: 0	18:20:43	20:45:34	23: 2:20	25:26:40	23:11:12
10	0:50:33	3:34: 0	5:49:39	8:12:54	10:35:15	13:12:58	15:50: 9	18:25:32	20:50:19	23: 6:44	25:31:44	23:16:44
11	0:55:33	3:39: 9	5:53:59	8:17:30	10:40: 9	13:18:11	15:55:22	18:30:21	20:54:40	23:11:36	25:36:53	23:22:17
12	1: 1: 0	3:44: 4	5:58:38	8:21:49	10:45: 5	13:23:26	16: 0:32	18:35:10	20:59:13	23:16:15	25:41:53	23:27:51
13	1: 6:33	3:49: 4	6: 3:18	8:26:27	10:50: 5	13:28:41	16: 5:42	18:39:57	21: 3:46	23:20:55	25:47: 0	23:33:25
14	1:12: 1	3:54: 0	6: 7:57	8:31: 6	10:54:59	13:33:55	16:10:52	18:44:44	21: 8:18	23:25:35	25:52: 7	23:39: 0
15	1:17:29	3:59: 0	6:12:36	8:35:46	11: 0: 4	13:39: 9	16:15:59	18:49:30	21:12:21	23:30:15	25:57:16	23:44:35
16	1:22:56	4: 3:53	6:17:14	8:40:25	11: 4:58	13:44:24	16:21: 5	18:54:16	21:17:23	23:34:57	26: 2:35	23:50:10
17	1:28:23	4: 8:45	6:21:52	8:45: 5	11: 9:56	13:49:41	16:26:11	18:59: 1	21:21:56	23:39:40	26: 7:35	23:55:46
18	1:33:48	4:13:41	6:26:30	8:49:48	11:14:57	13:54:57	16:31:21	19: 3:44	21:26:28	23:44:22	26:12:48	29: 1:22
19	1:39: 7	4:18:41	6:31: 7	8:54:30	11:19:58	14: 0:12	16:36:27	19: 8:28	21:31: 0	23:49: 6	26:18: 0	29: 6:58
20	1:44:37	4:23:34	6:35:44	8:59:11	11:25: 0	14: 5:28	16:41:37	19:13:10	21:35:33	23:53:50	26:23:14	29:12:35
21	1:49:59	4:28:27	6:40:22	9: 3:54	11:30: 0	14:10:44	16:46:37	19:17:52	21:40:25	23:58:45	26:28:29	29:18:11
22	1:55:33	4:33:18	6:45: 0	9: 8:20	11:35: 1	14:16: 0	16:51:52	19:22:33	21:44:37	24: 3:58	26:33:45	29:23:48
23	2: 0:47	4:38:18	6:49:37	9:13: 0	11:40:11	14:21:15	16:56:52	19:27:15	21:49:19	24: 8: 8	26:44:20	29:29:25
24	2: 6:12	4:42:58	6:54:17	9:18: 5	11:45:14	14:26:31	17: 1:47	19:31:55	21:53:42	24:12:44	26:49:39	29:35: 2
25	2:11:21	4:47:48	6:58:47	9:22:44	11:50:25	14:31:46	17: 6:49	19:36:34	21:58:14	24:17:44	26:54:58	29:40:15
26	2:16:39	4:52:35	7: 3:23	9:27:34	11:55:25	14:37: 2	17:11:49	19:41:13	22: 2:47	24:22:33	27: 0:19	29:46:15
27	2:21:57	5: 2: 9	7: 7:59	9:32:23	12: 0:38	14:42:17	17:16:49	19:45:52	22: 7:20	24:27:23	27: 5:41	29:51:52
28	2: 6: 2		7:12:39	9:37:37	12: 5:38	14:47:32	17:21:48	19:50:30	22:11:53	24:32:14	27:11:41	29:57:29
29	2:27:12		7:17:18	9:41:53	12:10:48	14:52:47	17:26:48	19:55:47	22:16:26	24:37: 2	27:16:28	30: 8:42
30	2:32:26		7:21:48	9:46:41	12:15:54	14:58: 2	17:31:46	19:59:44	22:21: 0	24:41:59	27:21:52	30: 8:42
31	2:42:52		7:26:24		12:21: 3		17:36:43	20: 4:21		24:46:53		30:14:18

1951   SSRY = 30: 4:46

	January	February	March	April	May	June	July	August	September	October	November	December
1	30: 4:46	2:46:38	5: 4:20	7:27: 9	9:46:20	12:19:14	14:55:12	17:32:13	19:58:15	22:13:38	24:38:28	27:17:27
2	0: 5:33	2:51:46	5: 9: 3	7:31:43	9:51: 6	12:24:41	15: 0:23	17:37: 6	20: 7:22	22:18:10	24:43:21	27:17:50
3	0:11: 5	2:56:54	5:13:45	7:36:17	9:55:53	12:29:49	15: 5:35	17:41:58	20:11:54	22:27:15	24:48:15	27:23:15
4	0:16:37	3: 2: 5	5:18:27	7:40:51	10: 0:40	12:34:57	15:10:46	17:46:50	20:16:57	22:27:15	24:53:10	27:28:40
5	0:22: 8	3: 7: 9	5:23:47	7:45:24	10: 5:27	12:45:15	15:15:57	17:51:42	20:20:59	22:40:55	26: 3: 0	27:33:32
6	0:27:38	3:12:10	5:27:48	7:50:10	10:10:18	12:50:24	15:21: 7	17:56:31	20:25:30	22:45:29	25: 8: 3	27:39:43
7	0:33:10	3:17:12	5:32:28	7:54:34	10:15: 7	12:55:34	15:26:16	18: 1:21	20:30: 2	22:50: 4	25:13: 0	27:44:59
8	0:38:40	3:22:14	5:37: 1	7:59: 9	10:19:58	13: 0:44	15:31:26	18: 6:10	20:34:33	22:54:39	25:18: 0	27:50:27
9	0:44: 8	3:27:15	5:41:46	8: 3:44	10:24:49	13: 5: 6	15:36:35	18:10:58	20:39: 4	22:59:14	25:23: 2	27:55:56
10	0:49:38	3:32:15	5:46:24	8: 8:18	10:29:39	13:10:16	15:41:47	18:15:46	20:43:34	23: 3:51	25:28: 4	28: 1:25
11	0:55: 8	3:37:15	5:51: 1	8:12:53	10:34:31	13:16:17	15:46:59	18:20:34	20:48: 4	23: 8:28	25:33: 7	28: 6:25
12	1: 0:33	3:42:10	5:55:38	8:17:31	10:39:23	13:21:29	15:51:59	18:25:17	20:52:35	23:13: 6	25:38:11	28:11:56
13	1: 6: 0	3:47:10	6: 0:16	8:22: 8	10:44:15	13:26:41	16: 2:12	18:30:32	20:57: 5	23: 3:28	25:43:17	28:17:56
14	1:11:26	3:52: 1	6: 4:53	8:26:44	10:49:15	13:31:53	16: 7:22	18:34:46	21: 1:35	23:13:13	25:48:23	28:23:27
15	1:16:51	3:57: 1	6: 9:29	8:31:22	10:54:10	13:37: 3	16:12:22	18:39:29	21: 6:34	23:17:43	25:53:30	28:28:59
16	1:22:15	4: 1:58	6:14: 5	8:35:59	10:59: 4	13:42:30	16:17:27	18:44:54	21:11: 1	23:22:22	26: 3:39	28:34:31
17	1:27:39	4: 6:48	6:18:40	8:40:37	11: 3:59	13:47:30	16:22:27	18:48:54	21:15:34	23:27:41	26: 8:59	28:40: 3
18	1:33: 1	4:11:40	6:23:15	8:45:15	11: 9: 0	13:52:42	16:27:34	18:58:17	21:19:34	23:31:41	26:14:11	28:45:36
19	1:38:23	4:16:32	6:27:50	8:49:54	11:13:58	13:57:55	16:32:39	19: 1:31	21:24:11	23:36:22	26:19:24	28:51: 9
20	1:43:44	4:21:22	6:32:24	8:54:33	11:18:52	14: 3:20	16:37:39	19: 7:36	21:28:33	23:41: 3	26:24:38	29: 2:16
21	1:49: 4	4:26:12	6:36:58	8:59:12	11:23:57	14: 8:33	16:42:39	19:11:58	21:33:18	23:45:45	26:24:52	29: 7:45
22	1:54:22	4:31:10	6:41:33	9: 3:52	11:28:57	14:13:46	16:47:40	19:16:53	21:37:33	23:50:52	26:30: 6	29:13:20
23	1:59:40	4:35:49	6:46: 7	9: 8:33	11:33:57	14:18:46	16:52:40	19:21:31	21:42: 3	23:55:12	26:35: 8	29:18:57
24	2: 4:57	4:40:36	6:50:41	9:13:14	11:38:59	14:23:46	16:57:50	19:26: 8	21:46:33	24: 0:25	26:40:25	29:24:31
25	2:10:14	4:45:22	6:55:14	9:17:56	11:44: 1	14:29:11	17: 2:37	19:30:45	21:51: 2	24: 4:29	26:45:43	29:30: 6
26	2:15:29	4:50: 8	6:59:48	9:22:38	11:49: 4	14:34:23	17: 7:50	19:35:40	21:55:34	24:14:17	26:51: 2	29:35:40
27	2:20:45	4:54:52	7: 4:21	9:27:21	11:54:11	14:39:40	17:12:40	19:40:21	22: 0:35	24:19:54	26:56:22	29:41:13
28	2:25:59	4:59:37	7: 8:55	9:32: 5	11:59: 3	14:44:48	17:17:28	19:44:32	22: 0:35	24:24:54	27: 1:43	29:46:45
29	2:31: 8		7:13:28	9:36:49	12: 4:21	14:50: 0	17:22:24	19:49: 1	22: 9: 7	24:28:45	27: 7: 4	29:52:21
30	2:36:19		7:18: 2	9:41:34	12: 9: 1	14:55: 9	17:27:19	19:53:41	22: 9: 7	24:33:36		29:57:54
31	2:41:29		7:22:36		12:14:27		17:27:19					

1952   SSRY = 30:14:14

	January	February	March	April	May	June	July	August	September	October	November	December
1	30:14:14	2:47:37	5:10:52	7:34:19	9:54:23	12:28:41	15: 5:11	17:47:47	20: 9:20	22:24:24	24:51:15	27:26:26
2	0: 5:34	2:52:47	5:15:36	7:38:54	9:59:11	12:33:50	15:10:24	17:47:47	20:13:54	22:29:58	24:56: 1	27:31:52
3	0:11: 9	2:57:56	5:20:19	7:43:30	10: 8:49	12:38:59	15:15:36	17:52:34	20:18:28	22:34:31	25: 6: 4	27:37:18
4	0:16:42	3: 3: 4	5:25: 2	7:48: 4	10: 8:49	12:44: 9	15:20:48	17:57:27	20:23: 2	22:39: 6	25:11: 2	27:42:45
5	0:22:11	3: 8: 7	5:29:43	7:52:41	10:13:59	12:49:20	15:25:58	18: 2:18	20:27:35	22:43:40	25:11: 2	27:48:13
6	0:27:40	3:13:10	5:34:25	7:57:17	10:18:49	12:54:31	15:31:11	18: 7:10	20:32: 8	22:48:14	25:16: 4	27:53:42
7	0:33:21	3:18:21	5:39: 6	8: 1:53	10:23:22	12:59:42	15:36:23	18:12: 0	20:36:41	22:52:47	25:21: 2	27:59:11
8	0:38:52	3:23:25	5:43:46	8: 6:29	10:28:14	13: 4:53	15:41:35	18:16:49	20:41:14	22:57:26	25:26: 3	28: 4:41
9	0:44:23	3:28:27	5:48:25	8:11: 6	10:33: 1	13:10: 5	15:46:43	18:21:38	20:45:46	23: 2: 3	25:31: 6	28:10:12
10	0:49:54	3:33:30	5:53: 3	8:15:43	10:38: 7	13:15:18	15:51:56	18:26:26	20:50:18	23: 6:39	25:36: 9	28:15:44
11	0:55:23	3:38:30	5:57:43	8:20:20	10:42:55	13:20:31	15:57: 8	18:31:13	20:54:50	23:11: 5	25:41:14	28:21:16
12	1: 0:52	3:43:30	6: 2:24	8:24:58	10:47:50	13:25:44	16: 2:10	18:36: 1	20:59: 4	23:15:26	25:46:19	28:26:48
13	1: 6:21	3:48:28	6: 7: 0	8:29:35	10:52:43	13:30:57	16: 7:18	18:40:46	21: 3:53	23:20:34	25:51:26	28:32:21
14	1:11:48	3:53:23	6:11:37	8:34:14	10:57:43	13:36:10	16:12:56	18:45:31	21: 8:24	23:25:53	26: 1:43	28:37:55
15	1:17:16	3:58:23	6:16:14	8:38:52	11: 2:40	13:41:24	16:17:33	18:50:15	21:12:56	23:30:34	26: 6:53	28:43:29
16	1:22: 4	4: 3:19	6:20:50	8:43:31	11: 7:36	13:46:38	16:22:39	18:54:59	21:17:27	23:34:34	26:12:17	28:49: 3
17	1:28: 7	4: 8:13	6:25:28	8:48:11	11:12:36	13:51:52	16:27:44	18:59:42	21:22: 8	23:39:58	26:17:44	28:54:38
18	1:33:31	4:13: 8	6:30: 6	8:52:51	11:17:36	13:57: 6	16:32:54	19: 4:25	21:26:30	23:43:41	26:22:30	29: 5:48
19	1:38:55	4:18: 1	6:34:40	8:57:32	11:22:36	14: 2:21	16:37:54	19: 9: 7	21:31: 1	23:48:41	26:27:44	29:11:23
20	1:44:17	4:22:53	6:39:16	9: 2:13	11:27:36	14: 7:35	16:42:58	19:13:48	21:40:35	23:53:25	26:33: 0	29:16:59
21	1:49:40	4:27:44	6:43:51	9: 6:54	11:32:39	14:12:50	16:48: 1	19:18:29	21:44:35	23:58: 2	26:38:16	29:22:35
22	1:55: 0	4:32:44	6:48:27	9:11:36	11:37:42	14:18: 4	16:53: 4	19:23:10	21:48:21	24: 2: 4	26:43:29	29:28:12
23	2: 0:20	4:37:25	6:53: 2	9:16:19	11:42:45	14:23:19	16:58: 6	19:27:48	21:52:48	24: 7:28	26:48:52	29:33:46
24	2: 5:39	4:42:14	6:57:38	9:21: 2	11:47:48	14:28:34	17: 3: 6	19:32:27	21:58:10	24:12:28	26:54:11	29:39:22
25	2:10:57	4:47: 2	7: 2:13	9:25:46	11:52:53	14:33:49	17: 8: 6	19:37: 6	22: 2:42	24:17:16	26:59:31	29:44:58
26	2:16:15	4:51:50	7: 6:48	9:30:31	11:57:58	14:39: 2	17:13: 6	19:41:44	22: 2:42	24:26: 4	27: 4:53	29:50:33
27	2:21:32	4:56: 36	7:11:23	9:35:16	12: 3: 5	14:44:16	17:18: 5	19:46:21	22: 7:14	24:26:54	27:10:15	29:56: 9
28	2:26:48	5: 1:50	7:15:58	9:40: 2	12: 8:12	14:49:30	17:23: 6	19:50:58	22:11:46	24:31:44	27:15:39	29:56: 9
29	2:32: 5	5: 6: 7	7:20:33	9:44:48	12:13:17	14:54:44	17:28: 0	19:55:34	22:16:18	24:36:41	27:21: 1	30: 7:19
30	2:37:13		7:25:10	9:49:35	12:18:24	14:59:58	17:32:56	20: 0:10	22:20:51	24:41:28		30:12:53
31	2:42:26		7:29:44		12:23:32		17:37:52	20: 4:45		24:46:21		

1953 SSRY = 30:13: 3

	January	February	March	April	May	June	July	August	September	October	November	December	
1	30:13: 3	2:47:11	5: 5:17	7:28:40	9:48:35	12:22:42	14:59: 5	17:36:40	20: 3:13	22:19:13	24:44:53	27:19:50	1
2	0: 5:34	2:52:20	5:10: 1	7:33:15	9:53:22	12:33:50	15: 4:38	17:41:32	20: 8:22	22:28:19	24:49:48	27:25:15	2
3	0:11:40	2:57:35	5:14:44	7:37:58	9:58:10	12:38:53	15: 9:45	17:46:24	20:12:22	22:32:53	24:54:44	27:30:41	3
4	0:16:33	3: 2:38	5:19:26	7:42:26	10: 2:50	12:43:19	15:14:30	17:51:20	20:16:26	22:37:28	24:59:41	27:36: 8	4
5	0:22:13	3: 7:41	5:24: 8	7:47: 1	10: 7:50	12:48:30	15:19:54	17:56:12	20:21:29	22:42: 3	25: 4:39	27:41:36	5
6	0:27:45	3:12:45	5:28:49	7:51:37	10:12:45	12:53:41	15:25: 6	18: 1: 3	20:26: 2	22:46:38	25: 9:38	27:47: 4	6
7	0:33:16	3:17:49	5:33:30	7:56:12	10:17:32	12:58:53	15:30:17	18: 5:54	20:30:35	22:51:14	25:14:38	27:52:34	7
8	0:38:47	3:22:52	5:38:10	8: 0:47	10:22:24	13: 4: 5	15:35:27	18:10:44	20:35: 7	22:55:50	25:19:39	28: 3:34	8
9	0:44:48	3:27:55	5:42:50	8: 5:22	10:27:24	13: 9:17	15:40:37	18:15:54	20:39:39	23: 0:27	25:24:41	28: 9: 5	9
10	0:49:48	3:32:55	5:47:29	8:10: 2	10:32:10	13:14:29	15:45:47	18:20:21	20:44:11	23: 5: 4	25:29:44	28:14:37	10
11	0:55:17	3:37:55	5:52: 8	8:14:39	10:37: 4	13:19:42	15:50:56	18:25:32	20:48:43	23: 9:42	25:34:48	28:20: 9	11
12	1: 0:45	3:42:54	5:56:46	8:19:16	10:41:59	13:24:46	15:56: 5	18:29:55	20:53:15	23:14:20	25:39:54	28:25:42	12
13	1: 6:13	3:47:53	6: 1:24	8:23:53	10:46:54	13:30: 9	16: 1:13	18:34:26	20:57:47	23:19:20	25:45: 1	28:31:15	13
14	1:11:40	3:52:51	6: 6: 1	8:28:31	10:51:50	13:35:23	16: 6:13	18:39:26	21: 1:20	23:23:39	25:50: 7	28:36:49	14
15	1:17:40	3:57:45	6:10:39	8:33:11	10:56:48	13:40:37	16:11:28	18:44:11	21: 6:49	23:28:20	25:55:16	28:42:22	15
16	1:22:32	4: 2:40	6:15:16	8:37:50	11: 1:46	13:45:51	16:16:30	18:48:55	21:10:51	23:33: 1	26: 0:25	28:47:57	16
17	1:27:56	4: 7:34	6:19:52	8:42:29	11: 6:45	13:51: 5	16:21:40	18:53:38	21:15:51	23:37:43	26: 5:36	28:53:31	17
18	1:33:20	4:12:21	6:24:29	8:47: 9	11:11: 0	13:56:19	16:26:46	18:58:20	21:20:22	23:42:25	26:10:48	28:59: 5	18
19	1:38:43	4:17:20	6:29: 4	8:51:49	11:16:44	14: 1:33	16:31:53	19: 3: 1	21:24:53	23:47:32	26:16: 0	29: 4:41	19
20	1:44: 6	4:22:10	6:33:40	8:56:49	11:21:44	14: 6:48	16:36:53	19: 7:43	21:29:24	23:51:52	26:21:14	29:10:16	20
21	1:49:26	4:27: 1	6:38:16	9: 1:12	11:26:46	14:12: 4	16:41:56	19:12:24	21:33:55	23:56:37	26:26:28	29:15:51	21
22	1:54:46	4:31:51	6:42:51	9: 5:53	11:31:48	14:17:16	16:46:58	19:17: 4	21:38:26	24: 1:22	26:31:44	29:21:26	22
23	2: 0: 5	4:36:40	6:47:27	9:10:36	11:36:50	14:22:34	16:52: 2	19:21:43	21:42:56	24: 6: 9	26:37: 1	29:27: 2	23
24	2: 5:23	4:41:28	6:52: 2	9:15:18	11:41:54	14:27:48	16:57: 1	19:26:22	21:47:26	24:10:56	26:42:19	29:32:37	24
25	2:10:40	4:46:16	6:56:37	9:20: 1	11:46:59	14:32:58	17: 2: 0	19:30:59	21:51:58	24:15:44	26:47:37	29:38:13	25
26	2:15:56	4:51: 2	7: 1:12	9:24:44	11:52: 6	14:38:12	17: 6:56	19:35:38	21:56:31	24:20:33	26:52:57	29:43:48	26
27	2:21:11	4:55:48	7: 5:46	9:29:30	11:57: 1	14:43:26	17:11:59	19:40:15	22: 1: 3	24:25:23	26:58:18	29:49:23	27
28	2:26:26	5: 0:33	7:10:21	9:34:15	12: 2:13	14:48:39	17:16:56	19:45:51	22: 6:15	24:30:14	27: 3:39	29:54:58	28
29	2:31:38		7:14:56	9:39: 1	12: 7:19	14:53:52	17:21:54	19:49:27	22:10:26	24:35: 4	27: 9: 2	30: 0:33	29
30	2:36:50		7:19:31	9:43:48	12:12:26	14:58:54	17:26:50	19:54:27	22:14:40	24:38:59	27:14:25	30: 6: 8	30
31	2:42: 1		7:24: 5		12:17:34		17:31:45	19:58:38					31

1954 SSRY = 30:11:30

	January	February	March	April	May	June	July	August	September	October	November	December	
1	30:11:30	2:47: 8	5: 5:13	7:28:31	9:48:15	12:22:10	14:58:24	17:35:56	20: 2:27	22:18:20	24:43:47	27:18:29	1
2	0: 5:34	2:52:18	5: 9:57	7:33: 6	9:53: 3	12:27:18	15: 3:50	17:40:41	20: 7: 2	22:22:23	24:48:42	27:23:13	2
3	0:11:40	2:57:28	5:14:40	7:37:39	9:57:54	12:32:27	15: 9: 5	17:45:44	20:11:35	22:27:26	24:53:37	27:29:13	3
4	0:16:30	3: 2:33	5:19:22	7:42:16	10: 2:40	12:37:37	15:14: 2	17:50:37	20:16: 9	22:32: 0	24:58:33	27:34:45	4
5	0:22:13	3: 7:39	5:24: 4	7:46:51	10: 7:30	12:42:47	15:19:14	17:55:28	20:20:42	22:36:34	25: 3:31	27:40:13	5
6	0:27:45	3:12:44	5:28:45	7:51:27	10:12: 1	12:47:57	15:24:25	18: 0:20	20:25:15	22:41: 8	25: 8:29	27:45:40	6
7	0:33:17	3:17:47	5:33:26	7:56: 3	10:17: 1	12:53: 8	15:29:36	18: 5: 0	20:29:27	22:45:43	25:13:28	27:51:20	7
8	0:38:48	3:22:50	5:38: 6	8: 0:39	10:21:58	12:58:20	15:34:46	18: 9:57	20:34: 2	22:50:19	25:18:28	28: 2: 8	8
9	0:44:48	3:27:53	5:42:46	8: 5:15	10:26:45	13: 3:31	15:40: 0	18:14:48	20:38:52	22:54:54	25:23:30	28: 7:39	9
10	0:49:48	3:32:53	5:47:25	8: 9:51	10:31:48	13: 8:42	15:45:15	18:19:36	20:43:23	22:59:30	25:28:33	28:13:10	10
11	0:55:17	3:37:53	5:52: 4	8:14:28	10:36:42	13:13:55	15:50:14	18:24:23	20:47:55	23: 4: 7	25:33:36	28:18:41	11
12	1: 0:45	3:42:49	5:56:46	8:19: 5	10:41:36	13:19: 2	15:55:23	18:29:10	20:52:26	23: 8:44	25:38:41	28:24:13	12
13	1: 6:13	3:47:49	6: 1:20	8:23:42	10:46:30	13:24:20	16: 0:33	18:33:57	20:56:57	23:13:22	25:43:53	28:29:45	13
14	1:11:40	3:52:45	6: 5:56	8:28:20	10:51:21	13:29:33	16: 5:45	18:38:41	21: 1:30	23:18: 2	25:48:53	28:35:19	14
15	1:17:35	3:57:42	6:10:34	8:32:58	10:56:21	13:34:49	16:10:45	18:43:25	21: 5:59	23:22:40	25:54: 4	28:40:52	15
16	1:22:31	4: 2:37	6:15:11	8:37:37	11: 1:19	13:39:59	16:15:51	18:48: 9	21:10:30	23:27:20	25:59:10	28:46:26	16
17	1:27:55	4: 7:31	6:19:47	8:42:15	11: 6:19	13:45:13	16:20:56	18:52:52	21:15: 3	23:32: 0	26: 4:20	28:52: 0	17
18	1:33:30	4:12:21	6:24:23	8:46:55	11:11:17	13:50:26	16:26: 4	18:57:34	21:19:31	23:36:42	26: 9:31	28:57:35	18
19	1:38:41	4:17:16	6:28:59	8:51:35	11:16:17	13:55:39	16:31: 9	19: 2:16	21:24: 2	23:41:24	26:14:43	29: 3:10	19
20	1:44:17	4:22: 4	6:33:37	8:56:15	11:21:17	14: 0:52	16:36:13	19: 7: 1	21:28:33	23:46: 8	26:19:56	29: 8:45	20
21	1:49:26	4:26:58	6:38:16	9: 1: 9	11:26:17	14: 6: 8	16:41:17	19:11:37	21:33: 4	23:50:50	26:25:11	29:14:20	21
22	1:54:43	4:31:47	6:42:44	9: 5:37	11:31:19	14:11:26	16:46:16	19:16:17	21:37:34	23:55:35	26:30:26	29:19:55	22
23	2: 0: 2	4:36:36	6:47:19	9:10:17	11:36:24	14:16:36	16:51:15	19:20:56	21:42: 5	24: 0:20	26:35:42	29:25:30	23
24	2: 5:20	4:41:24	6:51:53	9:15: 1	11:41:24	14:21:50	16:56:16	19:25:35	21:46:37	24: 5: 6	26:41: 0	29:31: 6	24
25	2:10:37	4:46:12	6:56:29	9:19:24	11:46:36	14:27: 4	17: 1:14	19:30:14	21:51: 8	24: 9:53	26:46:18	29:36:41	25
26	2:15:53	4:50:58	7: 1: 4	9:24:44	11:51:36	14:32:19	17: 6:16	19:34:51	21:55:39	24:14:41	26:51:38	29:42:16	26
27	2:21: 8	4:55:44	7: 5:38	9:29:12	11:56:36	14:37:31	17:11:16	19:39:28	22: 0:11	24:19:29	26:56:58	29:47:51	27
28	2:26:22	5: 0:29	7:10:12	9:33:57	12: 1:41	14:42:45	17:16:12	19:44: 5	22: 4:43	24:24:19	27: 2:19	29:53:26	28
29	2:31:35		7:14:47	9:38:42	12: 6:48	14:47:58	17:21: 9	19:48:41	22: 9:15	24:29:10	27: 7:41	29:59:26	29
30	2:36:47		7:19:22	9:43:29	12:11:55	14:53:11	17:26: 6	19:53:17	22:13:47	24:34: 1	27:13: 5	30: 4:35	30
31	2:41:58		7:23:56		12:17: 2		17:31: 1	19:57:52		24:38:54			31

1955   SSRY = 30:17:42

Day	January	February	March	April	May	June	July	August	September	October	November	December
1	0: 5:35	2:49:40	5:16:14	7:30:20	9:55:30	12:24:51	15: 6:36	17:44:33	20: 6:28	22:23: 9	24:49:36	27:24: 6
2	0:11:10	2:53: 9	5:15:58	7:34:55	9:55:18	12:30:10	15: 6:49	17:44:38	20:11:23	22:27:42	24:53:55	27:27:49
3	0:16:44	2:58: 9	5:19:31	7:39:31	10: 4:57	12:35:10	15:12: 3	17:49:33	20:15:58	22:31:16	24:58:51	27:31:28
4	0:22:17	3: 3:17	5:20:42	7:44: 7	10: 4:57	12:40:20	15:17:16	17:54:26	20:20:32	22:36:51	25: 3:48	27:34:58
5	0:27:51	3: 8:24	5:25:25	7:48:43	10: 9:47	12:45:31	15:22:28	17:59:19	20:25: 6	22:41:25	25: 8:46	27:40:25
6	0:33:30	3:13:30	5:30: 7	7:53:19	10:14:38	12:50:42	15:27:41	18: 4:11	20:29:40	22:56:36	25:13:46	27:45:53
7	0:38:55	3:18:35	5:34:49	7:57:52	10:18:38	12:55: 5	15:32:52	18: 9: 3	20:34:13	22:50:11	25:18:46	27:51:22
8	0:44:27	3:23:42	5:39:30	8: 2:32	10:24:22	13: 1: 5	15:38:12	18:13:53	20:43:20	22:55:12	25:23:47	27:56:52
9	0:49:58	3:28:44	5:44:10	8: 7: 9	10:29:15	13: 6:18	15:43:15	18:18:43	20:47:52	22:59:49	25:28:49	28: 7:53
10	0:55:28	3:33:44	5:48:50	8:11:47	10:34: 7	13:11:30	15:48:21	18:23:32	20:52:25	23: 9: 4	25:33:53	28:13:24
11	1: 0:56	3:38:45	5:53:30	8:16:24	10:39: 3	13:16:43	15:53:35	18:28:21	20:57:25	23:14:21	25:38:57	28:18:57
12	1: 6:24	3:43:45	5:58: 9	8:21:42	10:43:58	13:21:57	15:58:48	18:37:55	21: 1:30	23:18:21	25:44: 9	28:24:31
13	1:11:54	3:48:44	6: 2:48	8:25:44	10:48:51	13:27:11	16: 4: 1	18:42:47	21: 6:32	23:23: 0	25:49: 9	28:30:22
14	1:17:21	3:53:42	6: 7:26	8:30:19	10:53:51	13:32:25	16: 9: 3	18:47:22	21:11: 6	23:27:40	25:54:17	28:35:37
15	1:22:48	3:58:39	6:12: 4	8:34:58	10:58:48	13:37:39	16:14:11	18:52:12	21:15: 6	23:32:21	25:59:26	28:41:11
16	1:28:14	4: 3:36	6:16:42	8:39:37	11: 3:46	13:42:53	16:19:18	18:56:57	21:20:37	23:37: 3	26: 4:36	28:46:46
17	1:33:39	4: 8:31	6:21:19	8:44:17	11: 8:45	13:48: 8	16:24:36	19: 1:45	21:24:33	23:42: 9	26: 9:47	28:52:21
18	1:39: 3	4:13:26	6:25:58	8:53:38	11:13:45	13:53:23	16:29:44	19: 6:23	21:28:41	23:46:28	26:15: 0	28:57:56
19	1:44:26	4:18:19	6:30:33	8:58:19	11:18:45	13:58:38	16:34:52	19:11:18	21:33:13	23:51:12	26:20:12	29: 3:32
20	1:49:48	4:23:12	6:35:10	9: 3: 1	11:23:46	14: 3:53	16:39:41	19:15:47	21:37:45	23:55:56	26:25:26	29: 9: 8
21	1:55:10	4:28: 3	6:39:46	9: 7:43	11:28:48	14: 9: 8	16:44:46	19:20:20	21:41:48	24: 0:41	26:30:41	29:14:44
22	2: 0:30	4:32:55	6:44:22	9:12:26	11:33:51	14:14:39	16:49:46	19:25:33	21:46:48	24: 5:27	26:35:57	29:20:20
23	2: 5:50	4:37:45	6:48:58	9:17:9	11:38:54	14:19:39	16:54:52	19:30:49	21:46:48	24: 6:24	26:41:14	29:25:56
24	2:11: 8	4:42:35	6:53:33	9:21:50	11:43:58	14:24:50	16:59:56	19:34:28	21:51:52	24:14:51	26:46:30	29:31:32
25	2:16:26	4:47:52	6:58:10	9:26:38	11:49: 3	14:30:24	17: 5: 0	19:39:42	21:55:52	24:19:51	26:51:52	29:37: 8
26	2:21:42	4:52:10	7: 2:46	9:31:24	11:54: 2	14:35:39	17:10: 3	19:44:21	22: 0:25	24:24:30	26:57:12	29:42:45
27	2:26:58	4:56:57	7: 7:21	9:36: 9	11:59:13	14:40:53	17:14:56	19:48:22	22: 4:57	24:29:30	27: 2:33	29:48:21
28	2:32:12	5: 1:44	7:11:57	9:40:56	12: 4:20	14:45:53	17:19:55	19:52:52	22: 9:30	24:34:21	27: 7:55	29:53:57
29	2:37:26		7:16:33	9:45:43	12: 9:27	14:51: 8	17:24:53	19:56:56	22:14: 2	24:39:13	27:13:18	29:59:33
30	2:42:38		7:21: 8		12:14:34	14:56:22	17:29:56	20: 2:12	22:18:35	24:44: 6	27:18:41	30:10:44
31			7:25:44		12:19:42		17:34:47					

1956   SSRY = 30: 7:12

Day	January	February	March	April	May	June	July	August	September	October	November	December
1	30: 7:33	2:46:57	5: 9:39	7:32:36	9:52: 4	12:20:46	15: 5:40	17:48:38	20: 9:37	22:20:11	24:46:29	27:30:24
2	0: 7:33	2:51:35	5:19: 3	7:37:49	9:56:51	12:36: 6	15:12: 3	17:48:24	20:13:49	22:20:13	24:50:23	27:35:24
3	0:11:10	2:57:13	5:19: 3	7:41:41	9:56:58	12:36: 6	15:17:14	17:53:15	20:18:17	22:29:16	24:55:18	27:30:56
4	0:16:38	2: 2:20	5:23:45	7:46:15	10:11:16	12:41:11	15:17:14	17:58: 6	20:22:49	22:33:49	25: 0:15	27:36:20
5	0:22:10	3: 7:25	5:28:34	7:50:48	10:16:16	12:46:20	15:27:35	18: 2:56	20:27:22	22:38:23	25: 5:12	27:41:45
6	0:27:41	3:12:30	5:33:46	7:55:25	10:16:16	12:51:30	15:32:44	18:12:34	20:31:56	22:42:57	25:10:10	27:47:15
7	0:33:13	3:17:36	5:42:25	8: 0: 0	10:20:40	12:56:41	15:37:54	18:12:34	20:36:25	22:47:32	25:15:10	27:52:43
8	0:38:44	3:22:38	5:42:25	8: 4:35	10:30:40	13: 1:44	15:43: 3	18:17:22	20:40:56	22:52:37	25:20:11	27:58:12
9	0:44:12	3:27:38	5:47: 3	8: 9:11	10:35:32	13: 7: 2	15:48: 2	18:22:10	20:45:27	22:56:42	25:25:11	28: 3:42
10	0:49:42	3:32:39	5:51:41	8:13:47	10:40:26	13:12:14	15:53:20	18:26:55	20:49:58	23: 1:18	25:30:14	28: 9:12
11	0:55:10	3:37:38	5:56:21	8:18:23	10:40:26	13:17:25	15:53:20	18:31:51	20:54:29	23: 5:55	25:35:17	28:14:42
12	1: 0:38	3:42:37	6: 0:57	8:23: 0	10:45:15	13:22:37	15:58:33	18:31:51	20:58:58	23:10:32	25:40:22	28:20:14
13	1: 6:10	3:47:38	6:10:54	8:32:14	10:50:15	13:27:30	16: 8:41	18:41:10	21: 3:30	23:15:10	25:45:28	28:26:14
14	1:11:32	3:52:28	6:10:54	8:32:14	10:55:11	13:33:15	16: 8:41	18:45:53	21: 8: 0	23:19:48	25:50:34	28:31:45
15	1:16:58	3:57:28	6:14:47	8:36:52	11: 0: 5	13:43:27	16:13:46	18:50:36	21:12:30	23:24:27	25:55:42	28:36:50
16	1:22:23	4: 2: 4	6:19:23	8:41:30	11: 5: 4	13:43:27	16:18:52	18:55:19	21: 7: 0	23:29: 6	26: 0: 1	28:42:26
17	1:27:47	4: 7:16	6:23:34	8:46:9	11:10: 4	13:48:40	16:23:59	18:59:59	21:17: 7	23:33:46	26: 6:11	28:47:56
18	1:33:10	4:12: 1	6:28:34	8:50:48	11:14:59	13:53: 6	16:29: 7	19: 3:40	21:21:31	23:38:28	26:11:11	28:53:29
19	1:38:33	4:17:52	6:32:49	8: 5: 6	11:19:59	13:58:55	16:34: 9	19: 9:20	21:30:31	23:42:57	26:16:23	28:59:37
20	1:43:54	4:21:52	6:37:43	9: 4:48	11:24:59	14: 9:33	16:44: 7	19:13:59	21:35: 0	23:47:52	26:21:36	29: 4:37
21	1:49:35	4:26:43	6:42:18	9: 4:48	11:29:59	14: 9:33	16:49: 8	19:18:38	21:35: 0	23:52:35	26:26:50	29:10:11
22	1:54:35	4:31:32	6:46:53	9: 9: 1	11:40: 5	14:14:46	16:49: 8	19:23:16	21:44: 1	23:57:19	26:32: 5	29:15:45
23	1:59:53	4:36:21	6:51:27	9:14:11	11:40: 5	14:19:59	16:54: 9	19:28: 0	22: 2: 4	24: 2: 4	26:37:21	29:21:19
24	2: 5:10	4:41:36	6:56: 0	9:18:46	11:45: 5	14:25: 9	16:59:12	19:32:44	21:53:22	24: 6:50	26:42:38	29:26:54
25	2:10:36	4:45:55	7: 0:36	9:23:23	11:50: 8	14:30:12	17: 4:14	19:37:31	21:57:33	24:11:36	26:47:56	29:32:44
26	2:15:44	4:50:41	7: 5: 9	9:28:18	11:55:11	14:35:38	17: 9: 2	19:41:44	22: 2: 4	24:16:24	26:53:15	29:38:42
27	2:20:46	4:55:27	7: 5: 9	9:33: 2	12: 0:16	14:40:51	17:14: 2	19:46:19	22: 6:35	24:21:12	26:58:35	29:43:37
28	2:26:12	5: 0:11	7:14:16	9:37:46	12: 5:21	14:46: 3	17:14: 2	19:50:54	22:11: 7	24:26: 2	27: 3:56	29:49:11
29	2:31:15	5: 4:55	7:14:16	9:42:32	12:10:26	14:51:15	17:18:59	19:50:54	22:15:38	24:26:52	27: 9:18	29:54:45
30	2:36:44		7:18:50	9:47:17	12:15: 2	14:56:28	17:23:50	19:55:37	22:15:38	24:31:53	27:14:40	30: 5:52
31	2:41:47		7:27:58		12:20:39		17:33:45	20: 0: 3		24:40:36		

1957   SSRY = 30:10:55

	January	February	March	April	May	June	July	August	September	October	November	December	
1	30:10:55	2:46:59	5: 4:54	7:28: 7	9:47:53	12:21:49	14:58: 7	17:35:24	20: 1:46	22:17:36	24:43: 7	27:17:55	1
2	0: 5:34	2:52: 7	5: 9:38	7:32:42	9:52:40	12:26:54	15: 3:14	17:40:18	20: 6:20	22:22: 9	24:48: 9	27:23:15	2
3	0:11: 7	2:57:15	5:14:20	7:37:17	9:57:29	12:32: 2	15: 8:38	17:45:11	20:10:27	22:26:43	24:52:57	27:28:15	3
4	0:16:40	3: 2:22	5:19: 2	7:41:52	10: 2:18	12:37:16	15:13:38	17:50: 3	20:15:27	22:31:16	24:57:54	27:34:11	4
5	0:22:12	3: 7:28	5:23:42	7:46:28	10: 7: 7	12:42:26	15:18:50	17:55: 3	20:20: 0	22:35:50	25: 2:51	27:39:39	5
6	0:27:44	3:12:32	5:28:25	7:51: 3	10:11:58	12:47:36	15:24: 0	17:59:45	20:24:33	22:40:25	25: 7:50	27:45: 7	6
7	0:33:15	3:17:35	5:33: 6	7:55:39	10:16:49	12:52:47	15:29:11	18: 4:35	20:29: 5	22:44:59	25:12:49	27:50:35	7
8	0:38:46	3:22:38	5:37:46	8: 0:15	10:21:40	12:57:58	15:34:21	18: 9:24	20:33:37	22:49:35	25:17:50	27:56:34	8
9	0:44:16	3:27:39	5:42:25	8: 4:51	10:26:33	13: 3:10	15:39:30	18:14:13	20:38:10	22:54:10	25:22:51	28: 1: 5	9
10	0:49:45	3:32:40	5:47: 4	8: 9:27	10:31:26	13: 8:21	15:44:40	18:19: 1	20:42:41	22:58:47	25:27:54	28: 7: 5	10
11	0:55:14	3:37:39	5:51:42	8:14:24	10:36:19	13:13:33	15:49:48	18:23:47	20:47:12	23: 3:24	25:32:58	28:12:36	11
12	1: 0:42	3:42:37	5:56:20	8:18:46	10:41:14	13:18:46	15:54:56	18:28:34	20:51:43	23: 8: 1	25:38: 3	28:18: 8	12
13	1: 6: 9	3:47:35	6: 0:58	8:23:18	10:46: 9	13:23:58	16: 0: 4	18:33:19	20:56:14	23:12:39	25:43: 9	28:23:40	13
14	1:11:35	3:52:31	6: 5:37	8:27:56	10:51: 5	13:29:11	16: 5:11	18:38: 4	21: 0:44	23:17:18	25:48:16	28:29:11	14
15	1:17: 0	3:57:27	6:10:14	8:32:34	10:56: 2	13:34:24	16:10:17	18:42:48	21: 5:14	23:21:57	25:53:24	28:34:44	15
16	1:22:26	4: 2:21	6:14:51	8:37:12	11: 0:59	13:39:37	16:15:23	18:47:31	21: 9:47	23:26:37	25:58:33	28:40:19	16
17	1:27:50	4: 7:15	6:19:28	8:41:51	11: 5:57	13:44:51	16:20:28	18:52:14	21:14:17	23:31:18	26: 3:43	28:45:53	17
18	1:33:13	4:12: 8	6:24: 0	8:46:30	11:10:55	13:50: 4	16:25:32	18:56:56	21:18:48	23:35:59	26: 8:55	28:51:27	18
19	1:38:35	4:16:59	6:28:35	8:51:10	11:15:55	13:55:18	16:30:36	19: 1:38	21:23:19	23:40:42	26:14: 7	28:57: 2	19
20	1:43:57	4:21:50	6:33:16	8:55:51	11:20:56	14: 0:32	16:35:39	19: 6:18	21:27:50	23:45:25	26:19:21	29: 2:37	20
21	1:49:18	4:26:39	6:37:58	9: 0:33	11:25:57	14: 5:46	16:40:42	19:10:59	21:32:21	23:50: 9	26:24:35	29: 8:12	21
22	1:54:38	4:31:30	6:42:42	9: 5:13	11:30:57	14:11: 0	16:45:44	19:15:38	21:36:51	23:54:53	26:29:51	29:13:47	22
23	1:59:55	4:36:18	6:46:56	9: 9:55	11:36: 0	14:16:14	16:50:45	19:20:18	21:41:22	23:59:39	26:35: 7	29:19:22	23
24	2: 5:13	4:41: 6	6:51:30	9:14:38	11:41: 1	14:21:27	16:55:45	19:24:56	21:45:53	24: 4:25	26:40:25	29:24:57	24
25	2:10:29	4:45:53	6:56: 9	9:19:21	11:46:16	14:26:41	17: 0:46	19:29:34	21:50:24	24: 9:12	26:45:44	29:30:32	25
26	2:15:45	4:50:40	7: 0:40	9:24: 5	11:51:16	14:31:54	17: 5:45	19:34:11	21:54:56	24:14: 0	26:51: 3	29:36: 6	26
27	2:21: 0	4:55:25	7: 5:14	9:28:49	11:56:16	14:37: 1	17:10:43	19:38:49	21:59:28	24:18:49	26:56:24	29:41:42	27
28	2:26:14	5: 0:10	7:10:23	9:33:34	12: 1:21	14:42:15	17:15:41	19:43:25	22: 3:59	24:23:39	27: 1:45	29:47:17	28
29	2:31:27		7:14:23	9:38:20	12: 6:27	14:47:35	17:20:38	19:48: 1	22: 8:31	24:28:30	27: 7: 7	29:52:52	29
30	2:36:38		7:18:58	9:43: 6	12:11:34	14:52:48	17:25:34	19:52:36	22:13: 4	24:33:21	27:12:31	29:58:26	30
31	2:41:49		7:23:33		12:16:42		17:30:30	19:57:11		24:38:14		30: 4: 1	31

1958   SSRY = 30:18:41

	January	February	March	April	May	June	July	August	September	October	November	December	
1	30:18:41	2:47:47	5: 6:24	7:30:17	9:50:36	12:25: 8	15: 1:59	17:40: 6	20: 7:10	22:23:35	24:49:38	27:24:57	1
2	0: 5:35	2:52:57	5:11: 9	7:34:53	9:55:35	12:30:17	15: 7: 9	17:45: 2	20:11:45	22:28: 5	24:54:33	27:30:12	2
3	0:11: 7	2:58: 6	5:15:53	7:39:29	10: 0:14	12:35:27	15:12:22	17:49:56	20:16:20	22:32:43	24:59:31	27:35:29	3
4	0:16:40	3: 3:13	5:20:36	7:44: 5	10: 5: 3	12:40:38	15:17:33	17:54:49	20:20:55	22:37:18	25: 4:27	27:41:17	4
5	0:22:14	3: 8:17	5:25:19	7:48:41	10: 9:54	12:45:49	15:22:52	17:59:42	20:25:29	22:41:53	25: 9:26	27:46:45	5
6	0:27:50	3:13:27	5:30: 2	7:53:17	10:14:45	12:51: 0	15:28: 4	18: 4:34	20:30: 3	22:46:28	25:14:26	27:52:15	6
7	0:27:50	3:18:32	5:34:43	7:57:54	10:19:37	12:56:12	15:33:14	18: 9:26	20:34:36	22:51: 4	25:19:26	27:57:45	7
8	0:33:23	3:23:36	5:39:24	8: 2:31	10:24:30	13: 1:24	15:38:28	18:14:16	20:39:10	22:55:41	25:24:28	28: 3:15	8
9	0:38:55	3:28:39	5:44: 5	8: 7: 8	10:29:38	13: 6:37	15:43:38	18:19: 6	20:43:43	23: 0:18	25:29:30	28: 8:47	9
10	0:44:27	3:33:42	5:48:45	8:11:46	10:34:12	13:11:50	15:48:45	18:23:55	20:48:16	23: 4:55	25:34:34	2E:14:19	10
11	0:49:58	3:38:42	5:53:25	8:16:24	10:39: 8	13:17: 3	15:54: 0	18:28:44	20:52:49	23: 9:33	25:39:39	2E:19:51	11
12	0:55:28	3:43:42	5:58: 4	8:21: 2	10:44: 4	13:22:17	15:59: 9	18:33:31	20:57:21	23:14:12	25:44:45	2E:25:25	12
13	1: 0:57	3:48:41	6: 2:43	8:25:40	10:49: 1	13:27:31	16: 4:18	18:38:19	21: 1:54	23:18:51	25:49:53	2E:30:58	13
14	1: 6:26	3:53:39	6: 7:21	8:30:19	10:53:58	13:32:45	16: 9:27	18:43: 6	21: 6:28	23:23:32	25:55: 0	2E:36:30	14
15	1:11:54	3:58:36	6:11:59	8:34:58	10:58:57	13:37:59	16:14:35	18:47:50	21:11: 1	23:28:12	26: 0:10	28:42: 3	15
16	1:17:21	4: 3:31	6:16:37	8:39:38	11: 3:57	13:43:15	16:19:42	18:52:35	21:15:30	23:32:53	26: 5:20	28:47:42	16
17	1:22:48	4: 8:27	6:21:15	8:44:18	11: 8:57	13:48:30	16:24:49	18:57:20	21:20: 2	23:37:35	26:10:32	28:53:17	17
18	1:28:14	4:13:22	6:25:52	8:48:59	11:13:57	13:53:45	16:29:55	19: 2: 3	21:24:34	23:42:17	26:15:44	28:58:53	18
19	1:33:39	4:18:15	6:30:29	8:53:40	11:18:59	13:59: 0	16:35: 0	19: 6:46	21:29: 6	23:47: 1	26:20:58	29: 4:29	19
20	1:39: 3	4:23: 8	6:35: 6	8:58:22	11:24: 1	14: 4: 0	16:40: 6	19:11:28	21:33:38	23:51:45	26:26:12	29:10: 5	20
21	1:44:26	4:28: 0	6:39:42	9: 3: 4	11:29: 5	14: 9:31	16:45: 9	19:16:10	21:42:41	23:56:29	26:31:28	29:15:41	21
22	1:49:48	4:32:50	6:44:18	9: 7:47	11:34: 8	14:14:46	16:50:13	19:20:51	21:47:13	24: 1:15	26:36:44	29:21:17	22
23	1:55: 9	4:37:41	6:48:55	9:12:30	11:39: 8	14:20: 1	16:55:16	19:25:32	21:51:46	24: 6: 1	26:42: 1	29:26:53	23
24	2: 0:30	4:42:30	6:53:31	9:17:14	11:44:12	14:25:17	17: 0:18	19:30:11	21:56:18	24:10:48	26:47:20	29:32:30	24
25	2: 5:49	4:47:18	6:58: 8	9:21:58	11:49:17	14:30:32	17: 5:19	19:34:50	22: 0:50	24:15:36	26:52:40	29:38: 6	25
26	2:11: 8	4:52: 5	7: 2:43	9:26:43	11:54:23	14:35:48	17:10:19	19:39:29	22: 5:23	24:20:25	26:58: 0	29:43:43	26
27	2:16:25	4:56:53	7: 7:18	9:31:28	11:59:29	14:41: 1	17:15:19	19:44: 7	22: 9:55	24:25:15	27: 3:22	29:49:19	27
28	2:21:42	5: 1:39	7:11:54	9:36:14	12: 4:35	14:46:16	17:20:18	19:48:45	22:14:28	24:30: 5	27: 8:44	29:54:55	28
29	2:26:56		7:16:30	9:41: 1	12: 9:42	14:51:31	17:25:15	19:53:22	22:19: 2	24:34:57	27:14: 7	30: 0:31	29
30	2:32:11		7:21: 5	9:45:48	12:14:50	14:56:45	17:30:14	19:57:58		24:39:50	27:19:31	30: 6:37	30
31	2:37:24		7:25:41		12:19:59		17:35:11	20: 2:34		24:44:43		30:11:43	31

1959   SSRY = 30: 7:43

Day	January	February	March	April	May	June	July	August	September	October	November	December
1	30: 6:53	2:46:53	5: 4:46	7:27:49	9:47:14	12:20:45	14:56:39	17:33:53	20: 0: 3	22:15:45	24:40:49	27:15: 5
2	0: 5:33	2:52: 1	5: 9:28	7:32:23	9:52: 1	12:25:53	15: 1:51	17:38:47	20: 4:43	22:20:17	24:45:43	27:20:29
3	0:11: 6	2:57: 9	5:14:12	7:36:58	9:56:48	12:31: 1	15: 7: 2	17:43:40	20: 9:16	22:24:50	24:50:38	27:25:54
4	0:16:28	3: 2:15	5:18:54	7:41:32	10: 1:36	12:36:10	15:12:14	17:48:32	20:13:49	22:29:23	24:55:33	27:31:20
5	0:22:10	3: 7:21	5:23:35	7:46:47	10: 6:25	12:41:19	15:17:25	17:53:24	20:18:22	22:33:56	25: 0:30	27:36:46
6	0:27:41	3:12:25	5:28:56	7:50:47	10:11: 5	12:46:29	15:22:36	17:58:14	20:22:26	22:38:29	25: 5:26	27:42: 4
7	0:33:12	3:17:28	5:32:15	7:55:17	10:16: 5	12:51:39	15:27:46	18: 3:14	20:27:26	22:43:19	25:10:26	27:47:41
8	0:38:43	3:22:31	5:37:36	7:59:52	10:20:56	12:56:49	15:32:56	18: 7:53	20:31:58	22:47:39	25:15:26	27:53:10
9	0:44:13	3:27:33	5:42:15	8: 4: 9	10:25:48	13: 7:11	15:38: 6	18:12:42	20:36:30	22:52:14	25:20:26	27:58:39
10	0:49:42	3:32:33	5:46:54	8: 9: 4	10:30:40	13:12:23	15:43:15	18:17:29	20:41: 1	22:56:50	25:25:28	28: 4: 9
11	0:55:10	3:37:33	5:51:32	8:13:40	10:35:33	13:17:26	15:48:23	18:22:16	20:45:32	23: 1:26	25:30:30	28: 9:38
12	1: 0:38	3:42:31	5:56:10	8:18:26	10:40:27	13:22:47	15:53:31	18:27: 2	20:50: 2	23: 6:20	25:35:35	28:15:30
13	1: 6:38	3:47:29	6: 0:47	8:22:53	10:45:21	13:27:59	15:58:38	18:31:48	20:54:34	23:10:40	25:40:40	28:20:41
14	1:11:32	3:52:25	6: 5:24	8:27:31	10:50:16	13:33:12	16: 3:45	18:36:32	20:59: 4	23:15:18	25:45:45	28:26:13
15	1:16:58	3:57:21	6:10: 1	8:32: 8	10:55:12	13:38:24	16: 8:51	18:41:16	21: 3:34	23:19:56	25:50:52	28:31:45
16	1:22:22	4: 2:16	6:14:37	8:36:46	11: 0: 8	13:43:50	16:13: 5	18:45:59	21: 7:35	23:24:35	25:56: 0	28:37:18
17	1:27:46	4: 7: 9	6:19:13	8:41:24	11: 5: 4	13:48:37	16:19: 1	18:50:42	21:12:35	23:29:15	26: 1:20	28:42:50
18	1:33:46	4:12: 2	6:23:48	8:46: 4	11:10: 1	13:54: 4	16:24: 5	18:55: 4	21:17:35	23:33:57	26: 6:20	28:48:24
19	1:38:32	4:16:54	6:28:24	8:50:42	11:15: 0	13:59:16	16:29:10	19: 0: 5	21:21:35	23:38:37	26:11:31	28:53:58
20	1:43:53	4:21:45	6:32:59	8:55:22	11:20: 2	14: 4:30	16:34:13	19: 4:46	21:26: 5	23:43:19	26:16:43	28:59:32
21	1:49:13	4:26:35	6:37:34	9: 0: 2	11:25: 1	14: 9:43	16:39:15	19: 9:25	21:30:35	23:48: 1	26:21:56	29: 5: 6
22	1:54:33	4:31:24	6:42:43	9: 4:43	11:30: 1	14:14:57	16:44:17	19:14: 5	21:35:36	23:52:45	26:27: 9	29:10:40
23	1:59:51	4:36:12	6:46:43	9: 9:24	11:35: 7	14:20:29	16:49:18	19:18:45	21:39:36	23:57:30	26:32:26	29:16:14
24	2: 5: 9	4:41:12	6:51:17	9:14: 6	11:40: 6	14:25:32	16:54:18	19:23:22	21:44:36	24: 2:15	26:37:43	29:21:48
25	2:10:25	4:45:47	6:55:51	9:18:48	11:45: 0	14:30:35	16:59:17	19:27:59	21:48:37	24: 7: 1	26:43: 0	29:27:24
26	2:15:41	4:50:33	7: 0:25	9:23:31	11:50:12	14:35:48	17: 4:15	19:32:56	21:53:35	24:11:48	26:48:18	29:32:58
27	2:20:55	4:55:18	7: 4:59	9:28:14	11:55:16	14:41: 2	17: 9:14	19:37:13	21:57:39	24:16:36	26:53:38	29:38:33
28	2:26: 9	5: 0: 2	7: 9:32	9:32:58	12: 0:22	14:46:14	17:14: 9	19:41:48	22: 2:40	24:21:24	26:58:58	29:44: 2
29	2:31:22		7:14: 6	9:37:43	12: 5:28	14:51:26	17:19:11	19:46:24	22: 6:41	24:26:14	27: 4:20	29:49:41
30	2:36:33		7:18:41	9:42:28	12:10:32		17:24: 4	19:51: 8	22:11:13	24:31: 5	27: 9:42	29:55:16
31	2:41:43		7:23:15		12:15:38		17:28:59	19:55:34		24:35:57		30: 0:49

1960   SSRY = 30:16:48

Day	January	February	March	April	May	June	July	August	September	October	November	December
1	0: 5:35	2:47:50	5:11:16	7:34:55	9:55:12	12:29:44	15: 6:27	17:44:15	20:10:59	22:17:15	24:53:19	27:28:44
2	0:10:44	2:53: 0	5:16:10	7:39:31	10: 0: 0	12:34:54	15:11:41	17:49:10	20:15:34	22:21:49	24:58:14	27:34:10
3	0:16:14	2:58:10	5:20:44	7:44: 7	10: 4:50	12:40: 4	15:16:54	17:54: 4	20:20:49	22:26:23	25: 3:11	27:39:37
4	0:21:44	3: 3:18	5:25:27	7:48:43	10: 9:40	12:45:14	15:22: 6	17:58:56	20:24:43	22:30:57	25: 8: 9	27:45: 4
5	0:22:18	3: 8:25	5:30: 9	7:53:19	10:14:30	12:50:25	15:27:19	18: 3:49	20:29:16	22:35:32	25:13: 7	27:50:33
6	0:27:55	3:13:30	5:34:51	7:57:54	10:19:21	12:55:35	15:32:30	18: 8:40	20:33:49	22:40: 7	25:18: 7	27:56: 1
7	0:33:31	3:18:37	5:39:31	8: 2:32	10:24:14	13: 0:46	15:37:42	18:13:30	20:38:20	22:45:32	25:23: 8	28: 1:32
8	0:38:56	3:23:41	5:44:13	8: 7: 9	10:29: 6	13: 6: 0	15:42:53	18:18:20	20:42:56	22:50:19	25:28:10	28: 7: 3
9	0:44:27	3:28:44	5:48:53	8:11:46	10:34: 0	13:11:13	15:48: 3	18:23: 9	20:47:28	22:54:53	25:33:13	28:12:34
10	0:49:58	3:33:46	5:53:32	8:16:23	10:38:54	13:16:26	15:53:13	18:27:58	20:52: 0	22:59:19	25:38:17	28:18: 6
11	0:55:28	3:38:47	5:58:10	8:21: 3	10:43:48	13:21:39	15:58:22	18:32:42	20:56:33	23: 3:13	25:43:22	28:23:38
12	1: 0:58	3:43:47	6: 2:47	8:25:39	10:48:54	13:26:52	16: 3:30	18:37:30	21: 1: 5	23: 7:49	25:48:28	28:29:11
13	1: 6:27	3:48:44	6: 7:29	8:30:17	10:53:41	13:32: 6	16: 8:40	18:42:18	21: 5:37	23:12:30	25:53:35	28:34:44
14	1:11:57	3:53:44	6:12: 6	8:34:56	10:58:38	13:37:20	16:13:48	18:47: 4	21:10: 8	23:17:49	25:58:43	28:40:18
15	1:17:22	3:58:42	6:16:44	8:39:35	11: 3:35	13:42:34	16:18:55	18:51:49	21:14:40	23:21:49	26: 3:53	28:45:53
16	1:22:48	4: 3:38	6:21:21	8:44:14	11: 8:34	13:47:48	16:24: 2	18:56:33	21:19:12	23:26:31	26: 9: 3	28:51:28
17	1:28:14	4: 8:33	6:25:58	8:48:54	11:13:33	13:53:18	16:29: 9	19: 1:17	21:23:43	23:31:49	26:14:16	28:57:39
18	1:33:39	4:13:27	6:30:35	8:53:34	11:18:33	13:58:35	16:34:15	19: 6: 0	21:28: 8	23:36:31	26:19:29	29: 2:14
19	1:39:39	4:18:21	6:35:11	8:58:16	11:23:34	14: 3:32	16:39:18	19:10:42	21:32:46	23:41:55	26:24:41	29: 8:14
20	1:44:26	4:23:14	6:39:47	9: 2:57	11:28:35	14: 8:47	16:44:22	19:15:23	21:37:18	23:45:32	26:29:56	29:13:50
21	1:49:48	4:28: 6	6:44:23	9: 7:39	11:33:40	14:14: 2	16:49:25	19:20:45	21:41:50	23:50:38	26:35:12	29:19:26
22	1:55:30	4:32:56	6:48:59	9:12:22	11:38:48	14:19:17	16:54:28	19:24:45	21:46:22	23:55:23	26:40:29	29:25: 2
23	2: 1: 6	4:37:46	6:53:32	9:17: 5	11:43:48	14:24:47	16:59:31	19:29:34	21:55:22	24: 0: 8	26:45:47	29:30:39
24	2: 6:25	4:42:36	6:58:11	9:21:48	11:53:53	14:29:47	17: 4:32	19:34:22	22: 1: 3	24: 4:53	26:50:58	29:36:15
25	2:11:42	4:47:24	7: 2:46	9:26:33	11:58:58	14:35:32	17: 9:32	19:39:11	22: 9:58	24: 9:39	26:56:26	29:41:51
26	2:16:25	4:52:12	7: 7:22	9:31:18	12: 4: 5	14:40:17	17:14:32	19:43:21	22: 1:36	24:14:27	27: 1:46	29:47:27
27	2:21:42	4:56:59	7:11:57	9:36:43	12: 9:11	14:45:31	17:19:31	19:47:58	22: 9:26	24:19:16	27: 7: 8	29:53: 3
28	2:26:58	5: 1:46	7:16:31	9:41:10	12:14:18	14:50:49	17:24:30	19:52:36	22: 3:39	24:24:55	27:12:31	29:58:39
29	2:32:12	5: 6:31	7:21:18	9:45:49	12:19:27	14:56:56	17:29:27	19:57:32	22:18:35	24:28:55	27:17:54	30: 4:15
30	2:37:26		7:25:44	9:50:23	12:24:35	15: 1:14	17:34:24	20: 1:48	22:22:41	24:33:44	27:23:19	30: 9:50
31	2:42:38		7:30:20				17:39:20	20: 6:24		24:38:34		30:15:25

1961 SSRY = 30:18: 7

	January	February	March	April	May	June	July	August	September	October	November	December
1	0: 0: 0	2:47:39	5: 6: 7	7:29:55	9:50:14	12:24:48	15: 1:37	17:44:37	20: 6:33	22:22:54	24:48:59	27:24:23
2	0: 5:35	2:52:48	5:10:51	7:34:30	9:55: 4	12:29:57	15: 6:51	17:49:26	20:11: 8	22:27:28	24:53:55	27:29:49
3	0:11:10	2:57:56	5:15:35	7:39:36	9:59:55	12:35:57	15:12:17	17:54:19	20:15:42	22:32:32	24:58:52	27:35:16
4	0:16:43	3: 3: 5	5:20:19	7:48:18	10: 4:41	12:40:40	15:17:17	17:59:12	20:20:17	22:36:37	25: 3:50	27:40:44
5	0:22:16	3: 8:11	5:25: 1	7:52:55	10: 9:32	12:45:29	15:22:29	18: 4: 5	20:24:51	22:41:13	25: 8:48	27:46:13
6	0:27:48	3:13:17	5:29:43	7:57:31	10:14:23	12:50:40	15:27:42	18: 8:57	20:29:25	22:45:50	25:13:48	27:51:42
7	0:33:22	3:18:21	5:34:25	8: 2: 8	10:19:16	12:55:32	15:32:54	18:13:45	20:33:58	22:50:24	25:18:49	27:57:12
8	0:38:53	3:23:24	5:39: 6	8: 6:46	10:24: 8	13: 6:17	15:38: 5	18:18:35	20:38:32	22:55: 2	25:23:51	28: 2:43
9	0:44:25	3:28:26	5:43:46	8:11:23	10:29: 2	13:11:30	15:43:16	18:23:24	20:43: 5	22:59:38	25:28:54	28: 8:15
10	0:49:56	3:33:29	5:48:26	8:16: 0	10:33:56	13:16:46	15:48:26	18:28:12	20:47:37	23: 4:15	25:33:58	28:13:49
11	0:55:26	3:38:30	5:53: 5	8:20:39	10:38:51	13:21:58	15:53:36	18:32:59	20:52:12	23: 8:53	25:39: 2	28:19:21
12	1: 0:55	3:43:30	5:57:44	8:25:17	10:43:47	13:27:26	15:58:46	18:37:44	20:56:48	23:13:32	25:44: 9	28:24:52
13	1: 6:24	3:48:28	6: 2:23	8:29:55	10:48:43	13:32:26	16: 3:55	18:42:32	21: 1:15	23:18:11	25:49:17	28:30:26
14	1:11:52	3:53:26	6: 7: 1	8:34:30	10:53:41	13:37:41	16: 9: 3	18:47:18	21: 5:47	23:22:51	25:54:26	28:36: 0
15	1:17:19	3:58:23	6:11:39	8:39:16	10:58:39	13:48:10	16:14:11	18:52: 2	21:10:19	23:27:32	25:59:35	28:41:35
16	1:22:45	4: 3:19	6:16:17	8:43:56	11: 3:38	13:53:25	16:19:18	18:56:46	21:14:51	23:32:13	26: 4:45	28:47:10
17	1:28:11	4: 8:14	6:20:55	8:48:37	11: 8:37	13:59:23	16:24:25	19: 1:32	21:19:23	23:36:56	26: 9:55	28:52:45
18	1:33:35	4:13: 8	6:25:32	8:53: 2	11:13:37	13:56:55	16:29:31	19: 6:12	21:23:54	23:41:38	26:15: 6	28:58:20
19	1:38:59	4:18: 1	6:30: 9	8:58:14	11:18:37	14: 3:56	16:34:38	19:10:54	21:28:26	23:46:21	26:20:23	29: 3:56
20	1:44:44	4:22:54	6:34:45	9: 2:42	11:23:40	14: 9:11	16:39:40	19:15:35	21:32:58	23:51: 5	26:25:37	29: 9:32
21	1:49:44	4:27:45	6:39:21	9: 7:25	11:28:42	14:14:26	16:44:44	19:20:16	21:37:29	23:55:50	26:30:53	29:15: 8
22	1:55: 4	4:32:36	6:43:58	9:12: 8	11:33:45	14:19:41	16:49:47	19:24:56	21:42: 1	24: 0:35	26:36: 9	29:20:44
23	2: 0:25	4:37:26	6:48:34	9:16:51	11:38:48	14:24:56	16:54:50	19:29:35	21:46:33	24: 5:20	26:41:26	29:26:20
24	2: 5:44	4:42:14	6:53:10	9:21:35	11:43:52	14:30:11	16:59:52	19:34:14	21:51: 4	24:10: 9	26:46:44	29:31:57
25	2:11: 3	4:47: 2	6:57:45	9:26:21	11:48:57	14:35:26	17: 4:52	19:38:53	21:55:37	24:14:57	26:52: 2	29:37:33
26	2:16:19	4:51:50	7: 2:21	9:31: 6	11:54: 1	14:40:41	17: 9:52	19:43:31	22: 0: 9	24:19:46	26:57:26	29:43: 9
27	2:21:35	4:56:36	7: 6:57	9:35:52	11:59: 8	14:45:55	17:14:52	19:48: 8	22: 4:42	24:24:36	27: 2:47	29:48:45
28	2:26:49	5: 1:22	7:11:32	9:40:39	12: 4:15	14:51:23	17:19:50	19:52:45	22: 9:15	24:29:27	27: 8:10	29:54:21
29	2:32: 3		7:16: 8	9:45:26	12: 9:23	14:56:23	17:24:48	19:57:21	22:13:48	24:34:19	27:13:33	29:59:57
30	2:37:16		7:20:43		12:14:30		17:29:45	20: 1:57	22:18:21	24:39:11	27:18:58	30: 5:33
31	2:42:28		7:25:19		12:19:39		17:34:41	20: 6:31		24:44: 5		30:11: 9

1962 SSRY = 30:11:25

	January	February	March	April	May	June	July	August	September	October	November	December
1	0: 0: 0	2:47: 7	5: 5:11	7:28:30	9:48:15	12:22:19	14:58:25	17:45: 5	20: 6:23	22:18:15	24:43:43	27:18:24
2	0: 5:34	2:52:16	5:10: 2	7:33: 5	9:52:56	12:27:29	15: 3:37	17:49:55	20:10:57	22:22:49	24:48:37	27:23:49
3	0:10:57	2:57:24	5:14:38	7:37:40	9:57:51	12:32:28	15: 8:50	17:54:47	20:15:31	22:27:21	24:53:32	27:29:15
4	0:16:40	3: 2:31	5:19:20	7:42:15	10: 2:40	12:37:38	15:14: 2	17:59:40	20:20: 6	22:31:55	24:58:32	27:34:41
5	0:22:13	3: 7:37	5:24: 2	7:46:50	10: 7:30	12:42:48	15:19:14	18: 4:33	20:24:38	22:36:29	25: 3:26	27:40:36
6	0:27:45	3:12:42	5:28:44	7:51:26	10:12:20	12:47:58	15:24:25	18: 9:25	20:29:11	22:41: 6	25: 8:26	27:45:58
7	0:33:16	3:17:46	5:33:24	7:56: 2	10:17:13	12:53: 8	15:29:36	18:14:15	20:33:43	22:45:43	25:13:24	27:51: 5
8	0:38:47	3:22:49	5:38: 4	8: 0:37	10:22: 6	13: 3:32	15:34:46	18:19: 5	20:38:16	22:50:14	25:18:25	27:56:34
9	0:44:17	3:27:51	5:42:44	8: 5:14	10:27:13	13: 8:44	15:39:56	18:23:54	20:42:48	22:54:49	25:23:26	28: 2: 6
10	0:49:48	3:32:52	5:47:23	8: 9:50	10:31:48	13:13:56	15:45: 6	18:28:42	20:47:20	22:59:26	25:28:29	28: 7:34
11	0:55:16	3:37:51	5:52: 1	8:14:27	10:36:41	13:19: 8	15:50:15	18:33:29	20:51:53	23: 4: 1	25:33:32	28:13: 9
12	1: 0:45	3:42:50	5:56:40	8:19: 4	10:41:37	13:24:21	15:55:23	18:38:15	20:56:25	23: 8:38	25:38:38	28:18:37
13	1: 6:12	3:47:48	6: 1:17	8:23:41	10:46:33	13:29:34	16: 0:31	18:43: 0	21: 0:57	23:13:18	25:43:42	28:24: 9
14	1:11:39	3:52:44	6: 5:55	8:28:18	10:51:31	13:34:47	16: 5:38	18:47:44	21: 5:29	23:17:56	25:48:49	28:29:42
15	1:17: 5	3:57:41	6:10:32	8:32:57	10:56:24	13:40: 0	16:10:44	18:52:27	21:10: 1	23:22:35	25:53:57	28:35:15
16	1:22:30	4: 2:36	6:15:10	8:37:36	11: 1:22	13:45:14	16:15:50	18:57:10	21:14:33	23:27:15	25:59: 6	28:40:48
17	1:27:55	4: 7:30	6:19:45	8:42:15	11: 6:20	13:50:28	16:20:56	19: 1:51	21:19: 5	23:31:56	26: 4: 6	28:46:22
18	1:33:18	4:12:23	6:24:21	8:46:54	11:11:18	13:55:43	16:26: 1	19: 6:31	21:23:37	23:36:38	26: 9:16	28:51:57
19	1:38:41	4:17:16	6:28:58	8:51:34	11:16:18	14: 0:55	16:31: 6	19:11:11	21:28: 9	23:41:19	26:14:39	28:57:30
20	1:44: 2	4:22: 8	6:33: 8	8:56:14	11:21:18	14: 6: 9	16:36:11	19:15:50	21:32:41	23:46: 2	26:19:52	29: 3: 5
21	1:49:23	4:26:59	6:42:43	9: 0:55	11:26:18	14:11:23	16:41:11	19:20:28	21:37:13	23:50:45	26:25: 5	29: 8:40
22	1:54:43	4:31:49	6:47:18	9: 5:37	11:31:20	14:16:37	16:46:13	19:25: 6	21:41:45	23:55:30	26:30:22	29:14:15
23	2: 0: 2	4:36:38	6:51:53	9:10:19	11:36:22	14:21:51	16:51:14	19:29:43	21:46:17	24: 0:15	26:35:38	29:19:51
24	2: 5:19	4:41:23	6:56:27	9:15: 1	11:41:25	14:27: 5	16:56:15	19:34:20	21:50:49	24: 4:59	26:40:56	29:25:27
25	2:10:36	4:46:10	7: 1: 2	9:19:44	11:46:28	14:32:14	17: 1:15	19:38:56	21:55:22	24: 9:48	26:46:14	29:31: 1
26	2:15:52	4:50:56	7: 5:36	9:24:28	11:51:33	14:37:32	17: 6:15	19:43:31	22: 0: 6	24:14:36	26:51:33	29:36:36
27	2:21: 7	4:55:42	7:10:11	9:29:13	11:56:37	14:42:45	17:11:10	19:48: 6	22: 4:38	24:19:25	26:56:53	29:42:11
28	2:26:21	5: 0:27	7:14:46	9:33:57	12: 1:42	14:47:59	17:16:10	19:52:41	22: 9:10	24:24:14	27: 2:13	29:47:46
29	2:31:34		7:19:20	9:38:42	12: 6:49	14:53:12	17:21: 8	19:48:37	22:13:42	24:29:25	27: 7:37	29:53:21
30	2:36:46		7:23:55	9:43:29	12:11:56		17:26: 6	19:53:13		24:33:57	27:13: 0	29:58:56
31	2:41:57				12:17: 3		17:31: 0	19:57:48		24:38:49		30: 4:30

1983 SSRY = 30:16:42

	January	February	March	April	May	June	July	August	September	October	November	December
1	0: 0: 0	2:47:43	5: 6:17	7:30: 4	9:50:12	12:24:29	15: 1: 9	17:39:10	20: 6: 7	22:22:23	24:48:11	27:23:12
2	0: 5:35	2:52:53	5:11:46	7:34:35	9:55:45	12:29:38	15: 6:13	17:44: 5	20:10:42	22:26:57	24:53: 6	27:28:37
3	0:11:12	2:58: 2	5:16:44	7:39: 5	10: 0:39	12:34:29	15:11:16	17:49:59	20:15:51	22:31:31	24:58: 1	27:34: 4
4	0:16:43	3: 3:10	5:20:42	7:43:51	10: 4:38	12:39:59	15:16:40	17:53:45	20:19:51	22:36:31	25: 2:58	27:39:31
5	0:22:17	3: 8:17	5:25:42	7:48:27	10: 9:23	12:45:20	15:22: 1	17:58:45	20:24:25	22:40:39	25: 7:56	27:44:58
6	0:27:50	3:13:23	5:29:54	7:53: 3	10:14:19	12:50:20	15:27:13	18: 3:37	20:28:59	22:45:14	25:12:55	27:50:27
7	0:33:22	3:18:27	5:34:36	7:57:39	10:19:11	12:55:55	15:32:25	18: 8:28	20:33:32	22:49:50	25:17:55	27:55:56
8	0:38:54	3:23:31	5:39:57	8: 2:16	10:24: 3	13: 0:43	15:37:36	18:13:18	20:38: 5	22:54:26	25:22:56	28: 1:27
9	0:44:25	3:28:34	5:45:37	8: 6:53	10:28:59	13: 5:55	15:42:57	18:18: 7	20:42:38	22:59: 2	25:27:58	28: 6:57
10	0:49:56	3:33:36	5:48:37	8:11:30	10:33:44	13:11:34	15:48:16	18:22:57	20:47:10	23: 3:39	25:33: 1	28:12:27
11	0:55:26	3:38:37	5:53:17	8:16: 7	10:38:44	13:16:21	15:53:16	18:27:45	20:51:43	23: 8:16	25:38: 6	28:18: 1
12	1: 0:55	3:43:36	5:57:56	8:20:45	10:43:35	13:21:34	15:58:16	18:32:32	20:56:15	23:12:55	25:43:11	28:23:33
13	1: 6:24	3:48:35	6: 2:34	8:25:23	10:48:35	13:26:47	16: 3:25	18:37:19	21: 0:47	23:17:33	25:48:18	28:29: 6
14	1:11:52	3:53:32	6: 7:11	8:30: 1	10:53:28	13:32: 1	16: 8:33	18:42: 5	21: 5:19	23:22:13	25:53:25	28:34:40
15	1:17:19	3:58:30	6:11:50	8:34:44	10:58:28	13:37:15	16:13:48	18:46:51	21: 5:59	23:26:53	25:58:34	28:40:49
16	1:22:46	4: 3:26	6:16:28	8:39:20	11: 3:26	13:42:30	16:18:54	18:51:35	21:10:22	23:31:33	26: 3:44	28:46:49
17	1:28:10	4: 8:21	6:21: 5	8:43:59	11: 8:25	13:47:44	16:23:55	18:56:19	21:14:22	23:36:15	26: 8:54	28:51:24
18	1:33:35	4:13:15	6:25:42	8:48:40	11:13:25	13:52:59	16:29: 0	19: 1: 2	21:18:54	23:40:57	26:14: 6	28:56:59
19	1:38:59	4:18: 9	6:30:18	8:53:20	11:18:25	13:58:13	16:34: 6	19: 5:45	21:23:26	23:45:40	26:19:19	29: 2:34
20	1:44:21	4:23: 1	6:34:44	8:58: 1	11:23:28	14: 3:28	16:39: 6	19:10:27	21:27:57	23:50:24	26:24:33	29: 8:10
21	1:49:44	4:27:53	6:39:31	9: 2:43	11:28:28	14: 8: 1	16:44:10	19:15:27	21:32:29	23:55: 9	26:29:48	29:13:22
22	1:55: 5	4:32:44	6:44: 4	9: 7:25	11:33:30	14:13:58	16:49:18	19:20: 9	21:37: 0	24: 4:39	26:35: 4	29:19:22
23	2: 0:25	4:37:34	6:48:43	9:12: 8	11:38:33	14:19:13	16:54:20	19:24:50	21:41:32	24: 4:39	26:40:21	29:24:58
24	2: 5:44	4:42:23	6:53:19	9:16:52	11:43:37	14:24:28	16:59:18	19:29:10	21:46: 4	24: 9:25	26:45:39	29:30:34
25	2:11: 3	4:47:11	6:57:55	9:21:36	11:48:41	14:29:43	17: 4:23	19:33:49	21:50:36	24:14:13	26:50:58	29:36:10
26	2:16:20	4:51:59	7: 2:29	9:26:20	11:53:46	14:34:48	17: 9:25	19:38:27	21:55: 8	24:19: 1	26:56:18	29:41:46
27	2:21:36	4:56:46	7: 7: 6	9:31: 5	11:58:51	14:39:48	17:14:19	19:43:33	21:59:40	24:23:31	27: 1:39	29:47:22
28	2:26:52	5: 1:32	7:11:42	9:35:51	12: 3:56	14:45:27	17:19:22	19:47:43	22: 4:12	24:28:41	27: 7: 1	29:52:46
29	2:32: 6		7:16:17	9:40:37	12: 9: 5	14:50:41	17:24:20	19:52: 6	22: 8:44	24:33:32	27:12:24	29:58:58
30	2:37:19		7:20:53	9:45:24	12:14:13	14:55:55	17:29:18	19:56:56	22:13:17	24:38:24	27:17:48	30: 4:10
31	2:42:31		7:25:18		12:19:12		17:34:14	20: 1:32		24:43:17		30: 9:45

1964 SSRY = 30: 8:42

	January	February	March	April	May	June	July	August	September	October	November	December
1	0: 0: 0	2:47: 4	5: 9:52	7:32:53	9:52:33	12:26:25	15: 2:27	17:39:32	20: 5:37	22:21:15	24:46:41	27:21:25
2	0: 5:33	2:52:13	5:14:34	7:37:27	9:57:20	12:31:33	15: 7:39	17:44:26	20:10:10	22:25:48	24:51:36	27:26:50
3	0:11: 5	2:57:20	5:19:20	7:42:36	10: 2: 8	12:36:42	15:12:51	17:49:18	20:14:44	22:30:21	24:56:31	27:32:16
4	0:16:39	3: 2:27	5:23:58	7:46:36	10: 6:58	12:41:51	15:18: 3	17:54:11	20:19:18	22:34:54	25: 1:28	27:37:42
5	0:22:11	3: 7:33	5:28:39	7:51:11	10:11:46	12:47: 1	15:23:33	17:59: 2	20:23:49	22:39:27	25: 6:25	27:43:37
6	0:27:42	3:12:38	5:33:19	7:55:46	10:16:36	12:52:11	15:28:43	18: 3:51	20:28:24	22:44: 3	25:11:24	27:49: 6
7	0:33:13	3:17:42	5:37:59	8: 0:21	10:21:27	12:57:21	15:33:55	18: 8:40	20:32:54	22:48:38	25:16:24	27:54: 6
8	0:38:44	3:22:45	5:42:39	8: 4:57	10:26:19	13: 2:32	15:39: 5	18:13:29	20:37:25	22:53:13	25:21:24	27:59:35
9	0:44:14	3:27:47	5:47:18	8: 9:33	10:31:11	13: 7:43	15:44:17	18:18: 7	20:41:57	22:57:49	25:26:26	28: 0:35
10	0:49:44	3:32:47	5:51:56	8:14:10	10:36: 3	13:12:54	15:49:57	18:22:48	20:46:28	23: 2:25	25:31:28	28: 6:35
11	0:55:12	3:37:47	5:56:34	8:18:46	10:40:58	13:18: 7	15:54:10	18:27:51	20:50:59	23: 7: 2	25:36:33	28:16:35
12	1: 0:41	3:42:46	6: 1:12	8:23:23	10:45:52	13:23:19	15:59: 0	18:32:42	20:55:30	23:11:39	25:41:38	28:21:38
13	1: 6: 9	3:47:44	6: 5:49	8:28: 0	10:50:48	13:28:32	16: 4:25	18:37:22	21: 0: 1	23:16:17	25:46:43	28:27:10
14	1:11:35	3:52:42	6:10:26	8:32:38	10:55:44	13:33:44	16: 9:31	18:42:49	21: 4:32	23:20:56	25:51:50	28:32:42
15	1:17:35	3:57:37	6:15: 3	8:37:16	11: 0:41	13:39: 0	16:14:42	18:46:49	21: 9: 3	23:25:35	25:56:58	28:38:15
16	1:22:27	4: 2:32	6:19:39	8:41:55	11: 5:38	13:44:24	16:19:47	18:51:32	21:13:32	23:30:35	26: 2: 7	28:43:28
17	1:27:51	4: 7:26	6:24:14	8:46:34	11:10:36	13:49:24	16:24:47	18:56:15	21:18: 3	23:35:15	26: 7:17	28:48:42
18	1:33:14	4:12:19	6:28:50	8:51:13	11:15:35	13:54:37	16:29:51	19: 0:56	21:22:33	23:39:37	26:12:29	28:54:55
19	1:38:37	4:17:12	6:33:25	8:55:53	11:20:34	13:59:50	16:34:55	19: 5:37	21:27: 4	23:44:19	26:17:41	29: 0:29
20	1:43:59	4:22: 4	6:38: 1	9: 0:34	11:25:34	14: 5: 2	16:39:57	19:10:17	21:31:34	23:49: 1	26:22:54	29: 6: 4
21	1:49:19	4:26:54	6:42:35	9: 5:14	11:30:36	14:10:18	16:44:59	19:14:59	21:36: 5	23:53:45	26:28: 8	29:11:38
22	1:54:39	4:31:43	6:47:10	9: 9:55	11:35:38	14:15:31	16:50: 0	19:19:36	21:41:40	23:58:30	26:33:23	29:17:12
23	1:59:58	4:36:32	6:51:45	9:14:37	11:40:38	14:20:45	16:55: 1	19:24:14	21:45:35	24: 3:14	26:38:40	29:22:47
24	2: 5:16	4:41:20	6:56:19	9:19:19	11:45:41	14:25:58	17: 0: 1	19:28:52	21:50:16	24: 8: 0	26:43:57	29:28:22
25	2:10:33	4:46: 7	7: 0:53	9:24: 2	11:50:44	14:31:11	17: 5: 0	19:33:29	21:54: 6	24:12:47	26:49:15	29:33:56
26	2:15:50	4:50:54	7: 5:27	9:28:46	11:55:48	14:36:24	17: 9:58	19:38: 6	21:58:37	24:17:35	26:54:35	29:39:31
27	2:21: 4	4:55:39	7:10: 2	9:33:30	12: 0:53	14:41:37	17:14:56	19:42:43	22: 2:39	24:22:23	26:59:55	29:45: 6
28	2:26:12	5: 0:24	7:14:36	9:38:15	12: 5:58	14:46:50	17:19:53	19:47:18	22: 7:11	24:27: 8	27: 5:16	29:50:40
29	2:31:31	5: 5: 8	7:19:10	9:43: 0	12:11: 4	14:52: 2	17:24:44	19:51:53	22:11:43	24:31:56	27:10:38	29:56:14
30	2:36:43		7:23:44	9:47:46	12:16:11	14:57:15	17:29:44	19:56:28	22:16:43	24:36:55	27:16: 1	30: 1:48
31	2:41:54		7:28:18		12:21:18		17:34:39	20: 1: 3		24:41:48		30: 7:22

1965 SSRY = 30:12:16

	January	February	March	April	May	June	July	August	September	October	November	December
1	0: 0:0	2:47: 5	5: 5: 5	7:20:25	9:38:18	12:22:24	14:58:44	17:36:13	20: 2:39	22:18:35	24:44:12	27:19: 7
2	0: 0:34	2:47:41	5: 5:49	7:37:35	9:53: 6	12:27:32	15: 3:56	17:41: 0	20: 7:14	22:23: 8	24:49: 1	27:24:32
3	0: 6:11	2:57:22	5:14:32	7:37:35	9:57:54	12:32:42	15: 9: 9	17:46: 0	20:11:48	22:27:41	24:54: 3	27:29:58
4	0:10:40	3: 2:29	5:19:15	7:42:11	10: 0:47	12:37:51	15:14:21	17:50:53	20:16:21	22:32:15	25: 0:53	27:35:23
5	0:16:40	3: 7:34	5:23:56	7:46:46	10:17:33	12:43:12	15:19:33	17:55:58	20:20:57	22:36:49	25: 8:56	27:40:52
6	0:21:13	3:12:39	5:28:38	7:51:22	10:12:24	12:48:12	15:24:46	18: 5:25	20:25:27	22:41:24	25:13:56	27:46:20
7	0:27:45	3:17:43	5:33:18	7:55:58	10:17:24	12:53:23	15:29:55	18: 5:25	20:30: 2	22:45:59	25:18:57	27:51:49
8	0:33:17	3:22:47	5:37:58	8: 0:34	10:27: 0	12:58:35	15:35: 5	18:10:14	20:34:32	22:50:34	25:23:58	27:57:19
9	0:44:19	3:27:47	5:42:38	8: 5:10	10:27: 0	13: 3:46	15:40:15	18:15: 3	20:39: 4	22:55:10	25:29:47	28: 2:20
10	0:49:47	3:32:48	5:47:17	8: 9:47	10:31:53	13: 8:58	15:45:24	18:19:51	20:43:36	22:59:47	25:34: 5	28: 7:51
11	0:55:16	3:37:48	5:51:56	8:14:24	10:36:48	13:14:10	15:50:33	18:24:38	20:48: 8	23: 4:24	25:39:10	28:13:51
12	1: 0:45	3:42:46	5:56:34	8:19: 1	10:41:42	13:19:23	15:55:41	18:29:24	20:52:38	23: 9: 2	25:44:17	28:19:23
13	1: 6:16	3:47:44	6: 1:10	8:23:39	10:46:38	13:24:36	16: 0:49	18:34:10	20:57:10	23:13:40	25:49:24	28:24:55
14	1:11:39	3:52:40	6: 5:49	8:28:17	10:51:35	13:29:49	16: 5:56	18:38:55	21: 1:41	23:18:19	25:54:31	28:30:28
15	1:17:13	3:57:36	6:10:26	8:32:55	10:56:31	13:35: 3	16:11: 3	18:43:39	21: 6:12	23:22:58	25:59:41	28:36: 1
16	1:22:30	4: 2:31	6:15: 2	8:37:34	11: 1:28	13:40:16	16:16: 9	18:48:23	21:10:43	23:27:38	26: 4:52	28:41:35
17	1:27:54	4: 7:24	6:19:39	8:42:13	11: 6:26	13:45:30	16:21:15	18:53: 5	21:15:13	23:32:19	26:10: 4	28:47:10
18	1:33:17	4:12: 1	6:24:15	8:46:52	11:11:25	13:50:44	16:26:19	18:57:48	21:19:44	23:37: 1	26:15:16	28:52:44
19	1:38:39	4:17:24	6:28:50	8:51:33	11:16:25	13:55:58	16:31:23	19: 2:29	21:24:15	23:41:43	26:20:30	28:58:19
20	1:44:22	4:22:51	6:33:26	8:56:13	11:21:26	14: 1:12	16:36:26	19: 7:10	21:28:46	23:46:27	26:25:43	29: 3:54
21	1:49:22	4:26:51	6:38: 1	9: 0:54	11:26:27	14: 6:26	16:41:29	19:11:50	21:33:18	23:51:12	26:30:57	29: 9:27
22	1:54:41	4:31:40	6:42:36	9: 5:36	11:31:29	14:11:40	16:46:31	19:16:30	21:37:49	23:55:57	26:36:17	29:20:40
23	2: 0: 9	4:36:29	6:47:11	9:10:18	11:36:31	14:16:54	16:51:33	19:21:10	21:42:19	24: 0:41	26:41:35	29:26:15
24	2: 5:18	4:41:14	6:51:46	9:15: 1	11:41:35	14:22: 8	16:56:33	19:25:48	21:46:50	24: 5:28	26:46:54	29:31:51
25	2:10:35	4:45:58	6:56:22	9:19:44	11:46:38	14:27:22	17: 1:33	19:30:26	21:51:22	24:10:15	26:52:15	29:37: 6
26	2:15:51	4:50:50	7: 0:56	9:24:28	11:51:43	14:32:36	17: 6:33	19:35: 4	21:55:53	24:15:53	26:57:36	29:43: 2
27	2:21: 5	4:55:36	7: 5:31	9:29:13	11:56:48	14:37:50	17:11:31	19:39:41	22: 0:55	24:20:42	27: 2:58	29:48:37
28	2:26:19	5: 0:21	7:10:56	9:33:58	12: 1:54	14:43: 4	17:16:29	19:44:28	22: 5:24	24:24:33	27: 8:59	29:54: 2
29	2:31:32		7:14:40	9:38:44	12: 7: 1	14:48:17	17:21:26	19:48:35	22: 9:29	24:29:33	27: 2:50	29:59:46
30	2:36:50		7:19:23	9:43:31	12:12: 8	14:53:31	17:26:22	19:53:30	22:14: 2	24:34:25	27:13:43	30: 5:21
31	2:41:55		7:23:50		12:17:15		17:31:18	19:58: 5		24:39:18		30:13:25

1966 SSRY = 30:20:23

	January	February	March	April	May	June	July	August	September	October	November	December
1	0: 0: 0	2:47:56	5: 6:40	7:30:40	9:55:57	12:25:51	15: 2:52	17:41: 8	20: 8:19	22:24:51	24:51: 1	27:26:29
2	0: 0: 0	2:58:16	5:11:30	7:39:53	9:55:57	12:31: 1	15: 8: 6	17:46: 0	20:12:54	22:29:25	24:55:57	27:31:55
3	0: 5:35	2:58:16	5:16:20	7:39:53	10: 0:47	12:36:11	15:13:20	17:50:58	20:17:29	22:33:59	25: 0:53	27:37:23
4	0:11:10	3: 3: 4	5:16:20	7:44:29	10: 5:37	12:41:22	15:18:33	17:55:52	20:21:58	22:38:34	25: 5:51	27:42:51
5	0:16:50	3: 8:31	5:20:53	7:49: 6	10:10:28	12:46:33	15:23:46	18: 0:45	20:26:33	22:43: 9	25:10:50	27:48:19
6	0:22:19	3:13:37	5:25:36	7:53:42	10:15:20	12:51:44	15:28:59	18: 5:40	20:31: 8	22:47:45	25:15:50	27:53:49
7	0:27:52	3:18:42	5:30:18	7:58:18	10:20:12	12:56:56	15:34:11	18:10:29	20:35:46	22:52:21	25:20:51	27:59:17
8	0:33:25	3:23:44	5:35: 0	8: 2:56	10:25: 5	13: 2:10	15:39:23	18:15:20	20:40:20	22:56:58	25:25:53	28: 4:50
9	0:44:29	3:28:46	5:39:42	8: 7:34	10:29:58	13: 7:23	15:44:34	18:20:10	20:44:53	23: 1:35	25:30:56	28:10:24
10	0:50: 0	3:33:52	5:44:22	8:12:12	10:34:48	13:12:36	15:49:45	18:24:59	20:49:26	23: 6: 3	25:36: 1	28:15:57
11	0:55:31	3:38:53	5:49: 3	8:16:51	10:39:48	13:17:49	15:54:55	18:29:47	20:53:58	23:10:41	25:41: 5	28:21:24
12	1: 1: 0	3:43:53	5:53:43	8:21:28	10:44:44	13:23: 3	16: 0: 5	18:34:33	20:58:30	23:15:30	25:45:44	28:27: 0
13	1: 6:30	3:48:53	5:58:22	8:26: 8	10:49:40	13:28:18	16: 5:15	18:39:23	21: 1:37	23:20: 2	25:51:19	28:32:34
14	1:11:58	3:53:51	6: 1: 1	8:30:48	10:54:38	13:33:33	16:10:24	18:44: 8	21: 7:37	23:24:49	25:56:28	28:38: 9
15	1:17:25	3:58:44	6: 7:40	8:35:26	10:59:36	13:38:48	16:15:32	18:48:55	21:12: 9	23:29:30	26: 1:37	28:43:44
16	1:22:52	4: 3:44	6:12:18	8:40: 6	11: 4:35	13:44: 3	16:20:40	18:53:41	21:16:40	23:34:10	26: 6:48	28:49:19
17	1:28:18	4: 8:40	6:16:55	8:44:46	11: 9:35	13:49:18	16:25:48	18:58:26	21:21:12	23:38:55	26:12: 9	28:54:55
18	1:33:43	4:13:34	6:21:34	8:49:27	11:14:36	13:54:33	16:30:53	19: 3:10	21:25:46	23:43:37	26:17:12	29: 0:31
19	1:39:10	4:18:31	6:26:11	8:54: 9	11:19:38	13:59:49	16:35:59	19: 7:52	21:30:18	23:48:20	26:22:26	29: 6: 7
20	1:44:31	4:23:13	6:30:49	8:58:50	11:24:40	14: 5: 5	16:41: 4	19:12:34	21:34:50	23:53: 4	26:27:41	29:11:43
21	1:49:54	4:28:13	6:35:26	9: 3:33	11:29:44	14:10:20	16:46: 9	19:17:16	21:39:22	23:57:50	26:32:57	29:17:20
22	1:55:15	4:33: 1	6:40: 2	9: 8:16	11:34:44	14:15:36	16:51:13	19:21:57	21:43:55	24: 1:35	26:38:14	29:22:56
23	2: 0:36	4:37:54	6:44:39	9:12:59	11:39:48	14:20:52	16:56:15	19:26:37	21:48:27	24: 6:22	26:43:32	29:28:33
24	2: 5:55	4:42:33	6:49:15	9:17:43	11:44:57	14:26: 8	17: 1:18	19:31:18	21:52:59	24:11: 2	26:48:51	29:34:11
25	2:11:15	4:47:17	6:53:28	9:22:28	11:50: 1	14:31:23	17: 6:19	19:35:57	21:57:32	24:16:58	26:54:10	29:39:47
26	2:16:32	4:52:21	6:57:59	9:27:13	11:55: 3	14:36:38	17:11:20	19:40:36	22: 2: 4	24:21:47	26:59:31	29:45:23
27	2:21:48	4:57: 8	7: 2:18	9:31:59	12: 0:10	14:41:53	17:16:20	19:45:15	22: 6:37	24:26:37	27: 4:56	29:51:36
28	2:27:14	5: 1:54	7: 7:40	9:36:46	12: 5:17	14:47: 8	17:21:19	19:49:52	22:11:13	24:31:47	27:15:39	30: 1:36
29	2:32:18		7:16:52	9:41:32	12:10:25	14:52:23	17:26:19	19:54:40	22:15:13	24:36:24	27:15:39	30: 7:49
30	2:42:44		7:16:52	9:46:20	12:15:33	14:57:38	17:31:15	19:59:37	22:20:17	24:41:13	27:21: 4	30:13:25
31	2:42:44		7:26: 4		12:20:41		17:36:12	20: 3:43		24:46: 6		

1967 SSRY = 30: 6:59

	January	February	March	April	May	June	July	August	September	October	November	December
1	0: 0: 0	2:46:48	5: 4:37	7:27:36	9:46:59	12:20:28	14:56:19	17:33:29	19:59:40	22:15:12	24:40:13	27:14:26
2	0: 5:33	2:51:56	5: 9:20	7:32:11	9:51:46	12:25:36	15: 1:31	17:38:23	20: 8:47	22:19:44	24:45: 7	27:19:50
3	0:11: 5	2:57: 3	5:14:15	7:41:19	9:56:23	12:30:54	15: 6:42	17:43:16	20: 8:47	22:24:17	24:50: 1	27:25:15
4	0:16:37	3: 2:10	5:18:44	7:41:19	10: 1:23	12:36:12	15:11:53	17:48:59	20:13:50	22:28:23	24:54:57	27:25:40
5	0:22: 9	3: 7:15	5:23: 6	7:45:54	10: 6:51	12:41:11	15:17:15	17:57:49	20:17:53	22:37:52	25: 4:51	27:41:34
6	0:27:40	3:12: 6	5:28: 6	7:50:29	10:10:59	12:46:11	15:22:15	18: 2:39	20:22:25	22:37:52	25: 9:50	27:47: 2
7	0:33:11	3:17:23	5:32:26	7:55:39	10:15:40	12:56:31	15:27:25	18: 7:28	20:26:57	22:47: 5	25:14:49	27:52:30
8	0:38:41	3:22:25	5:37:26	7:59:39	10:20:40	13: 6:52	15:32:35	18:12:16	20:31:29	22:51:40	25:19:52	27:57:59
9	0:44:11	3:27:26	5:42:26	8: 8:50	10:25:52	13: 6:53	15:37:42	18:17:54	20:36: 0	22:56:16	25:24:52	28: 3:29
10	0:49:40	3:32:26	5:46:44	8:13:26	10:30:24	13:12: 4	15:42:45	18:21:51	20:40:31	23: 0:52	25:34:58	28: 3:29
11	0:55: 9	3:37:26	5:51:22	8:13:26	10:35:17	13:17:17	15:48:10	18:26:37	20:45:33	23: 0:52	25:34:58	28:14:30
12	1: 0:36	3:42:24	5:55:59	8:18: 3	10:40:11	13:22:29	15:53:10	18:31:22	20:49:33	23:10: 6	25:40: 9	28:20: 1
13	1: 6: 3	3:47:22	6: 0:37	8:22:39	10:45: 5	13:27:41	15:58:17	18:36:50	20:54: 3	23:14:44	25:45: 9	28:25:33
14	1:11:30	3:52:14	6: 4:26	8:27:17	10:50:56	13:33: 6	16: 3:24	18:40:50	21: 3: 4	23:19:22	25:50:15	28:31: 5
15	1:16:55	3:57:14	6: 9: 5	8:31:55	10:55:53	13:38: 6	16: 8:30	18:45:45	21: 3: 4	23:23:41	25:55:23	28:36:37
16	1:22:20	4: 2: 8	6:14:26	8:36:32	10:59:53	13:43:45	16:13:40	18:50:55	21:16:34	23:28:41	26: 5:42	28:42:11
17	1:27:44	4: 7: 2	6:19: 2	8:41:10	11: 4:50	13:48:42	16:18:40	18:54:57	21:16:34	23:33:21	26: 5:42	28:53:17
18	1:33: 7	4:11:54	6:23:37	8:45:49	11: 9:48	13:53:45	16:23:44	18:59:38	21:20:34	23:38: 2	26:16: 6	28:53:17
19	1:38:29	4:16:46	6:28:13	8:50:28	11:14:47	13:58:58	16:28:48	19: 4:19	21:25:34	23:42:44	26:16: 6	29: 4:25
20	1:43:50	4:21:36	6:32:48	8: 5: 8	11:19:46	14: 4:12	16:33:51	19: 9: 9	21:30:34	23:47:27	26:21:19	29: 9:59
21	1:49:10	4:26:27	6:37:27	9: 4:28	11:24:46	14: 9:24	16:38:52	19:13: 9	21:34:34	23:52: 9	26:26:30	29:15:33
22	1:54:29	4:31:16	6:41:57	9: 4:28	11:29:47	14:14:37	16:43:53	19:18:18	21:39:42	23:56:55	26:31:48	29:21: 7
23	1:59:48	4:36: 4	6:46:31	9: 9:10	11:34:48	14:19:50	16:48:55	19:22:54	21:43:34	24: 1:40	26:37: 5	29:21:17
24	2: 5: 5	4:40:52	6:51: 5	9:13:51	11:39:50	14:25: 4	16:53:55	19:27:32	21:48: 5	24: 6:26	26:42:20	29:26:42
25	2:10:21	4:45:38	6:55:39	9:18:33	11:44:52	14:30:14	16:58:54	19:32: 9	21:48: 5	24:11:13	26:47:40	29:32:16
26	2:15:37	4:50: 0	7: 0: 4	9:23:28	11:49:55	14:35:24	17: 3:53	19:32:45	21:52:35	24:16: 0	26:52:59	29:37:50
27	2:20:51	4:55: 0	7: 4: 0	9:28:10	11:55: 0	14:40:42	17: 8:51	19:37: 6	21:56:36	24:20:49	26:58: 9	29:43:24
28	2:26: 4	4:59:53	7: 9:21	9:32:44	12: 0: 4	14:45:54	17:13:48	19:45:32	22: 2: 7	24:25:39	27: 3:23	29:48:59
29	2:31:17		7:13:51	9:37:44	12: 5: 4	14:40:42	17:18:44	19:45:56	22: 6: 9	24:30:29	27: 9: 3	29:54:33
30	2:36:28		7:18:29	9:42:13	12:10:15	14:51: 7	17:23:40	19:50:31	22:10:40	24:35:21	27: 9: 3	30: 0: 6
31	2:41:38		7:23: 2		12:15:21		17:28:35	19:50: 6		24:35:21		30: 9:31

1968 SSRY = 30:10:51

	January	February	March	April	May	June	July	August	September	October	November	December
1	0: 0: 0	2:47:16	5:10:13	7:33:24	9:53:14	12:27:18	15: 3:31	17:40:47	20: 7: 2	22:22:50	24:48:27	27:23:22
2	0: 5:34	2:52:25	5:14:56	7:37:59	9:58: 2	12:32:26	15: 8:44	17:45:39	20:11:35	22:27:23	24:53:21	27:28:47
3	0:16:40	2:57:33	5:24:21	7:42:33	10: 2:50	12:37:36	15:13:56	17:50:34	20:16: 9	22:31:56	24:58:17	27:34:13
4	0:16:40	3: 2:40	5:24:21	7:42:33	10: 7:38	12:42:55	15:19:11	17:50:34	20:16: 9	22:36:30	25: 3:14	27:39:40
5	0:22:13	3: 7:47	5:29: 2	7:51:44	10:12:29	12:48: 5	15:24:18	18: 0:21	20:20:45	22:41:38	25:13:10	27:45:35
6	0:27:45	3:12:56	5:33:43	7:56:19	10:17:20	12:53: 6	15:29:30	18: 9:57	20:29:47	22:45:38	25:18:10	27:56:35
7	0:33:16	3:17:56	5:38:23	8: 0:55	10:22: 9	13: 3:27	15:34:40	18: 9:57	20:34:20	22:50:13	25:23:11	28: 1:34
8	0:38:48	3:22:59	5:43: 2	8: 5:31	10:27: 3	13: 8:39	15:39:50	18:14:46	20:38:51	22:54:49	25:28:13	28: 7: 4
9	0:44:18	3:28: 2	5:43: 2	8:10:44	10:31:55	13: 3:27	15:45:10	18:19:34	20:43:23	22:59:25	25:28:13	28:12:35
10	0:49:48	3:33: 3	5:47:41	8:10:44	10:36:55	13:13:51	15:50:13	18:24:21	20:47:55	23: 4: 1	25:33:16	28:18: 6
11	0:55:18	3:38: 3	5:52:21	8:15: 0	10:41:44	13:19: 5	15:55: 5	18:29: 8	20:52:25	23: 4:38	25:38:20	28: 9:10
12	1: 0:46	3:43: 2	5:56:59	8:19:21	10:46:37	13:24:15	16: 0:24	18:33:54	20:56:57	23:17:38	25:43:23	28:24: 9
13	1: 6:13	3:48: 3	6: 1:37	8:23:58	10:51:32	13:29:15	16: 5:32	18:38:39	21: 1:28	23:17:54	25:48:31	28:29:40
14	1:11:40	3:52:57	6: 6:14	8:33:13	10:56:29	13:34:41	16:10:38	18:43:23	21: 5:59	23:22:33	25:53:39	28:34:43
15	1:17:56	3: 2:48	6:10:28	8:37:51	11: 1:25	13:39:54	16:15:44	18:48:21	21:10:29	23:27:12	25:58:47	28:40:16
16	1:22:32	4: 2:48	6:15:29	8:37:51	11: 6:20	13:45: 2	16:20:50	18:57:33	21:10:29	23:31:53	26: 3:57	28:45:24
17	1:27:56	4: 7:43	6:20:16	8:47: 0	11:11:21	13:50:21	16:25:56	18:57:33	21:19:32	23:36:33	26:14:19	28:50:55
18	1:33:20	4:12:36	6:24:40	8:51:48	11:16:20	13:55:35	16:30:59	19: 2:15	21:24: 2	23:41:15	26:14:19	28:56:24
19	1:38:43	4:17:28	6:29:16	8:56:28	11:21:20	14: 0:48	16:36: 1	19: 6:56	21:28:32	23:45:58	26:19:32	29: 1:55
20	1:44:12	4:22:20	6:33:50	9: 1:19	11:26:20	14: 6: 8	16:41: 6	19:11:37	21:33: 3	23:50:41	26:24:46	29: 8: 8
21	1:49:26	4:27:11	6:38:26	9: 5:59	11:31:23	14:11:16	16:46: 8	19:16:13	21:33: 3	23:55:25	26:30: 1	29:13:43
22	1:54:46	4:32:11	6:43: 4	9:10:44	11:36:28	14:16:30	16:51:10	19:20:53	21:37: 8	24: 0:56	26:35:16	29:19:18
23	2: 0: 6	4:37:50	6:47:37	9:15:28	11:41:26	14:21:44	16:56:10	19:25:35	21:42:36	24: 4:56	26:35:16	29:19:18
24	2: 5:24	4:41:38	6:52:42	9:24:40	11:46:29	14:26:58	17: 1:11	19:30:12	21:47: 7	24: 9:42	26:45:51	29:24:38
25	2:10:41	4:46:26	6:56:46	9:24:40	11:51:33	14:32:12	17: 6:11	19:34:51	21:51:57	24:14:29	26:51:10	29:30:13
26	2:15:57	4:51: 3	7: 1:21	9:29:25	11:56:38	14:37:22	17:11:10	19:39:42	21:55:38	24:19:18	26:56:30	29:36: 8
27	2:21:13	4:55: 9	7: 5:56	9:34: 9	12: 1:43	14:42:36	17:16:10	19:44:41	22: 0:56	24:24: 7	27: 1:51	29:41:38
28	2:26: 1	5: 0:44	7:10:56	9:38:54	12: 6:49	14:47:52	17:21: 8	19:48:41	22: 6:32	24:28:57	27: 7:12	29:47:13
29	2:31:41	5: 5:29	7:15:56	9:43:40	12:11:55	14:53:19	17:26: 2	19:53:17	22:13:15	24:33:40	27:12:12	29:52:48
30	2:36:54		7:19:39	9:48:26	12:17: 2	14:58:19	17:30:58	19:57:52	22:18:17	24:38:40	27:17:58	30: 3:57
31	2:42: 5		7:24:14		12:22:10		17:35:53	20: 2:27		24:43:33		30: 9:31

1969   SSRY = 30:14:17

	January	February	March	April	May	June	July	August	September	October	November	December
1	30:14:17	2:47:16	5: 5:25	7:28:54	9:48:57	12:23:14	14:59:44	17:37:23	20: 3:58	22:20: 2	24:45:50	27:20:56
2	0: 5:34	2:52:25	5:10: 9	7:33:29	9:53:45	12:28:22	15: 4:57	17:42:17	20: 8:33	22:24:36	24:50:45	27:26:22
3	0:11:41	2:57:32	5:14:52	7:38:36	9:58:34	12:33:29	15:10: 9	17:47:10	20:13: 7	22:29:11	24:55:42	27:31:48
4	0:17:41	3: 2:45	5:19:44	7:47:16	10: 8:13	12:43:52	15:20:31	17:56:55	20:17:47	22:38:18	25: 0:53	27:37:45
5	0:22:13	3: 7:39	5:24:16	7:47:51	10:13: 4	12:49:43	15:20:33	17:56:55	20:22:14	22:42:53	25: 5:37	27:42:12
6	0:27:46	3:12:50	5:28:58	7:56:28	10:17:55	12:54:14	15:30:56	18: 1:46	20:26:47	22:47:29	25:10:36	27:47:10
7	0:33:17	3:17:54	5:33:39	8: 1: 4	10:22:48	12:59:26	15:36: 7	18:11:26	20:31:20	22:52: 5	25:15:36	27:53:41
8	0:38:48	3:22:34	5:38:18	8: 5:41	10:27:41	13: 4:38	15:41:17	18:16:15	20:35:53	22:56:41	25:20:38	27:59:12
9	0:44:19	3:27:59	5:42:58	8:10:55	10:32:34	13: 9:15	15:46:27	18:25:51	20:40:25	23: 1:18	25:25:40	28: 4:42
10	0:55:18	3:38: 0	5:52:17	8:15:55	10:37:24	13:15: 0	15:51:36	18:30:37	20:44:57	23: 5:56	25:30:44	28: 0:14
11	1: 0:47	3:42:59	5:56:55	8:19:32	10:42:24	13:20:16	15:56:46	18:30:37	20:49:29	23:10:34	25:35:48	28:10:18
12	1: 6:14	3:47:57	6: 1:33	8:28:49	10:52:17	13:25:30	16: 1:53	18:35:24	20:54: 1	23:19:52	25:40:54	28:26:51
13	1:11:42	3:52:54	6: 6:11	8:33:28	10:57:14	13:30:44	16: 7: 1	18:40: 6	20:58:33	23:24:32	25:46: 1	28:32:25
14	1:17:42	3:57:52	6:10:49	8:38:28	11: 2: 7	13:35:55	16:12: 8	18:40:45	21: 3: 4	23:29:12	25:51: 9	28:37:59
15	1:22:33	4: 2:49	6:15:28	8:42:47	10:57:12	13:41: 8	16:17:14	18:45:45	21: 7:36	23:33:54	25:56:17	28:43:33
16	1:27:33	4: 7:39	6:20: 2	8:47:27	11: 7:11	13:46:26	16:22:17	18:54:21	21:16:38	23:38:36	26: 6:38	28:49: 7
17	1:27:58	4:12:33	6:24:39	8:52: 4	11:12:11	13:56:55	16:27:25	18:59: 4	21:21: 9	23:43:19	26:11:50	28:54:42
18	1:33:45	4:17:25	6:29:15	8:56:49	11:17:11	14: 2:30	16:32:30	19: 3:46	21:25:41	23:48: 2	26:17: 3	29: 0:17
19	1:38:45	4:22:17	6:33:51	9: 6:12	11:22:12	14: 7:34	16:37:30	19: 8:27	21:30:12	23:48:42	26:22:17	29: 5:52
20	1:44:26	4:27: 8	6:43:12	9:10:55	11:32:14	14:12:38	16:42:39	19:13:48	21:35:14	23:57:32	26:27:36	29: 7:28
21	1:54:49	4:31:58	6:47:38	9:15:38	11:37:19	14:17:53	16:47:42	19:18:22	21:43:46	24: 7: 4	26:32:43	29:18: 5
22	2: 0: 6	4:36:47	6:52:13	9:20:22	11:42:23	14:23: 7	16:52:49	19:22:27	21:48:17	24:11:52	26:37:58	29:28:14
23	2: 5:26	4:41:35	6:56:49	9: 9: 6	11:47:27	14:33:50	17: 2:41	19:27: 6	21:57:20	24:16:40	26:43:23	29:33:26
24	2:10:43	4:46:23	7: 1:59	9:24:50	11:52:32	14:33:56	17: 7:42	19:36:22	21:57:20	24:21: 2	26:48:42	29:34:26
25	2:16:15	4:51:35	7:10:34	9:34:37	11:57:32	14:38:50	17:17:36	19:41:26	22: 2:18	24:26:20	26:54: 2	29:40:36
26	2:26:29	4:55:55	7:15: 9	9:39:23	12: 2:43	14:44: 4	17:22:36	19:45:35	22: 6:24	24:31:11	27: 5:23	29:46:17
27	2:31:42	5: 0:41	7:19:44	9:42:10	12: 7:50	14:49:17	17:27:36	19:50:12	22:10:57	24:36: 1	27:10: 8	29:56:12
28	2:36:54		7:24:19		12:12:57	14:54:31	17:32:28	19:54:48	22:15:29	24:40:56	27:15:32	30: 7:21
29	2:42: 5				12:18: 5			19:59:23				
30												
31												

1970   SSRY = 30: 9:21

	January	February	March	April	May	June	July	August	September	October	November	December
1	30: 9:21	2:46:54	5: 4:47	7:27:54	9:47:32	12:21:19	14:57:23	17:34:41	20: 0:57	22:16:39	24:41:58	27:16:31
2	0: 5:33	2:52: 2	5: 9:30	7:32:29	9:52:19	12:26:27	15: 2:35	17:39:34	20: 5:31	22:21:12	24:46:52	27:21:56
3	0:11:30	2:57:10	5:14:12	7:37: 4	9:57:15	12:31:34	15: 7:47	17:44:27	20:10: 4	22:25:45	24:51:47	27:27:22
4	0:17:39	3: 2: 9	5:19: 6	7:46:14	10: 6:45	12:41:35	15:17:58	17:54:19	20:14:38	22:30:58	24:56:44	27:32:48
5	0:22:11	3: 3:22	5:23:36	7:46:49	10:11:35	12:47: 5	15:18:14	17:59: 1	20:19:18	22:35:24	25: 1: 9	27:32:45
6	0:27:40	3:12:22	5:28:17	7:55:24	10:16:26	12:52:15	15:23:21	17:59: 1	20:23:43	22:39:26	25: 6:39	27:38:14
7	0:33:13	3:17:30	5:32:57	8: 0: 0	10:21:20	12:57:26	15:28:32	18: 3:51	20:28:15	22:44: 1	25:11:38	27:43:40
8	0:38:48	3:22:32	5:37:37	8: 4:36	10:26: 9	13: 2:37	15:33:42	18: 8:40	20:32:47	22:48:36	25:16:38	27:49:11
9	0:44:14	3:27:34	5:42:16	8:13:49	10:30:56	13: 7:48	15:38:51	18:13:29	20:37:19	22:53:11	25:21:40	28: 0: 9
10	0:55:12	3:37:34	5:51:34	8:18:49	10:35:56	13:13: 1	15:44: 0	18:18:18	20:41:50	22:57:24	25:26:44	28: 5:39
11	1: 0:40	3:42:39	5:56:11	8:18:26	10:40:50	13:18:13	15:49: 9	18:23: 7	20:46:22	23: 7:21	25:31:49	28: 5:39
12	1: 6:?	3:47:39	6: 0:49	8:27:40	10:45:45	13:28:38	15:54:17	18:27:49	20:50:53	23:11:39	25:41:45	28:16:41
13	1:11:34	3:52:26	6: 5:26	8:32:18	10:50:41	13:33:30	15:59:24	18:32:19	20:55: 2	23:16:17	25:47: 1	28:22: 3
14	1:16:59	3:57:21	6:10: 3	8:36:18	10:55:37	13:33:51	16: 4:31	18:37:19	20:59:54	23:20:56	25:52: 9	28:27:45
15	1:22: 4	4: 2:21	6:14:42	8:41:35	10:50:24	13:39: 1	16: 9:37	18:42: 2	21: 4:24	23:25:35	25:57:18	28:38:51
16	1:27:48	4: 7:16	6:19: 5	8:46:15	11: 5:32	13:44:17	16:14:43	18:51:29	21: 8:55	23:30:22	26: 2:38	28:38:55
17	1:33:35	4:12: 2	6:23:51	8:50:54	11:10:30	13:49:31	16:19:48	18:56:11	21:13:26	23:34:57	26: 7:38	28:44:26
18	1:38:33	4:16:54	6:28:26	8:55:34	11:15:30	13:54:44	16:24:54	19: 0:53	21:17:56	23:39:38	26:12:50	28:55:32
19	1:43:54	4:21:45	6:33: 3	9: 0:56	11:20: 9	13:59:57	16:29:56	19: 5:33	21:22:56	23:44:21	26:18: 3	29: 1: 7
20	1:49:34	4:26:30	6:42:36	9: 0:56	11:25:12	14: 5: 1	16:40: 0	19:10:13	21:31:27	23:49: 4	26:23:17	29: 6:41
21	1:54:52	4:31:28	6:46:46	9:14:20	11:30:31	14: 5: 7	16:45: 3	19:14:47	21:36: 2	23:53:43	26:38:24	29:12:16
22	2: 5:10	4:36:12	6:51:22	9:19: 2	11:35:31	14:15:40	16:50: 8	19:19:31	21:40:28	24: 8: 6	26:44:23	29:17:46
23	2:10:26	4:41: 0	6:55:54	9:23:46	11:40:35	14:20:52	16:55: 4	19:24:39	21:44:58	24:12:53	26:49:42	29:23:25
24	2:15:46	4:45:47	7: 0:49	9:28:24	11:45:39	14:31:18	17: 0: 4	19:33:24	21:49:29	24: 8: 6	26:55: 2	29:34:35
25	2:21: 3	4:50:33	7: 5:29	9:33:14	11:50:43	14:26:52	17: 5: 4	19:38:38	21:54: 0	24:17:12	27: 0:22	29:34:35
26	2:26:10	5: 0: 3	7: 9:59	9:38: 8	11:55:47	14:31:56	17:10: 4	19:43:24	21:58:32	24:21:42	27: 5:49	29:40:26
27	2:31:22		7:14:31	9:42:45	12: 0:52	14:42:58	17:15:58	19:47:12	22: 2:35	24:27:21	27: 6:45	29:45:49
28	2:36:34		7:18:46		12: 6: 0	14:52:10	17:21: 5	19:51:48	22:12: 7	24:32:12	27:11: 8	29:56:54
29	2:41:44		7:23:20		12:11: 4		17:24:51	19:56:22		24:37: 5		30: 2:28
30					12:16:11		17:29:46					
31												

1971   SSRY = 30:19: 0

Day	January	February	March	April	May	June	July	August	September	October	November	December
1	30:19: 0	2:47:54	5: 6:37	7:35:34	9:50:54	12:25:25	15: 2:17	17:40:29	20: 7:35	22:24: 1	24:50: 0	27:25:15
2	0: 5:35	2:53: 4	5:11:22	7:40:10	9:55:42	12:30:35	15: 7:35	17:45:24	20:12:11	22:28:35	24:54:52	27:30:41
3	0:10:14	2:58:13	5:16:10	7:44:22	10: 0:31	12:35:45	15:12:53	17:50:18	20:16:48	22:33:10	24:59:49	27:36: 4
4	0:16:14	3: 3:21	5:20:51	7:48:59	10: 5:21	12:40:55	15:17:55	17:55:12	20:21:24	22:37:43	25: 4:49	27:41:35
5	0:22:52	3: 8:29	5:25:34	7:53:35	10:10:12	12:46: 6	15:23:11	18: 0: 5	20:26: 0	22:42:18	25: 9:47	27:47: 4
6	0:27:52	3:13:36	5:30:16	7:58:12	10:15: 3	12:51:18	15:28:23	18: 4:57	20:30:35	22:46:53	25:14:47	27:52:33
7	0:33:25	3:18:41	5:34:58	8: 2:49	10:19:55	12:56:29	15:33:35	18: 9:49	20:35: 4	22:51:29	25:19:47	27:58: 3
8	0:38:50	3:23:45	5:39:39	8: 7:26	10:24:48	13: 1:42	15:38:47	18:14:39	20:39:35	22:56: 5	25:24:49	28: 3:34
9	0:44:29	3:28:48	5:44:20	8:12: 4	10:29:41	13: 6:54	15:43:58	18:19:29	20:44: 8	23: 0:45	25:29:52	28: 9: 4
10	0:50:20	3:33:50	5:49: 0	8:16:42	10:34:35	13:12: 7	15:49: 9	18:24:18	20:48:41	23: 5:20	25:34:55	28:14:36
11	0:55:30	3:38:51	5:53:40	8:21:20	10:39:30	13:17:21	15:54:19	18:29: 7	20:53:14	23: 9:57	25:40: 0	28:20: 9
12	1: 1: 0	3:43:51	5:58:19	8:25:58	10:44:26	13:22:34	15:59:29	18:33:54	20:57:46	23:14:36	25:45: 5	28:25:42
13	1: 6:29	3:48:51	6: 2:58	8:30:16	10:49:22	13:27:48	16: 4:38	18:38:41	21: 2:18	23:19:15	25:50:10	28:31:15
14	1:11:54	3:53:46	6: 7:37	8:35:16	10:54:19	13:33: 2	16: 9:46	18:43:13	21: 6:48	23:23:55	25:55:40	28:36:49
15	1:17:24	3:58:41	6:12:15	8:39:56	10:59:17	13:38:17	16:14:54	18:48:13	21:11:23	23:28:35	26: 0:29	28:42:24
16	1:22:51	4: 3:42	6:16:53	8:44:36	11: 4:15	13:43:32	16:20: 2	18:52:58	21:15:55	23:33:16	26: 5:40	28:47:59
17	1:28:17	4: 8:38	6:21:30	8:49:16	11: 9:14	13:48:46	16:25: 8	18:57:43	21:20:27	23:37:58	26:10:51	28:53:34
18	1:33:42	4:13:32	6:26: 7	8:53:57	11:14:14	13:54: 1	16:30:15	19: 2:26	21:24:59	23:42:40	26:16: 1	28:59:10
19	1:39: 6	4:18:26	6:30:44	8:58:38	11:19:15	13:59:17	16:35:20	19: 7:10	21:29:30	23:47:23	26:21: 8	29: 4:46
20	1:44:29	4:23:17	6:35:21	9: 3:21	11:24:16	14: 4:32	16:40:25	19:11:53	21:34: 6	23:52: 6	26:26:31	29:10:22
21	1:49:29	4:28:10	6:39:58	9: 8: 4	11:29:18	14: 9:47	16:45:30	19:16:33	21:38:34	23:56:52	26:31:47	29:15:58
22	1:55:13	4:33: 2	6:44:34	9:12:47	11:34:21	14:15: 3	16:50:33	19:21:15	21:43: 6	24: 1:38	26:37: 3	29:21:35
23	2: 0:33	4:37:52	6:49:10	9:17:31	11:39:24	14:20:18	16:55:36	19:25:55	21:47:38	24: 6:24	26:42:21	29:27:12
24	2: 5:53	4:42:41	6:53:47	9:22:15	11:44:29	14:25:34	17: 0:38	19:30:35	21:52:11	24:11: 1	26:47:39	29:32:48
25	2:11: 2	4:47:30	6:58:23	9:27: 0	11:49:34	14:30:49	17: 5:40	19:35:13	21:56:43	24:15:58	26:52:58	29:38:26
26	2:16:29	4:52:16	7: 2:58	9:31:45	11:54:40	14:36: 4	17:10:40	19:39:53	22: 1:15	24:20: 8	26:58:16	29:44: 2
27	2:21:46	4:57: 5	7: 7:34	9:36:31	11:59:45	14:41:19	17:15:40	19:44:32	22: 5:48	24:25:38	27: 3:34	29:49:38
28	2:27: 2	5: 1:52	7:12:10	9:41:18	12: 4:52	14:46:34	17:20:40	19:49: 9	22:10:21	24:30:28	27: 9: 3	29:55:14
29	2:32:16		7:16:46	9:46: 6	12: 9:59	14:51:49	17:25:38	19:53:47	22:14:54	24:35:20	27:14:26	30: 0:51
30	2:37:30		7:21:22		12:15: 7	14:57: 3	17:30:36	19:58:23	22:19:27	24:40:12	27:19:50	30: 6:27
31	2:42:42		7:25:58		12:20:16		17:35:33	20: 3: 0		24:45: 6		30:12: 2

1972   SSRY = 30:13:46

Day	January	February	March	April	May	June	July	August	September	October	November	December
1	30:13:46	2:47:31	5:10:42	7:34: 6	9:54:11	12:28:31	15: 5: 0	17:42:30	20: 8:56	22:24:57	24:50:48	27:25:59
2	0: 5:34	2:52:41	5:15:25	7:38:42	9:58:59	12:33:40	15:10:12	17:47:24	20:13:31	22:29:31	24:55:43	27:31:25
3	0:10:41	2:57:49	5:20: 8	7:43:17	10: 3:48	12:38:50	15:15:25	17:52:17	20:18: 6	22:34: 9	25: 0:37	27:36:52
4	0:15:49	3: 2:57	5:24:50	7:47:52	10: 8:38	12:44: 0	15:20:35	17:57: 9	20:22:41	22:38:43	25: 5:37	27:42:19
5	0:22:14	3: 8: 4	5:29:32	7:52:28	10:13:28	12:49:10	15:25:49	18: 2: 1	20:27:12	22:43:13	25:10:35	27:47:47
6	0:27:47	3:13: 9	5:34:13	7:57: 4	10:18:19	12:54:21	15:31: 0	18: 6:52	20:31:45	22:47:48	25:15:35	27:53:16
7	0:33:19	3:18:14	5:38:54	8: 1:40	10:23:11	12:59:32	15:36: 1	18:11:42	20:36:18	22:52:24	25:20:35	27:58:46
8	0:38:50	3:23:17	5:43:34	8: 6:17	10:28: 3	13: 4:44	15:41:21	18:16:31	20:40:50	22:57: 3	25:25:37	28: 4:16
9	0:44:51	3:28:20	5:48:14	8:10:54	10:32:56	13:10: 9	15:46:31	18:21:20	20:45:26	23: 1:36	25:30:39	28: 9:48
10	0:49:51	3:33:22	5:52:53	8:15:30	10:37:50	13:15:20	15:51:41	18:26: 8	20:49:58	23: 6:13	25:35:43	28:15:18
11	0:55:21	3:38:22	5:57:53	8:20: 8	10:42:45	13:20:22	15:56:50	18:30:55	20:54:26	23:10:51	25:40:48	28:20:50
12	1: 0:50	3:43:22	6: 2:10	8:24:46	10:47:40	13:25:35	16: 1:59	18:35:42	20:58:58	23:15:29	25:45:54	28:26:23
13	1: 6:20	3:48:21	6: 6:48	8:29:24	10:52:36	13:30:49	16: 7: 7	18:40:28	21: 3:29	23:20: 8	25:51: 1	28:31:56
14	1:11:46	3:53:18	6:11:26	8:34: 2	10:57:33	13:36: 2	16:12:14	18:45:13	21: 8: 1	23:24:47	25:56: 9	28:37:30
15	1:17: 3	3:58:15	6:16: 4	8:38:42	11: 2:30	13:41:16	16:17:21	18:49:57	21:12:33	23:29:28	26: 1:17	28:43: 3
16	1:22:39	4: 3: 0	6:20:43	8:43:21	11: 7:28	13:46:30	16:22:27	18:54:41	21:17: 3	23:34: 9	26: 6:28	28:48:37
17	1:28: 5	4: 8: 0	6:25:17	8:48: 0	11:12:28	13:51:44	16:27:33	18:59:24	21:21:34	23:38:50	26:11:39	28:54:12
18	1:33: 5	4:12:55	6:29:53	8:52:40	11:17:28	13:56:59	16:32:38	19: 4: 6	21:26: 6	23:43:32	26:16:51	28:59:46
19	1:38:53	4:17:53	6:34:29	8:57:21	11:22:28	14: 2:13	16:37:42	19: 8:48	21:30:36	23:48:15	26:22: 4	29: 5:21
20	1:44:37	4:22:45	6:39: 5	9: 2: 2	11:27:31	14: 7:28	16:42:46	19:13:29	21:35: 8	23:52:59	26:27:18	29:10:56
21	1:49:37	4:27:37	6:43:41	9: 6:44	11:32:31	14:12:42	16:47:48	19:18: 9	21:39:36	23:57:42	26:32:33	29:16:32
22	1:54:58	4:32:27	6:48:16	9:11:26	11:37:33	14:17:56	16:52:49	19:22:49	21:44: 8	24: 2:28	26:37:49	29:22: 7
23	2: 0:18	4:37:17	6:52:51	9:16: 9	11:42:36	14:23:10	16:57:51	19:27:28	21:48:41	24: 7:14	26:43: 7	29:27:43
24	2: 5:37	4:42:15	6:57:27	9:20:52	11:47:40	14:28:24	17: 2:52	19:32: 6	21:53:12	24:12: 0	26:48:25	29:33:18
25	2:10:55	4:46:53	7: 2: 2	9:25:36	11:52:44	14:33:39	17: 7:52	19:36:44	21:57:43	24:16:48	26:53:44	29:38:54
26	2:16:12	4:51:42	7: 6:37	9:30:20	11:57:48	14:38:53	17:12:50	19:41:22	22: 2:17	24:21:26	26:59: 4	29:44:29
27	2:21:27	4:56:27	7:11:12	9:35: 5	12: 2:55	14:44: 8	17:17:49	19:45:59	22: 6:47	24:26:26	27: 4:25	29:50: 5
28	2:26:42	5: 1:13	7:15:47	9:39:51	12: 8: 1	14:49:20	17:22:48	19:50:35	22:11:15	24:31:16	27: 9:48	29:55:41
29	2:31:56	5: 5:57	7:20:22	9:44:37	12:13: 8	14:54:34	17:27:44	19:55:11	22:15:51	24:36: 8	27:15:11	30: 1:15
30	2:37: 9		7:24:56	9:49:24	12:18:15	14:59:47	17:32:42	19:59:46	22:20:24	24:41: 0	27:20:35	30: 6:50
31	2:42:20		7:29:31		12:23:23		17:37:35	20: 4:22		24:45:54		30:12:25

1973 SSRY = 30:14:36

	January	February	March	April	May	June	July	August	September	October	November	December
1	30:14:36	2:47:17	5:15:28	7:28:59	9:49: 4	12:23:24	14:56:56	17:31:35	20: 8:11	22:20:16	24:51: 5	27:21:13
2	0:16:34	2:53: 3	5:14:55	7:36:10	9:53:41	12:33:43	15:10:34	17:47:23	20:13:20	22:29:23	24:55:57	27:32: 5
3	0:16:38	2:57:42	5:19:38	7:38:10	9:58:41	12:33:43	15:16:34	17:50: 8	20:17:54	22:33:58	25: 0:54	27:32: 5
4	0:22:15	3: 7:48	5:24:20	7:47:22	10: 8:22	12:44: 3	15:20:46	17:57: 8	20:22:27	22:38:32	25: 5:52	27:43: 1
5	0:27:47	3:12:53	5:29: 2	7:51:53	10:13:13	12:49:15	15:25:58	18: 1:59	20:27: 1	22:43: 7	25:10:52	27:48:29
6	0:33:19	3:17:57	5:33:43	7:56:34	10:18: 5	12:54:26	15:36: 9	18: 6:49	20:31:37	22:47:43	25:15:53	27:53:29
7	0:38:50	3:23: 0	5:38:23	8: 5:48	10:27:50	13: 4:50	15:41:30	18:11:39	20:36: 6	22:52:19	25:20:53	27:53:29
8	0:44:21	3:28: 2	5:43: 3	8: 5:48	10:27:50	13: 4:50	15:46:40	18:16:28	20:40:38	22:56:55	25:25:55	28: 4:59
9	0:49:51	3:33: 3	5:47:43	8:10:25	10:32:44	13:10: 3	15:51:49	18:21:16	20:45:10	23: 1:32	25:30:59	28:10:30
10	0:55:21	3:38: 3	5:52:22	8:15: 2	10:37:38	13:15:15	15:56:58	18:26: 3	20:49:42	23: 6: 9	25:36: 3	28:16: 2
11	1: 0:49	3:43: 0	5:57: 0	8:19:40	10:42:34	13:20:28	16: 2: 7	18:30:50	20:54:15	23:10:47	25:41: 9	28:21:35
12	1: 6:17	3:47:57	6: 1:39	8:24:18	10:47:30	13:25:42	16: 7:13	18:35:37	20:58:49	23:15:26	25:46:15	28:27:10
13	1:11:44	3:52:57	6: 6:16	8:28:56	10:52:26	13:30:55	16:12:20	18:40:21	21: 3:17	23:20:25	25:51:23	28:32:41
14	1:17:11	3:57:53	6:10:54	8:33:35	10:57:24	13:36: 8	16:17:26	18:45: 6	21: 7:48	23:24:45	25:56:32	28:38:15
15	1:22:36	4: 2:49	6:15:31	8:38:14	11: 2:22	13:41:23	16:22:32	18:49:50	21:12:19	23:29:25	26: 1:41	28:43:49
16	1:28: 1	4: 7:43	6:20: 7	8:42:54	11: 7:20	13:46:37	16:27:37	18:54:33	21:16:50	23:34: 7	26: 6:52	28:49:23
17	1:33:24	4:12:36	6:24:44	8:47:34	11:12:20	13:51:51	16:32:41	18:59: 5	21:21:19	23:38:49	26:12: 3	28:54:58
18	1:38:47	4:17:28	6:29:20	8:52:15	11:17:21	13:57: 6	16:37:45	19: 3:38	21:25:52	23:43:33	26:17:15	29: 0:33
19	1:44: 9	4:22:20	6:33:56	8:56:55	11:22:21	14: 2:20	16:42:48	19: 8:10	21:30:24	23:48:15	26:22:31	29: 6:10
20	1:49:30	4:27:10	6:38:31	9: 1:37	11:27:23	14: 7:34	16:47:51	19:13:19	21:34:55	23:52:59	26:27:47	29:11:44
21	1:54:50	4:32: 0	6:43: 7	9: 6:19	11:32:25	14:12:49	16:52:52	19:17:59	21:39:26	23:57:45	26:33: 3	29:17:20
22	2: 0: 9	4:36:49	6:47:42	9:11: 1	11:37:28	14:18: 3	16:57:52	19:22:22	21:43:48	24: 1:20	26:38:20	29:22:56
23	2: 5:27	4:41:37	6:52:16	9:15:44	11:42:31	14:23:18	17: 2:53	19:26:51	21:48:15	24: 6: 2	26:43:38	29:28:32
24	2:10:45	4:46:25	6:56:53	9:20:28	11:47:36	14:28:34	17: 7:53	19:31:56	21:53:21	24:12: 6	26:48:58	29:34: 7
25	2:16: 1	4:51:12	7: 1:28	9:25:13	11:52:41	14:33:47	17:12:52	19:36:54	21:57:33	24:16:54	26:54:18	29:39:43
26	2:21:16	4:55:58	7: 6: 3	9:29:58	11:57:46	14:39: 1	17:17:50	19:41:11	22: 2: 5	24:21:44	26:59:39	29:45:19
27	2:26:30	5: 0:43	7:10:38	9:34:43	12: 2:53	14:44:14	17:22:47	19:46:25	22: 6:37	24:26:34	27: 5: 1	29:50:55
28	2:31:44		7:15:13	9:39:30	12: 7:59	14:49:29	17:27:43	19:51:38	22:11:10	24:31:25	27:10:24	29:56:30
29	2:36:57		7:20:47	9:44:17	12:13:29	14:54:44	17:32:40	19:56:50	22:15:43	24:36:17		30: 2: 6
30	2:42: 9		7: 6: 3		12:18:15			19:59:36		24:41:11		30: 7:40
31	2:42: 7		7:24:24				17:32:40					30:13: 7

1974 SSRY = 30:20: 6

	January	February	March	April	May	June	July	August	September	October	November	December
1	30:20: 6	2:47:53	5:16:25	7:30:35	9:51: 4	12:30:47	15: 8:47	17:40:59	20: 8: 6	22:20:36	24:47:46	27:28:13
2	0:26:35	2:53: 3	5:16: 5	7:36:12	9:55:53	12:30:47	15: 8:47	17:45:55	20:12:42	22:24:36	24:55:41	27:36:10
3	0:11:10	2:58:13	5:16: 2	7:39:48	10: 0:43	12:36: 8	15:13:15	17:50:49	20:17:17	22:33:44	25: 0:38	27:37: 7
4	0:16:43	3: 3:21	5:25:31	7:44:24	10: 5:33	12:41:18	15:18:28	17:55:42	20:21:51	22:38:19	25: 5:36	27:42:30
5	0:22:18	3: 8:28	5:25:31	7:49: 1	10:10:24	12:46:30	15:23:41	18: 0:36	20:26:26	22:42:54	25:10:35	27:48: 3
6	0:27:52	3:13:34	5:30:54	7:53:38	10:15:15	12:51:41	15:28:53	18: 5:29	20:30:59	22:47:30	25:15:52	27:53:33
7	0:33:25	3:18:40	5:35:37	7:58: 2	10:20: 6	13: 1: 9	15:39:17	18:10:22	20:40: 7	22:52:49	25:25:37	28: 4:34
8	0:38:57	3:23:43	5:39:37	8: 2:52	10:25: 1	13: 1: 9	15:39:17	18:15:10	20:40: 7	22:56:43	25:30:40	28: 4:34
9	0:44:29	3:28:46	5:44:18	8: 7:29	10:29:55	13: 7:19	15:44:28	18:20: 0	20:44:40	23: 1:20	25:35:45	28:10: 5
10	0:50: 0	3:33:48	5:48:58	8:12: 6	10:34:49	13:12:32	15:49:39	18:24:49	20:49:13	23: 5:57	25:40:50	28:15:38
11	0:55:30	3:38:49	5:53:38	8:16:45	10:39:44	13:17:46	15:54:49	18:29:37	20:53:46	23:10:36	25:45:56	28:21:11
12	1: 0:59	3:43:48	5:57:56	8:21:23	10:44:39	13:23: 1	16: 0:17	18:34:25	20:58:19	23:15:54	25:51: 4	28:26:44
13	1: 6:29	3:48:49	6: 7:56	8:26: 1	10:49:34	13:28:14	16: 5:25	18:39:12	21: 2:51	23:19:54	25:56:12	28:37:52
14	1:17:24	3:53:47	6: 7:55	8:30:41	10:54:34	13:33:28	16:10:17	18:43:57	21: 7:23	23:24:34	26: 1:22	28:37:52
15	1:17:24	3:58:44	6:12:13	8:35:21	10:59:32	13:38:44	16:15:25	18:48:44	21:11:55	23:29:15	26: 6:32	28:43:27
16	1:22:51	4: 3:40	6:16:51	8:40:41	11: 4:31	13:43:56	16:20:33	18:53:29	21:16:28	23:33:56	26:11:44	28:49: 2
17	1:28:17	4: 8:36	6:21:29	8:44:42	11: 9:31	13:49:14	16:25:40	18:58:13	21:21: 0	23:38:38	26:16:57	28:54:38
18	1:33:42	4:13:30	6:26: 5	8:49:24	11:14:32	13:54:30	16:30:48	19: 2:57	21:25:32	23:43: 5	26:22: 9	29: 0:15
19	1:39:42	4:18:24	6:30:40	8:54:24	11:19:32	13:59:46	16:35:40	19: 7:40	21:30: 4	23:48: 5	26:22: 9	29: 5:54
20	1:44:29	4:23:17	6:35:20	8:58:46	11:24:34	14: 5: 0	16:40:57	19:12:23	21:34:36	23:52:49	26:27:25	29:11:26
21	1:55:13	4:28: 9	6:39:57	9: 3:28	11:29:37	14:10:16	16:46: 5	19:17: 5	21:39: 8	23:57:34	26:32:41	29:17: 5
22	1:55:13	4:33: 0	6:44:34	9: 8:11	11:34:40	14:15:32	16:51: 5	19:21:46	21:43:40	24: 2:20	26:37:58	29:22:43
23	2: 0:34	4:37:50	6:49:10	9:12:55	11:39:44	14:20:47	16:56: 9	19:26:28	21:48:12	24: 7: 7	26:43:16	29:28:16
24	2: 5:55	4:42:40	6:53:47	9:17:41	11:44:49	14:26: 3	17: 6:10	19:31: 9	21:52:45	24:11:55	26:48:35	29:33:52
25	2:11:12	4:47:28	6:58:23	9:22:29	11:55: 1	14:36:34	17:11: 6	19:35:46	21:57:17	24:16:43	26:53:55	29:39:30
26	2:16:29	4:52:16	7: 2:59	9:27:29	12: 0: 6	14:36:34	17:16:12	19:40:40	22: 1:50	24:21:32	26:59:16	29:45:36
27	2:21:46	4:57: 3	7: 7:35	9:31:55	12: 6:13	14:41:49	17:21:17	19:45:43	22: 6:23	24:26:22	27: 4:37	29:50:43
28	2:27:17	5: 1:50	7:12:11	9:36:41	12: 6:13	14:47: 2	17:26: 9	19:49:40	22:10:56	24:31:13	27:10: 0	29:56:19
29	2:32:16		7:16:47	9:41:28	12:10:21	14:52:18	17:31:14	19:54:54	22:15:29	24:36: 5	27:15:24	30: 1:55
30	2:42:42		7:21:23	9:46:16	12:15:29	14:57:33	17:36: 3	20: 3:30	22:20: 2	24:45:51	27:20:48	30:13: 7
31	2:42:42		7:25:59		12:20:38		17:36: 3					

1975 SSRY = 30: 7: 4

Day	January	February	March	April	May	June	July	August	September	October	November	December
1	30: 7: 4	2:46:44	5: 4:36	7:27:36	9:47: 2	12:20:34	14:56:25	17:33:34	19:59:42	22:15:14	24:40:16	27:14:31
2	0: 5:33	2:51:55	5: 9:19	7:32:10	9:51:49	12:24:42	15: 1:37	17:38:27	20: 4:16	22:15:42	24:45:10	27:19:55
3	0:11:35	2:57: 2	5:14:43	7:36:45	9:56:24	12:30:58	15: 1:49	17:43:20	20: 8:49	22:28:51	24:50: 5	27:24:40
4	0:16:30	3: 2: 9	5:19:18	7:45:54	10: 6:13	12:41: 7	15:17:11	17:53: 3	20:17:55	22:37:58	24:59:57	27:30:45
5	0:22: 9	3: 7:14	5:28: 5	7:50:29	10:11: 3	12:46:17	15:22:21	17:57:53	20:22:27	22:42:33	25: 4:54	27:36:11
6	0:27:40	3:12:17	5:33:24	7:55: 5	10:15:53	12:51:27	15:27:31	18: 2:43	20:26:59	22:47:42	25: 9:53	27:41:38
7	0:33:11	3:17:21	5:37:24	7:59:39	10:20:44	12:56:37	15:32:41	18: 7:32	20:31:31	22:52:52	25:14:53	27:47: 5
8	0:38:41	3:22:23	5:42:52	8: 8:50	10:25:35	13: 6:59	15:42:59	18:17:20	20:36:31	23: 2: 1	25:19:53	27:52:33
9	0:44:11	3:27:25	5:47:18	8:13:27	10:30:28	13:12:11	15:48: 8	18:21:54	20:40:33	23: 6:11	25:24:55	27:58: 4
10	0:49:40	3:32:25	5:51:20	8:18: 3	10:35:21	13:17:23	15:53:16	18:26:48	20:45: 4	23: 0:54	25:29:58	28: 9: 4
11	0:55: 8	3:37:24	5:55:58	8:22:40	10:40:15	13:22:35	15:58:23	18:31:25	20:54:36	23: 5:31	25:35: 2	28: 3:34
12	1: 0:36	3:42:23	6: 0:35	8:27:47	10:45: 9	13:27:47	16: 3:30	18:36: 6	20:54:36	23:10:46	25:40: 7	28:20: 6
13	1: 6: 3	3:47:20	6: 5:12	8:32:17	10:50: 4	13:33:40	16: 8:36	18:40:54	20:59:36	23:19:25	25:45:13	28:31:30
14	1:11:29	3:52:16	6:10:43	8:37:55	10:55: 0	13:38:47	16:13:41	18:45:37	21: 2: 6	23:24: 4	25:50:20	28:36:43
15	1:16:54	3:57:12	6:14:25	8:36:33	10:59:57	13:43:25	16:18:46	18:50:19	21:12: 6	23:33:24	25:55:28	28:42:15
16	1:22:19	4: 2: 7	6:19: 0	8:41:11	11: 4:55	13:48:38	16:23:50	18:55: 1	21:16:36	23:38:47	26: 0:37	28:47:49
17	1:27:43	4: 7: 0	6:23:36	8:45:50	11: 9:53	13:53:51	16:28:53	18:59:42	21:21:12	23:38:47	26: 5:47	28:53:56
18	1:33: 6	4:11:53	6:28:11	8:50:30	11:14:51	13:58:58	16:33:58	19: 4:22	21:30:36	23:47:30	26:10:58	28:59: 4
19	1:38:28	4:16:44	6:32:46	8:55: 9	11:19:51	14: 3:59	16:39: 2	19: 9:31	21:30:45	23:52: 6	26:16:10	29: 4:30
20	1:43:49	4:21:35	6:37:21	8: 4:30	11:24:51	14: 9:18	16:44: 6	19:13:41	21:34:36	23:56:58	26:21:23	29:10: 4
21	1:49: 9	4:26:25	6:41:56	9: 9:12	11:29:52	14:14:44	16:49: 0	19:18:19	21:39: 8	24: 1: 6	26:26:37	29:15:38
22	1:54:28	4:31:14	6:46:30	9:13:53	11:34:53	14:19:57	16:54: 0	19:22:57	21:43:36	24: 6:11	26:31:53	29:21:11
23	1:59:47	4:36: 0	6:51: 4	9:18:36	11:39:55	14:25:10	16:59: 9	19:27:35	21:48:37	24:11:19	26:37: 9	29:26:41
24	2: 5: 5	4:40:50	6:55:39	9:23:18	11:44:58	14:30:16	17: 3:56	19:32:25	21:48:37	24:16: 6	26:42:26	29:32:21
25	2:10:20	4:45:37	7: 1:43	9:28:12	11:55: 0	14:35:36	17: 8:50	19:36:48	21:50: 2	24:20:52	26:47:45	29:36:41
26	2:15:36	4:50:23	7: 4:47	9:32:54	11:55: 0	14:40:49	17:13:53	19:41:23	22: 1:39	24:25:42	26:53: 4	29:43:29
27	2:20:50	4:55: 8	7: 9:20	9:37:31	12: 0:10	14:46: 1	17:18:49	19:45:59	22: 6:10	24:30:34	26:58:24	29:49: 3
28	2:26: 3	4:59:52	7:14:53	9:42:16	12: 5:15	14:46: 1	17:23:45	19:50:34	22: 6:10	24:35:24	27: 3:45	29:54:37
29	2:31:16		7:18:28		12:10:21	14:51:13	17:28:34	19:55: 8	22:10:42		27: 9: 8	30: 0:11
30	2:36:27		7:23: 2		12:15:27							
31	2:41:37											

1976 SSRY = 30:10:12

Day	January	February	March	April	May	June	July	August	September	October	November	December
1	30:10:12	2:47:10	5:10: 3	7:33:11	9:53:11	12:32: 4	15: 3:15	17:40:26	20: 6:34	22:22:19	24:47:53	27:22:46
2	0: 5:34	2:52:19	5:14:46	7:37:46	9:57:48	12:32:13	15: 8:27	17:45:19	20:11: 4	22:22:47	24:52:47	27:28:11
3	0:11: 7	2:57:35	5:19:28	7:42:41	10: 7:26	12:37:48	15:19:39	17:50:12	20:15:39	22:35:58	25: 2:40	27:39: 3
4	0:16:40	3: 7:41	5:24:10	7:47:41	10:12:12	12:42:52	15:24: 1	17:55: 2	20:24:47	22:45: 7	25: 7:37	27:44:31
5	0:22: 4	3: 7:41	5:28:52	7:51:31	10:17: 6	12:47:41	15:29:12	18: 4:45	20:24:47	22:45: 7	25:12:36	27:49:59
6	0:27:44	3:12:50	5:33:32	7:56: 7	10:17:58	12:52:52	15:34:22	18: 9:34	20:33:52	22:49:47	25:17:36	27:55:27
7	0:33: 7	3:17:50	5:38:13	8: 0:43	10:26:58	12:58: 2	15:39:32	18:14:23	20:38:25	22:54:57	25:22:39	28: 0:55
8	0:38:40	3:22:53	5:42:52	8: 5:19	10:26:58	13: 3:14	15:44:42	18:19:12	20:42:58	23: 8: 6	25:27:39	28: 6:27
9	0:44:11	3:27:56	5:47:30	8: 9:55	10:36:35	13:13:37	15:49:50	18:23:58	20:47:26	23:17:20	25:32:41	28:11:57
10	0:49:47	3:32:55	5:52: 6	8:14:31	10:41:29	13:24: 1	15:54:59	18:28:44	20:51:57	23: 8: 6	25:37:45	28:17:29
11	0:55: 5	3:37:56	5:56:48	8:19: 8	10:46:24	13:24: 1	16: 0: 6	18:33:30	20:56:28	23:17:22	25:42:51	28:23: 0
12	1: 0:44	3:42:55	6: 1:26	8:23:45	10:51:19	13:29:14	16: 5:13	18:38:15	21: 0:59	23:27:20	25:47:57	28:28:32
13	1: 6:12	3:47:52	6: 6: 4	8:28:23	10:51:19	13:34: 9	16:10:25	18:42:59	21: 5:30	23:27:20	25:53: 4	28:34:12
14	1:11:38	3:52:49	6:10:43	8:37:38	10:56:10	13:39:40	16:15:20	18:47:43	21:10: 0	23:31:20	25:58:12	28:39:38
15	1:17: 3	3:57:45	6:15:21	8:37:38	11: 6:10	13:44:53	16:20:31	18:52:27	21:14:31	23:36: 1	26: 3:22	28:45:12
16	1:22:30	4: 2:40	6:19:53	8:42:17	11: 1:16	13:50:50	16:25:36	18:57:20	21:19: 1	23:40:42	26: 8:32	28:50:46
17	1:27:54	4: 7:35	6:24:29	8:46:56	11:16: 7	13:55:30	16:30:40	19: 1:50	21:19: 1	23:45:23	26:13:44	28:56:20
18	1:33:17	4:12:28	6:29:4	8:51:36	11:21: 6	14: 0:33	16:35:44	19: 6:34	21:23:32	23:50: 6	26:18:56	29: 1:54
19	1:38:40	4:17:20	6:33:40	8:56:56	11:26: 7	14: 0:39	16:40:49	19:11:16	21:28: 3	23:54:52	26:24: 9	29:18:39
20	1:44: 2	4:22:11	6:38:20	9: 1:16	11:31: 8	14: 6:15	16:45:49	19:15:51	21:32:45	23:59:37	26:29:25	29:13: 4
21	1:49:23	4:27: 1	6:42:50	9: 5:37	11:36:10	14:11: 1	16:50:51	19:20:30	21:37: 4	24: 4:22	26:34:41	29:24:14
22	1:54:43	4:31:52	6:47:25	9:10:19	11:41:13	14:21:29	16:55:51	19:25: 9	21:46:20	24: 9: 9	26:39:58	29:29:49
23	1:59:47	4:36:41	6:52: 0	9:15: 1	11:46:16	14:26:42	17: 0:51	19:29:47	21:46:20	24:13:46	26:45:15	29:35:26
24	2: 5: 5	4:41:29	6:56:34	9:19:44	11:51:20	14:31:56	17: 5:51	19:34:25	21:50:37	24:18:44	26:50:34	29:41: 4
25	2: 5:20	4:46:16	7: 1: 9	9:24:27	11:51:20	14:37:36	17:10:51	19:39:25	21:55:39	24:13:46	26:55:12	29:46:34
26	2:10:33	4:51: 3	7: 1:44	9:29: 9	11:56:24	14:42:23	17:15:47	19:43:39	22: 0:13	24:23:40	27: 1: 5	29:52: 8
27	2:16: 8	4:55:49	7:10:18	9:33:56	12: 1:29	14:47:36	17:20:44	19:48:15	22: 4:43	24:28:23	27: 6:36	29:57:43
28	2:21:49	5: 0:34	7:14:53	9:38:41	12: 6:35	14:52:49	17:25:41	19:52:50	22:13:14	24:28:23	27:11:59	30: 3:17
29	2:26:23	5: 5:19	7:19:27	9:43:27	12:11:41	14:58: 2	17:30:37	19:57:25	22:13:14	24:33:14	27:17:22	30: 8:51
30	2:31:54		7:24:52	9:48:13	12:16:48		17:35:32	20: 2: 0	22:17:46	24:38:16		
31	2:42: 0		7:28:36		12:21:56					24:42:59		

1977 SSRY = 30:16: 4

#	January	February	March	April	May	June	July	August	September	October	November	December
1	30:16: 4	2:47:24	5: 5:40	7:29:18	9:49:31	12:23:59	15: 0:40	17:38:27	20: 5: 9	22:21:20	24:47:17	27:22:33
2	0: 5:34	2:52:33	5:10:24	7:33:53	9:54:19	12:29: 9	15: 5:53	17:43:17	20: 9:44	22:25:54	24:52:12	27:27:59
3	0:11: 8	2:57:41	5:15: 8	7:38:25	9:57:49	12:34:18	15:11:16	17:48:15	20:14:18	22:30:28	24:57: 6	27:33:25
4	0:16:42	3: 2:48	5:19:33	7:47:41	10: 3:58	12:49:39	15:16:18	17:55:59	20:23:52	22:39:37	25: 1:26	27:44:21
5	0:22:16	3: 7:54	5:24:33	7:52:17	10: 8:58	12:49:50	15:26:42	18: 2:51	20:27:59	22:44:12	25: 5: 4	27:49:50
6	0:27:47	3:12:59	5:29:14	7:56:53	10:13:40	12:55: 2	15:31:54	18: 7:41	20:32:32	22:48:48	25:12: 7	27:55:20
7	0:33:19	3:18: 4	5:33:55	8: 1:30	10:18:32	13: 0:14	15:37: 4	18:12:31	20:37: 5	22:53:24	25:17: 5	28: 0:50
8	0:38:50	3:23: 7	5:38:36	8: 6: 7	10:23:24	13: 5:27	15:42:15	18:17:20	20:41:38	22:58:14	25:22: 1	28: 6:21
9	0:44:21	3:28: 9	5:43:16	8:10:44	10:28:18	13:10:40	15:47:25	18:22:25	20:46:38	22:40:38	25:27:13	28:11:53
10	0:49:51	3:33:10	5:47:55	8:15:22	10:33: 6	13:15:52	15:52:34	18:26:57	20:50:42	23: 3:18	25:32:13	28:17:25
11	0:55:21	3:38:10	5:52:34	8:20: 0	10:37:55	13:21:12	15:57:44	18:31:44	20:55:14	23:11:54	25:37:18	28:22:58
12	1: 0:50	3:43: 9	5:57:13	8:24:38	10:43: 2	13:26:20	16: 2:52	18:36:30	20:59:46	23:11:13	25:42:31	28:28:31
13	1: 6:18	3:48: 7	6: 1:51	8:29:17	10:52:55	13:31:34	16: 8: 7	18:41:16	21: 4:18	23:21: 3	25:52:39	28:34: 5
14	1:11:45	3:53: 5	6: 6:29	8:33:56	10:47:58	13:36:48	16:18: 5	18:46:15	21: 7:49	23:30:33	25:52:59	28:39:39
15	1:17:12	3:58: 1	6:11: 6	8:38:36	10:52:55	13:42: 3	16:23: 9	18:50:45	21:12:24	23:35:16	26: 8:10	28:45:14
16	1:22:37	4: 2:57	6:15:44	8:43:15	11: 2:51	13:47:17	16:23:20	18:55:28	21:17:53	23:39:59	26:13:22	28:50:49
17	1:28: 2	4: 7:51	6:20:21	8:47:56	11: 7:51	13:52:32	16:28:26	19: 0:11	21:22:24	23:44:42	26:18:36	28:56:24
18	1:33:26	4:12:45	6:24:58	8:52:37	11:17:51	13:57:47	16:33:31	19: 4:53	21:26:56	23:49:25	26:23:50	29: 1:59
19	1:38:50	4:17:38	6:29:35	8:57:18	11:22:53	14: 3: 1	16:38:35	19: 9:35	21:31:27	23:54: 8	26:29: 4	29: 7:35
20	1:44:12	4:22:29	6:34:11	9: 1:58	11:27:54	14: 3:16	16:43:39	19:14:16	21:35:58	23:58:56	26:34:18	29:13:11
21	1:49:33	4:27:20	6:38:47	9: 6:43	11:32:58	14: 8:31	16:48:41	19:18:56	21:40:30	24: 3:39	26:39:32	29:18:47
22	1:54:54	4:32:11	6:43:23	9:11:26	11:38: 1	14:13:46	16:53:44	19:23:36	21:45: 2	24: 8:22	26:34:22	29:24:22
23	2: 0:13	4:37: 0	6:47:59	9:16:10	11:43: 6	14:24: 1	16:58:44	19:28:15	21:49:33	24: 8:29	26:39:39	29:29:58
24	2: 5:32	4:41:49	6:52:35	9:20:54	11:48:10	14:29:16	17: 3:44	19:32:54	21:54: 5	24:13: 7	26:44:58	29:35:34
25	2:10:50	4:46:36	6:57:10	9:25:38	11:53:15	14:34:30	17: 8:45	19:37:32	21:58:37	24:18:25	26:50:17	29:41: 9
26	2:16: 6	4:51:23	7: 1:45	9:30:38	11:58:16	14:39:59	17:13:43	19:42:10	22: 3: 9	24:23:25	26:55: 9	29:46:46
27	2:21:22	4:56:10	7: 6:21	9:35:52	12: 3:35	14:44:43	17:18:42	19:46:46	22: 7:42	24:28: 9	27: 6:21	29:52:21
28	2:26:36	5: 0:55	7:10:56	9:39:56	12: 8:35	14:50:13	17:23:39	19:51:22	22:12:14	24:32:37	27:11:44	29:57:57
29	2:31:50		7:15:32	9:44:43	12:18:51	14:55:26	17:28:36	19:55:58	22:16:47	24:37:29	27:17: 8	30: 3:32
30	2:37: 2		7:15:32				17:33:31	20: 0:34				30: 9: 7
31	2:42:13		7:24:42							24:42:23		

1978 SSRY = 30:11:30

#	January	February	March	April	May	June	July	August	September	October	November	December
1	30:11:30	2:47: 4	5: 5: 6	7:28:24	9:48:13	12:22:13	14:58:29	17:35:57	20: 2:22	22:18:14	24:43:43	27:18:28
2	0: 5:34	2:52:13	5: 9:49	7:32:59	9:53: 4	12:32:30	15: 3:41	17:40:51	20: 6:57	22:22:47	24:48:38	27:23:53
3	0:11: 7	2:57:21	5:14:32	7:37:34	9:57:49	12:32:30	15: 8:54	17:45:44	20:11:31	22:22:54	24:53:33	27:29:19
4	0:16:40	3: 2:27	5:19: 9	7:46:45	10: 2:28	12:42:50	15:14: 6	17:50:28	20: 6: 4	22:36:24	24:58:30	27:34:45
5	0:22:12	3: 7:33	5:23:55	7:51:20	10:12:18	12:48: 1	15:24:29	17:55:28	20:20:28	22:36:28	25: 3:26	27:40:11
6	0:27:44	3:12:38	5:28:37	7:55:56	10:17: 9	12:53:11	15:24:29	18: 0:19	20:25:10	22:45:37	25: 8:27	27:45:41
7	0:33:15	3:17:42	5:33:18	8: 0:32	10:17: 9	12: 3: 3	15:34:50	18: 5:10	20:29:43	22:50:13	25:13:26	27:51: 9
8	0:38:46	3:22:45	5:37:58	8: 5: 8	10:26:54	13: 3:35	15:40: 0	18: 9:59	20:38:47	22:54:49	25:18:26	27:56:39
9	0:44:16	3:27:46	5:42:38	8: 9:45	10:31:46	13:13:59	15:45:10	18:14:48	20:38:47	22:59:25	25:23:28	28: 2: 9
10	0:49:46	3:32:46	5:47:18	8:14:22	10:36:41	13:13:59	15:50:20	18:19:35	20:43:20	23: 4: 1	25:28:28	28: 7:39
11	0:55:15	3:37:45	5:51:58	8:19:59	10:41:36	13:24:24	15:55:27	18:24:23	20:47:59	23: 8:39	25:33:34	28:13:10
12	1: 0:44	3:42:42	5:56:34	8:23:37	10:41:36	13:29:38	16: 0:35	18:33:55	20:56:53	23:13:17	25:38:39	28:18:41
13	1: 6:11	3:47:43	6: 1:12	8:28:15	10:46:31	13:24:24	16: 5:42	18:38:40	21: 1:24	23:17:56	25:43:45	28:24:14
14	1:11:38	3:52:40	6: 5:49	8:32:53	10:51:27	13:29:38	16:10:48	18:43:24	21: 1:24	23:17:56	25:48:52	28:29:47
15	1:17: 4	3:57:36	6:10:30	8:37:22	10:56:22	13:34:51	16: 5:42	18:43:24	21: 5:54	23:22:35	25:53:54	28:35:20
16	1:22:29	4: 2:31	6:15:21	8:42:11	11: 6:20	13:45:18	16:21: 0	18:52:50	21:10:26	23:31:53	25:53:54	28:40:53
17	1:27:53	4: 7:25	6:19:39	8:46:51	11: 6:20	13:50: 3	16:26: 4	18:57:32	21:14:56	23:36:32	26: 4:19	28:46:27
18	1:33:17	4:12:18	6:24:15	8:51:31	11:16:18	13:55:17	16:31: 9	19: 2:14	21:19:26	23:36:32	26: 9:30	28:52: 1
19	1:38:39	4:17:10	6:28:51	8:56:11	11:21:18	14: 0:31	16:36:12	19: 6:55	21:23:57	23:41:19	26:14:42	28:57:36
20	1:44: 1	4:22: 1	6:33:27	9: 0:52	11:26:18	14: 0:59	16:41:16	19:11:35	21:28:28	23:46: 2	26:19:55	29: 3:11
21	1:49:22	4:26:52	6:38:37	9: 5:33	11:31:21	14: 6:13	16:46:16	19:16:15	21:32:28	23:50:46	26:25:30	29: 8:46
22	1:54:41	4:31:41	6:42:59	9:10:15	11:36:23	14:16:41	16:51:18	19:20:54	21:37:30	23:55:40	26:30:41	29:14:21
23	2: 0: 0	4:36:30	6:47:12	9:14:58	11:41:26	14:21:55	16:56:18	19:25:32	21:42: 0	24: 5: 1	26:35:41	29:19:56
24	2: 5:18	4:41:18	6:51:47	9:19:41	11:46:30	14:27:10	17: 1:18	19:30:10	21:46:31	24: 4:36	26:51:36	29:36:41
25	2:10:34	4:46: 5	6:56:22	9:24:25	11:51:34	14:32:22	17: 6:17	19:34:48	21:51: 2	24:14:36	26:51:36	29:41:51
26	2:15:50	4:50:51	7: 0:56	9:24:25	11:56:35	14:38: 3	17:11:16	19:39:24	21:55:32	24:14:36	26:56:28	29:47:51
27	2:21: 4	4:55:37	7: 5:30	9:33:52	12: 1:55	14:42:50	17:16:13	19:44:21	22: 4: 3	24:19:14	26:51:36	29:52: 1
28	2:26:19	5: 0:22	7:10: 5	9:33:54	12: 6:45	14:42:50	17:21:10	19:48:57	22: 2: 9	24:24:17	27: 2:18	29:58:51
29	2:31:32		7:14:40	9:38:40	12:11:58	14:48: 3	17:26: 7	19:53:13	22: 9: 9	24:28: 9	27: 7:41	30: 3:26
30	2:36:43		7:19:15	9:43:26	12:17: 5	14:53:16	17:26: 7	19:57:48	22:13:41	24:29:57	27:13: 4	30: 9:14
31	2:41:54		7:23:49				17:31: 2			24:38:50		30: 4:35

1979 SSRY = 30:14:11

Day	January	February	March	April	May	June	July	August	September	October	November	December	Day
1	0:0:0	2:47:26	5:5:46	7:29:20	9:49:19	12:23:27	14:59:55	17:37:41	20:4:24	22:20:27	24:46:4	27:20:55	1
2	0:5:34	2:52:35	5:10:31	7:33:56	9:54:7	12:28:36	15:5:9	17:42:35	20:8:58	22:25:0	24:50:59	27:26:20	2
3	0:11:8	2:57:44	5:15:14	7:38:31	9:58:56	12:33:32	15:10:21	17:47:29	20:13:32	22:29:34	24:55:54	27:31:46	3
4	0:16:42	3:2:51	5:19:57	7:43:7	10:3:46	12:38:45	15:15:36	17:52:24	20:18:6	22:34:8	25:0:58	27:37:13	4
5	0:22:47	3:7:58	5:24:40	7:47:42	10:8:35	12:43:16	15:20:47	17:57:15	20:22:40	22:38:42	25:5:52	27:42:43	5
6	0:27:47	3:13:3	5:29:21	7:52:18	10:13:25	12:48:56	15:25:57	18:2:6	20:27:13	22:43:16	25:10:47	27:48:8	6
7	0:33:19	3:18:8	5:34:2	7:56:54	10:18:17	12:54:27	15:31:9	18:6:56	20:31:46	22:47:52	25:15:47	27:53:37	7
8	0:38:51	3:23:12	5:38:43	8:1:30	10:23:0	12:59:39	15:36:19	18:11:46	20:36:18	22:52:27	25:20:48	27:59:7	8
9	0:44:22	3:28:13	5:43:23	8:6:17	10:28:13	13:4:51	15:41:30	18:16:35	20:40:51	22:57:2	25:25:49	28:4:37	9
10	0:49:53	3:33:15	5:48:3	8:11:0	10:32:45	13:10:0	15:46:40	18:21:23	20:45:23	23:1:47	25:30:52	28:10:8	10
11	0:55:21	3:38:13	5:52:42	8:15:44	10:37:39	13:15:13	15:51:49	18:26:11	20:49:55	23:6:47	25:35:56	28:15:40	11
12	1:0:50	3:43:14	5:57:20	8:20:28	10:42:43	13:20:28	15:56:58	18:30:58	20:54:26	23:10:54	25:41:1	28:21:12	12
13	1:6:18	3:48:12	6:1:58	8:24:36	10:47:39	13:25:41	16:2:6	18:35:44	20:58:58	23:15:33	25:46:7	28:26:44	13
14	1:11:45	3:53:10	6:6:36	8:29:14	10:52:35	13:30:55	16:7:14	18:40:30	21:3:29	23:20:12	25:51:14	28:32:17	14
15	1:17:12	3:58:2	6:11:14	8:33:53	10:57:32	13:36:8	16:12:21	18:45:14	21:8:0	23:24:51	25:56:22	28:37:51	15
16	1:22:37	4:2:57	6:15:51	8:38:32	11:2:28	13:41:22	16:17:29	18:50:0	21:12:32	23:29:32	26:1:32	28:43:25	16
17	1:28:2	4:7:50	6:20:27	8:43:11	11:7:28	13:46:36	16:22:33	18:54:42	21:17:3	23:34:13	26:6:42	28:49:0	17
18	1:33:26	4:12:50	6:25:4	8:47:51	11:12:29	13:51:50	16:27:39	18:59:25	21:21:34	23:38:54	26:11:54	28:54:34	18
19	1:38:49	4:17:43	6:29:40	8:52:31	11:17:27	13:57:3	16:32:47	19:4:7	21:26:5	23:43:37	26:17:6	29:0:9	19
20	1:44:12	4:22:35	6:34:16	8:57:10	11:22:34	14:2:19	16:37:47	19:8:49	21:30:36	23:48:20	26:22:20	29:5:44	20
21	1:49:33	4:27:26	6:38:52	9:2:0	11:27:30	14:7:26	16:42:53	19:13:30	21:35:7	23:53:3	26:27:35	29:11:20	21
22	1:54:54	4:32:26	6:43:28	9:6:35	11:32:31	14:12:34	16:47:57	19:18:10	21:39:38	23:57:49	26:32:50	29:16:56	22
23	2:0:14	4:37:5	6:48:3	9:11:18	11:37:34	14:18:3	16:52:56	19:22:50	21:44:10	24:2:34	26:38:7	29:22:33	23
24	2:5:32	4:41:54	6:52:39	9:16:1	11:42:37	14:23:17	16:57:57	19:27:29	21:48:42	24:7:21	26:43:25	29:28:11	24
25	2:10:50	4:46:42	6:57:14	9:20:45	11:47:42	14:28:42	17:2:58	19:32:8	21:53:13	24:12:8	26:48:43	29:33:43	25
26	2:16:6	4:51:29	7:1:49	9:25:29	11:52:46	14:33:46	17:7:57	19:36:46	21:57:44	24:16:56	26:54:3	29:39:18	26
27	2:21:22	4:56:16	7:6:24	9:30:14	11:57:51	14:38:57	17:12:55	19:41:23	22:2:16	24:21:44	26:59:24	29:44:54	27
28	2:26:37	5:1:1	7:10:52	9:34:59	12:3:0	14:44:13	17:17:52	19:46:0	22:6:49	24:26:35	27:4:25	29:50:30	28
29	2:31:51		7:15:35	9:39:45	12:8:4	14:49:28	17:22:53	19:50:37	22:11:22	24:31:26	27:10:8	29:56:5	29
30	2:37:3		7:20:10	9:44:32	12:13:10	14:54:42	17:27:55	19:55:13	22:15:54	24:36:18	27:15:31	30:1:40	30
31	2:42:15		7:24:45		12:18:19		17:32:46	19:59:48		24:41:11		30:7:15	31

1980 SSRY = 30:10:31

Day	January	February	March	April	May	June	July	August	September	October	November	December	Day
1	0:0:0	2:47:11	5:10:5	7:33:15	9:53:6	12:27:11	15:3:23	17:40:35	20:6:45	22:22:32	24:48:8	27:23:4	1
2	0:5:34	2:52:20	5:14:48	7:37:50	9:57:54	12:32:19	15:8:35	17:45:28	20:11:19	22:27:5	24:53:3	27:28:29	2
3	0:11:39	2:57:28	5:19:31	7:42:24	10:2:42	12:37:23	15:13:47	17:50:21	20:15:52	22:31:38	24:57:59	27:33:55	3
4	0:17:39	3:2:41	5:24:9	7:47:0	10:7:31	12:42:38	15:18:58	17:55:13	20:20:26	22:36:12	25:2:55	27:39:22	4
5	0:22:44	3:7:45	5:28:54	7:51:35	10:12:21	12:47:48	15:24:9	18:0:3	20:25:0	22:40:45	25:7:53	27:44:49	5
6	0:27:44	3:12:46	5:33:14	7:56:10	10:17:11	12:52:58	15:29:20	18:4:54	20:29:31	22:45:20	25:12:52	27:50:17	6
7	0:33:15	3:17:50	5:38:14	8:0:46	10:22:2	12:58:9	15:34:30	18:9:43	20:34:3	22:49:55	25:17:52	27:55:46	7
8	0:38:41	3:22:53	5:42:54	8:5:22	10:26:54	13:3:20	15:39:40	18:14:32	20:38:35	22:54:31	25:22:53	28:1:16	8
9	0:44:16	3:27:55	5:47:33	8:10:10	10:31:47	13:8:32	15:44:50	18:19:21	20:43:7	22:59:7	25:27:56	28:6:46	9
10	0:49:44	3:32:55	5:52:12	8:14:58	10:36:38	13:13:56	15:49:59	18:24:8	20:47:38	23:3:44	25:32:59	28:12:17	10
11	0:55:21	3:37:56	5:56:50	8:19:34	10:41:29	13:19:2	15:55:7	18:28:55	20:52:10	23:8:21	25:38:3	28:17:49	11
12	1:0:43	3:42:53	6:1:28	8:24:10	10:46:29	13:24:8	16:0:15	18:33:41	20:56:41	23:12:58	25:43:8	28:23:21	12
13	1:6:11	3:47:53	6:6:6	8:28:26	10:51:26	13:29:21	16:5:23	18:38:26	21:1:12	23:17:37	25:48:15	28:28:53	13
14	1:11:38	3:52:50	6:10:42	8:33:4	10:56:21	13:34:35	16:10:29	18:43:10	21:5:43	23:22:16	25:53:22	28:34:26	14
15	1:17:4	3:57:47	6:15:25	8:37:43	11:1:15	13:39:48	16:15:34	18:47:54	21:10:14	23:26:55	25:58:31	28:39:59	15
16	1:22:29	4:2:30	6:20:8	8:42:22	11:6:15	13:45:1	16:20:46	18:52:37	21:15:15	23:31:36	26:3:35	28:45:33	16
17	1:27:54	4:7:36	6:24:32	8:47:1	11:11:15	13:50:15	16:25:50	18:57:20	21:19:16	23:36:16	26:8:40	28:51:7	17
18	1:33:18	4:12:30	6:29:8	8:51:41	11:16:14	13:55:28	16:30:54	19:2:2	21:23:46	23:40:58	26:14:2	28:56:41	18
19	1:38:41	4:17:22	6:33:43	8:56:21	11:21:14	14:0:43	16:35:54	19:6:43	21:28:16	23:45:41	26:19:15	29:2:15	19
20	1:44:3	4:22:14	6:38:16	9:1:2	11:26:15	14:5:56	16:40:59	19:11:23	21:32:47	23:50:24	26:24:29	29:7:49	20
21	1:49:24	4:27:9	6:42:49	9:5:43	11:31:16	14:11:9	16:45:59	19:16:2	21:37:17	23:55:8	26:29:43	29:13:24	21
22	1:54:44	4:31:55	6:47:29	9:10:25	11:36:18	14:16:22	16:51:2	19:20:42	21:41:48	23:59:52	26:34:59	29:18:59	22
23	2:0:4	4:36:44	6:52:4	9:15:7	11:41:20	14:21:38	16:56:2	19:25:21	21:46:18	24:4:24	26:40:16	29:24:34	23
24	2:5:22	4:41:32	6:56:39	9:19:50	11:46:24	14:26:52	17:1:2	19:29:59	21:50:50	24:9:24	26:45:33	29:30:9	24
25	2:10:39	4:46:19	7:1:13	9:24:33	11:51:27	14:32:6	17:6:1	19:34:37	21:55:21	24:14:2	26:50:52	29:35:44	25
26	2:15:55	4:51:6	7:5:48	9:29:17	11:56:32	14:37:19	17:11:0	19:39:14	21:59:52	24:18:49	26:56:12	29:41:18	26
27	2:21:5	4:55:52	7:10:23	9:34:1	12:1:36	14:42:32	17:16:2	19:43:26	22:4:23	24:23:37	27:1:54	29:46:52	27
28	2:26:25	5:0:37	7:14:57	9:38:47	12:6:41	14:47:45	17:21:1	19:48:26	22:8:43	24:28:26	27:6:54	29:52:26	28
29	2:31:38	5:5:22	7:19:31	9:43:32	12:11:49	14:52:58	17:25:51	19:53:1	22:13:27	24:33:21	27:12:16	29:58:2	29
30	2:36:50		7:24:5	9:48:19	12:16:56	14:58:10	17:30:40	19:57:36	22:17:59	24:38:22	27:17:39	30:3:36	30
31	2:42:1		7:28:40		12:22:3		17:35:41	20:2:11		24:43:14		30:9:10	31

1981 SSRY = 30:10:15

Day	January	February	March	April	May	June	July	August	September	October	November	December
1	0: 0: 0	2:46:51	5: 4:40	7:27:50	9:47:37	12:21:35	14:57:45	17:35: 1	20: 1:15	22:17: 0	24:42:30	27:17:18
2	0: 5:33	2:51:59	5: 9:23	7:32:25	9:52:33	12:26:44	15: 2:58	17:39:55	20: 5:49	22:21:33	24:47:25	27:22:43
3	0:11: 6	2:57: 7	5:14: 6	7:37: 0	9:57:13	12:31:53	15: 8:11	17:44:47	20:10:56	22:36:40	24:52:11	27:28: 5
4	0:16:39	3: 2:13	5:18:48	7:41:35	10: 1:42	12:37: 4	15:13:21	17:49:39	20:19:29	22:35:14	24:57:17	27:33:35
5	0:22:12	3: 7:18	5:23:29	7:45:10	10: 6:33	12:42:12	15:18:33	17:54:31	20:24: 1	22:39:49	25: 2:15	27:39:32
6	0:27:43	3:12:23	5:28:10	7:50:46	10:11:42	12:47:23	15:23:44	17:59:21	20:28:33	22:44:23	25: 7:13	27:44:30
7	0:33:14	3:17:26	5:32:51	7:55:22	10:16:33	12:52:34	15:28:54	18: 4:11	20:33: 5	22:48:59	25:12:13	27:49:59
8	0:38:44	3:22:28	5:37:31	7:59:58	10:21:25	12:57:45	15:34: 4	18: 9: 0	20:37:37	22:53:35	25:17:14	27:55:28
9	0:44:14	3:27:30	5:42:10	8: 4:34	10:26:17	13: 2:56	15:39:14	18:13:48	20:42:38	22:58:11	25:22:18	28: 6:28
10	0:49:43	3:32:29	5:46:49	8: 8:47	10:31: 9	13: 8: 6	15:44:31	18:18:36	20:46:40	23: 2:48	25:27:18	28:11:59
11	0:55:12	3:37:29	5:51:27	8:13:47	10:36: 5	13:13:20	15:49:31	18:23:22	20:51:11	23: 7:25	25:32:22	28:17:31
12	1: 0:40	3:42:27	5:56: 6	8:18:24	10:40:59	13:18:33	15:54:41	18:28: 8	20:55:41	23:12: 2	25:37:27	28:23: 3
13	1: 6: 7	3:47:25	6: 0:42	8:23: 2	10:45:55	13:23:45	15:59:46	18:32:53	21: 0:12	23:16:42	25:42:32	28:28:35
14	1:11:33	3:52:21	6: 5:20	8:27:39	10:50:51	13:28:58	16: 4:53	18:37:38	21: 5: 9	23:21: 2	25:47:39	28:34: 5
15	1:16:59	3:57:16	6: 9:56	8:32:18	10:55:47	13:34:11	16: 9:55	18:42:22	21: 9:13	23:26:21	25:47:57	28:39:42
16	1:22:24	4: 2:11	6:14:33	8:37: 0	11: 0:43	13:39:21	16:15: 2	18:47:25	21:13:44	23:30:41	26: 3: 7	28:45:15
17	1:27:47	4: 7: 4	6:19: 9	8:41:35	11: 5:43	13:44:38	16:20:10	18:51:47	21:18:14	23:35:23	26: 8:18	28:50:49
18	1:33:10	4:11:57	6:23:44	8:46:15	11:10:41	13:49:51	16:25:14	18:56:29	21:22:45	23:40:45	26:13:30	28:56:24
19	1:38:32	4:16:48	6:28:20	8:50:54	11:15:42	13:55: 5	16:30:18	19: 1:51	21:27:46	23:44:38	26:18:44	29: 1:58
20	1:43:53	4:21:39	6:32:55	8:55:35	11:20:41	14: 0:18	16:35:20	19: 6:51	21:31:46	23:49:31	26:23:58	29: 7:38
21	1:49:13	4:26:29	6:37:30	8:59:57	11:25:41	14: 5:16	16:40:23	19:10:51	21:37:46	23:54:16	26:29:14	29:13:18
22	1:54:33	4:31:18	6:42: 4	9: 4:39	11:30:44	14:10: 6	16:45:23	19:15:10	21:40:47	23:59: 1	26:34:30	29:18:43
23	1:59:51	4:36: 6	6:46:40	9: 9:39	11:35:46	14:15:59	16:50:25	19:19:49	21:45:18	24: 3:48	26:39:48	29:24:18
24	2: 5: 8	4:40:54	6:51:14	9:14:22	11:40:49	14:21:13	16:55:25	19:24:23	21:49:49	24: 8:35	26:45: 2	29:29:53
25	2:10:24	4:45:40	6:55:49	9:19: 5	11:45:53	14:26:27	17: 0:25	19:29: 2	21:49:49	24:13:21	26:50:26	29:35:28
26	2:15:40	4:50:26	7: 0:23	9:23:48	11:50:56	14:31:40	17: 5:22	19:34:42	21:58:52	24:18:12	26:55:46	29:41: 3
27	2:20:54	4:55:11	7: 4:57	9:28:31	12: 1: 0	14:36:53	17:10:22	19:39:43	22: 3:24	24:23: 1	27: 1:30	29:46:37
28	2:26: 7	4:59:56	7: 9:32	9:33:18	12: 6:13	14:42:47	17:15:19	19:42:30	22: 7:56	24:27:52	27: 6:30	29:52:12
29	2:31:20		7:14: 6	9:38: 3	12:11:20	14:47:20	17:20:16	19:47:50	22:12:28	24:32:44	27:11:53	29:57:46
30	2:36:31		7:18:41	9:42:50	12:16:28	14:52:33	17:25:11	19:52:40		24:37:37		30: 3:21
31	2:41:42		7:23:16		12:21:28		17:30: 7	19:57:16				

1982 SSRY = 30:17:43

Day	January	February	March	April	May	June	July	August	September	October	November	December
1	0: 0: 0	2:47:38	5: 6: 8	7:29:56	9:50:15	12:24:47	15: 1:35	17:39:34	20: 6:28	22:22:46	24:48:46	27:24: 4
2	0: 5:35	2:52:48	5:10:53	7:34:32	9:55:33	12:29:57	15: 6:49	17:44:29	20:11: 3	22:27:20	24:53:42	27:29:30
3	0:11: 9	2:57:57	5:15:36	7:39: 8	9:59:53	12:35: 7	15:12:15	17:49:23	20:15:37	22:32:14	24:58:38	27:34: 4
4	0:16:43	3: 3: 4	5:20:19	7:43:43	10: 4:33	12:40:17	15:17:29	17:54: 8	20:20: 9	22:36:29	25: 3:35	27:40:24
5	0:21: 9	3: 8:11	5:25: 2	7:48:20	10: 9:13	12:45:12	15:22:43	17:59: 8	20:24:45	22:41: 4	25: 8:34	27:45:52
6	0:26:43	3:13:17	5:29:44	7:52:57	10:14:24	12:50:39	15:27:39	18: 4: 0	20:29:19	22:50:15	25:13:33	27:45:21
7	0:27:50	3:18:18	5:34:26	7:57:33	10:19:16	12:55:51	15:32:53	18: 8:51	20:33:52	22:50:15	25:18:34	27:56:51
8	0:33:22	3:23:25	5:39: 9	8: 2:10	10:24: 9	13: 1: 3	15:38:12	18:13:41	20:38:25	22:54:51	25:23:35	23: 2:21
9	0:38:54	3:28:25	5:43:47	8: 6:47	10:29: 2	13: 6:16	15:43:13	18:18:30	20:42:31	22:59:26	25:28:36	23: 7:51
10	0:44:25	3:33:30	5:48:27	8:11:24	10:33:51	13:11:26	15:48:42	18:23:19	20:46:56	23: 3:43	25:33:46	23:13:24
11	0:49:55	3:38:30	5:53:26	8:16: 0	10:38:51	13:16:42	15:53:43	18:28:19	20:52:33	23: 8:43	25:38:47	23:18:57
12	0:55:25	3:43:29	5:57:45	8:20:40	10:43:43	13:27:10	15:58:42	18:32:55	21: 1: 7	23:13:21	25:43:53	23:24:30
13	1: 0:55	3:48:28	6: 2:24	8:25:19	10:48:43	13:27:10	16: 3:51	18:37:41	21: 5:39	23:18: 0	25:49: 0	23:30: 3
14	1: 6:23	3:53:26	6: 7: 2	8:29:57	10:53:36	13:32:20	16: 8:59	18:42:27	21:10:12	23:22:40	25:54: 8	23:35:37
15	1:11:51	3:58:22	6:11:40	8:34:37	10:58:43	13:37:38	16:14:14	18:47:12	21:14:43	23:27:20	25:54:27	23:40:47
16	1:17:18	4: 3:18	6:16:20	8:39:15	11: 3:36	13:42:50	16:19:14	18:51:57	21:19:11	23:32: 0	26: 4:27	23:46:17
17	1:22:44	4: 8: 9	6:20:55	8:43:56	11: 8:37	13:48: 2	16:24:31	18:56:41	21:23:47	23:36:43	26: 9:39	23:52:22
18	1:28:12	4:13: 0	6:25:39	8:48:37	11:13:37	13:53: 8	16:29:31	19: 1:24	21:28:18	23:41:26	26:14:51	23:57:57
19	1:33:34	4:18: 0	6:30: 9	8:53:18	11:18:37	13:58:37	16:34:31	19: 6: 7	21:32:50	23:46: 9	26:20: 4	29: 3:33
20	1:38:57	4:22:53	6:34:45	8:58: 0	11:23:38	14: 3:52	16:39:36	19:10:49	21:37:21	23:50:53	26:25:15	29: 9: 8
21	1:44:20	4:27:45	6:39:27	9: 2:44	11:28:38	14: 9: 6	16:44:46	19:15:40	21:41:54	23:55:44	26:30:15	29:14:45
22	1:49:42	4:32:36	6:44: 7	9: 7:24	11:33:38	14:14:20	16:49:57	19:20:31	21:46:26	24: 0:23	26:35:51	29:20:21
23	2: 0:23	4:37:25	6:48:54	9:12: 7	11:38:47	14:19:38	16:54:46	19:24:51	21:55:30	24: 5:10	26:41: 9	29:25:58
24	2: 5:42	4:42:14	6:53:10	9:16:51	11:43:47	14:24:53	16:59:47	19:29:31	21:55:30	24:14:45	26:46:28	29:31:34
25	2:11: 0	4:47: 2	6:57:44	9:21:36	11:48:56	14:30: 8	17: 4:48	19:34:10	22: 0: 2	24: 9:57	26:51:47	29:37:10
26	2:16:17	4:51:50	7: 2:21	9:26:21	11:54: 5	14:35:23	17: 9:47	19:38:48	22: 4:34	24:14:45	26:57: 8	29:42:46
27	2:21:33	4:56:12	7: 7: 1	9:31: 2	11:59: 4	14:40:30	17:14:47	19:43:26	22: 9: 7	24:19:24	27: 1: 9	29:48:23
28	2:26:43		7:11:33	9:35:52	12: 4: 9	14:45:27	17:19:47	19:48: 3	22:13:40	24:24:14	27: 7:51	29:53:59
29	2:32: 2		7:16:13	9:40:39	12: 9:14	14:51: 7	17:24:42	19:52:40	22:13:40	24:29:14	27:13:15	29:59:35
30	2:37:15		7:20:44	9:45:27	12:14:30	14:56:21	17:29:42	19:57:16	22:18:13	24:34: 6	27:18:39	30: 5:10
31	2:42:27		7:25:20		12:19:38		17:34:38	20: 1:52		24:43:52		30:10:46

1983 SSRY = 30:12: 5

Day	January	February	March	April	May	June	July	August	September	October	November	December
1	0: 0: 0	2:47:13	5: 5:24	7:28:47	9:48:37	12:22:35	14:58:53	17:36:27	20: 2:58	22:18:51	24:44:19	27:19: 1
2	0: 5:34	2:52:22	5:10:17	7:33:22	9:53:24	12:27:44	15: 4: 8	17:41:21	20: 7:32	22:23:24	24:49:15	27:24:25
3	0:11: 9	2:57:30	5:15:10	7:37:58	9:58:13	12:32:53	15: 9:18	17:46:14	20:12: 6	22:27:58	24:54:12	27:29:51
4	0:16:40	3: 2:37	5:19:53	7:42:32	10: 3: 1	12:38: 2	15:14:28	17:51: 7	20:16:40	22:32:31	24:59:11	27:35:18
5	0:22:13	3: 7:43	5:24:17	7:47: 8	10: 7:49	12:43:12	15:19:38	17:55:59	20:21:13	22:37: 5	25: 4:12	27:40:45
6	0:27:45	3:12:48	5:28:56	7:51:43	10:12:41	12:48:23	15:24:53	18: 0:50	20:25:46	22:41:40	25: 9:14	27:46:13
7	0:33:16	3:17:52	5:33:37	7:56:19	10:17:32	12:53:33	15:30: 4	18: 5:40	20:30:19	22:46:15	25:14:18	27:51:42
8	0:38:47	3:22:55	5:38:17	8: 0:55	10:22:24	12:58:45	15:35:15	18:10:30	20:34:51	22:50:50	25:19:23	27:57:11
9	0:44:17	3:27:58	5:42:56	8: 5:32	10:27:16	13: 3:56	15:40:25	18:15:19	20:39:23	22:55:26	25:24:30	28: 2:42
10	0:49:47	3:32:59	5:47:36	8:10: 9	10:32: 8	13: 9: 8	15:45:35	18:20: 6	20:43:55	23: 0: 2	25:29:38	28: 8:12
11	0:55:17	3:37:59	5:52:14	8:14:45	10:37: 1	13:14:21	15:50:44	18:24:54	20:48:27	23: 4:39	25:34:47	28:13:43
12	1: 0:45	3:42:58	5:56:54	8:19:22	10:41:58	13:19:34	15:55:52	18:29:41	20:52:58	23: 9:17	25:39:14	28:19:15
13	1: 6:13	3:47:56	6: 1:32	8:24: 0	10:46:54	13:24:47	16: 1: 0	18:34:27	20:57:30	23:13:55	25:44:20	28:24:48
14	1:11:40	3:52:53	6: 6: 9	8:28:38	10:51:50	13:30: 0	16: 6: 8	18:39:12	21: 2: 1	23:18:34	25:49:27	28:30:20
15	1:17: 6	3:57:49	6:10:47	8:33:16	10:56:46	13:35:14	16:11:15	18:43:57	21: 6:32	23:23:13	25:54:35	28:35:54
16	1:22:32	4: 2:45	6:15:24	8:37:55	11: 1:44	13:40:27	16:16:21	18:48:41	21:11: 2	23:27:53	25:59:44	28:41:28
17	1:27:57	4: 7:39	6:20: 0	8:42:35	11: 6:43	13:45:41	16:21:27	18:53:24	21:15:34	23:32:34	26: 4:53	28:47:21
18	1:33:21	4:12:32	6:24:36	8:47:14	11:11:42	13:50:55	16:26:32	18:58: 6	21:20: 4	23:37:15	26:10: 3	28:52:35
19	1:38:43	4:17:24	6:29:12	8:51:54	11:16:42	13:56: 9	16:31:36	19: 2:48	21:24:36	23:41:57	26:15:17	28:58:10
20	1:44: 5	4:22: 7	6:33:48	8:56:35	11:21:43	14: 1:23	16:36:40	19: 7:29	21:29: 6	23:46:40	26:20:30	29: 3:44
21	1:49:27	4:27: 7	6:38:24	9: 1:16	11:26:43	14: 6:37	16:41:43	19:12: 9	21:33:36	23:51:23	26:25:45	29: 9:19
22	1:54:47	4:31:57	6:42:59	9: 5:58	11:31:44	14:11:51	16:46:45	19:16:49	21:38: 7	23:56: 7	26:31: 0	29:14:55
23	2: 0: 6	4:36:46	6:47:34	9:10:40	11:36:49	14:17: 5	16:51:46	19:21:29	21:42:38	24: 0:53	26:36:15	29:20:29
24	2: 5:24	4:41:34	6:52: 9	9:15:22	11:41:49	14:22:19	16:56:47	19:26: 7	21:47: 9	24: 5:39	26:41:32	29:26: 5
25	2:10:41	4:46:23	6:56:44	9:20: 5	11:46:53	14:27:33	17: 1:46	19:30:45	21:51:40	24:10:25	26:46:51	29:31:40
26	2:15:57	4:51: 2	7: 1:19	9:24:49	11:51:57	14:32:47	17: 6:45	19:35:23	21:56:11	24:15:13	26:52:10	29:37:15
27	2:21:13	4:55:54	7: 5:54	9:29:33	11:57: 3	14:38: 0	17:11:46	19:40: 0	22: 0:42	24:20: 1	26:57:31	29:42:50
28	2:26:27	5: 0:39	7:10:29	9:34:18	12: 2: 8	14:43:14	17:16:43	19:44:36	22: 5:15	24:24:51	27: 2:51	29:48:20
29	2:31:40		7:15: 3	9:39: 4	12: 7:14	14:48:27	17:21:40	19:49:12	22: 9:47	24:29:42	27: 8:13	29:54:20
30	2:36:52		7:19:38	9:43:50	12:12:18	14:53:40	17:26:36	19:53:48	22:14:19	24:34:33	27:13:37	29:59:35
31	2:42: 3		7:24:13		12:17:28		17:31:32	19:58:23		24:39:25		30: 5:10

1984 SSRY = 30:14: 6

Day	January	February	March	April	May	June	July	August	September	October	November	December
1	0: 0: 0	2:47:31	5:10:42	7:34: 8	9:54:16	12:28:41	15: 5:11	17:42:42	20: 9: 8	22:25: 9	24:51: 2	27:26:17
2	0: 5:34	2:52:40	5:15:25	7:38:44	9:59: 5	12:33:50	15:10:24	17:47:36	20:13:42	22:29:42	24:55:57	27:31:43
3	0:11: 8	2:57:48	5:20: 6	7:43:19	10: 3:54	12:39: 0	15:15:37	17:52:29	20:18:16	22:34:16	25: 0:54	27:37: 9
4	0:16:42	3: 2:55	5:24:51	7:47:55	10: 8:44	12:44:21	15:20:49	17:57:21	20:22:50	22:38:50	25: 5:51	27:42:37
5	0:22:15	3: 8: 1	5:29:33	7:52:31	10:13:34	12:49:32	15:26: 0	18: 2:13	20:27:23	22:43:25	25:10:50	27:48: 5
6	0:27:48	3:13:10	5:34:14	7:57: 7	10:18:25	12:54:43	15:31:12	18: 7: 4	20:31:56	22:48: 0	25:15:49	27:53:34
7	0:33:20	3:18:10	5:38:55	8: 1:43	10:23:17	12:59:54	15:36:23	18:11:54	20:36:28	22:52:35	25:20:50	27:59: 3
8	0:38:52	3:23:19	5:43:35	8: 6:20	10:28:10	13: 4:55	15:41:34	18:16:43	20:41: 1	22:57:11	25:25:51	28: 4:33
9	0:44:22	3:28:21	5:48:16	8:10:57	10:33: 5	13:10: 7	15:46:44	18:21:31	20:45:33	23: 1:48	25:30:54	28:10: 4
10	0:49:53	3:33:23	5:52:57	8:15:34	10:37:59	13:15:20	15:51:56	18:26:19	20:50: 4	23: 6:25	25:35:57	28:15:35
11	0:55:23	3:38:23	5:57:38	8:20:11	10:42:52	13:20:32	15:57: 3	18:31:16	20:54:36	23:11: 3	25:41: 1	28:21: 7
12	1: 0:52	3:43:22	6: 2:11	8:24:49	10:47:43	13:25:46	16: 2:11	18:35:52	20:59: 8	23:15:40	25:46: 8	28:26:40
13	1: 6:21	3:48:22	6: 6:49	8:29:27	10:52:43	13:30:59	16: 7:18	18:40:38	21: 3:39	23:20:19	25:51:14	28:32:13
14	1:11:48	3:53:19	6:11:27	8:34: 4	10:57:40	13:36:12	16:12:25	18:45:23	21: 8:10	23:24:58	25:56:22	28:37:46
15	1:17:15	3:58:16	6:16: 7	8:38:43	11: 2:38	13:41:26	16:17:32	18:50: 7	21:12:41	23:29:38	26: 1:31	28:43:20
16	1:22:41	4: 3:12	6:20:47	8:43:23	11: 7:36	13:46:40	16:22:38	18:54:50	21:17:12	23:34:19	26: 6:41	28:48:54
17	1:28: 6	4: 8: 0	6:25:17	8:48: 3	11:12:35	13:51:53	16:27:43	18:59:33	21:21:44	23:39:10	26:11:53	28:54:28
18	1:33:30	4:13:10	6:29:54	8:52:43	11:17:34	13:57: 3	16:32:48	19: 4:16	21:26:15	23:43:43	26:17: 5	29: 0: 3
19	1:38:53	4:17:53	6:34:30	8:57:24	11:22:37	14: 2:23	16:37:52	19: 8:57	21:30:46	23:48:26	26:22:18	29: 5:39
20	1:44:15	4:22:36	6:39: 4	9: 2: 5	11:27:36	14: 7:51	16:42:56	19:13:38	21:35:17	23:53: 9	26:27:33	29:11:14
21	1:49:37	4:27:26	6:43:41	9: 6:47	11:32:37	14:12:51	16:48: 0	19:18:18	21:39:48	23:57:54	26:32:48	29:16:50
22	1:54:58	4:32:16	6:48:16	9:11:29	11:37:41	14:18: 5	16:53: 0	19:22:58	21:44:19	24: 2:39	26:38: 5	29:22:25
23	2: 0:18	4:37:16	6:52:52	9:16:12	11:42:43	14:23:20	16:58: 2	19:27:37	21:48:51	24: 7:26	26:43:22	29:28: 1
24	2: 5:36	4:42: 5	6:57:27	9:20:55	11:47:47	14:28:35	17: 3: 2	19:32:16	21:53:22	24:12:13	26:48:41	29:33:37
25	2:10:53	4:46:53	7: 2:11	9:25:44	11:52:51	14:33:49	17: 8: 0	19:36:54	21:57:54	24:17: 1	26:54: 0	29:39:13
26	2:16:11	4:51:44	7: 6:32	9:30:34	11:57:56	14:39: 3	17:13: 0	19:41:32	22: 2:26	24:21:49	26:59:21	29:44:48
27	2:21:27	4:56:26	7:11:12	9:35: 0	12: 3: 2	14:44:17	17:18: 0	19:46: 9	22: 6:58	24:26:32	27: 4:42	29:50:24
28	2:26:42	5: 1:12	7:15:47	9:39:55	12: 8: 9	14:49:31	17:22:58	19:50:46	22:11:30	24:31:30	27:10:42	29:55:59
29	2:31:56	5: 5:57	7:20:21	9:44:41	12:13:16	14:54:44	17:27:55	19:55:22	22:16: 3	24:36:30	27:15:28	30: 1:35
30	2:37: 9		7:24:58	9:49:28	12:18:24	14:59:58	17:32:51	19:59:58	22:20:36	24:41:14	27:20:52	30: 7:10
31	2:42:20		7:29:33		12:23:32		17:37:47	20: 4:33		24:46: 8		30:12:45

1985 SSRY = 30:18:48

	January	February	March	April	May	June	July	August	September	October	November	December
1	0: 0: 0	2:47:39	5: 6:52	7:39:58	9:50:25	12:35: 9	15: 2:13	17:41: 3	20: 6:56	22:23:19	24:59:25	27:30: 0
2	0: 0:35	2:51:28	5:11:36	7:43:57	9:54:54	12:35:18	15: 6:17	17:44:57	20:16: 9	22:29:53	24:59:22	27:30:27
3	0:11: 9	2:57:54	5:14:56	7:43:47	10: 4:54	12:38:32	15:12:30	17:49:51	20:16:32	22:35:54	25: 4:20	27:35:54
4	0:16:43	3: 3: 5	5:20:19	7:43:47	10: 9:45	12:40:39	15:17:43	17:54:45	20:20:41	22:37: 2	25: 9:19	27:41:22
5	0:27:50	3: 8:11	5:20:55	7:48:23	10: 9:45	12:45:51	15:22:58	17:59:37	20:25:15	22:40:13	25:14:19	27:46:50
6	0:27:50	3:13:17	5:29:44	7:53: 0	10:14:36	12:51: 2	15:28:58	18: 4:29	20:29:48	22:46:13	25:19:20	27:52:50
7	0:33:22	3:18:22	5:34:25	7:57:36	10:19:30	12:56:14	15:33:14	18: 9:10	20:34:55	22:50:26	25:24:22	28: 3:21
8	0:44:25	3:23:28	5:38:56	8: 2:14	10:24:22	13: 6:40	15:38:31	18:16:59	20:43:28	23: 4:41	25:24:30	28: 8:53
9	0:49:56	3:28:28	5:43:46	8: 6:51	10:29:16	13: 6:40	15:43:42	18:18:59	20:48: 0	23: 4:41	25:34:30	28:14:25
10	0:55:26	3:33:29	5:53: 6	8:16:47	10:34:10	13:11:53	15:48:52	18:23:48	20:52:33	23: 9:19	25:39:35	28:19:58
11	1: 0:55	3:38:30	5:53: 6	8:16:47	10:39: 5	13:17: 7	15:54:12	18:28:36	20:57:35	23:13:58	25:44:49	28:25: 3
12	1: 0:55	3:43:29	6: 2:26	8:20:45	10:44: 6	13:22:20	15:59:11	18:33:24	21: 1:38	23:18:51	25:49:49	28:31: 5
13	1:11:52	3:48:28	6: 7:40	8:30:24	10:48:56	13:27:33	16: 4:26	18:37:58	21: 6:10	23:23:17	26: 0: 7	28:36:39
14	1:17:19	3:53:26	6:11:40	8:34:42	10:53:56	13:33:49	16: 9:29	18:42:56	21:10:42	23:27:58	26: 0: 7	28:42:14
15	1:22:45	3:58:22	6:16:18	8:39:22	10:53:56	13:43:19	16:14:36	18:47:42	21:15:14	23:32:39	26: 5:18	28:47:49
16	1:28:10	4: 3:18	6:20:55	8:44: 3	11: 3:53	13:48:34	16:24:50	18:52:26	21:19:46	23:37:21	26:10:30	28:53:25
17	1:33:35	4: 8:13	6:25:32	8:48:45	11: 8:52	13:53:49	16:29:56	18:57:10	21:24: 8	23:42:10	26:15: 3	28:59: 3
18	1:38:58	4:13: 0	6:30: 8	8:53:26	11:13:53	13:53:49	16:35: 1	19: 1:36	21:28:48	23:46:48	26:20:57	29: 4:36
19	1:44:21	4:17:57	6:34:48	8:58: 7	11:18:54	14: 4:19	16:40: 6	19: 6:18	21:33:21	23:51:32	26:26:12	29:10:13
20	1:49:43	4:22:53	6:39:23	9: 2:50	11:23:56	14: 9:35	16:45:10	19:10:59	21:37:53	23:56:17	26:31:28	29:15:49
21	1:55: 4	4:27:44	6:43:59	9: 7:33	11:28:58	14:14:50	16:50:15	19:15:40	21:42:25	24: 1: 3	26:36:45	29:21:25
22	2: 0:24	4:32:35	6:48:35	9:12:16	11:34: 1	14:20: 6	16:55:15	19:20:40	21:46:57	24: 5:50	26:42: 3	29:27:3
23	2: 5:43	4:37:25	6:53: 9	9:17:15	11:39: 4	14:25:21	17: 0:15	19:25:20	21:51:29	24: 5:50	26:42:38	29:32:38
24	2:11: 1	4:42:14	6:57:17	9:21:45	11:44:10	14:30:36	17: 0:18	19:30:39	21:56:20	24:10:26	26:52:41	29:38:14
25	2:16:18	4:47: 1	7: 2:23	9:26:30	11:49: 0	14:35:51	17:10:18	19:39:17	22: 0:34	24:20:15	26:58: 2	29:43:51
26	2:21:34	4:51:49	7: 6:59	9:31:13	11:54:21	14:41: 6	17:15:17	19:43:55	22: 5: 7	24:25: 5	27: 3:24	29:49:27
27	2:26:49	4:56:36	7:11:35	9:36: 4	11:59:28	14:46:21	17:20:16	19:48:32	22: 9:39	24:34:48	27: 8:47	29:55: 3
28	2:32: 3	5: 1:22	7:16:11	9:40:49	12: 4:35	14:51:35	17:25:16	19:53:14	22:14:12	24:34:48	27:14:10	3C: 0:15
29	2:37:16		7:20:47	9:45:37	12: 9:42	14:56:49	17:30:16	19:57:45	22:18:46	24:44:35	27:19:35	3C: 6:38
30	2:42:28		7:25:42	9:45:37	12:14:59		17:35:17	20: 2:21		24:44:35		3C:11:51
31			7:26:42		12:16:59			20: 2:21				3C:11:51

1986 SSRY = 30:13:53

	January	February	March	April	May	June	July	August	September	October	November	December
1	0: 0: 0	2:47:17	5: 5:29	7:28:59	9:49: 1	12:23:15	14:59:43	17:37:22	20: 3:57	22:19:58	24:45:39	27:26:37
2	0: 6:34	2:57:34	5:10:17	7:33: 0	9:49:49	12:33:44	15:15:21	17:47:10	20: 8:51	22:19:58	24:55:34	27:26:31
3	0:11: 8	2:57:34	5:14:58	7:38:39	9:58:33	12:35:44	15:15:21	17:47:10	20:13: 9	22:26: 5	25: 0:27	27:31:29
4	0:16:41	3: 2:41	5:19:39	7:42:44	10: 8:17	12:38:44	15:20:45	17:52: 2	20:17:39	22:33:39	25: 5:25	27:36:56
5	0:16:41	3: 7:47	5:24:21	7:47:21	10:13: 8	12:43:54	15:25:45	17:56:54	20:26:46	22:38:13	25: 5:27	27:47:52
6	0:27:46	3:12:53	5:29: 3	7:51:57	10:13: 8	12:49: 5	15:30:46	18: 1:46	20:31:19	22:42:48	25:10:24	27:47:52
7	0:33:18	3:18: 0	5:33:44	7:56:34	10:27:45	12:54:16	15:36:18	18: 6:38	20:35:25	22:57:53	25:15:26	27:58:51
8	0:38:49	3:23: 3	5:38:24	8: 5:47	10:27:45	13: 4:40	15:41: 1	18: 6:15	20:40:24	22:56:30	25:20:25	28: 3:21
9	0:44:20	3:28: 6	5:43: 4	8: 5:47	10:32:38	13: 9:53	15:46:27	18:16:15	20:44:56	23: 1:12	25:30:31	2E: 9:53
10	0:49:50	3:33: 8	5:47:44	8:10:24	10:37:33	13:15: 8	15:51:37	18:21: 3	20:49:28	23: 5:50	25:35:35	2E:15:25
11	0:55:19	3:38: 8	5:52:23	8:15: 4	10:42:33	13:20:18	15:56:44	18:25:51	20:53:59	23:10:28	25:40:40	2E:20:27
12	1: 0:48	3:43: 6	5:57: 1	8:19:39	10:47:33	13:30:30	16: 1:54	18:30:38	20:58:31	23:15:45	25:50:54	2E:25:59
13	1:11:43	3:52:58	6: 6:17	8:24:55	10:57:21	13:35:59	16: 7: 4	18:40:24	21: 7:33	23:24:25	25:56: 2	2E:32:36
14	1:17:10	3:57:54	6:10:55	8:33:13	10:57:21	13:41:13	16:12: 2	18:44:53	21: 7:33	23:29: 5	26: 1:11	26:37:36
15	1:22:35	4: 2:49	6:15:32	8:38:13	11: 7:16	13:41:13	16:17:15	18:49:37	21:12: 2	23:33:46	26: 6:22	26:43:10
16	1:28: 0	4: 7:44	6:24:45	8:47:33	11:12:15	13:51:41	16:22:25	18:54:20	21:16:35	23:38:28	26:11:33	26:48:44
17	1:33:24	4:12:37	6:24:45	8:47:33	11:12:15	13:56:27	16:27:25	18:59: 3	21:21: 6	23:43: 7	26:16:35	27: 5:29
18	1:44: 7	4:17:30	6:29: 8	8:52:11	11:17:15	14: 2:56	16:32:25	19: 3:45	21:25:37	23:47:46	26:21:40	29: 5:29
19	1:44:30	4:22:22	6:33:57	8:56:54	11:22:17	14: 7:24	16:37:30	19: 8:26	21:30: 7	23:52:37	26:27:14	29:11: 4
20	1:49:30	4:27:17	6:38:37	9: 1:36	11:27:17	14:12:36	16:42:39	19:13: 6	21:34:39	23:57:27	26:32:30	29:11: 4
21	1:54:50	4:32: 2	6:43:19	9: 6:18	11:32:19	14:17:53	16:47:39	19:17:46	21:39:10	24: 2: 8	26:37:47	29:22:15
22	2: 0: 9	4:36:51	6:47:44	9:11: 0	11:37:22	14:23: 7	16:52:40	19:22:26	21:43:41	24: 2: 8	26:43: 5	29:27:50
23	2: 5:27	4:41:39	6:52:19	9:15:43	11:42:24	14:28:21	16:57:41	19:27:43	21:48:13	24: 6:54	26:43:26	29:33:26
24	2:10:45	4:46:28	6:57:17	9:20:17	11:47:26	14:33:35	17: 2:43	19:32: 9	21:52:44	24:11:30	26:53:44	29:39: 1
25	2:16: 1	4:51:13	7: 1:29	9:25:11	11:52:34	14:38:49	17: 7:41	19:37:16	21:57:16	24:16:30	26:59: 4	29:44:37
26	2:21:16	4:55:59	7: 6: 4	9:29:50	11:57:39	14:44: 3	17:12:39	19:40:58	22: 1:48	24:21:19	27: 4:26	29:50:13
27	2:26:30	5: 0:45	7:10:39	9:34:41	12: 2:45	14:44:17	17:17:37	19:45:34	22: 6:20	24:26: 0	27: 9:49	29:55:48
28	2:31:43	5: 0:45	7: 6: 4	9:39:27	12: 7:52	14:49:17	17:22:37	19:50:51	22:10:52	24:31: 9	27: 9:49	29:55:48
29	2:36:56		7:10:39	9:44:14	12:12:59	14:54:30	17:27:31	19:54:46	22:15:25	24:35:52	27:15:13	30: 1:23
30	2:36:56		7:19:49	9:44:14	12:18: 7	14:54:30	17:32:27	19:59:22	22:15:25	24:40:45	27:15:13	30: 6:58
31			7:24:24		12:18: 7		17:32:27	19:59:22		24:40:45		30: 6:58

1987   SSRY = 30:11: 3

Day	January	February	March	April	May	June	July	August	September	October	November	December	Day
1	0: 5:34	2:47:18	5: 5:13	7:33:33	9:48:19	12:24:14	14:58:27	17:45:54	20: 6:53	22:18: 6	24:43:30	27:18: 6	1
2	0:11:37	2:52:23	5:10:40	7:37:43	9:57:55	12:32:32	15: 3:39	17:50:34	20:11:27	22:22:40	24:48:24	27:23:30	2
3	0:16:40	2:57:25	5:15:40	7:42:18	9:57:55	12:32:32	15: 8:52	17:45:41	20:16: 0	22:27:13	24:53:19	27:28:56	3
4	0:22:13	3: 2:32	5:19:23	7:42:49	10: 7:34	12:42:51	15:19:15	17:50:34	20:20:33	22:31:46	24:58:15	27:34:22	4
5	0:27:45	3: 7:38	5:24: 5	7:46:54	10:12:42	12:48:12	15:24:26	18: 1: 6	20:25:38	22:36:20	25: 3:12	27:39:49	5
6	0:33:46	3:12:42	5:28:46	7:51:29	10:17:24	12:53:23	15:29:38	18: 4:28	20:29:38	22:45:29	25: 8:10	27:45:16	6
7	0:44:47	3:17:46	5:33:27	7:56:13	10:22:15	12:58:23	15:34:47	18: 9:55	20:34:10	22:45:29	25:13: 9	27:50:45	7
8	0:49:47	3:22:49	5:38:27	8: 0:41	10:26:59	13: 3:34	15:39:57	18:14:44	20:38:42	22:50:24	25:18: 9	27:56:14	8
9	0:55:16	3:27:51	5:42:46	8: 5:17	10:31:51	13: 8:46	15:45: 6	18:19:32	20:43:13	22:54:39	25:23:11	28: 1:44	9
10	1: 0:44	3:32:52	5:47:25	8: 9:53	10:36:43	13:13:58	15:50:15	18:24:19	20:47:45	22:59:15	25:28:13	28: 7:14	10
11	1: 6:44	3:37:51	5:52: 4	8:14:30	10:41:45	13:19: 7	15:55: 6	18:28:15	20:52:47	23: 3:52	25:33:16	28:12:45	11
12	1:11:38	3:42:50	5:56:42	8:19: 7	10:46:35	13:24:23	16: 0:31	18:33:50	20:56:47	23: 8:29	25:38:35	28:18:16	12
13	1:17: 4	3:47:50	6: 1:57	8:23:44	10:51:30	13:29:36	16: 5:38	18:38:35	21: 1: 5	23:13: 7	25:43:26	28:23:49	13
14	1:22:29	3:52:44	6: 6:34	8:28:22	10:56:27	13:34:49	16:10:44	18:43:20	21: 5:48	23:17:45	25:48:33	28:29:21	14
15	1:27:53	3:57:41	6:15:11	8:37:39	11: 1:24	13:40: 2	16:15:50	18:48: 3	21:10:50	23:22:25	25:53:41	28:34:54	15
16	1:33:39	4: 2:36	6:19:47	8:42:18	11: 6:22	13:45:16	16:20:50	18:52:46	21:14:50	23:27: 5	25:58:50	28:40:27	16
17	1:44:22	4: 7:30	6:24:23	8:46:57	11:11:22	13:50:39	16:26:50	18:57:28	21:19:26	23:31:45	26: 4: 1	28:46: 1	17
18	1:49:22	4:12:23	6:29:13	8:51:57	11:16:20	13:55:43	16:31:10	19: 2:10	21:23:51	23:36:26	26: 9:12	28:57:10	18
19	1:54:41	4:17:13	6:33:10	8:56:17	11:21:20	14: 0:57	16:36: 8	19: 6:51	21:28:22	23:41:48	26:14:23	29: 2:45	19
20	2: 0: 1	4:22:16	6:38:10	9: 0:58	11:26:15	14: 6:11	16:41:10	19:11:31	21:32:58	23:45:51	26:19:36	29: 8:19	20
21	2: 5:18	4:26:57	6:42:45	9: 5:40	11:31:23	14:11:25	16:46:13	19:16:11	21:37:23	23:50:34	26:24:50	29:13:55	21
22	2:10:35	4:31:46	6:47:20	9:10:22	11:36:25	14:16:39	16:51:15	19:20:50	21:41:48	23:55:19	26:30: 5	29:19:30	22
23	2:15:52	4:36:35	6:51:55	9:15: 4	11:41:35	14:21:53	16:56:15	19:25:29	21:46:28	24: 0: 4	26:35:21	29:25: 3	23
24	2:21: 1	4:41:24	6:56:30	9:19:47	11:46:31	14:27:53	17: 1:13	19:30:27	21:50:56	24: 4:50	26:40:36	29:30:40	24
25	2:26:21	4:46:12	7: 1: 3	9:24:31	11:51:31	14:32:20	17: 6:14	19:35:16	21:55:28	24: 9:37	26:45:57	29:36:15	25
26	2:31:34	4:50:58	7: 5:39	9:29:15	11:56: 4	14:37:34	17:11:13	19:39:21	21:59:59	24:14:24	26:51:16	29:41:50	26
27	2:36:46	4:55:43	7:10:14	9:34: 0	12: 1:46	14:42:48	17:16: 1	19:43:58	22: 4:31	24:19:13	26:56:36	29:47:25	27
28	2:41:57	5: 0:29	7:14:49	9:38:46	12: 6:52	14:48:14	17:21: 8	19:48:34	22: 9: 3	24:24: 2	27: 1:57	29:53: 0	28
29			7:19:54	9:43:32	12:12: 5	14:53:14	17:26: 8	19:53:10	22:13:35	24:28:53	27: 7:19	29:58:35	29
30			7:23:58		12:17: 7		17:30:59	19:57:44		24:33:44	27:12:42	30: 4: 9	30
31			7:28: 4							24:38:36			31

1988   SSRY = 30:12:13

Day	January	February	March	April	May	June	July	August	September	October	November	December	Day
1	0: 5:34	2:47:19	5:10:20	7:33:38	9:53:39	12:33:56	15: 4:18	17:46:37	20:17:53	22:23:45	24:49:30	27:20:36	1
2	0:10:34	2:52:27	5:15:34	7:38:16	9:58:16	12:38:14	15:14:42	17:46:31	20:17: 1	22:23:45	24:54:25	27:26:5	2
3	0:16:40	2:57:37	5:19:44	7:42:44	10: 3:16	12:38:14	15:19:54	17:51:23	20:21:34	22:32:52	24:59:21	27:30:27	3
4	0:22:13	3: 2:44	5:24:28	7:47:24	10: 8: 6	12:43:34	15:25: 5	17:56:15	20:26:37	22:37:26	25: 4:18	27:40:54	4
5	0:27:45	3: 7:50	5:29:10	7:51:59	10:12:56	12:48:34	15:30:16	18: 1: 6	20:30:39	22:42:40	25: 9:16	27:40:54	5
6	0:33:46	3:12:56	5:33:51	7:56:39	10:17:47	12:53:45	15:40:16	18: 5:57	20:34:23	22:46:35	25:14:16	27:45:51	6
7	0:44:47	3: 8: 5	5:38:31	8: 1:47	10:27:30	12:58:45	15:40:37	18:10:36	20:39:44	22:46:35	25:19: 7	27:51:51	7
8	0:49:48	3:28: 5	5:42:50	8: 5:47	10:27:30	13: 3:56	15:45:47	18:15:36	20:39:44	22:51:46	25:24:17	28: 2:50	8
9	0:55: 5	3:33: 8	5:47:50	8:10:24	10:32:23	13: 9:19	15:50:56	18:20:24	20:44:16	23: 0:22	25:29:20	28: 8:21	9
10	1: 0:46	3:33: 6	5:52:29	8:15: 1	10:37:17	13:14:32	15:56: 6	18:25:12	20:48:48	23: 4:59	25:34:23	28:13:52	10
11	1: 5:28	3:38: 7	5:57: 8	8:19:38	10:42: 8	13:19:44	15:56: 6	18:29:59	20:53:19	23: 9:37	25:39:28	28:19:24	11
12	1:11:41	3:43: 4	6: 1:46	8:24:15	10:47: 0	13:24:57	16: 1:13	18:34:45	20:57:51	23:14:15	25:44:34	28:24:56	12
13	1:17: 8	3:53: 1	6: 6:23	8:28:52	10:51:55	13:30:11	16: 6:13	18:34:45	21: 2:24	23:18:53	25:49:40	28:30:29	13
14	1:22:33	3:53: 1	6:11:21	8:33:32	10:56:54	13:35:24	16:11:28	18:44:15	21: 6:57	23:23:33	25:54:48	28:36: 2	14
15	1:27:58	3:57:58	6:15:38	8:38:10	11: 1:57	13:40:38	16:16:34	18:48:59	21:11:24	23:28:13	25:59:57	28:41:36	15
16	1:33:22	4: 2:53	6:20:14	8:42:50	11: 6:55	13:51: 5	16:21:40	18:53:43	21:15:55	23:32:53	26: 5: 7	28:47:10	16
17	1:38: 5	4: 7:48	6:24:51	8:47:29	11:11:54	13:56:20	16:26:45	18:58:25	21:20:26	23:37:34	26:10:18	28:52:44	17
18	1:44: 9	4:12:42	6:29:27	8:52:50	11:16:55	13:56:20	16:26:45	19: 3: 7	21:24:57	23:42:20	26:15:30	28:58:18	18
19	1:49:29	4:22:28	6:38:33	8: 9:31	11:21:55	14: 2: 6	16:41:57	19: 7:48	21:29:28	23:46:59	26:20:42	29: 3:53	19
20	1:54:50	4:22:28	6:38:33	9: 6:13	11:26:55	14: 6:48	16:41:57	19:12:29	21:33:58	23:51:42	26:25:57	29: 9:28	20
21	2: 0:28	4:27:18	6:43:14	9: 9: 1	11:31:59	14:12: 2	16:46:49	19:17:29	21:38:22	23:56:27	26:31:12	29:15: 3	21
22	2:10:42	4:32: 8	6:47:49	9:15:37	11:42: 4	14:17:16	16:52: 1	19:21:48	21:43: 0	24: 1:12	26:36:28	29:20:38	22
23	2:16: 2	4:36:57	6:52:29	9:15:37	11:42: 2	14:22:30	16:57: 2	19:26:27	21:47:31	24: 5:57	26:41:45	29:26:13	23
24	2:21:17	4:41:46	6:57: 6	9:24:51	11:47: 9	14:27:44	17: 2: 1	19:31: 5	21:52: 4	24:10:44	26:47: 2	29:31:48	24
25	2:26:32	4:46:36	7: 1:49	9:29:31	11:52:10	14:32:58	17: 7: 2	19:35:43	21:56:33	24:15:32	26:52:22	29:37:24	25
26	2:31:45	4:51:20	7: 6:30	9:34:14	11:57:13	14:38:12	17:12: 1	19:40:20	22: 1: 5	24:20:20	26:57:42	29:43:00	26
27	2:36:58	4:56: 2	7:10:44	9:38:57	12: 2:20	14:43:26	17:16:59	19:44:57	22: 5:36	24:25: 9	27: 3: 3	29:48:34	27
28	2:42:59	5: 0:52	7:15:20	9:43:41	12: 7:26	14:48:39	17:21:56	19:49:33	22:10: 8	24:29:59	27: 8:25	29:54: 9	28
29	2:38:58	5: 5:36	7:19:54	9:44:52	12:12:33	14:53:52	17:26:52	19:54:44	22:14:40	24:34:51	27:13:47	29:59:43	29
30			7:24: 4		12:22:48	14:59: 2	17:31:47	20: 3:19	22:19:13	24:44:36	27:19:11	30:10:52	30
31			7:28: 4				17:36:43						31

1989 SSRY = 30:12:24

	January	February	March	April	May	June	July	August	September	October	November	December
1	30:12:24	2:47: 2	5: 5: 0	7:28:20	9:48:18	12:22:31	15:18:53	17:44:19	20: 2:41	22:22:39	24:44:15	27:19:15
2	0: 5:34	2:52:10	5: 9:43	7:32:25	9:53:55	12:32:40	15: 9:18	17:46: 6	20: 7:50	22:27:42	24:49:10	27:24:40
3	0:10:40	2:57:18	5:14:26	7:37:31	9:57:55	12:32:49	15:14:31	17:46: 6	20:11:50	22:27:42	24:54: 6	27:30: 6
4	0:16:40	3: 2:28	5:19: 8	7:42: 6	10: 7:35	12:43:10	15:19:42	17:50:59	20:20:56	22:36:50	25: 4: 2	27:41: 1
5	0:22:12	3: 7:30	5:23:50	7:46:42	10: 7:35	12:48:20	15:24:54	17:55:50	20:25:29	22:41:25	25: 9: 1	27:46:28
6	0:27:44	3:12:35	5:28:31	7:51:17	10:12:17	12:58:43	15:30:15	18: 5:31	20:30: 2	22:46: 2	25:14: 7	27:51:28
7	0:33:16	3:17:39	5:33:12	7:55:54	10:17:10	13: 3:55	15:35:15	18:10:20	20:34:34	22:50:36	25:19: 2	27:57:28
8	0:38:47	3:22:43	5:37:52	8: 0:30	10:22: 0	13: 9: 8	15:40:25	18:15: 9	20:39: 6	22:55:12	25:24: 2	2E: 2:58
9	0:44:19	3:27:41	5:42:32	8: 5:33	10:27:10	13:14:20	15:45:34	18:19:57	20:43:38	22:59:49	25:29: 1	2E: 8:29
10	0:49:47	3:32:43	5:47:11	8: 9:43	10:31:56	13:19:33	15:50:43	18:24:44	20:48: 9	23: 4:26	25:34:11	2E:14:21
11	0:55:16	3:37:43	5:51:50	8:14:21	10:36:51	13:24:46	15:55:59	18:29:30	20:52:42	23: 9: 2	25:39:16	2E:19:53
12	1: 0:44	3:42:42	5:56:28	8:18:58	10:41:46	13:29:33	16: 0:59	18:34:16	20:57:14	23:13:42	25:44:23	2E:25: 3
13	1: 6:16	3:47:39	6: 1: 6	8:23:14	10:46:36	13:34:13	16: 6: 6	18:39:30	21: 1:43	23:18:21	25:49:30	2E:30:38
14	1:11:38	3:52:36	6: 5:43	8:27:48	10:51:35	13:35:13	16:11:13	18:43:44	21: 6:13	23:23: 0	25:54:38	26:36:12
15	1:17:08	3:57:31	6:10:20	8:32:53	10:56:35	13:40:27	16:16:10	18:48:28	21:10:44	23:27:41	25:59:48	26:41:45
16	1:22:22	4: 2:26	6:14:57	8:37:32	11: 1: 6	13:45:40	16:21:24	18:53:10	21:15:15	23:32:22	26: 4:58	26:47:19
17	1:27:53	4: 7:20	6:19:33	8:42:11	11: 6:32	13:50:53	16:26:28	18:58:18	21:15:15	23:36:28	26:10: 6	26:52:54
18	1:33:16	4:12:13	6:24:10	8:46:51	11:11:32	13:56: 5	16:31:28	19: 2:34	21:24:16	23:41:46	26:15:23	26:58:28
19	1:38:30	4:17:06	6:28:46	8:51:31	11:16:31	14: 1:22	16:36:38	19: 7:14	21:28:47	23:46:29	26:20:30	29: 3:38
20	1:43:59	4:21:59	6:33:21	8:56:12	11:21:32	14: 6:36	16:41:38	19:11:55	21:33:18	23:51:13	26:25:51	29: 9:38
21	1:49:30	4:26:46	6:37:56	9: 0:53	11:26:41	14:11:51	16:46:40	19:16:34	21:37:49	23:55:58	26:31: 2	29:15:14
22	1:54:40	4:31:35	6:42:32	9: 5:35	11:31:35	14:17: 5	16:51:44	19:21:13	21:42:20	24: 0:39	26:36:24	29:20:46
23	1:59:59	4:36:24	6:47: 7	9:10:18	11:36:38	14:22:19	16:56:44	19:26: 3	21:46:52	24: 0:39	26:41:42	29:26:24
24	2: 5:36	4:41:12	6:51:42	9:14:44	11:41:41	14:27:33	17: 1:41	19:30:30	21:51:22	24:10:17	26:47: 1	29:32: 4
25	2:10:45	4:46:11	6:56:14	9:19:44	11:46:45	14:32:46	17: 6:40	19:35: 7	21:55:54	24:15: 6	26:52:21	29:37:35
26	2:15:49	4:50:45	7: 0:51	9:24:28	11:51:50	14:38: 0	17:11:39	19:39:44	22: 0:26	24:19:55	26:57:42	29:43:10
27	2:21: 3	4:55:31	7: 5:26	9:29:13	11:56:55	14:43:14	17:16:42	19:44:20	22: 0:26	24:24:45	27: 3: 4	29:48:46
28	2:26:17	5: 0:15	7:10: 1	9:33:58	12: 1: 1	14:48:27	17:21:25	19:49: 0	22: 4:58	24:29:34	27: 8:26	29:54:14
29	2:31:30		7:14:35	9:38:44	12: 6: 7	14:53:40	17:26:23	19:53:32	22: 9:30	24:34:28	27:13:50	29:59:55
30	2:37: 1		7:19: 1	9:43:31	12:12: 8		17:31:25	19:58: 7	22:14: 2	24:39:21		30: 5:30
31	2:41:52		7:23:45		12:17:23							

1990 SSRY = 30:16:31

	January	February	March	April	May	June	July	August	September	October	November	December
1	30:16:31	2:47:30	5: 5:54	7:29:36	9:49:51	12:24:20	15: 6: 1	17:43:55	20:10:16	22:26:54	24:47:48	27:26:28
2	0: 5:34	2:52:40	5:10:39	7:33:42	9:49:51	12:24:40	15: 6: 1	17:43:50	20:14:51	22:26:28	24:52:43	27:28:26
3	0:10:38	2:57:49	5:15:22	7:38:48	9:59:29	12:34:40	15:11:30	17:48:44	20:19:25	22:31: 1	24:57:39	27:33:52
4	0:16:31	3: 2:56	5:20: 5	7:43:24	10: 9: 1	12:45: 1	15:16:43	17:53:37	20:23:59	22:35:36	25: 2:37	27:39:20
5	0:22:16	3: 8: 3	5:24:47	7:48: 0	10: 9: 1	12:50:12	15:21:55	17:58:29	20:28:32	22:40:10	25: 7:35	27:44:48
6	0:27:49	3:13: 8	5:29:29	7:52:36	10:14: 3	13: 0:34	15:27:17	18: 3:32	20:33: 5	22:44:45	25:12:36	27:50:16
7	0:33:21	3:18:13	5:34:11	7:57:13	10:18:53	13: 5:46	15:32:28	18: 8:22	20:37:38	22:49:20	25:17:38	27:55:46
8	0:38:47	3:23:18	5:38:52	8: 1:49	10:23:15	13: 5:48	15:37:50	18:13:11	20:42:10	22:53:57	25:22:38	28: 1:16
9	0:44:23	3:28:19	5:43:32	8: 6:27	10:28:38	13:11: 4	15:42:50	18:17:50	20:46:43	22:58:33	25:27:38	28: 6:47
10	0:49:54	3:33:20	5:48:12	8:11: 4	10:33:32	13:16:14	15:47:50	18:22:39	20:51:15	23: 3:11	25:32:42	28:12:19
11	0:55:23	3:38:20	5:52:51	8:15:42	10:38:27	13:21:28	15:53: 1	18:27:39	20:55:48	23: 7:48	25:37:47	28:17:51
12	1: 0:52	3:43:19	5:57:29	8:20:18	10:43:23	13:26:42	15:58: 8	18:32:13	21: 0:21	23:12:26	25:42:59	28:23:24
13	1: 6:18	3:48:18	6: 2: 6	8:24:58	10:48: 8	13:31:45	16: 3: 8	18:36:41	21: 4:50	23:17: 6	25:48:13	28:28:51
14	1:11:54	3:53:14	6: 6:44	8:29:36	10:53: 6	13:37: 9	16: 8:25	18:41:45	21: 9:22	23:21:45	25:53: 7	28:34:31
15	1:17:14	3:58:12	6:11:24	8:34:15	10:58:13	13:37:37	16:13:39	18:46:30	21: 1:45	23:26:25	26: 3:18	28:40: 5
16	1:22:40	4: 3: 8	6:16: 1	8:38:55	11: 3:12	13:42:24	16:18:39	18:51:14	21: 9:25	23:31: 6	26: 3:26	28:45:39
17	1:28:30	4: 8: 2	6:20:39	8:43:35	11: 8:11	13:47:38	16:23:45	18:55:58	21:18:25	23:35:48	26: 8:37	28:51:14
18	1:33:30	4:12:56	6:25:15	8:48:15	11:13: 8	13:52:53	16:28:45	19: 0:24	21:22:38	23:40:29	26:13: 3	28:56:48
19	1:38:15	4:17:48	6:29:51	8:52:56	11:18: 8	13:58: 8	16:33:50	19: 5: 0	21:27:28	23:45:13	26:19: 3	29: 3:14
20	1:44:15	4:22:41	6:34:28	8:57:36	11:23:13	14: 3:23	16:39: 0	19: 9:46	21:32: 0	23:49:57	26:24:17	29: 8: 1
21	1:49:37	4:27:32	6:39: 4	9: 2:20	11:28:15	14: 8: 8	16:44: 0	19:14:18	21:36:31	23:54:41	26:29:33	29:13:37
22	1:54:58	4:32:22	6:43:40	9: 7: 2	11:33:17	14:13:53	16:49: 7	19:19:27	21:41: 3	23:59:27	26:34:49	29:19:13
23	2: 0:17	4:37:12	6:48:16	9:11:45	11:38:21	14:19: 8	16:54:13	19:24:17	21:45:34	24: 4:13	26:40:27	29:24:49
24	2: 5:36	4:42:49	6:52:51	9:16:29	11:43:30	14:24:23	16:59:11	19:29:18	21:54:38	24: 9:13	26:45:25	29:30:26
25	2:10:56	4:47:41	6:57:27	9:20:58	11:48:35	14:34:53	17: 4:11	19:33:25	21:59:10	24:13:48	26:50:44	29:41:37
26	2:16:14	4:51:36	7: 2: 3	9:25:43	11:53:48	14:40: 7	17: 9:11	19:38:25	22: 3:43	24:18:37	26:56: 5	29:47:13
27	2:21:27	4:56:23	7: 6:38	9:30:28	11:58:48	14:45:22	17:14:10	19:42:41	22: 8:16	24:23:26	27: 1:26	29:52:49
28	2:26:41	5: 1: 8	7:11: 1	9:35:09	12: 3:48	14:50:36	17:19: 9	19:47:18	22:12:15	24:28:17	27: 6:48	29:58:24
29	2:31:55		7:15:49	9:40: 3	12: 8:55	14:50:50	17:24: 4	19:51:55	22:12:48	24:33: 8	27:12:11	30: 4: 4
30	2:37:08		7:20: 1	9:40: 3	12:13: 6		17:29: 2	19:56:35	22:17:21	24:42:54	27:17:35	30: 9:35
31	2:42:20		7:25: 1		12:19:12		17:34: 0	20: 1: 6				

1991 SSRY = 30:10:33

	January	February	March	April	May	June	July	August	September	October	November	December
1	30: 6:33	2:52: 3	5: 6:49	7:32:22	9:52:54	12:22: 0	14:58:10	17:36:35	20: 1:52	22:27:44	24:43: 4	27:23:39
2	0: 5:33	2:57:22	5:14:38	7:37:57	9:57:54	12:32:17	15: 2:23	17:41:22	20: 6:57	22:31:23	24:47:59	27:28:29
3	0:11: 6	3: 2:26	5:19:14	7:42:37	10: 2:31	12:37:26	15: 7:22	17:45:22	20:10:39	22:36:57	24:52:54	27:33:55
4	0:16:39	3: 7:37	5:23:56	7:46:42	10: 7:20	12:47:46	15:13:47	17:50:14	20:15:39	22:40:31	24:57:50	27:39:22
5	0:22:11	3:12:37	5:28:37	7:51:17	10:12:10	12:52:57	15:18:35	17:55: 6	20:20:12	22:45: 6	25: 2:47	27:44:50
6	0:27:43	3:17:40	5:33:31	7:55:53	10:17:53	12:58: 7	15:24: 9	17:59:57	20:24:44	22:49:41	25: 7:45	27:50:49
7	0:33:14	3:22:45	5:37:55	8: 0:58	10:21:53	13: 3:19	15:29:30	18: 4:36	20:29:49	22:54:17	25:12:45	27:55:48
8	0:38:44	3:27:40	5:42:37	8: 5: 5	10:26:48	13: 8:31	15:34:30	18: 9:36	20:33:45	22:58:53	25:17:45	28: 1:18
9	0:44:15	3:32:42	5:47:16	8: 9:41	10:31:41	13:13:43	15:39:40	18:14:25	20:38:21	23: 3:29	25:22:47	28: 6:48
10	0:49:44	3:37:45	5:51:55	8:14:18	10:36:32	13:18:55	15:44:30	18:19: 6	20:42:52	23: 8: 5	25:27:47	28:12:19
11	0:55:13	3:42:42	5:56:33	8:18:53	10:41:26	13:24: 7	15:49:58	18:24: 0	20:47:24	23:12:41	25:32:53	28:17:51
12	1: 0:41	3:47:39	6: 0:48	8:23:33	10:46:14	13:29:21	15:54:21	18:28:46	20:51:55	23:18:47	25:37:57	28:23:22
13	1: 6: 9	3:52:32	6: 5:48	8:28:11	10:51:17	13:34:35	15:59:12	18:33:46	20:56:57	23:17:23	25:43: 0	28:28:53
14	1:11:35	3:57:36	6:10:25	8:32:49	10:56:14	13:39:48	16: 5:34	18:38:17	21: 0:57	23:21:57	25:48: 9	28:34:28
15	1:17: 1	4: 2:30	6:15: 2	8:37:27	11: 1:11	13:45: 2	16:10:54	18:43: 7	21: 5:28	23:26:42	25:53:17	28:40: 2
16	1:22:27	4: 7:24	6:19:38	8:42: 6	11: 6: 9	13:50:29	16:15:34	18:47:45	21:10:29	23:31:23	26: 3:36	28:45:35
17	1:27:51	4:12:11	6:24:26	8:46:41	11:11: 8	13:55:38	16:20:40	18:52: 6	21:14:20	23:36:46	26: 8:51	28:51:11
18	1:33:15	4:17: 1	6:28:50	8:51:22	11:16: 8	14: 0:43	16:25:44	18:57:51	21:19:30	23:45:46	26:19:11	29: 2:18
19	1:38:37	4:21: 9	6:33:26	8:56: 6	11:21: 8	14: 5:57	16:30:58	19: 6:32	21:24:30	23:45:28	26:19:11	29: 7:52
20	1:43:59	4:26:37	6:38: 1	9: 0:47	11:26: 9	14:11:11	16:35:52	19:15:12	21:32:31	23:50:11	26:24:25	29:13:27
21	1:49:20	4:31:41	6:42:36	9: 5:29	11:31:10	14:16:24	16:40:54	19:20:31	21:37: 2	23:54:56	26:34:56	29:19: 2
22	1:54:40	4:36:30	6:47:16	9:10:11	11:36:13	14:21:38	16:45:56	19:25: 9	21:41:32	23:59:40	26:40:13	29:24:38
23	1:59:58	4:41:18	6:51:56	9:15:10	11:41: 6	14:26:52	16:50:58	19:29:47	21:45:33	24: 4: 9	26:45:31	29:30:12
24	2: 5:16	4:46: 5	6:56:21	9:19:36	11:46:10	14:32: 9	16:55:57	19:34:24	21:50: 4	24:14: 0	26:50:50	29:35:46
25	2:10:33	4:50:51	7: 0:55	9:24:20	11:51:23	14:37:19	17: 0:58	19:39: 1	21:55: 6	24:18:48	26:56:10	29:41: 0
26	2:15:49	4:55:37	7: 5:30	9:29:24	11:56:10	14:42:32	17: 5:53	19:43:37	21:59:36	24:23:38	27: 1:31	29:46:56
27	2:21: 4	5: 0:22	7:10: 4	9:33:49	12: 1:33	14:47:45	17:10:49	19:48:13	22: 4: 8	24:28:28	27: 6:53	29:52:21
28	2:26:18		7:14:46	9:38:54	12: 6:37	14:52:58	17:15:53	19:52:58	22:13:11	24:38:11	27:12:15	29:55:32
29	2:31:31		7:19:18	9:43:20	12:10:49		17:20:49	19:57:23				30: 0:31
30	2:36:43		7:10: 4		12:16:52		17:25:45					30: 3:39
31	2:41:53		7:23:48		12:16:52		17:30:41					

1992 SSRY = 30: 7:59

	January	February	March	April	May	June	July	August	September	October	November	December
1	30: 7:59	2:52:55	5:14:38	7:32:33	9:52:15	12:36:10	15: 2:10	17:39: 7	20: 5: 3	22:20:36	24:46: 2	27:20:46
2	0: 5:33	2:57: 4	5:14:38	7:37: 8	9:57: 2	12:36:27	15: 7:22	17:48:53	20: 9: 0	22:25:59	24:55:56	27:25:41
3	0:11: 6	3: 2: 1	5:19:12	7:41:42	10: 1:51	12:41:37	15:12:45	17:53:44	20:14:19	22:31:37	25: 0:48	27:31:37
4	0:16:38	3: 7:24	5:23:42	7:46:17	10: 6:40	12:46:46	15:17:45	17:58:34	20:18:42	22:34:15	25: 5:46	27:37: 3
5	0:22:11	3: 2:18	5:28:42	7:50:52	10:11:29	12:51:57	15:22:16	18: 3:24	20:23:14	22:43:23	25:10:44	27:42:30
6	0:27:42	3: 7:24	5:33:22	7:55:28	10:16:20	12:57: 7	15:28:16	18: 8:13	20:27:46	22:44:58	25:15:44	27:47:58
7	0:33:12	3:12:29	5:37:43	8: 4:39	10:21: 9	13: 2:19	15:33:26	18:13:13	20:32:18	22:49:52	25:20:45	27:53:26
8	0:38:44	3:17:32	5:42:35	8: 9:15	10:26: 0	13: 7:29	15:38:34	18:17:49	20:36:48	22:54:56	25:25:46	27:59: 4
9	0:44:13	3:22:35	5:47: 9	8:13:51	10:30:55	13:12:41	15:43:34	18:22:36	20:41:21	22:57:32	25:30:48	28: 4:25
10	0:49:43	3:27:36	5:51:39	8:18:28	10:35:42	13:17:53	15:48:43	18:27:22	20:45:51	23: 1:44	25:35:52	28: 9:55
11	0:55: 1	3:32:37	5:56:17	8:23: 5	10:40:42	13:23: 5	15:53:50	18:32:27	20:50:22	23: 6:21	25:40:57	28:15:26
12	1: 0:39	3:37:37	6: 0:38	8:27:41	10:45: 0	13:28:12	15:58:58	18:37:22	20:54:53	23:10:58	25:46: 0	28:20:57
13	1: 6: 6	3:42:35	6: 5:38	8:32:12	10:50:18	13:33:29	16: 4:11	18:42:52	20: 9:53	23:15:36	25:51:10	28:26:29
14	1:11:33	3:47:35	6:10:38	8:36:57	10:55:27	13:38:42	16: 9:21	18:46:19	21: 3:23	23:20:51	25:56:18	28:31:59
15	1:16:58	3:52:29	6:15:29	8:41:36	11: 0: 5	13:43:55	16:14:16	18:51: 1	21: 7:54	23:34:14	26: 1:27	28:37:34
16	1:22:23	3:57:25	6:19:21	8:46:16	11: 5:21	13:49: 8	16:24:24	18:55:43	21:12:54	23:38:55	26: 6:37	28:43: 7
17	1:27:47	4: 2:19	6:23:56	8:50:54	11:10:16	13:54:21	16:24:24	19: 0:24	21:17:24	23:43:20	26:11:48	28:48:40
18	1:33:32	4: 7:13	6:28:32	8:55:28	11:15:18	13:59:34	16:29:29	19: 9:45	21:21:54	23:48:55	26:16:50	28:54:14
19	1:38:42	4:12: 6	6:33: 7	9: 0: 9	11:20:18	14: 4:48	16:34:37	19: 9:45	21:26:24	23:43: 0	26:22:14	28:59:48
20	1:43:59	4:16:58	6:37:41	9: 4:55	11:25:17	14:10: 1	16:39:34	19:14:24	21:30:54	23:57: 0	26:27:28	29: 5:23
21	1:49:21	4:21:49	6:42:16	9: 9:36	11:30:18	14:15:14	16:44:36	19:19:41	21:35:25	23:53:48	26:38: 0	29:10:56
22	1:54:43	4:26:39	6:46:51	9:14:18	11:40:22	14:20:28	16:49:37	19:23:41	21:39:55	24: 2:33	26:38: 0	29:16:31
23	1:59:52	4:31:38	6:51:25	9:19:23	11:40:22	14:25:41	16:54:37	19:28:56	21:44:25	24: 1:27	26:43:18	29:22: 6
24	2: 5: 0	4:36: 4	6:56:17	9:23:43	11:45:27	14:30:54	16:59:39	19:33:56	21:48:56	24: 2:19	26:48:36	29:27:40
25	2:10:26	4:41:41	7: 5: 8	9:28:11	11:50:28	14:36: 7	17: 4:31	19:38:56	21:53: 7	24:16:54	26:53:49	29:33:49
26	2:15:42	4:45:51	7: 5: 8	9:33:11	11:55:32	14:41:20	17: 9:34	19:42:40	21:57:58	24:16:54	26:59:16	29:38:49
27	2:20:56	4:50:37	7:10:12	9:37:56	12: 0:52	14:46:33	17:14:31	19:46:44	22: 2:29	24:21:43	27: 4:37	29:44:24
28	2:26:10	4:55:23	7:14:16	9:42:42	12: 5:43	14:51:46	17:19:28	19:51:20	22: 7: 1	24:26:33	27: 9:59	29:49:58
29	2:31:24	5: 0: 8	7:19:21	9:47:28	12:10:49	14:56:58	17:24:24	19:55:24	22:11:32	24:31:24	27:15:23	29:55:32
30	2:36:35	5: 4:52	7:23:24		12:16: 1		17:29:24	20: 0:29	22:16: 4	24:41: 8		30: 0:33
31	2:41:45		7:27:59		12:21: 3		17:34:14					30: 6:40

Bibliography

Addey, John M. *Harmonics in Astrology.* Green Bay: Cambridge Circle, Ltd., 1976.

_____. *Harmonic Anthology.* Green Bay: Cambridge Circle, Ltd., 1976.

Allen, Garth. "Murder Will Out!" *American Astrology,* February 1957

_____. "Perspectives". *American Astrology,* September 1973.

Allen, Garth, and Gary Duncan. "Angularity potential scales." *American Astrology,* April 1974

American Astrology, March 1957

American Astrology, March 1974

"Astro-Dream Analysis." *American Astrology.*

Bradley, Donald A. *Solar and Lunar Returns.* Los Angeles: Llewellyn Foundation for Astrological Research, 1948.

Clark, Katherine, Allen Gilchrist, Janice Mackey, and Charles Dorminy. *Contemporary Sidereal Horoscopes, Book I.* San Francisco: Sidereal Research Publications, 1976.

De Luce, Robert. *Complete Method of Prediction.* New York: ASI Publishers, 1978.

Dobyns, Zipporah Pottenger. *Finding the Person in the Horoscope.* Los Angeles: Tia Publications, 1973.

Ebertin, Reinhold. *The Combination of Stellar Influences.* Translated by Dr. Alfred G. Roosedale and Linda Kratzch. Aalen, Germany: Ebertin-verlag, 1972.

Elwell, Dennis. "An Astrologer's Viewpoint on Death". *American Astrology Digest,* 1978.

Eshelman, James A. *The Sidereal Handbook.* Anaheim, Ca.: Stymie Publications, 1975.

_____. "Upheavals in World Structures." *American Astrology,* March 1974.

Eshelman, James A., and Tom Stanton. *The New Instant Astrologer.* Los Angeles: The Astro Press, 1976.

Fagan, Cyril. "Solunars." *American Astrology.*

Fagan, Cyril, and Brig. R. C. Firebrace. *Primer of Sidereal Astrology.* Isabella, Mo.: Littlejohn Publishing Co., 1971.

Gauquelin, Michel. *Cosmic Influences on Human Behavior.* Translated by Joyce E. Clemow. New York: Stein & Day, 1973.

Hand, Robert. *Planets in Transit.* Gloucester, Ma.: Para Research, Inc., 1976.

Howard, Andrew B. "Angles vs. Houses: A Realignment of Priorities." *Astrology Now*. Vol. 1 No. 9, December 1975.

Jansky, Robert. *Interpreting the Eclipses*. San Diego: ACS Publications, Inc., 1980.

Jones, J. Allen, Jr. *Easy Tables*. Hollywood, Ca: Golden Seal Research Headquarters, 1973.

Michelsen, Neil F. *The American Book of Tables*. San Diego, Ca: ACS Publications, Inc., 1976.

_____. *The American Ephemeris 1931to 1980 & Book of Tables*. San Diego, Ca.: ACS Publications, Inc., 1982.

_____. *The American Ephemeris 1981 to 1990*. San Diego, Ca.: ACS Publications, Inc., 1977.

_____. *The American Sidereal Ephemeris 1976-2000*. San Diego, Ca: ACS Publications, Inc., 1985.

Nelson, John H. *Cosmic Patterns*. Washington, DC: American Federation of Astrologers, 1974.

Paige, Bob. "A Bonanza of Solar and Lunar Returns." *Astrology Now*. Vol. 1 No. 9, December 1975.

Rudhyar, Dane. *The Lunation Cycle*. Berkeley, Ca.: Shambala, 1971.

The Astronomical Almanac. Washington, DC.: U.S. Naval Observatory, Annual.

The Complete Planetary Ephemeris, 1950-2000 A.D. Medford, MA.: Hieratic Publishing Co., 1975.

Wynn. *The Key Cycle*. Tempe, Az.: American Federation of Astrologers, Inc., 1970.

RETURNS GALORE!

Astro Computing offers every kind of **Return** chart for your use! All the options described by Jim Eshelman (and more!) can be ordered through Astro.

SOLAR RETURN — Specify the location and year of the Solar Return and give complete natal data or the Sun's exact position (sign, degree, minute and second) in your natal chart **$2.00**

DEMI-SOLAR RETURN —Computed for when the transiting Sun opposes the natal solar longitude. This represents the last half of the Solar Return year.. **$2.00**

QUARTI-SOLAR RETURN — Computed for the time when the transiting Sun squares the natal Sun. This horoscope symbolizes the three months following its inception — until the next conjunction or opposition **$2.00**

ENNEAD CHART — There are eight Enneads per year. They occur every 40° from the position of the natal Sun.................................... **$2.00**

SOLAR RETURN & 8 ENNEADS — This special bulk rate is available for black-and-white charts only **$12.00**

LUNAR RETURN — Computed for when the transiting Moon returns to its natal position. This horoscope symbolizes trends for 27 days.............. **$2.00**

DECILIUM CHART — Charts computed for 10° intervals (within the Ennead period). Each chart is symbolic of a 10-day period...................... **$2.00**

ANLUNAR RETURN — Computed for the return of the transiting Moon to the exact longitude of the Moon in the Solar Return. These charts occur every 27.3 days.. **$2.00**

DEMI-ANLUNAR — Each chart covers approximately a two-week period.... **$2.00**

QUARTI-ANLUNAR — Each chart covers approximately a one-week period . **$2.00**

1 YEAR OF ANLUNARS — This special bulk rate is available for black-and-white charts only **$15.00**

> For all of the above, you provide the date in which you are interested, and Astro will calculate the nearest Demi-Solar, Quarti-Solar, Ennead, Solar Monthly, Lunar Return, Decilium Chart, Anlunar Return, Demi-Anlunar or Quarti-Anlunar. Give the location of the Return. Provide complete natal data or the exact natal position (sign, degree, minute and second) of the natal Sun and Moon.

SOLAR QUOTIDIAN CHART — One method of examining progressions to the Solar Return chart **$2.00**

PROGRESSED SIDEREAL SOLAR RETURN — Another method of examining progressions to the Solar Return chart. Specify the day, month and year to which you want the Return progressed. Give the location and the complete natal data or the Sun's exact position in your natal chart **$2.00**

DAY-BY-DAY PSSR PER YEAR — Day-by-day listing of aspects to natal as well as Solar Return planets from the progressed positions................ **$2.00**

DAY-BY-DAY SOLAR QUOTIDIAN PER YEAR — Day-by-day listing of aspects to natal as well as Solar Return planets from the progressed positions. Specify the year desired. (Day-by-day positions will commence with your birthday of that year.) Give the location and complete natal data or the Sun's exact position in your natal chart **$2.00**

> All of the above — **except** the day-by-day options and the bulk rate offers — are available in the aesthetic (four-color) format for $2.00 per chart.

Phone orders: 800-826-1085 (excluding Alaska and Hawaii). In California: **800-525-1786**.

To order by mail: Send the complete data required. Include your name and address. Add $2.00 for postage and handling and mail a check or money order to:

ASTRO COMPUTING SERVICES, DEPT SR•PO BOX 16430•SAN DIEGO, CA 92116-0430

Major References

<table>
<tr><td align="center">

THE AMERICAN ATLAS

US Latitudes and Longitudes
Time Changes and Time Zones

</td><td align="center">

THE INTERNATIONAL ATLAS

World Latitudes, Longitudes
and Time Changes

</td></tr>
</table>

compiled and programmed by
Thomas G. Shanks

Over 190,000 Birthplaces • The complete clock-setting history of every major city (and most minor ones) in the world.

Time Changes and Time Zones from 1850 to 2000 • Every geographical entry is referenced to a Standard/Daylight Time Change and Time Zone Table.

Supersede All Other Sources • Complete and comprehensive summaries with original sources researched for complete and accurate documentation. Three times as many localities included as any previous source. Computer typesetting eliminates transcription errors.

Published by ACS Publications, Inc. • The perfect companion volumes to *The American Ephemeris for the 20th Century 1900 to 2000* for **$25.00** and **$29.95** respectively.

AMERICAN EPHEMERIS SERIES

ACS Publications is
STILL pioneering new territory with
the best ephemerides in the world!

The American Ephemeris for the 20th Century 1900 to 2000

Features 101 years INCLUDING the year 2000, calculated for GMT, *not* ephemeris time — Gives Sun and Moon to seconds of arc; planets to tenths of a minute of arc; sign ingresses; lunar phases; station's times; void-of-course Moon; with True and Mean Lunar Nodes.

Provides detailed eclipse information and an outer planet aspectarian. **$15.95, Paper**

<table>
<tr><td>

The American Ephemeris for the 21st Century 2001 to 2100

Just like *The American Ephemeris for the 20th Century*, but a hundred years beyond it. This is the first, and presently **the only**, complete ephemeris available anywhere for the entire next century. Quality calculation of planets, eclipses, Chiron, etc., combine with easy portability to make this a **must** for every mundane astrologer — or for anyone else interested in life even **a few years from now.** **$19.95**

</td><td>

The American Sidereal Ephemeris 1976-2000

No ephemeris of **any type** has ever offered the detail and precision of this Sidereal masterwork. Daily right ascension and declination, plus longitudes of all planets to **seconds of arc** make this a superb buy for Tropical and Sidereal astrologers alike. Introduction by James A. Eshelman and Kenneth Irving. **$19.50**

</td></tr>
</table>

Order from:

ACS Publications, Inc., P.O. Box 16430, San Diego, CA 92116-0430.
Add $2.00 for postage and handling for up to three books,
plus 25¢ for each additional book.